MUSIC IN THE SERVICE
OF THE KING

France in the Seventeenth Century

MUSIC IN THE SERVICE
OF THE KING

France in the Seventeenth Century

ROBERT M. ISHERWOOD

Cornell University Press

ITHACA AND LONDON

Cornell University Press gratefully acknowledges a grant from the
Andrew J. Mellon Foundation that aided in bringing this book to publication.

First published 1973 by Cornell University Press.
Published in the United Kingdom by Cornell University Press Ltd.,
2-4 Brook Street, London W1Y 1AA.

International Standard Book Number 0-8014-0734-6
Library of Congress Catalog Card Number 72-3842
Composition by St. Catherines Press, Ltd.

Printed in the United States of America
by Vail-Ballou Press, Inc.

*Librarians: Library of Congress cataloging information
appears on the last page of the book.*

TO NITA

Preface

The development of music in the context of French political and social history is the basic subject of my book. It attempts to bring music into the mainstream of general history and, in particular, to follow musical history from the standpoint of the essential political, social, religious, and artistic functions of musical productions in the age of royal absolutism. The French court often determined musical subjects and forms, and although I will not press the point too vigorously, the composers' use of stylistic elements seems closely related to nonmusical factors.

Many historians treat the arts and especially music as the frills of history and relegate them to the periphery of their studies of the past. The arts are neatly set apart from such important matters as wars, commerce, and society and are treated in the form of abbreviated lists of names and works, a few sweeping generalizations about style, and a handful of judiciously chosen adjectives. Musicologists, on the other hand, tend to write for each other, using a terminology that baffles the historian and the general reader. Moreover, they tend to work from the assumption that musical forms and styles develop according to a logic of their own, unrelated to nonmusical factors. Although there are exceptions, neither historians nor musicologists have found a thread tying general historical development to the history of music. My book attempts in part to locate that thread during the century when French culture rose to preeminence in Europe and the power of the French monarchy reached its apogee.

Although a portion of Chapter 1 deals with musical philosophy before the age of absolutism and Chapter 2 centers on the Valois court of the sixteenth century, the heart of the book concerns the reign of Louis XIV. I have devoted considerable attention to the musical history of the period preceding Louis XIV's reign in the belief that the historical association of music and monarchy must be seen as a continuous development beginning with the Valois and climaxing in Louis XIV's reign.

As the title suggests, my book is not a history of music in the traditional sense. Music constitutes simply the common ingredient in the many forms of royal *spectacle* and entertainment which the book describes. These forms include musical productions such as ballets and operas, royal entries, pageants, ceremonies, balls, and a wide range of entertainments known to the seventeenth century as *divertissements*, where music was only one ingredient, though perhaps the most important one. In short, I have discussed composers and musical style only in connection with those productions, sponsored by the French monarchy, that in some way entailed the use of music.

The reader may find my view of Louis XIV different from his own and from that of older studies of the reign. I believe that the king was more rational and calculating than he is often portrayed as having been, especially in his pleasures and ceremonious manner of living. Furthermore, I contend that he and Colbert had a grasp of the interrelationship of different kinds of state policies, programs, and activities; that they deliberately worked to achieve a relationship between pleasure and politics, between art and commerce. I am also persuaded that Louis' pursuit of *gloire* was prompted less by personal pride and vanity than by reasons of state: music and the other arts were essential to the deliberate creation of a mystique of kingship symbolic of France's strength and unity.

The research and writing of my book was made possible by the generous financial assistance of the Department of History of the University of Chicago and the Research Council of Vanderbilt University. I am deeply grateful to both. I would like to thank the following libraries for their kind assistance: Harper Library, Newberry Library, the Archives Nationales, and the Bibliothèques du Conservatoire, de l'Opéra, and de l'Arsenal. My greatest debt is to the entire staff of the Bibliothèque Nationale; their expertise and patience have facilitated my research at every turn. For his assistance in locating engravings, Roger-Armand Weigert deserves my special thanks.

For the weaknesses of my book, I claim sole responsibility. For its strengths, I am indebted to those in the departments of history and music of the University of Chicago who gave me encouragement and guidance. In this regard, may I especially thank Leonard B. Meyer. At a later stage, the manuscript benefited greatly from the suggestions of H. L. Koenigsberger of Cornell University. I am also grateful to the staff of Cornell University Press.

Whatever value my book may possess, whatever I am as a historian, I owe to Donald F. Lach. I have benefited more than I can express from his knowledge and inspiration. I have been bolstered by his confidence and warmed by his understanding.

Finally, my wife shared every stage of the research and writing of my book. She typed and edited the manuscript in several versions and has given invaluable aid, especially in the task of searching for and selecting the illustrations. Nothing I have done would have been possible without her helpful criticism, her patience, and her ability to renew my confidence.

ROBERT M. ISHERWOOD

Nashville, Tennessee

Contents

Illustrations

MUSIC IN THE SERVICE
OF THE KING

France in the Seventeenth Century

Musical Philosophy

The seventeenth century held a lofty conception of the meaning and power of musical experience. Music, it was believed, reflected the harmonious universe and linked the cosmos and finite man. Musical harmonies were analogous to the harmony of the spheres. Thus, in making music, man was touching the universe itself; he was reaching toward a divine realm through the most sublime means of self expression. In the words of René François, a religious adviser for Louis XIII, music "is the refrain and the echo of the harmonious songs of heaven and an ingenious collection of all the proportions which nature has disseminated for the scope of this universe."[1]

François' distinguished contemporaries Marin Mersenne and René Descartes elaborated this idea. In his *Compendium musicae* Descartes presented a systematic classification of musical sounds and calculated the degrees of the scale including semitones. He contended that the sounds and rhythms of music suggested the rational harmony of the universe and that man's emotions could be correlated with each sound in the scale of intervals.[2] In his monumental work *Harmonie universelle* Mersenne pursued Descartes' interest in a science of sound and attempted the codification of harmonic and rhythmic principles. Believing in man's affinity with the universe through music, Mersenne likened harmonic principles to the principles governing astronomical motion, bodily functions, poetic meters, and architectural design. Music was the foundation of the entire encyclopedia of knowledge. Indeed, Mersenne set forth a series of propositions explaining how the study of harmony was beneficial to all occupations and classes, having particular utility for soldiers, monarchs, priests, and engineers. He declared that "kings and all the greatest powers on earth can draw from the utility of our harmonic treatises."[3] Moreover, for both Descartes and Mersenne, the basis of their claims for the utility of music and the consequence of their belief in the rapport between musical harmony and universal harmony was the deeply held conviction that music has a profound effect on the spiritual well-being, the moral conduct, and the emotions of men. Embracing both rhythms and harmonies, Descartes' compendium related slow rhythmical beats to feelings of languor and sadness, whereas swift rhythms, it said, evoke the lively emotions of joy and anger. Mersenne likened certain consonant chords to the virtues of faith, hope, and charity. Because such chords can help purge man of his passions and vices, musical harmonies are useful in preserving a peaceful society, according to Mersenne. René François was more precise in his expression of the same idea. After analyzing the mathematical and physical properties of musical sounds, François tried to demonstrate how every sound filters through the ear to the mind, capturing the senses and emotions in its passage. François contrasted the effects of the Dorian mode, which "kindles in our hearts the love of chastity and illuminates the innocent flames of virginity," with those of the Phrygian mode, which "puts the heart to gallop, the sword to hand, . . . stirs the spirits, bends the arms, and hurls so much souphre into our veins that we want nothing more vehemently than conflict and the din of war."[4] In music lay the power of giving mankind a "foretaste of paradise"; its effects were those of a sonic elixir.

The common elements in most seventeenth-century books and treatises on music were the idea that the harmony of man, nature, and the cosmos was reproduced in music; that music had a profound effect on conduct and temperament; and that it therefore could be useful in creating and preserving a peaceful, orderly society. This last conclusion was perhaps the most important in the musical life of the age of royal absolutism. It was fully developed as a concept in a corpus of historical and analytical literature on music, becoming the dogmatic fulcrum of the musical thought and practice of the century. Whether the widely held assumptions about music of writers such as Mersenne actually influenced the musical policies of the Bourbon kings and their ministers is not very important. Probably the assumptions of the savants were more of a justification of, than an influence on, royal policy. The musical philosophy of the age was, however, a substantial intellectual underpinning for the extravagant musical productions, entertainments, and ceremonies sponsored by the rulers of France, and it provided an intellectual climate sustained in large part by clerics, notably Jesuits, in which music could be bent to the purposes of kings.

The seventeenth-century writers, to whom we shall return later, inherited their musical philosophy from the ancient Greeks, the Church Fathers, and from the Neo-Platonism and humanism of the Italian and French Renaissance. Some of the fundamental ideas and assumptions of this rich tradition must be considered if the meaning and power attributed to music in the seventeenth century are to be grasped. Mersenne's predecessors and descendants avowedly interpreted music from a Platonic and a Neo-Platonic point of view and used antiquity not only as a model for their lofty conception of the nature of music, but as a weapon to overwhelm the opposition to their musical ideology and to explain the musical course followed by the crown.

The seventeenth century took its musical philosophy from Plato directly and from his innumerable interpreters in the Middle Ages and the Renaissance. Four closely related concepts of Plato were especially important. First, in the *Timaeus*, where he propounds a theory of genesis and a cosmology based on Pythagoras, Plato envisages a vast harmonious order in which the motion of celestial bodies is akin to that of the human soul. The human soul and the world soul originate in the same source, the one participating in the harmony of the other. In effect, the celestial harmony is reproduced in the harmonious relationships of the elements and the seasons, and in the proportions of the human soul. Musical harmony imitates celestial harmony and expresses the harmonious relationship between soul and body. Music, therefore, is not to be taken lightly as a mere source of pleasure.

So much music as is adapted to the sound of the voice and to the sense of hearing is granted to us for the sake of harmony. And harmony, which has motions akin to the revolutions of our souls, is not regarded by the intelligent votary of the Muses as given by them with a view to irrational pleasure, which is deemed to be the purpose of it in our day, but as means to correct any discord which may have arisen in the courses of the soul, and to be our ally in bringing her into harmony and agreement with herself, and rhythm too was given by them for the same reason, on account of the irregular and graceless ways which prevail among mankind generàlly, and to help us against them.[5]

Thus, in making music, man is literally tuning in to the source of celestial intelligence and imitating the course of the heavens and of his own soul and body. Plato's logic then led him to two contentions, which constitute the second and third important facets of his musical philosophy: music has the power to eradicate discord and restore order to the soul; because of this power, music should hold the primary place in education and be carefully controlled by the laws.

No Platonic idea had a greater impact on the development of musical thought than the idea that music affects man's temperament, inducing predictable physical and moral responses. Plato explained this idea in the parts of the *Republic* and the *Laws* where he dealt with education, because he believed that music could have a decisive influence on the formation of the habits and morals of children. A proper musical education was especially mandatory for the guardian of the republic: "Our guardians must lay the foundation of their fortress in music. . . . By the help of music [they] have gained the habit of good order."[6]

Education must begin early in life because the young child learns quickly to associate virtue and vice with his natural feeling of pleasure and pain. If these associations, formed in the soul, follow the right course, when the child later reaches the age of understanding his feelings and emotions will be consonant with his reason. He will have developed a love of virtue and a hatred of vice through "a rightly disciplined state of pleasures and pains."[7] Plato emphasized that man's earliest education "comes through the Muses and Apollo"; that we are given the capacity to perceive and enjoy rhythm and melody before we can reason;

that through this perception we acquire a love of order. "Amid fair sights and sounds, Beauty shall flow into ear and eye and insensibly draw the soul from earliest years into likeness and sympathy with the beauty of reason."[8] Music's role in the educational process is far greater than that accorded the visual arts, because, for Plato, the painter operates on a more distant level of reality than the musician does. In his analogy of beds, Plato explained that, while the primary level of reality is God's idea of a bed, and the secondary level is any particular bed made by a carpenter, the artist works on a level three times removed from reality because he only imitates what the first two have made. Even the poet is an imitator of reality. Music, however, leads man directly to an intuition of the harmony of the world. "Musical training," Plato declared, "is a more potent instrument than any other, because rhythm and harmony find their way into the inward places of the soul, on which they mightily fasten."[9]

To support his belief in the potency of music, Plato followed two lines of thought: the first was rooted in Pythagorean number theory; the second involved an explicit statement of the actual effects of musical harmonies and rhythms on moral conduct. It was the second that led him to postulate the laws governing music in the republic. With Pythagoras, Plato believed that the universe consisted of numerical proportions and intervals; that the very nature of number is comprehended in the total scheme of the universe. Day and night follow a sequence expressed in the "lore of one and two";[10] the moon passes through a cycle every fifteen nights; the year consists of four recurring seasons and a sequence of twelve months; man orders his life and rotates his crops by number. Intervals of number, thus, lie behind the divine order of the universe. Knowledge of numerical proportions and relations is, therefore, essential to wisdom and is perhaps God's greatest gift to man. It enables man to leave the world of sense experience in favor of the world of ideas. Accepting the gift of number, man may "let his mind expatiate over the whole heavenly circuit."[11] If number were banished from mankind, man could never be wise; his soul could never attain virtue. Unable to recognize two and three, odd and even, man would be a creature of sensation and memory, lacking wisdom, without the capacity to become virtuous and happy. But to gain a knowledge of number is to impress on the soul the right, the good, and the virtuous. Since everything consists of numbers, knowledge of number may be gained by studying the various arts. Plato referred most often, however, to music, doubtless because of its power to enter and affect the soul before the development of reason. Music consists of numerical intervals of pitch and rhythm. The distinguishing of levels of pitch begins with the determination of one tone and proceeds to the determination of two, three, or more levels of sound. Thus, in hearing music, man is in effect discovering the number and nature of all the intervals formed by high and low pitch and is led to a discovery of the notes that comprise the intervals and the scales.[12] Music, therefore, is a superior avenue to the knowledge of number and interval, and to know number through music is to gain virtue and to draw the soul toward divine contemplation. "All musical effects manifestly depend upon the numeration of motions and tones. Unregulated, disorderly, ungainly, unrhythmical, tuneless movement, and all else that partakes of evil, is destitute of all number."[13]

In the *Republic,* Plato explained the effects of music more concretely by commenting on the influence of particular musical modes on morals and temperament. The Ionian and Lydian modes are harmful and, since they produce indolence, softness of character, and are associated with drunkenness, must be banished from the republic. The warlike Dorian and Phrygian modes, however, produce effects suited to the state. They inspire courage and resolution and enable man to survive blows of fortune. Plato associated another mode, which he was unable to identify, with peace, obedience, and religious piety. The effects of the modes are clear. Music need have no recourse to more complex harmonies and scales, or multi-stringed instruments. The four notes of the tetrachord are sufficient to compose all suitable harmonies. Rhythms must also be kept simple. Ruling out "complex systems of metre," Plato identifies three basic ratios of meter—3/2, 2/2, and 2/1. Plato was unsure, however, about the exact relationship between meters and morals. The musician Damon, on whom Plato relied in musical matters, must be consulted to determine which rhythms express meanness, insolence, and fury, and which their opposites. We must discover "what rhythms are the expressions of a courageous and harmonious life."[14] Although Plato was unable to be specific, he did not hesitate to state the following principle: the style must conform to the subject, while the meter follows the style, to the end that "the simplicity and harmony of the soul should be reflected in them all." This in turn meant that the music of a composition is adapted to the words: "We shall adapt the foot and the melody to words having a like spirit, not the words to the foot and the melody."[15]

This principle can be regarded as the fourth major element of Plato's musical philosophy. It was revived by the theorists of the sixteenth and seventeenth centuries, who regarded it as the primary means of re-creating ancient music and the effects it supposedly produced. There is no doubt that Plato strongly emphasized this principle, for he returned to it again and again. Uncertain about the exact relationship of particular rhythms to particular effects, Plato was sure that order or discord were produced by rhythm, that the best rhythms, like the best harmonies, were simple, and that "rhythm and harmony are regulated by the words, and not the words by them." Thus, the text of a song not only assumes primary importance, but governs in some way the purely musical ingredients. "The melody and the rhythm will depend upon the words."

The musical education of youths was balanced by gymnastics, which Plato characterized as the twin sister of music. Allowing "music to play upon him and to pour into his soul through the funnel of his ears" is essential to temper and make useful man's passion and spirit. But gymnastics is equally essential to prevent him from becoming soft—a feeble warrior. "He who mingles music with gymnastic in the fairest proportions, and best attempers them to the soul, may be rightly called the true musician and harmonist in a far higher sense then the tuner of the strings."[16]

In Book IV of the *Republic*, Plato returned to the duties of the ruler, stressing the necessity of preserving music and gymnastics "in their original form."[17] Any sort of musical innovation must be prohibited, he warned, because it "is full of danger to the whole

State." Citing Damon again as his authority, Plato stated that "when modes of music change, the fundamental laws of the State always change with them." Lawlessness sets in as what seem like harmless kinds of musical amusements produce license and disorder. Plato even had in mind a particular musician, Marsyas, to whom he refers disparagingly in the *Republic*. Marsyas played the flute, an instrument that Plato rejected, along with multi-stringed instruments, as being unnecessarily complicated. In the *Symposium*, Plato returned to the dangers of Marsyas' music. Alcibiades, in a drunken state, interrupts Socrates' banquet, and relates how Marsyas "charmed the souls of men by the power of his breath, as the performers of his music do still."[18] Alcibiades complains of the effect of Marsyas' music which causes him to neglect "the wants of my soul" and to be discontented with life.

It was his belief in the effects of music that led Plato to take up again in the *Laws* the subject of controlling music and musical education. Since music is the gift of Apollo and the Muses and has the power to instill and to express vice or virtue, its effect must not be left to chance. Unfortunately men derive pleasure from musical expressions of vice either because they have been poorly educated or because they have a bad temperament. Laws governing the "choric art" of the Muses are, therefore, necessary. Plato pointed to Egypt as the sole country that long ago recognized that "poses and melodies must be good, if they are to be habitually practiced by the youthful generations of citizens."[19] The Egyptians wisely forbade innovations. Their legislators created musical and artistic models that are still copied after thousands of years.

No doubt one could find grounds for censure in other Egyptian institutions, but in this matter of music, at least, it is a fact, and a thought-provoking fact, that it has actually proved possible, in such a sphere, to canonize melodies which exhibit an intrinsic rightness permanently by law. That must have been the doing of a god, or a godlike man—as, in fact, the local tradition is that the melodies which have been preserved for so many ages were the work of Isis. So, . . . if we can but detect the intrinsically right in such matters, in whatever degree, we should reduce them to law and system without misgiving, since the appeal to feeling which shows itself in the perpetual craving for novel musical sensation can, after all, do comparatively little to corrupt choric art, once it has been consecrated, by deriding it out of fashion.[20]

Plato acknowledged grudgingly that pleasure was the current basis of judging the arts, but he pointed out that since youths and adults do not derive pleasure from the same kinds of entertainments, the real question is pleasure for which audience. Thus, there is an ultimate basis for judging music; "the finest music is that which delights the best men, the properly educated, that, above all, which pleases the one man who is supreme in goodness and education."[21] In the final analysis, the good judge stands against the audience, rather than following it, and opposes performers who resort to improper ways of giving pleasure. Plato concluded that pleasure should be learned from laws governing music. These laws will be set by the oldest and wisest men; they will stand against musical fads and innovations and uphold a music that is right, not one that is pleasing. The right music is that which "reproduces the proportions and quality" of the universal harmony of the world soul of which man's music is an image. And again in the *Laws*, Plato insisted that the right music, the music which is worthy of the Muses, is the one where masculine language is set to masculine tunes; where melodies fit for free men are joined to appropriate rhythms; where melodies never lack vocal accompaniment (Plato opposed voiceless music composed for flutes and citharas); above all, where melody and rhythm follow the meter and sense of the words.

Plato dwelt on the problem of coordinating harmony, rhythm, and words because he regarded their coordination as the key to unlocking the good effects of music and poetry. He was thoroughly hostile to the music and poetry of Athens in his own time. The poets and musicians were producing bad effects because they catered to the pleasure of untrained youth and disregarded the proper adjustment of melody to rhythm, and music to words. "They divorce rhythm and figure from melody, and melody and rhythm from words, by their employment of cithara and flute without vocal accompaniment, though it is the hardest of tasks to discover what such wordless rhythm and tune signify, or what

model worth considering they represent."[22] This license is contrasted with the order and law of Athens during the time of its
earliest constitution, when "it was not permissible to misuse one
kind of melody for another" and when poets and musicians
worked under the laws rather than in response "to the catcalls
and discordant outcries of the crowd."[23] The public submitted
to the judgment and strict control of educated legislators. But in
later years this control broke down, and a contempt for musical
law set in. The "evil sovereignty of the audience" took hold as
poets and composers assumed that there was no standard of right
or wrong. The result was "a universal confusion of forms,"
musical anarchy, and loss of virtue. Plato laid down two rules
for the future: public standards for song, choric performance,
and ritual will be fixed by law; all poets must conform to the
laws, submitting their compositions to the "legislators for music."[24]
Moreover, the laws will not only ensure the proper combination
of musical elements as adjusted to the moral virtues with which
they are associated, they will also determine what compositions
are suitable for the various festival days of the year. Each
composition will have a corresponding social signification in the
calendar of ceremonies and festivals.

Finally, to the great satisfaction of its seventeenth-century
admirers, Plato's musical philosophy made dancing a natural,
necessary ally of music and poetry. In the *Laws*, Plato acknowledged the importance of dancing in the cycle of religious festivals.
He also contended that dancing, like singing, is a natural activity
of man. Therefore, in the educational program the laws must
provide for a kind of choric training which "embraces both dance
and song."[25] One half of this training is devoted to the rhythms
and melodies of the voice, and the other half to bodily movement,
which has rhythm in common with the movements of the voice.
The training of voice and body completes the musical education.
Furthermore, dancing is the link between music and gymnastics.
As dancing is related to music through the element of rhythm,
dancing is related to gymnastics through the element of bodily
rhythm and gesticulation. A man is educated when he can
express what he apprehends to be good through song and dance,
without feeling pleasure in the good or dislike of the bad. And

we can judge whether a man has a cowardly or a manly soul by the particular dances, figures, and melodies he performs. "Universally all postures and melodies connected with goodness of soul or body—whether with such goodness itself or with some image of it—are good, and those connected with badness universally the reverse."[26] As with song, dancing can have salutary effects by "reproducing the motions of comely bodies," or it can have unfortunate effects such as those associated with the frenzied dances of orgies and bacchanals. In the same way that Plato commended the Dorian and Phrygian modes, he identified two basic species of dance, one of which represents the movements of the "valiant soul in battle" by depicting motions of leaping, attacking, and yielding; the other species comprises dances of peace, representing the soul in a state of prosperity, good fortune, or well-being. It is natural that the movements of each species will be different, that they will accompany singing, and that they will produce opposing effects. It is the duty of the legislator to distinguish among the various dances and to ban those that are neither warlike nor pacific and, thus, serve no useful purpose. He must also combine dancing "with the rest of music," assigning to each ceremony its appropriate music and dance and ruling out all innovations.

To sum up, Plato's musical philosophy, which was the basis for Western musical thought until the eighteenth century, comprised four interrelated parts: the notion that musical harmonies and rhythms echoed the harmony of the spheres and reproduced the harmony of body and soul; the belief in music's power to exercise a profound effect on man's temperament and morality; the conviction that music must be governed under the laws of the republic; and the contention that the proper musical effects are produced only through establishing a careful relationship between the elements of harmony, rhythm, words, and dance, with the subject of the text and the words as the governing elements.

A variety of commentators, especially the Christian Neo-Platonists, transmitted Plato's musical ideas to modern times. In his commentary on Cicero's interpretation of Plato's *Timaeus*, the fifth-century writer Macrobius kept alive the notion of the harmony of the universe. The theory also appears in the mysticism of Pseudo-Dionysius. The scholars of Chartres studied carefully the Latin translation of the *Timaeus* by Chalcidius, and through them it became known to the Parisian intellectuals associated with the Abbey of Saint Victor and to the French poets of the Pléiade.[27]

Plato's important concept of the moral effects of music, especially as joined to Pythagorean philosophy and to the musical ideas of Plutarch (*De Musica*), had numerous adherents among the Alexandrian Greeks, who transmitted it to the Italian and French humanists. Alexandrians such as Iamblichus tended to seek intellectual inspiration from pre-Platonic Greek thought, in which music was closely related to religion and magic, and stories were told of Orpheus' power to cast spells with his hymns. Tying the doctrine of the effects to Pythagoras' explanation of the universe as harmony and number, they related how the Pythagoreans induced morals and manners through songs. Imbued with Alexandrian ideas, the Church Fathers replaced Orpheus with David as the microcosmic symbol of the universal harmony. And David was said by Ambrose and others to have drawn from the music of the universe when he composed the psalms as a means of helping man raise himself.[28] Indeed, legends of the musical effects associated with Orphic hymns, Hebrew chants, the Pythagorean school, and eventually the Alexandrians themselves became part of medieval lore. These tales of the Middle Ages were a main channel through which the doctrine of the effects passed from antiquity to the seventeenth century. They appear and reappear in the musical writings of the humanists; they were still taken seriously by Mersenne, and even surfaced again in the eighteenth century in the music history of Sir John Hawkins. The favorite story, the most popular version of which in the sixteenth and seventeenth centuries came from Saint Basil, dealt with the effects of Timotheus' music on Alexander. The king challenged his chief musician Timotheus to verify his boast that he could arouse the passions, making sad men happy, quiet men furious, by alternating the modes on his lyre. Timotheus commenced with a grave sound, producing melancholy in the king, then changed abruptly to a joyful tune, causing the king to dance. Changing modes, he then provoked such a rage in Alexander that guards had to be called to restrain him from attacking his guests. This story was believed and told in many versions by the musical writers of the sixteenth and seventeenth centuries, because "modern parallels had been recorded which supposedly confirmed its truth and proved that the ancients after all had not been so hyperbolical in their accounts of the power of music."[29]

The two most illustrious subscribers to the Pythagorean-Platonic effects theory in the Middle Ages were Augustine and Boethius. Believing with Plato in the necessity of a union of poetry and music and embracing Pythagoras' view that the meaning of the universe and of man's soul is expressed in number, Augustine wrote: "All the passions of our soul have, in accordance with the differences between them, certain sounds in the voice and in song which are proper to them, and by which they are excited through I know not what occult relationship."[30] Augustine actually questioned whether the Church, whose music was based on the Greek modes, dared to employ music and poetry, so powerful were their effects, though he believed strongly in the moral utility of a proper musical education. Since later musical theorists turned to Augustine as well as to Plato, it should be noted that Augustine gave poetic meter the same importance as musical harmony. Both express the proportions and consonances of celestial harmony and both ravish the soul; both are in essence measured intervals and proportions, the stuff of the universe itself. And in responding to the proportions of classical feet, whether they be dactyls, spondees, iambs, or anapests, we are expressing our love of God and our search for a proportioned soul.[31]

No less than Augustine, Boethius helped to preserve the ancient musical philosophy in the Middle Ages. He arrived at the idea of the effects in his complex universal system (*De institutione musica*) through a sequence of musical triads.[32] There are three types of music—world music, human music, and instrumental music. World music has three parts; one is contained in the elements, the second in the celestial bodies, and the third in times. The music of the elements, in turn, exists in weight, number, and measure. The world music contained in celestial bodies exists in position, motion, and nature. The world music contained in times exists in years (the four seasons), in months (the moon's cycle), and in days (alternation of light and darkness). The second type of music, human music, is contained in the body, the soul, and in the connection between soul and body. The music of the body is partly vegetative, partly in humours, partly in operations. The vegetative exists in all living things, while the music in the humours belongs to the sensitive nature and the music in operations belongs to the rational nature. The music of the soul is partly in powers such as anger and reason, and partly in virtues such as justice and fortitude. The music contained in the connection between soul and body resides in the natural friendship, rather than in the corporeal chain, which ties soul to body. Finally, the third type of music, instrumental music, is contained in striking (strings and timbrels), in wind (pipes and organ), and in the voice (songs and chants). Through this comprehensive universal musical system, Boethius could easily demonstrate how celestial harmony relates to man's musical harmony, how virtue can be awakened in the soul by harmonic effects, and even how man is affected physically by music. Boethius was an important source for later theorists.

It is essential to understand that although Boethius and other writers of late antiquity and the Middle Ages worked within a musical framework, their understanding of ancient thought involved a comprehensive conception of the effects of heavenly bodies on human life. They believed man's fate was governed by the stars, and they inherited the tendency to mythologize the celestial bodies from Homer and the early Greeks.[33]

In Cicero's time it was believed that the stars, sun, and moon were divinities; when the names of the gods were given to the stars, they took on divine personalities and powers. The association of constellations with the myths of the gods led eventually to a connection between the signs of the zodiac and the gods (the lion, for example, became the Nemean lion killed by Hercules). Thus, a complete fusion of mythology and astronomy occurred. The fusion became more complex when exotic constellations such as the Egyptian genii were added, and when the planets came to be identified with gods from the Seleucid Empire. Eventually, the Alexandrians simplified the nomenclature, naming each planet by its physical characteristic. By the third century, the belief that the planets actually contained divinity within them had become part of Alexandrian religion. The tradition of linking celestial bodies and gods, which helped perpetuate the old mythology for so long, was diffused throughout the Greek world by the Stoics, carried to Rome, and reinforced by the spread of Eastern astrological and religious beliefs, especially the Persian cult of the sun. The notion that the stars are gods who must be pacified by the use of amulets and talismans was further strengthened by the credulity of the Neo-Platonists and the compromises the Christians made with paganism and astrology. The will of God is supreme, but the stars have power through God and can be signs of His purpose. Thus, in absorbing so much of the culture of pagan antiquity, Augustine and other Church Fathers accepted the astrological premises of pagan science, and, believing that all physical things were related to the zodiac, they established relationships between the planets and the earth, connecting Mars to fire, Jupiter to air, and Mercury to water. Writers of the Middle Ages carried these relationships further by linking the planets and zodiacal signs to the elements, the seasons, the humours, the virtues, the liberal arts, and the Muses. These relationships were intended to indicate how man is dependent on cosmic forces and how the proportions of his own make-up follow the proportions of the universe. From the Neo-Platonists, Boethius derived the idea of man as a microcosm of the universe. This idea was then passed to Bernard of Tours, who applied it to medicine. By the twelfth and thirteenth centuries, it was in fact widely believed that the signs of the zodiac ruled parts of the body and that each limb and organ was governed by a planet. Astrology gained further credence with the introduction into the west of Arabic science and philosophy, which taught that certain planetary conjunctions caused famine, war, and disease, and that man could conciliate the celestial divinities through prayer, magic, and special gems used as amulets. This entire body of thought was taken up by the Renaissance humanists, who continued to believe in the effects of the heavenly bodies but also stressed that man had enough freedom and intelligence to influence his own destiny. Music was brought in as both an expression of the universal harmony that links man physically, intellectually, and morally to the celestial bodies and intelligences, and as a means, along with talismans and other devices, to draw out and channel celestial emanations.

The whole musical philosophy of ancient and medieval Europe, as derived from Pythagoras and Plato and as conveyed by the Neo-Platonists and Church Fathers, together with the complex corpus of theory linking astrology, mythology, and mysticism, was absorbed and transmitted by the Florentine humanists of the fifteenth century. Used by Plato and his descendants as a cornerstone of philosophy, music was central to the Renaissance Neo-Platonists' understanding of man's relationship to the universe. The return to antiquity of the fifteenth-century philosophers "is above all a return to the Alexandrian, to that neo-Pythagorean atmosphere in which the mystical associations of music are emphasized. For Ficino, as for Plotinus, music is a way of approach to the divine."[34] And without question, the pivotal mind in this development belonged to the leading light of Lorenzo de Medici's Platonic Academy, Marsilio Ficino.[35]

Two avenues lead to the musical philosophy of Ficino. Beginning at a colossal monument to Plato, they are lined with statues of Plotinus, Proclus, Iamblichus, Boethius, Pseudo-Dionysius, Macrobius, and Augustine. The avenues are intersected by streets bearing the names of *prisca theologia*, Zoroaster, Egypt, and Aristotle, and perhaps an alley named madness. The first avenue is paved with the smooth stones of Ficino's related concepts of beauty and love; the second with the more jagged stones of his idea of the relation between soul and body. In his commentary on Plato's *Symposium* and in the *De Amore* where he follows Plotinus, Ficino defined beauty as "the splendour of divine goodness." Existing as pure idea imminent in the mind of God, beauty is diffused throughout all the spheres of the universe by means of celestial energy. It passes through the realm of the angels, who are given the power by it to perceive celestial bodies as pure ideas. The divine splendor then radiates through the stars and planets, assuming many forms and gradations of quality before it finally reaches the four levels of human existence—mind, soul, nature, and matter. Although willful acts of contemplation and cognition are necessary, the mind and soul of man are ready to receive beauty because impressions of the idea of beauty, like all ideas, are inherent in the soul before they exist in the body.[36]

Beauty is manifested in each level, though when celestial energy has reached the level of nature, it has been broken up, and pure idea is disfigured by material influences. Imbued with an idea of beauty from preexistence, mind, on the other hand, is influenced directly by celestial energy and, thus, is a receptacle of divine beauty through its power of contemplation and intuitive apprehension. The mind becomes an "accumulator of modified super-celestial energy."[37] The soul, man's middle zone, has a higher part (i.e., reason) which lacks the mind's intuitive power but which can communicate the mind's illumination to the lower grades of life. The lower part of the soul is made up of imagination and the five senses, plus the faculties of nutrition, growth, and procreation. Since the only path to infinite goodness, love, and beauty is through the mind, the reasoning faculty of the soul must open itself to the influences of the mind and, thereby, to celestial energy. At rare moments, ecstatic fury arises from contemplation, and the mind and soul are released from the body, becoming a "tool of the divine."[38] Man is impelled by love in the act of contemplation or cognition toward reunion with God. Used by God as the means of effusing his beauty into the world, love, inversely, is the cause of man's search for divine goodness. But only when love is directed toward an ultimate goal by the rational faculty of the soul, rather than by bodily desire, does it actually attain its goal. Love, therefore, is a "desire for the fruition of beauty."

Insisting always that love of beauty is an act of contemplation and cognition, Ficino distinguishes three types of beauty—beauty of bodies, of sounds, and of souls. The love of each is attainable only by using the senses of seeing, hearing, and thinking. The lower senses have nothing to do with love of beauty because they can have no apprehension of something that has an incorporeal origin and whose corporeal images in sounds and colors have as their essence qualities of consonance and proportion. These qualities of beauty, which are perceived only when the Soul has freed itself from the body by an act of contemplation, can be brought to reality in the corporeal world through artistic and musical representations. Following Augustine, Ficino held that in approving a particular sight or sound, man was relating that representation to an inner perception of beauty by the soul, and through the mind to the primary idea of beauty in God. By the same token, the creator of art merely gives some form or substance to an idea in his mind of proportion and consonance. Ficino had little more to say about the arts *per se*, but it is clear that as a practicing musician, he was more concerned with sound than sight. Equating the qualities of proportion in visual art and consonance in music, he explained that although music is a corporeal phenomenon, it originates in the musician's soul, affects the listener's soul, and embodies the essential quality of beauty. Ficino put the matter on a personal level: "Serious music preserves and restores the consonance of the parts of the soul, as Plato and Aristotle say and as we have experienced frequently. . . . I frequently dedicate myself to the more serious strings and songs after the study of theology or medicine, in order to neglect the other pleasures of the senses, to expel the troubles of Soul and body, and to elevate the mind as much as possible to sublime things and God."[39] In order to clarify just why music in particular has the power of elevating the mind, Ficino reverted to the old Platonic-Pythagorean concept of the universal harmony. "The celestial spheres, attuned to each other according to the rules of consonance, produce a divine music imperceptible to us; and human music being an earthly imitation of the celestial sounds, through its admirable effect induces the Soul to elevate itself into the realm of celestial harmony."[40]

Plato had argued that the effects can only be achieved through a union of harmony, rhythm, and words. Ficino clung to this important idea, but he took it one step further by contending that poetry was superior to music. Poetry enters the ear like music, but it also speaks directly to the mind. Therefore, poetry originates in the divine mind itself, rather than in the celestial harmony, and its effects draw man directly to God. Although he relied on Plato's notion of poetic fury, Ficino held that an inner ecstasy of the spirit, rather than thought, induces poetic inspiration and that poetry is a heavenly gift whose effect is the genuine separation of mind from body. Ficino's accentuation of the power of poetry "underlies the great importance attached by musical humanists to the audibility of the words in the union of poetry and music."[41]

Despite their importance for his total philosophy, Ficino's aesthetics and metaphysics reveal less about his conception of music than do his views on medicine and astrology. That Ficino thought of music less in aesthetic terms than as a medical and theurgic device to prepare the soul for contemplation of God is explained in his commentary on Plato's *Timaeus*, which contains his most extensive writing on music, and the *De Triplici Vita*.[42] Music has an effect on the *spiritus*, whose function is to link man's soul with his body. In physical terms, the *spiritus* is a vapor of the blood, formed by the heat of the heart. It passes from the heart to the brain, taking with it the material of the senses. Thus, the *spiritus* is the blood vapor of man's body which the higher part of the soul (reason) uses to carry the lower part (the senses). Being very hot, fine, and agile, the *spiritus* can ignite, especially in philosophers and poets who constantly drain it from the heart in acts of thought and imagination. When ignited, the *spiritus* produces mania, then melancholy. It may be nourished, however, by certain foods and smells, and by music. Music is the most effective nourishment because both music and *spiritus* are essentially special sorts of living air. Musical melody, itself a kind of *spiritus*, is animated air which enters man's ear, blends with the vapor of the *spiritus*, and transforms the soul. "Musically moved air is alive, like a disembodied human *spiritus*, and therefore naturally has the most powerful effect possible on the hearer's *spiritus*."[43] And because music also has a text, it shares with *spiritus* the power of carrying thoughts to the rational soul. But whereas melody impresses only the sensible part of the soul, as the *spiritus* merely carries sensation and imagination, the text influences the rational soul. Thus, music, working through air and transmitting intellectual content through a text, affects the superior sense of hearing, as the *spiritus*, itself a rarified and subtle air, carries the material derived from the senses, especially hearing, to the rational faculties of the soul. Music has a far more powerful effect on man than visual or tactile objects because, whereas visual impressions must be transmitted to the *spiritus* by some other sense, sounds pass directly through the ear to the *spiritus*, which in turn conveys them to the whole body and soul of man. To reinforce his belief, Ficino used Plato's idea of the similarity between musical consonance and the soul, both of which have motion in common. Musical consonance "reaches the ears through . . . spherical motion," while the soul is the source of circular motion. Whereas visual impressions "lack the effectiveness of motion," music penetrates the *spiritus* through the ears by means of motion; thus, it "preeminently corresponds with the soul."[44] Moreover, both music and soul act as transmitters: the soul transmits sense impressions to its rational faculty and to the mind; music transmits the emotions and thoughts of the musician's soul to the listener's soul. In short, music's power rests in its direct impact on the soul through the *spiritus* that unites body and soul, and its ability to effect the whole of man by working on the senses and on the mind. And because music—unlike vision, which is static—possesses motion, it affects man's emotions and morals: they are infused with the motions of soul and *spiritus* as well as with the motions of the body. In the motion of music lies its power. Music affects morals because of all sensed things, only sound has motion or movement, movement is the same as action, and actions have a moral character.

Ficino's belief in astrology led him still further down the mystical path linking music and *spiritus*. To begin with, he believed that every man from birth was under the influence of a planet which fixed his moral and physical nature.[45] In *De Triplici Vita*, Ficino explained that each constellation, however, offers several different possibilities for life, leaving man free to choose among them. Saturn, for example, which was Ficino's star, induced melancholy, but also intelligence and contemplation. Man can willfully attract the good influence and repel the bad, or he can absorb both. Depending upon the inner disposition of man's will and his pursuit of divine contemplation, Saturn's influence can be used to develop virtue and happiness or the reverse. Though man is predominately influenced by one planet, he can draw upon the influence of other planets. This increases the factor of choice considerably. Ficino brought the *spiritus* into his astrology by contending that the celestial bodies are connected to the corporeal world by a flowing, cosmic *spiritus*. Resembling Aristotle's incorruptible *aether*, cosmic *spiritus* infuses its energy, a sort of divine fury, into the planets and into subcelestial bodies. Because the cosmic *spiritus* is like man's *spiritus*, man can attract it and use it to purify his own *spiritus*. Following Pythagoras and Plato, Ficino held that the spheres were bound by harmonic proportions akin to the harmony of soul and body and reproduced in music. Man can attract the cosmic *spiritus* by tuning his *spiritus* to the number and proportion of the celestial body. The problem is to find the exact means of attracting and receiving astral *spiritus*. Ficino got at this by contending that since music both affects and imitates emotions and morals, the planets can be imitated by music because the planets bear the emotions and morals of the gods. In the act of imitation, music can attract celestial influences.

Ficino laid down three rules governing imitation and attraction.[46] First, devise musical texts praising the positions, powers, and effects attributed to any given star. Second, set these texts to the musical modes which appear in the songs of different peoples and regions, and use these modes to attract whatever star rules over that region or people. Third, after watching the positions of the stars, imitate musically the morals and actions that accompany these various positions. Finally, Ficino outlined his own musical system for attracting the *spiritus*. He believed the sun's influence carried the greatest benefits for man's body and soul, and that Apollo could be imitated, hence attracted, by any sort of music. The best songs, however, are those which are simple, serious, gracious, and sweet. Jupiter's influence is summoned by grave music, Mercury's by gay and vigorous music; Venus was attracted by soft, voluptuous music. Thus, by performing any one of these various harmonies (Ficino apparently had in mind astrological modes corresponding to the Greek modes), the musician and his listeners will attract the planet's *spiritus* and will acquire the moral character associated with the music he plays or sings. A man can use the ethical and therapeutical power of music to tune his soul to the harmony of the spheres.

According to Ficino, music was the most effective means of repelling the melancholic effects of his own planet, Saturn, while at the same time conditioning the soul in both its rational and its sensible-imaginative parts for acts of religious contemplation. In the *Epistolarium* and in his commentary on Plotinus, he indicated vaguely the kind of music he himself used to achieve these effects.[47] He sang and played monodic chants written in the modes on an instrument he called his Orphic lyre while burning incense and drinking wine (odors and foods attract the planets). Conceivably, his songs were based on plain chant, and he probably improvised and sang them as recitative.[48] What he sang were Orphic hymns, whose verses supposedly contained precious religious truths from Orpheus. The ancient master of Pythagoras, Orpheus was ranked with Zoroaster, Moses, Hermes, and Plato as a divine theologian inspired by all four Furies—poetic, bacchic, prophetic, and amorous.[49] To Ficino, Orpheus was especially important because legend held that with his music he could cast a spell over trees, rocks, and animals and could civilize barbaric peoples. Thus Orpheus, the divine poet and theologian, was also the musical sorcerer.[50] Ficino's point was that anyone who sings or listens to these hymns is inspired by Orpheus' Furies and so is led to religious revelation, prophetic insight, and love of God—all through the power of music. For Ficino the Orphic hymns were plainly a theurgic device, the best practical means he had hit upon to draw the magical power of the astral *spiritus*. He chanted to the sun and other planets texts full of poetic fury and infused with the hidden meanings of the antique religion from which Platonism had stemmed and in which the Christian religion had been foreseen. His aim was to attract "something vital from the soul of the world and the souls of the spheres and stars."[51] No greater claim has ever been made for the power of music.[52] In Ficino's work, the doctrine of the effects was for the first time fully explained and applied. This was possible because of Ficino's knowledge of Plato and because of his belief in astrology and theurgy.

Ficino's writings served as the principal channel for the musical philosophy of antiquity.[53] His ideas permeated the circle of Marguerite de Navarre, which included the humanist Lefèvre d'Étaples and the poet and valet of François I, Clément Marot. Ficino's greatest influence was on Catholic writers. Chief among these were Symphorien Champier and Guy Lefèvre de la Bodérie.[54] La Bodérie, who was steeped in Greek mythology and in the *prisca theologia*, translated and published Ficino's works. The influence of the musical effects theory on La Bodérie is seen in his *Hymnes ecclésiastiques*. In dedicating this collection to Henri III, La Bodérie attacked Clément Marot's version of the Psalter (which the Huguenots would later use) for corrupting the people by musical effects that led them to the reformed religion. La Bodérie contended that his collection of Catholic hymns and spirituals would win back by song and verse people who have strayed from the faith. The collection contained a French translation of three Orphic hymns, one of which was the "Hymn of the Sun." Moreover, La Bodérie gave an unusual patriotic twist to the *prisca theologia*. In his *La Galliade, ou de la révolution des arts et sciences* (1578), he claimed that modern attempts to write poetry and music were just the latest chapter in a historical tradition dating to ancient Egypt, Greece, Judaea, and Italy, and especially to ancient Gaul. The ancient Druid theologians, La Bodérie declared, had invented such a powerful music that it could tranquilize two armies on the verge of battle.

Of the two Catholic writers, Champier came the closer to sharing Ficino's astrology. He believed in the influence of planets and was imbued with the theories in Ficino's *De triplici*. Yet, he carefully avoided discussing the *spiritus* and astral music because he knew these ideas were threatening to the Church, which had its own theurgy and its own definition of *spiritus*. Indeed, while Ficinian astrology remained firm in the thought of such writers as Claude Le Jeune and Pierre de Ronsard and at the court of Catherine de Medici,[55] the concept of the *spiritus* tended to disappear in the sixteenth century without, however, diminishing the popularity of the belief in the moral effects of music. Despite their caution with some aspects of Ficino's philosophy, French Catholic writers of the sixteenth century found a secure place for it in their own thought.

Ficinian Neo-Platonism was carried to the French academic movement of the middle and later half of the sixteenth century by the Pléiade poets. Ficino had stressed the importance of poetic inspiration for acts of contemplation, and he had pointed to the religious truths hidden in the poetic imagery of fables and ancient texts such as the *Orphica*. These elements of his thought, along with his idea of love and beauty, were taken up by the Pléiade, and later by Baïf and the academicians. But the two aspects of Ficino's thought (one should add the thought of the musical humanists) which exercised the strongest influence on the Pléiade and their descendants were the idea of the union of poetry and music and "the desire to revive the ethical power of ancient music."[56] They supported their belief in the power of music with Ficino's theories, the classical sources, and the literature of Neo-Platonism and musical humanism. Their aim was to create a musical poetry in the antique style which would actually bring to practical realization the musical power described by Plato and his intellectual descendants. Thus, the study of musical philosophy must now encompass not only the theories of universal harmony and the effects, but also the attempts to forge a likeness of the actual union of poetry and music in antiquity. That union, which from Plato to Ficino had been the real way to get the effects, was achieved by the poets and composers of Baïf's academy in the period of France's religious wars (see Chapter 2). But the Pléiade had already laid a theoretical and practical foundation founded in humanism. The practical side of the task was difficult because the poets had almost no actual examples of Greek music.[57] They had to rely, therefore, on the descriptions of music in classical literature and on the emphasis given to the union of dramatic and lyric poetry and music found in Plato, Plutarch, and others.[58]

The chief theoretician of the Pléiade, who was himself a musical humanist and a funnel for Ficino's ideas into France, was Pontus de Tyard, the Bishop of Chalon-sur-Saône. Tyard's *Solitaire second, ou discours de la musique* (1552) is one of the strongest statements of the effects theory in the sixteenth century; it reveals the Pléiade's commitment to the union of music and poetry. Besides relating in it all the familiar legends, including the

Alexander-Timotheus story, about music's unique power, Tyard added a new one told to him by a Milanese named Vintinelli, who at a banquet had heard a lute player take command of the souls of the guests and then restore them to normal through the alternations of his music.[59]

In his two works, *Solitaire premier* and *Solitaire second*, Tyard explained that the entire hierarchy of human knowledge was symbolized by the union of music and poetry. In his quest for release from the material world and for knowledge of God, the Solitary first masters the rational disciplines; he then attains a second level in the hierarchy, wherein he apprehends the unity of the sciences and arts, uses a symbolic language, and intuitively perceives the union of music and poetry. His progression to a higher level of knowledge is symbolized by that perception. Thus, the union was the most important element in man's whole intellectual and spiritual development. Furthermore, in *Solitaire premier*, Tyard echoed Plato's contention that music and poetry awaken the spiritually directed part of the soul by expelling discord. Having cleansed the soul, the union then became the first step (labelled poetic enthusiasm and associated with the Muses) in the soul's ascent from rational knowledge to the higher level of reality where the soul intuitively grasps the whole. Three remaining steps lead to knowledge of hidden religious truths (associated with Apollo), prophetic ravishment (Dionysius), and love (Aphrodite and Eros). These steps are equivalent to the four Furies discussed by Plato and Ficino. The image of the Muses as the guide of poetic fury was particularly important to Tyard because it enabled him to show how all knowledge is comprehended in the union of poetry and music and how the union ultimately reflects the harmony of the universe. From each of the three primary Muses—philosophy, rhetoric, and mathematics—Tyard created three subdivisions, respectively: theology, moral philosophy, and natural philosophy; demonstrative, deliberative, and judicial rhetoric; arithmetic, music, and geometry. The nine Muses personified all the branches of knowledge. Tyard assigned a planet to each of eight Muses, and to the ninth, the task of presiding over all of the planets. Thus, the Muses are both images of human knowledge in its totality and of the cosmic harmony.

They form one comprehensive whole, which is grasped in a state of poetic fury. Tyard added the figure of Apollo as the leader of the Muses' choir. His imagery was completed by the figure of Pasithée, of whom the Solitary has a vision in his poetic fury. "Measuring odes to her lyre," Pastithée is the object of the Solitary's love and the spirit of the Muses. The Solitary's adoration of Pasithée is expressed by the singing of measured verses, producing great effects on both of them, and this adoration symbolizes the Solitary's devotion to knowledge.[60]

Tyard's musical philosophy was completed in *Solitaire second*, which is, in effect, a musical treatise based on Chalcidius' interpretation of Plato's *Timaeus*, wherein musical proportions form the unity of world soul and human soul. In this dialogue, Pasithée represents the human harmonies of the microcosm, and a character called the Curieux represents the universal harmony of the macrocosm. Noting that the music of the spheres is inaudible to humans, the Curieux expounds on the harmonious relationships of the four seasons and the four elements. The Solitary points to the harmonious proportions of man's body and virtuous character. Through music, the soul acquires a balance of virtues and passions. Ignorance of music produces a lame soul. Thus, blending Plato and Ficino with his own imagery, Pontus de Tyard summed up the musical philosophy of the Pléiade. Under the influence of the poetic fury and following the mastery of the encyclopedia of knowledge, man enters the first level of his spiritual enlightenment where the union of music and poetry are intuitively apprehended.

Next to Tyard, the best exponent of the musical and poetic philosophy of the Pléiade was Pierre de Ronsard.[61] Court poet for Charles IX, purveyor of antique fables as poetic images of reality, enthusiast of the Counter Reformation, Ronsard espoused most of the tenets of the musical philosophy of antiquity. Ronsard, whose poetry was more frequently set to music than that of any other sixteenth-century poet, had read Plato, Plutarch, Boethius, and Ficino. In *Préface sur la musique* (1562) and in his poems he allied himself with the Platonic belief that music mirrors the harmony of the universe and of earth; he told again the standard stories about the effects of ancient music. That Ronsard did not link the effects exclusively to ancient Greek music is indicated by the fact that his *Préface* introduced a volume of popular French songs, most of which date to the fifteenth and early sixteenth centuries. Moreover, Ronsard believed that he was inspired by all four Furies, and that his own poems in the musical setting of Jacques Maudit, Orlando di Lasso, and Clément Janequin would revive the effects. The spirits of the listeners would be raised and lowered as the musicians reflected the harmonies of heaven and underscored the melancholy love of Dido and Aeneas and the heroics of the duc de Guise. In striving for the effects, Ronsard fitted the ordinary accents and rhymes of French verse to the musical settings by using alternating meters, regularity of line arrangement, and other techniques. He stopped short of adapting the quantitative meter of classical poetry to his compositions; that radical step would be taken by Baïf. In all other respects, however, Ronsard believed his musical poetry was a sufficiently close rendition of the antique to be effective in inculcating morality, and he saw the effects of his poetry as a force for the Catholic cause.

The pagan imagery of Ronsard's poems continued the mythological traditions of antiquity in conventionally moralistic ways. His preoccupation with the concealed moral meanings of pagan myths was anchored in the same medieval tradition that had attached the gods to the planets and the physical world. The early Christian Neo-Platonists, borrowing from Stoic analysis, had analyzed allegorically the Homeric tales of the gods, finding hidden moral truths.[62] They attributed philosophical and moralistic meanings to pagan legends, just as Plato himself had used the gods metaphorically and Virgil had endowed them with morality and given divine form to such abstractions as fortune, discord, victory, and remorse. Moreover, allegorical analysis of mythology was congenial to the Church Fathers, who used it to probe the hidden meanings of Scripture and found it convenient for didactic purposes. The allegorical method flourished in the Carolingian period, when treatises were written on the philosophical interpretation of fables. By the eleventh century some fables were believed to contain prefigurations of Christian truths, and by the twelfth, allegory was "the universal vehicle of all pious expression." The *Metamorphoses* of Ovid had replaced Virgil as the richest source of hidden truths; in one collection of extracts from the *Metamorphoses*, the gods are represented as priests, the goddesses as nuns. The use of the allegorical method reached its climax in the fourteenth-century work, *Ovide moralisé*, attributed to Philippe de Vitry, bishop of Meaux; the author explained the whole of Christian morality through Ovid: Actaeon is Jesus; Phaëton is Lucifer; Diana is the Trinity; the peacock symbolizes vanity; and Ceres' search for Proserpina is the Church's quest to win back the souls of Christians who have strayed from the faith. With a commentary by Colart Mansion on the morality of the fables, *Ovide moralisé* was translated into French from Pierre Bersuire's *Reductorium morale* and published in Bruges in 1484. The allegorical moralization of myth continued to be popular with humanists and Neo-Platonists of the Italian and French Renaissance, who found in Ovid not only a hidden morality but the whole of Christian doctrine. In the spirit of syncretism, relationships were found between Biblical truth and pagan myths, and Christian revelation was discovered in Homer, Socrates, the Persian Magi, and the prophets of Israel. Hidden and disguised in order to avoid vulgarization and profanation, the many sources of Christian revelation were uncovered through the use of allegory for the purpose of revealing the common truths of all religions. Finally, influenced by their study of Egyptian hieroglyphics and cryptograms, the humanists created emblems or pictures with concealed moral lessons that were explained by an accompanying text. In the first collection of emblems (*Emblamatum liber*, 1531) Andrea Alciati portrayed virtues, vices, and moral truths as Hercules, Minerva, Juno, Bacchus, the Graces, and the entire range of pagan deities. Images drawn from the Latin fabulists and poets—for example, Bellerophon, representing intelligence and courage overcoming obstacles, and Cupid in his lion-drawn chariot representing love's irresistable power—became common, almost stereotyped devices for teaching morality and reconciling Christianity with pagan mythology. These allegorical images and figures cropped up in Mannerist and Baroque art, in the festivals and processions of the Valois and Bourbon courts, and later in the operas of the

seventeenth century; they found a home in the Counter Reformation and were the stock in trade of the sixteenth- and seventeenth-century poets. Thus, Ronsard, following an old, accepted
tradition, could load his poems with fabulous stories containing
moral truths. He could portray the defeat of the mythological
giants by the gods as the victory of Catholics over Huguenots.
All his poetic fables, many of which were set to music, were meant
as images and allegories of higher spiritual truths and were at
the service of the Catholic faith. Ronsard saw himself as a poet-
theologian, another Orpheus, capable of stirring the deepest
passions of man. Along with Amadis Jamyn, Olivier de Magny,
and the other poets of the Pléiade, Ronsard believed that poetry
must be sung and be accompanied by a lyre in the ancient manner.
But although Ronsard wanted to have all of his odes and sonnets
set to music (most were) and fully accepted the ideas of union
and the effects, he had no clear conception of music or the relation
of music and text.[63] He simply assumed that music accompanies
the poem and moves the listener in some indeterminate way.
He assumed, as the ancients had said, that there must be a union,
but its nature eluded him. Thus, his fuzziness about the precise
role and use of music prevented him from putting into practice
the Platonic and humanist theory of music.

Theory and practice were finally combined in the work of
Jean-Antoine de Baïf and his circle at the Académie de musique
et de poésie, founded in 1570. In the interest of reviving ancient
effects and ancient music, Baïf took a step that went beyond the
Pléiade, that harkened back to Ficino, and that, ironically,
may have been a perversion of classical musical philosophy
itself. The rhythms and moods of the text were not to be united
with music, but to dominate music. Responding as much to the
influence of the musical humanists, who laid enormous emphasis
on the ethical effects of music,[64] as to the actual influence of
ancient authors, Baïf and his circle believed that the only way to
enable music to stir the passions, instill morality, and even to
"ensure the stability of the state," was to put melodies and
rhythms in the service of an affective language; to use harmony
in such a way that the text was audible and vividly rendered.[65]
It should be emphasized that this innovation was more one of

practice than of theory, since it had been suggested by Plato and Ficino among others, and that it sprang directly from the old belief in the effects and from the desire to revive music's ethical power.

Although no theoretical treatise on music by Baïf and his associates survives, their commitment to Platonic ideas is indicated in the Lettres patentes and statutes of the Académie and in the writings of Marin Mersenne, who learned a great deal about the Académie from his friend Jacques Maudit, one of its principal composers.[66] Invoking the authority of Plato and at times paraphrasing Books III and IV of the *Republic*, Baïf's Lettres call for the strict legislation of musical style. Offering instruction in all branches of knowledge, the Académie would specialize in musical composition based on that of antiquity. The academicians would follow uniform rules in the knowledge, as Plato had written, that only certain specified harmonies, rhythms, and texts could foster virtue in the soul and order in the society. Once firmly established, the new style, based on the closest possible union of poetry and music, would be imposed from above by the Académie acting on royal authority for, as Plato had said, music must not be left to the fickle judgment of the masses, but must be under the laws and entrusted to the best minds. Such careful regulation was necessary because the fundamental assumption of Baïf, the academicians, and Charles IX himself, was that music can raise or lower the spirits; that it has an incomparable ethical power, "for as every reader of Plato and Aristotle knows, music has an intimate relation to morals."[67] Serving as the fountain of knowledge, music will purge the soul of disorder, instill virtue and manners in the youth, soften spiritual elation, exhilarate spiritual depression, and according to Mersenne, "drive barbarism from Gaul." The regulation of music must be the chief concern of the modern guardian of the republic because, as the ancient and modern philosophers have said, "it is important for the morals of the citizens of a town that the music current and used in the country should be retained under certain laws, for the minds of most men are formed and their behavior influenced by its character, so that where music is disordered, there morals are also depraved, and where it is well ordered, there men are well disciplined morally."[68]

Although the religious wars of the reign of Henri III snuffed out the Académie's life and the experiments of Baïf, some French writers at the turn of the century believed that the Baïfian circle had succeeded more perfectly than the ancients in producing the effects. In his commentary on *Philostrate* (1611), the French writer Artus Thomas recounted the familiar legend of Timaeus and Alexander and compared the power of Timaeus' ancient music with that of Claude Le Jeune, one of the leading composers of Baïf's Académie. Thomas explained that the music of Le Jeune, "who has far surpassed . . . the musicians of former ages," so deeply affected people that on one occasion a gentleman of the court was moved to attack another listener, injuring him, but that when Le Jeune changed the modes, the gentlemen became tranquil. Noting that several observers confirmed the story, Thomas concluded: "Such is the force and power over the mind of the modulation and movement of voices joined together."[69] Thomas' story was repeated by many seventeenth-century writers, but it was altered in the version of the composer Jéhan Titelouze, who told it to Mersenne, so that rhythm replaced harmony as the source of the power of Le Jeune's music.

The particular musical and poetic means used by Baïf to recover the ancient effects, and the fate of his academy, will be discussed in Chapter 2. Baïf's circle brought to its fullest practical application the musical philosophy of antiquity. This philosophy acquired prestige because Catherine de Medici and the Valois rulers approved of it, and because it conformed to the moral and didactic tone of the Counter Reformation. To a monarchy locked in religious warfare and social anarchy, the promise of turning men from violence to peace, from a mood of anger and revenge to a state of gentleness, temperance, and tranquillity, must have been appealing. It is not surprising that Charles IX supported Baïf's academy. Catherine and her sons may conceivably have viewed Baïf's efforts to create musical effects that would calm the spirit as a way out of the religious turmoil of the time. The breach between Catholic and Protestant did not appear so irreparable, despite the Council of Trent, to the Gallican and conciliatory French crown and to the poets of the Pléiade and the academy who favored religious reconciliation and reunion. Thus, the revival of the ancient effects complimented the prevailing mood at the court, which favored means other than war to heal the religious wounds. As Frances Yates has expressed it:

The yearning of the poet-theologians of the Pléiade for a return to the music of the ancients and its effects, should be related to the dreams of reuniting French Christians without bloodshed by such means as a revival of liturgical forms used in the early Church, or the singing of psalms in French, which were floating in the air at the time of the Colloquy of Poissy and the Council of Trent. . . . In the academic atmosphere of Ficinian neo-Platonism, with its view of all religions as containing some part of divine truth, the ferocious discords of the day may still have seemed unreal and capable of being soothed away by a love song.[70]

In this spirit, Baïf in fact did try to use the power of sacred music by advocating that French versions of the psalms be sung outside the churches. Baïf and other poets produced French translations of the psalms which Jacques Maudit and Claude Le Jeune set to music, following the principles believed to underlie ancient composition. Their avowed aim was to reform morals, to counter the psalmody of the Huguenots, and to arm Catholics with the powerful and tranquillizing effects of music. Unlike the psalms used by the Huguenots, which were the rhymed versions in French by Clément Marot and Théodore Bèze, Baïf's were in the quantitatively measured verse that he felt reproduced the effects of antiquity. But although Baïf appealed to Pope Gregory XIII in 1573 for approval of his rendition of the psalms as a Counter Reformation measure, he and his musicians viewed the psalms mainly as conciliatory devices that would promote the harmony of the faiths. Perhaps for this reason the Pope denied Baïf the right to publish his psalms. The Saint Bartholomew's Day Massacre spoiled any immediate hope for conciliation, but through musical and artistic means, the idea of religious purification and conciliation, at least of opposing Catholic groups, survived in the penitential processions, academies, and court entertainments of Henri III.[71] And this idea was reintroduced in the seventeenth century in the thought of Marin Mersenne.

Although he lived and wrote years after Baïf's death (1589) and the termination of the Académie de musique et de poésie,

Mersenne was the main channel to the seventeenth century for the musical philosophy of the sixteenth century. His musical ideas were no less firmly fixed to Plato than those of the Church Fathers, the Neo-Platonists, and the humanists had been. He wrote: "Since the perfect musician ought to know everything appertaining to harmony, it is right that he should consider what the Platonists have said concerning it, for their manner of reasoning is approved by many and especially by the early Fathers of the Church who preferred it to the manner of the peripatetics."[72] Thus, in the *Quaestiones Celeberrimae in Genesim* (1632) and later in *Harmonie universelle* (1634) he repeated the relevant concepts of Plato and his commentators, referred frequently to Ficino as the foremost interpreter of Plato's musical philosophy, and put forth again all of the expectations of the Pléiade and of Baïf in renewing the effects of ancient music. He stressed repeatedly that this revival would serve the needs of the monarch and the Church. How strongly Mersenne tied musical effects to religion can be seen in the preface to the *Harmonie*, where he notes that the early Christians portrayed Christ with a pastoral flute under the image of Orpheus. In imitating Christ, modern Christians should behave like Orpheuses, inducing people to forsake passion in favor of virtue. Mersenne even used as a frontispiece a picture of Orpheus charming the animals with his music, with verses from the 150th Psalm beneath the picture.[73] Mersenne dwelt especially on the ethical power of musical versions of the psalms. He included ten of Baïf's psalms in his *Quaestiones*, remarking on their sacred power. Mersenne not only became the major exponent of the doctrine of the effects in the first half of the seventeenth century, but, like Baïf, he tied this doctrine to the promotion of religious piety. The religious revival was in turn pinned to the revival of a Baïfian type of academy incorporating the entire body of sixteenth-century musical philosophy. Mersenne wrote: "Would that that Academy might drive its roots into our own time and put forth flowers and fruits, never ceasing from divine praises and bringing forth musical persons, each of whom would make music with his whole heart."[74]

Revealing his personal passion for science, Mersenne held that the study of music should begin with an analysis of the properties of sound. Everything in the world consists of weight, number, and measure, and sounds embody all three; musical sound, therefore, reproduces the essence of the world, and music is the image of the encyclopedia of knowledge. Furthermore, through the study of metrics, rhythms, and the modes (Mersenne opted for Zarlino's modal system), the academicians would work to restore ancient music, which would be used to inculcate virtue, praise God, and repel atheists. Supported by the Catholic kings of Europe and by the Papacy, the academy would have branches in several European countries and employ theologians, mathematicians, philosophers, alchemists, experts in medicine and jurisprudence, and a battery of scientists.

All of Mersenne's thoughts on an academy were set down in his book *Quaestiones*, dedicated to Jean-François de Gondi, archbishop of Paris. It was a highly important book for the transmission of the musical philosophy of antiquity since it preserved the memory of Baïf's academy as well as the Baïf-Maudit psalms; it restated all the concepts surrounding the doctrine of the effects, lacing them with quotations and references to Plato, Augustine, Ficino, and Tyard; and, in the spirit of Ronsard and Baïf, it created a new social and psychological framework for the old musical philosophy—that of Catholic reformation and revival. In order to steer clear of dangerous ideas and avoid the censors, Mersenne dropped the astrological and theurgic explanation of music so dear to Ficino, and he made less out of the imagery of pagan myths and fables that had been so useful to earlier Western writers in their conceptualization and description of ancient culture. Music was to be used for pious ends, associated with Christian instead of pagan images, and employed as a healing device.

Many of the ideas of the *Quaestiones* reappeared in Mersenne's more ambitious work, *Harmonie universelle*. The book, which contains an analysis of the old theory of the harmony of the spheres, is almost a nostalgic look backward to the Valois era. Dedicated to Louis de Valois, the grandson of Charles IX and Marie Touchet, *Harmonie* dwelt on the virtues of the Valois, paying particular notice to Charles' love of music. Mersenne reiterated his arguments for an academy, pointing out with

regret that there was still no academy for musical study, despite
the knowledge that the right sort of music is necessary for religion
and for the good of the state.

In other respects, however, the *Harmonie* represents an advance
in Mersenne's thought. In the *Quaestiones* he had still been tied
strongly to the rather rigid formulae and prescriptions of the
Baïfian circle. Not only was the *Harmonie* more scientific than
earlier musical treatises in its analysis of sound, intervals, scales,
and so forth, it revealed a tendency to free musical expression
from the requirements imposed on it by the humanists and poets.
While the union of text and music was still considered the key
to the effects, Mersenne did not insist that Baïf's system was the
only way to revive the musical power of antiquity. Indeed,
Mersenne challenged Baïf's assumption that in antiquity musical
rhythm was identical with poetic meter and that, therefore, the
effects can be achieved only if music rigidly follows the text.
In contrast to the Baïfian perspective of his *Quaestiones*, Mersenne
in the *Harmonie* invoked the authority of Dionysius of Halicarnas-
sus in arguing that poetic and musical rhythm were separate in
ancient music. He denied that Greek music followed the rhythms
of spoken verse or preserved the meter of the text, a point on which
earlier theorists had insisted.[75] Moreover, Mersenne's whole
conception of musical rhythm itself had changed since the
Quaestiones. In the *Quaestiones* he had reiterated the Augustinian
(and Baïfian) view that the impact of musical rhythm was on the
mind; that it was the number, proportion, and consonance of the
universe which rhythm embodied and which it impressed on
man's reason. The effect produced by poetic meter was also
based on the proportion and number inherent in classical feet.
"In the constitution of the feet excellent proportions of harmony
are found to be measured."[76] Relating musical consonances to
the proportions of the feet, Mersenne equated a fifth with iambic,
an octave with a mixture of pyrrhic and spondee, and a fourth
with iambic and spondee. In the *Harmonie*, however, Mersenne
seems to have succumbed to the Cartesian view that musical
proportions have no affinity with the mind, because musical
pleasure is a matter of subjective taste, not a matter of absolute
rational determination. Mersenne thus abandoned his notion of

a rational music based on a rapport between musical proportions and the mind in favor of a conception of musical effects based on the relationship between rhythmical figures and human passions. "If he could not achieve his moral aim of tempering the soul by means of music addressed to reason he could attempt the same end by addressing it to the passions."[77] The impact of musical rhythm was felt in the motions of the passions rather than in the mind's knowledge of mathematical proportions. Proportion, consonance, and number were reserved for the intellect; musical and poetic rhythms operated on the passions, which responded involuntarily to motions similar to their own. Unsure of the exact correlations between rhythms and passions, Mersenne simply called for rhythmic analysis, psychological investigations, and study of the blood and other humours. His conclusions reflect the seventeenth-century tendency to analyze human nature as much in terms of emotions as of reason, and they reflect the belief of most of the theorists and musicians of Mersenne's time that they were restoring the power of music without having to follow to the letter the requirements of the humanists or the laws of Baïf's academy. Finally, Mersenne's emphasis on rhythm is an indication of the growing importance of ballet in the seventeenth century. With the other theorists, Mersenne clung tenaciously, however, to the fundamental Platonic concepts of the universal harmony and the power of music to inculcate morality through its effects on the emotions; and, though less rigid than Baïf, he believed in the union of music and poetry.

Although Mersenne failed to establish an academy, his cell in the convent of the Minimes on the Place Royal became a center of learning from which ideas were disseminated throughout France and Europe. His own life "was itself a kind of informal and unorganized academy."[78] All the leading writers, scientists, and musicians of the time visited Mersenne. He continued to plead for an academy to study the universal harmony and acted to transmit the ancient musical philosophy to the seventeenth-century theorists. The assumptions and arguments of that philosophy were echoed in innumerable musical treatises and histories of the seventeenth century. Indeed, the entire musical thought of the age of royal absolutism revolved around the four central principles of Plato's musical philosophy and the subsequent elaborations of these principles by writers such as Augustine, Boethius, Ficino, Tyard, Baïf, and Mersenne. But there was a unique, though Platonic, twist in the seventeenth-century literature. Plato had insisted on the importance of music to the Guardian and on the necessity of laws governing its composition and its educational and moral role in the life of the republic. Using a Platonic rationale, Baïf had won royal support for the revival of ancient music in the expectation that it would promote order, virtue, and tranquillity. Imbued with the doctrine of the effects, the musical theorists of the seventeenth century laid their greatest stress on the moral and social utility of music for an orderly, enlightened, and well-governed state. Their aim was not so much to reproduce the actual music of antiquity, because they believed that French music, especially that of Lully, had successfully united poetry, music, and dance, and that the salutary effects of French music were self-evident. Rather, by explaining how important musical *spectacles*[79] had been in ancient societies, they hoped to show how beneficial the *spectacles* were for their own society, and why, in fact, they were receiving such considerable attention from the crown. In Platonic thought, as in Aristotelian, public and private morality were closely related and both were strongly affected by music. Music induced harmony in the individual's soul which, through the development of his rational and intuitive powers, resulted in a virtuous life. Music also helped to establish harmony in the state, serving the magistrates in the maintenance of order and justice. In the context of the evolving royal absolutism, it was the second of these two closely related Platonic ideas that the seventeenth-century musical theorists stressed. A collection of discourses on musical subjects by several anonymous writers published in the 1660's shows the typical outlook of mid-century France.[80] Drawing from Plato and Pythagoras as well as from Mersenne, whose book on harmony one author called "no less great than the Bible,"[81] these writers hold that since music reproduces the harmonious motion of the universe, it has the power to instill in man a love of order, a courageous spirit, and feelings of loyalty and devotion.

Musical influences are, therefore, valuable to a monarch seeking to win the loyalty of his subjects and to preserve the social balance among the estates.

In the second half of the seventeenth century, the assumptions of the musical philosophy of antiquity had become so commonplace as to appear regularly in the pages of the *Mercure galant*, the chief organ of court news and gossip. The views expressed by the poet Rault de Rouën in the October 1680 issue typified the *Mercure's* outlook.[82] Harmony is a divine creation, he wrote. It expresses the notion of the planets and the essence of nature. In creating musical harmony, the composer, therefore, is providing humanity with the principle of life itself. Indeed, he is providing the basis of government. This truth, so clearly perceived and explained by the ancient philosophers and churchmen, has been recognized by Louis XIV, who alone is responsible for reviving the musical *spectacles* of the ancients and for restoring political and musical harmony to the world.

When seventeenth-century writers referred to *spectacles*, they at first had in mind chiefly the ballets and later the operas, which became the favorite musical and dramatic media. Thus, the up-to-date *Mercure* repeatedly tied the ideas of universal harmony, the effects, and "the union" to the dance, and accentuated the social and moral utility of the dance. In an essay on the origin of the dance published in the *Mercure* in April 1680, a writer named Tournelle defined the dance as "a certain disposition of the body which, by its proportional movements and postures, following the sound of instruments or the voice, is animated and is led to the cadence, and which, according to the numbers, the modes and the measures of the art, imitates and expresses the passions of the spirit and the actions of the body."[83] Setting up numerical correlations between the tones of the diatonic scale and the planets, and metaphysical relationships between celestial motion and danced motion, Tournelle concluded in the accepted Platonic fashion that both instrumental harmony and the harmonious movements of the ballet are imitations of the universe. He rejected the idea that music may be a purer reflection of the universe than the dance, or that the dance is a more recent invention than musical harmony. Having emerged "from the shaking of the heavens and from their harmony," the dance is as old as the world and has always been cultivated together with music. The ancients devised three distinctive styles of dancing: a noble and grave style to express glory and heroism; a free style to represent the varying customs of men; and a lively style danced by sylvans and satyrs to represent peace and joy. Each reflects the celestial harmony; each expresses and affects human emotions; and each has been used, as they are used again today, in threatrical productions, public *spectacles*, and royal ceremonies, because the rulers of antiquity, like the rulers of modern France, affirmed the "utility [of the dance] as necessary to public welfare and the preservation of their states." Explaining that in the ancient societies of Greece, Rome, Ethiopia, and Egypt the dance was valued as both a good preparation for war and a worthy form of relaxation, Tournelle drew the obvious parallel to his own society and underscored his theme of utility. The dance, he wrote, "is so appropriate to dress the body, to form grace, and to elevate the actions of young seigneurs or princes, that one does not hesitate to instruct them according to the merit of their birth and the dignity of their persons; it is that [the dance] which is practiced in every European court as much for utility as for the entertainment of crowned heads."[84]

The pages of the *Mercure* were full of essays like Tournelle's which reiterated the fundamental tenets of Western musical philosophy and invoked the authority of the Bible, Pythagoras, and Plato, the Neo-Platonists, humanists, and French poets. The writers pointedly rejected the notion that the idea of the harmony of the spheres was meant as a metaphor by the ancient and modern philosophers, and they reaffirmed the power of music to inculcate morality, calling it a "divine science." They developed an arsenal of arguments, ranging from Platonic concepts and a chronicle of ancient musical customs to the authoritative opinions of French kings, to emphasize the social utility of music. The views of the *Mercure*, which the aristocratic and intellectual elite of French society shared, were best summarized in an article on harmony by a writer named Marpalu.[85] Marpalu set forth three interrelated contentions: first, music expresses the consonance and symmetry of the world and reflects man's affinity with celestial bodies ("the music of the earth is . . . a shadow of the harmony of the heavens"); second, philosophers since the time of Pythagoras and Plato have associated certain types of music with the temperaments of man and have believed in music's power to affect beneficially man's moral, emotional, and physical state; third, from the example of great men such as Alexander, from the teaching of the Chinese ("one famous Chinese held that a state could not be well governed without music, that is to say without Justice and Equity, which must create harmony"), and from the revival of music by François I, Henri II, and especially Louis XIV, Frenchmen have learned the value of music for casting off their coarseness and barbarity and for achieving a well-mannered, harmonious state. French musicians, he concluded, "are obliged to conserve the honor of music; because whether it has taken birth in France or was received and cultivated by our ancient Gauls, there is no nation which has more interest in maintaining it in its purity and in working for its perfection."

As royal absolutism reached its apex in the reign of Louis XIV, the musical philosophy of antiquity was explained more and more from a practical and utilitarian point of view and was more closely associated with the prestige of the monarchy. It was pointed out that the guardians of great states throughout history had sponsored musical productions not only to instill social order, tranquillity, and morality, but as signs that such things in fact prevailed in their states. Samuel Chappuzeau, a Protestant lawyer of the Parlement of Paris, wrote: "The pompous *spectacles* have always been the noble amusement of Great Men, when they desired to give themselves some relaxation from the attentions which occupy them incessantly for the welfare and the glory of states. It is that which does the most to manifest their felicity, and when one observes the sovereign's and the people's joy, it is a certain sign that the inside is tranquil, and that one does not fear at all the tumult from without."[86] French writers laid particular emphasis on Chappuzeau's last points. Lavish musical productions were a sign to foreign enemies that France was prosperous and comfortable, and in an age of wars of attrition, might depress the enemy and cause him to shorten his efforts. To continue *spectacles* during war, the poet Philippe Quinault wrote, is to "give some well marked evidence that it (the state) has inexhaustible treasures and men left; that the perils and the labors of a campaign . . . change neither the spirit nor the humor nor the courage of those who impose these armies; that they (the armies) are delighted to undertake great things in the gala season, since they can remember them with so much pleasure during the winter; that their conquests can contribute well to their glory, and not to their felicity, which seems to be already acquired."[87] The *Mercure* belabored this point in its regular reports of the king's entertainments. The arts and pleasures do not usually flourish in a state at war, the *Mercure* wrote in 1677. But the arts have never been more brilliant than they are now; although the king is occupied with the problems of Europe, he never ceases working for the glory of the arts.[88] In 1680, The *Mercure* pointedly observed that in the heated fury of war with an infinite number of enemies to fight, France still enjoys prosperity as the pleasures of the court reveal.[89] And in 1703, during the War of the Spanish Succession when France was suffering military and economic reversals, the *Mercure* noted that the entertainments of the carnival season had not been curtailed.[90] A letter Colbert sent in 1672 to Charles Errard, the director of the French Academy in Rome, indicates that the *Mercure* reflected royal policy. You must observe, he stated, "that the king has not decided to discontinue his protection of the arts despite the great wars with which his Majesty is at present occupied." Instead, Colbert continued, the king will cultivate the arts with renewed vigor because he realizes that "they can be used to eternize his grand and glorious deeds."[91]

Many French writers also noted the value of musical *spectacles* as a means of distracting the potentially mischievous nobility. Reflecting the king's memory of the Fronde, Abbé Du Guet wrote: "The *spectacles*, according to the politicians, are necessary to amuse a number of useless citizens who are always found in the large cities and who could create disorder . . . against the state if they did not have an amusement."[92] In his history of Louis' reign, Henri-Philippe de Limiers suggested that the king had learned how to use various sorts of *divertissements* to keep the nobles amused and submissive from Cardinal Mazarin, who used them to distract the young Louis.[93] The nobles were bound to raise trouble as long as they were idle, and since they cannot be forced to work, they must be constantly distracted. Ceremonies and *spectacles* were ideally suited to hold them to a virtuous, orderly routine. The pleasure of the *spectacles*, wrote Philippe Quinault, "draws them there without violence; the hours of their repose slip away without regret; they lose all thoughts of doing evil, and their idleness itself is occupied."[94] Louis' purposes were not lost on foreign visitors to the French court. Estimating that Louis spent over 100,000 écus annually on music alone, Primi Visconti, comte de San-Maiolo, observed that the king had "a natural garden . . . in which he fostered the cultivation of the arts and sciences, but more for political reasons than for pleasure."[95] Ézéchiel Spanheim, the ambassador from Brandenburg, came close to the heart of the matter. Louis not only used the arts to divert the nobles, but to impress them as well. The key to Louis' encouragement of artistic *spectacles*, Spanheim wrote, is that they helped to "elevate him not only above the heroes of his race or those of other peoples, but beyond the scope and the boundaries of the mortal condition."[96] Spanheim noted that Colbert must have concurred with Louis' view since he filled the treasury with funds to be used for the king's magnificent fetes and edifices. On one occasion, however, when Colbert reportedly criticized Louis' lavish expenditures on musical *divertissements*, the king supposedly replied: "My glory, monsieur, one must remember is more important to me than anything else."[97]

Louis might have said, "my glorious image." Of all the arguments used to buttress the contention that musical and artistic productions were socially useful, the one which appeared most frequently in seventeenth-century literature was that the arts demonstrated the kingdom's grandeur and created a glorious image of the monarchy. This was certainly the uppermost idea in Louis' own mind. In his *Mémoires* he wrote that the unifying element behind all of his policies was "the same passion for the grandeur of the state." Often criticized for his vanity and pride, Louis held the view that whatever contributed to his own personal glory, his own heroic image, benefited the whole society. "The luster of one man redounds to the luster of the entire state," he wrote;

"the brilliant image of the grandeur in which he is elevated is carried to all parts on the wings of his fame."[98] The people must have someone to emulate and someone in whom the splendor of their society is reflected. This attitude explains why he supervised closely the work of his musicians and painters, why he used the arts to project his image, and why he believed that his *divertissements* were "both useful and glorious." Besides, whether as spectators or participants, the people derived pleasure from the ceremonies, operas, and *divertissements* of the monarch. "The public *spectacles,* having always created diversions for the most ordinary of peoples, and having been able to contribute to their happiness as well as to their relaxation and abundance, we do not content ourselves with watching over the tranquillity of our subjects through our constant attentions; we want to contribute even more through the public *divertissements*."[99]

The *Mercure galant* reinforced the king's views. Royal *spectacles,* wrote the *Mercure,* are expressions of the public joy in the king's conquests. Those who work for them and participate in them, "can do nothing which points up the grandeur of France more, the abundance which it has of everything, and the calm that it enjoys as a result."[100] The king's attention to the arts, the *Mercure* wrote in 1682, has made France celebrated throughout the world. In previous times the Italians aroused enthusiasm for their *spectacles.* Now it is France that attracts the curiosity of travelers from every nation, the *Mercure* continued.[101] Louis has never spared expense to insure the glory of his nation; "to this end he finds it necessary to support the fine arts."[102] That support was also undertaken so that "posterity will see his victories."[103]

The usefulness of the arts in creating an illustrious image of Louis for the benefit of posterity was a recurring theme in seventeenth-century literature. It constituted yet another argument in support of the utilitarian function of musicians, poets, and painters as image makers. No less noteworthy a writer than Pierre Bayle wrote: "Great warriors and the Muses need each other; it is the warriors' job to obtain peace and security for the Muses; it is the Muses job to immortalize in songs the beautiful deeds of heroes."[104] It seemed quite natural to seventeenth-century writers that artists should serve their patron by eulogizing him and guaranteeing him lasting fame. If there was any notion that royal patronage entailed an unwanted loss of artistic freedom, it was not expressed. Seventeenth-century musicians and artists apparently saw no harm in using the king's exploits for their inspiration and subject matter; it seemed logical to those who wrote about cultural ideas and events that the arts performed their proper social role and justified their royal support when they "hasten to render famous to posterity a name . . . so glorious for those who will follow him one day, so terrible to his enemies, so useful to his allies, so venerable to all peoples who have the good fortune of being the witnesses of his surprising actions and wise behavior."[105]

Although it is not always obvious, the intellectual underpinning of all the arguments advanced by seventeenth-century writers in support of the utility of music and the arts was the old theory of the moral effects of music and the other related elements of the ancient musical philosophy. The seventeenth-century writers, working within the framework of absolutism, simply equated morality with patriotic devotion to the king and seized upon opera, a modern invention and the king's favorite diversion, as the ideal instrument to achieve the effects through a perfect integration of harmony, poetry, and the dance. The Abbé Jean Terrasson, a strong defender of the moderns in the debate between the ancients and the moderns, gave probably the clearest expression to this development. The aim of politics, he wrote, is the maintenance of order and tranquillity. In pursuit of that aim, wise rulers must instill civil and moral virtue in themselves and in their subjects. Although the state cannot make men pious, it can keep them from barbarity and malevolence; it can induce loyalty and peacefulness. Music, especially opera, Terrasson continued, is an excellent means to instill virtuous sentiments. Presenting contented shepherds on the stage, operas create a mood of joy and calm. The shepherds urge us to be loving and faithful. Indeed, the prevalence of the love theme in operas contributes to the plan of God, who gave man the natural desire of procreation. Thus, while clerics may turn to piety and abstinence, musicians and poets must aid princes in promoting love and life. Moreover, operas present heroic characters who inspire the virtues of courage, sacrifice, and loyalty, inviting the audience to emulate the heroes of the stage. Thus, the musicians and poets "who work on the *spectacles* can regard themselves in a certain sense as the first or perhaps the only masters of morality whom the king will have."[106] "Opera will ordinarily be more useful to princes than tragedy," Terrasson declared, because it has greater power to inculcate popular virtues. Presented in an opera, virtue acquires a charm which it does not otherwise possess. It is more advantageous to present duty to princes under the guise of pleasure, because "sweetness (*douceur*) is more appropriate to instruct even than austerity and dryness." Opera possesses the charm necessary to make virtue attractive and is, therefore, the perfect vehicle of public morality.

Terrasson's views, which provided a well-constructed bridge joining the ancient musical philosophy to the society of absolutist France, were shared by other writers of the period. Addressing the Académie royale des belles-lettres, François Charpentier called attention to the way in which the animated music of Louis XIV's musicians has proven capable of arousing the finest sentiments of the human spirit.[107] Charpentier's colleague, Titon du Tillet, wrote that music is valued by the nation which recognizes that it is "capable of making the most lively impressions on the spirit and on the human heart, and of inspiring the most elevated sentiments."[108] Claude Menestrier, a prominent Jesuit priest and writer and an authority on the musical philosophy of antiquity, called attention to the unique union of music and poetry in opera. The text, he declared, causes us "to love virtue . . . by singing the praises of heroes and by representing that which they have made more worthy of immortality."[109] The music penetrates the soul directly, filling it with moral inspiration. Finally, another cleric, the Abbé Du Guet, labeled the opera a school of morality because it reaches such a large audience. "Does it not attract all the estates," he asked; "and do the workers not leave their shops, the men of war their camp, the merchants their companies, the magistrates their benches; do not the seigneurs leave the court and the kings their throne in order to come to hear them?"[110] The musical theater supports virtue, he declared. The power of music gives life to the heroic sentiments of verse. Together they "charm the ears, penetrate the heart, and enflame the emulation for glory; . . . the theater of the opera is an appropriate school for re-creating the spirit and at the same time inciting it to virtue."

Thus, the writers of the age of absolutism transformed the musical philosophy of antiquity. They politicized the concept of the universal harmony and the doctrine of the effects by tying opera to the harmony of the state, by equating morality with loyalty to the monarchy, and by converting Plato's ideas on the importance of music to the guardian and to the Republic into a grand justification of music's role in embellishing the grandeur of the state and the heroic image of the monarch. The musical thought that dominated the West, from the time of Plato and the Church Fathers to that of the Ficinian Neo-Platonists and French academicians, is sometimes difficult to discern in the literature of the seventeenth century, so much of which was written to propagate the utilitarian value of music. But seventeenth-century literature on the history of music does show how deeply the ideas and the example of antiquity were entrenched in the thought of the period. Indeed, the historical approach to the music of the ancients perhaps constitutes the century's greatest innovation. The seventeenth-century writers retained all the fundamental ingredients of Platonist musical philosophy. They accentuated the doctrine of the effects because it fitted in so nicely with their idea of the utility of music. Following Mersenne, they were less concerned about reviving ancient music than about underscoring the social and political value of music per se, especially dramatic and ceremonial music; they doubtless believed that French composers, notably Jean-Baptiste Lully, had already achieved the closest possible union of music and poetry in opera. "The effects of Lully's operas were regarded as having a potency equal to that attributed to the music of the ancients."[111] Besides, the union was enriched by the added attraction of the dance and visual spectacle. Where the seventeenth century writers really parted company with earlier writers was in their preference for a historical approach to ancient music over the metaphysical, aesthetic, and astrological approach of the Ficinian Neo-Platonists and the Pléiade. The ancient, medieval, and Renaissance philosophy of music was part of their intellectual heritage and was carried about as a piece of necessary luggage. But in the age of absolutism, the musical writers did not need a metaphysical rationale to convince scholars of the significance of music; they needed a body of historical examples to justify the musical enterprises of the monarchy to the general public. French writers, therefore, drew parallels between the musical practices of the ancient Greeks and Romans and those of their own time. Although the literature is extensive, the work of four writers stands out: Philippe Quinault, Michel de Pure, Claude Menestrier, and Jacques Bonnet.[112]

Concentrating mainly on the development of ancient and modern *spectacles*, Pure and Quinault traced the spread of musical and theatrical pageants, chariot races, and combats in the arena from Roman society to the societies of Africa, Asia, and Europe. Both writers emphasized the political utility of *spectacles* for ancient governments, contending that republican magistrates, emperors, and wealthy seigneurs had sponsored them as gestures of beneficence to their subjects and as demonstrations to conquered peoples that their rule was not tyrannical. The *spectacles* were designed to inspire popular admiration of the ruler, to honor the gods, and to divert the nobles and senators. Pure and Quinault underscored the music as an essential part of the show. "All kinds of music were known to them and performed at their games."[113] Chants and symphonies were performed at their fetes by musicians who held a high rank in the society. Music was especially important in the mamouth processions hailing the return of conquering heroes, in which trumpeters, flutists, and oboists joined soldiers' choruses in acclaiming the hero's deeds. Dramatic pageants also always included dances and concerts. All of these ancient *spectacles*, according to Pure and Quinault, constituted the origin and model for those of the modern era. Revived by Cardinal Richelieu, the grand *spectacles* of antiquity had been perfected by Louis XIV, who imitated Caesar in his entertainments as in his conquests. Quinault, however, acknowledged the difference between ancient and modern *spectacles* by noting the absence of chariot races and bestial contests in modern times and pointing to the refinement and dignity of Louis XIV's *spectacles*. Pure, on the other hand, accentuated the similarity of ancients and moderns, pointing to the parallels in antiquity of the tournaments, aquatic fetes, hunts, and musical dramas of the seventeenth century. The two writers agreed that, although the *spectacles* had been improved, their social and political value for both ancient and modern eras was the same.

Of the many varieties of *spectacles* treated by seventeenth-century writers, those commanding the most serious attention were the dance *spectacles*. The French court attached enormous social prestige to dancing skills, and ballet occupied the primary place in the musical and dramatic productions of the court. As a result, the writers were especially interested in the parallels between ancient and modern dance. In his essay on the ancients and moderns, Michel de Pure stressed what he believed to be the close similarity between French ballet and the dances of the Greeks and Romans. Pure maintained in particular that the dance served a parallel function for both societies. Both incorporated dancing into poetic dramas in order to celebrate great historical events and to represent "the most profound mysteries of nature and morality."[114] Moreover, both moderns and ancients recognized that ballet increases man's sensitivity, that it is a grace worthy of distinguished nobles and "a political virtue of a royal talent."

The most comprehensive histories of the ballet were written by Claude Menestrier[115] and Jacques Bonnet.[116] Menestrier identified three fundamental reasons for the widespread use of the dance in Greek society, each of which was equally noted for modern France: the ballet was an effective way of portraying significant historical events; it was an animated, colorful form of public celebration; and it served as an excellent physical preparation for combat. Menestrier then tied each of these social functions to the philosophy of Pythagoras and Plato, especially to the idea that the universe was comprised of harmonious and numerical proportions which could be imitated in measured cadences. From Pythagoras the Greeks learned that dances are consonant with celestial motion; they are an image of the cosmic order, reflecting the dance of the stars. Menestrier also cited Lucien's belief that the dance was primordial, originating at the same time as the

universe itself. More important, Menestrier, using Plato as an
authority, related the dance to the moral effects of music. Dancing
counteracts dangerous passions and aids music in forming
harmony in the souls of both performers and spectators. Did not
Agamemnon prove the validity of Plato's belief, Menestrier
asked, by providing dances for his wife in which the virtues of
illustrious women were represented, instilling in her a love of
virtue? (In light of what Agamemnon's wife did to her husband
after virtue had been instilled in her, one wonders if both Agamemnon and Menestrier did not underestimate the affective power
of the dances.) The Jesuit writer concluded that in conjunction
with song and poetry, the dance in antiquity contributed to the
moral development of man, expressed the virtues of the gods,
and therefore, performed a vital religious function, not only for
the Greeks but for Indians, Persians, Jews, and especially
Christians. John the Evangelist used the image of a concert to
describe the glory of the saints and the order of heaven, and Saint
Denys explained the celestial hierarchy through music. The
Church Fathers provided an excellent example for moderns:
they used the choirs and dances of the patriarchs, prophets, and
martyrs to express the perfection of the Church. Menestrier
pointed to the worthiness in modern times of Baïf's attempt to
imitate the ancients, but he criticized Baïf incorrectly for failing
to blend dancing and other ingredients used in "early operas"
with music and poetry. Presumably the royal musicians and the
Jesuits, who taught ballet and music in their schools, did a better
job. Menestrier was determined to associate the morally efficacious
effects of ballet with religious traditions and practices in antiquity
and in the present. Nevertheless, with an eye to the practical
outlook of his readers in courtly circles, Menestrier emphasized
the physical and emotional relaxation associated with dancing.
"The *divertissement* is no less necessary to the mind in order to
relax it, than nourishment is to the body in order to maintain it.
It is for that reason that Plato, after having formed the idea of a
perfect republic, desired that the legislator introduce some fetes
and public celebrations, festins, dances, and *spectacles* in order
to unite the people and to give the magistrates a rest from their
assiduous devotion to duty."[117] Although he realized that dancing

was necessary to good health and social unity, Plato also understood that dancing mollified dangerous passions and fostered man's sense of order, proportion, and harmony. Through Plato, Menestrier joined his moral and religious interpretation of the dance to the physical and relaxing benefits of dancing; the idea of the harmony of soul and body provided the connecting link.

Reiterating many of Menestrier's contentions, Jacques Bonnet located the origins of the dance in the mystery religions of the ancient Egyptians and Greeks. Although dancing has always had a recreational value, its moral utility was what concerned the ancient philosophers and rulers. Instead of using the dance as just a simple form of pleasure, "the first legislators made use of it for the perfection of morals" and the ancient heroes "viewed it as the first element in the art of war."[118] It was only after its religious significance, military utility, and emotional and physical value had been accepted that dancing came to play a part in Greek entertainments. Eventually, Sophocles and Euripides employed dancing, with choruses and instrumental music, in the theater. By Aristotle's time, ballet was accepted as a proper means of imitating nature and representing fables. Bonnet joined Menestrier in affirming that after centuries of neglect, French kings had finally learned to appreciate the utility of the dance. Among all the public *spectacles* of modern times, the ballets "must hold the first rank, because they are an older institution than most of the other *spectacles* which the Greeks and the Romans created for the people's enjoyment and . . . for the magnificence of their fetes and ceremonies."[119] The ballet, Bonnet enjoined, exists in its present state as a dramatic dance accompanied by music and poetry. In the union of elements and in its social use by modern kings as a means of entertaining the people, the ballet represents a true return to the golden age of Greece. Then, as now, the ballet reflects the moral well-being of the people and the magnificence of rulers.

Menestrier and Bonnet, in their earnest attempt to find historical precedents for the French delight in *spectacles*, delved into the traditions of other people besides the Greeks and Romans, including the Hebrews, the early Christians, and the Chinese. Menestrier drew scraps of evidence from the Bible. Moses, he declared, after crossing the Red Sea, danced with drums to the air of a hymn in order to thank God for saving his people. The prophet Jeremiah received God's promise to reestablish Jerusalem for the suffering Hebrews and to restore their ancient songs, ceremonies, and dances. The Jesuit historian even discovered that many of the ceremonies described in the Bible actually resembled musical dramas. David's dramatic songs thanking God for his victories were the original operas, according to Menestrier. The dancing and singing which followed Moses' crossing of the Red Sea blended musical elements in the way that "the musical performances are today composed of récits and ballets."[120] Along with concerts of voices, flutes, harps, and lutes, musical ballets were danced after David and Saul defeated the Philistines. The Hebrews had a form of recitative for their musical *divertissements*, as Solomon revealed in Ecclesiastes. In fact, he composed his own marriage music, in which allegorical characters acted out a musical play. Religious passion plays, which were celebrations of God and the ruler, made their appearance later in history, when the Church became the main source of dramatic music. First introduced during pilgrimages to Jerusalem, devotional music dramas depicted Christ's life and the miracles of the saints. Later on, townspeople began performing musical mystery plays on feast days "both for the instruction of the people and for their diversion." These perform-ances served as the celebrations for the entry of princes into the cities.[121] Eventually, the performances were given in theaters, and in the seventeenth century religious music dramas were performed before the popes. Menestrier concluded that the modern associa-tion of music with ceremony, celebration, and drama grew out of several centuries of development, rooted as much in the Judeo-Christian tradition as in pagan antiquity. The important func-tion of music in the modern state and church is a natural out-growth of its function in biblical times and in the Middle Ages. The Jesuit Father thus gave his blessing to the revival of musical *spectacles* representing the highest aspirations and values of French society and produced by a king "who has a very fine taste and discernment."

During the seventeenth and eighteenth centuries, the interest

of Europeans in the non-European world was mounting. Both
Menestrier and Bonnet treated Chinese conceptions and uses of
music. Menestrier acknowledged that the Chinese had long
possessed "most of the things which are used in Europe," and he
stressed the historical importance of music to Chinese rulers. The
laws and political maxims of Chinese government were expressed
through secret chants known only to the ruling families. Ling U,
who once ruled a part of China and who wanted to learn the laws
governing other areas of China, sent envoys to study the music
of the Cheve family to learn the secrets of government.[122] Bonnet
noted that the Chinese attributed the invention of music to an
ancient prince, resembling Jesus Christ, who invented a thirty-six
chord instrument in order to soften the fierce humor of his subjects
and to accustom them to beneficial entertainments. Music was
essential to Chinese government. For the ancient imperial families
of China, music constituted "the science of civil and political
laws, without which a prince could scarcely succeed to the
empire."[123] Furthermore, music retained a political significance
in modern China. "Those who possess the top jobs of the empire
are profoundly erudite and avail themselves of the rules of music
as a key to government." Bonnet concluded that the Chinese
continue to heed the advice of Confucius, who said that one could
not alter music without harming the government and believed
that music helped to instill morality.

It seemed to Bonnet that sleep alone was unaccompanied by
music in China. Though music is performed constantly, the annual
public fetes for agricultural laborers and the festivals of the
lanterns are the principal occasions for musical performances.
"Everyone in the entire empire illuminates so many fires and
lanterns during the evening that everything in the kingdom seems
like a universal incendiary, which is animated by the concerts
that are heard from every direction."[124] The king and the court
receive special attention from the concerts of voices and instruments, Bonnet contended. In the moon festivals and other
celebrations music is the main *divertissement*, and all the people
participate. "The Chinese regard these kinds of fetes as an amusement of politics." To illustrate his contention, Bonnet told a story
about the Emperor Lieupang, who ruled two hundred years

before Christ. After finding that certain villages would not submit to his rule, Lieupang prepared for their devastation. Having camped the night before the attack in order to rest and to survey the land, Lieupang suddenly heard to his astonishment a great concert of voices and instruments. He reportedly told his officers that these people must be ruled well since they love music and that their resistance to him was a testimony to their sense of duty. Consequently, he revoked his orders and granted them life and liberty. The resisting peoples, having "found their salvation in music," then praised Lieupang with entertainments. Thus, Bonnet contributed a Chinese legend to the ever-growing catalogue of stories about the effects of music. His purpose in telling it was clear: he wanted to point out the utility and importance that the Chinese attached to music in order to justify the importance that Louis XIV and his court gave to it. Bonnet added a single note of caution: "The history of China is filled with many examples of emperors who have been deposed from the empire for having too much attachment to music, which caused them to neglect the needs of the empire."

Bonnet drew his examples from the Gauls as well as from Greek, Roman, and Chinese civilizations. He asserted that the Gauls, having performed music since the year 2140 B.C., used it to educate their youth and to accompany their armies. Bonnet contended that early Gallic hymns were sung to stir up the army during battle or to placate generals when peace came. Clovis and Charlemagne employed music at ceremonies and public celebrations to entertain the court. François I gave the real thrust to music, however, by founding the Collège Royal, whose mathematics division featured the study of music. Under Charles IX a royal academy of music was founded, and once a week the king and his court attended its concerts. Musical activity in France reached its zenith in the seventeenth century, according to Bonnet, when the monarchy introduced it into every phase of national life.

Thus, present was linked to past, and a musical history of antiquity was joined to the musical philosophy of antiquity. France's picture of itself as the descendant of ancient Greece and Rome was complete. The musical mania of the French court was justified by the example of revered peoples and civilizations and by the belief in the moral effects of music, which was transformed into a doctrine of its social and political utility. The union of music and poetry was realized fully in the opera, and music was secure under the laws of Louis XIV's absolute state.

⚜ 2

Music and the Monarchy
before the Reign of Louis XIV

Musical Pageantry at the Valois Court

The French monarchy's interest in music can be traced to the fifth century, when King Clovis reportedly used music in his coronation; after defeating the Goths in 507, he insisted that Theodoric supply him with musicians.[1] Subsequent Frankish princes held militant musical celebrations in order to foster warlike emotions. During Pépin's reign a body of musicians was organized for the royal chapel, and in later years Charlemagne cultivated music and heard the deeds of his predecessors sung in verse.[2] The itinerant troubadours and jongleurs made musical entertainments so commonplace in the seats of power of the Frankish empire that the comte d'Anjou reportedly said to Louis IV: "Know, Sire, that a king without any taste for music is a crowned ass."[3] By the twelfth century, the troubadours were mixing music with poetry, and the jongleurs accompanied themselves on instruments. The first medieval theaters for musical-dramatic performances were probably established by pilgrims or crusaders, who in the fourteenth century presented religious dramas with musical interludes that were called mystères. Charles VI was a patron of these pilgrims; some of them in 1402 formed a group and took the name of Confrères de la Passion. Gradually the mystères became less solemn, and nonreligious *divertissements* were added to them.[4]

At the princely courts, meanwhile, the momerie and the mascarade made their appearance in the fourteenth and fifteenth centuries and are regarded as the prototypes of the ballet de cour.

[55]

The momeries were associated from their inception with coronations, solemn entries of princes, and royal marriages. They
were "species of ballets for two or three disguised persons, miming
a role, singing verses, and dancing."[5] The subjects of these
productions were allegorical, biblical, or taken from legends of
chivalry.[6] One of the earliest momeries was danced on January
29, 1392, at the Hôtel Reine Blanche to celebrate the marriage
of a knight of the house of Vermandois to a lady of the household
of Queen Isabelle of Bavaria. Composed by one of the king's
favorites, Hugonin de Janzay, this momerie included among the
participants Charles, the comte de Jouy, Charles de Poitiers,
and three additional courtiers. Dressed in skintight costumes,
each sewed to the other and each covered with hair, the six
performers rushed into the assembly hall, roaring, screaming, and
dancing like savages. Unable to recognize these masked characters, who created quite a stir among the nobles and ladies at
the banquet table, the king's brother lunged at the weird-looking
dancers with a torch and accidentally set fire to their costumes.
The queen, quickly recognizing her husband, covered him with
her robe and smothered the flames. Charles VI, however, fell
into an incurable madness after the incident.[7]

The mascarades, which also foreshadowed the court ballets,
were performed with increasing frequency in the sixteenth century.
In some cases the mascarades were unpretentious entertainments
mingling poetry, dancing, and music and given for small groups
of nobles in a royal château. They had loosely structured plots
and often took the form of a procession. Copies of the spoken
or sung verses were distributed among the guests, and members
of the audience frequently joined the dancers. These performances
usually concluded with an entrée danced by the king and queen
and the execution by the masked performers of figured dances.
Under Catherine de Medici, Pompeo Diobono, Virgilio Bracesco,
and other Italians came to France and added figured dances
such as the brando and the ballo.[8] The mascarades grew more
spectacular when the Italian *mascherata*, in which masked dancers
on floats acted out allegories and delivered verses of praise to
the ruler, were introduced to the French court in the middle
of the sixteenth century and came to be used in conjunction with

court ceremonies. Indeed, the mascarade, a loosely defined species of musical and danced theater, cannot be disassociated from the social and artistic setting in which it appeared or the events which it commemorated. Music in general, and the ballet in particular, became an important part of the life of the sixteenth-century monarchy mainly through its use along with the other arts in the ceremonial pageants of the Valois rulers. Music can be said to have served the monarchy in the sense that the royal entries, processions, and festivals of the Valois were "part of the build-up of these monarchs as 'Roman emperors,' descendants of the ancient Trojan line."[9] For such spectacular events musicians and artists transformed the city of Paris into an ancient shrine bedecked with theaters, triumphal arches, and obelisks. A fairy-tale atmosphere was created in which pagan rites mingled with chivalrous Christian ceremonies of an earlier era. The artists used legend and allegory to create a heroic image of a modern king in antique garb. The imagery of the sculpted figures on triumphal arches, like the characters of the ballets and the masked figures of the processions and carrousels, cast the Valois rulers as the descendants of Hercules, Ulysses, and Jason. The tableaux, whether painted or acted, recounted the great deeds and moral character of the kings to a bedazzled public.[10]

Henri II's entry into Paris in 1549 set the tone of royal pageantry for the next half century. The elaborate procession climaxed in a tiltyard where the chevaliers, masked as Amazons, danced a ballet. Along the route an artistic *spectacle* had been arranged by the poets of the Pléiade, the sculptor Jean Goujon, the king's musicians, and the architect Jean Martin. Their use of classical imagery and motifs perpetuated a practice that François I had begun but that Henri II, who was obsessed by his own apotheosis, carried to extremes, as the court acted out the drama of Olympus in its ceremonies, festivals, and ballets. The Gallic Hercules, a symbol of France and her kings in royal ceremonies, was represented in a triumphal arch (Figure 1) at the Porte de Saint Denys.[11] The power of the Gallic Hercules, in contrast to the Hercules of the Emperor Charles V, rested in his eloquence rather than in his physical strength. Instead of a club the Gallic Hercules held a lance wrapped in a serpent, and a laurel branch

Figure 1. Arch surmounted by the Gallic Hercules constructed for Henri II's entry into Paris in 1549. Plate engraved in wood, attributed to Jean Goujon; reprinted from *C'est l'ordre qui a ésté tenu à la nouvelle et joyeuse entrée que* ... *le Roy* ... *Henry deuzième* ... *a faicte en sa bonne ville* ... *à Paris* ... *le seizième jour de juin* 1549 (Paris, 1549), p. A4. (Photograph courtesy of the Bibliothèque Nationale, département de réserve imprimée.)

symbolizing victory through prudence. Chains were loosely strung from his mouth to the ears of four figures representing nobility, the church, council, and labor. The chains' looseness conveyed the idea that the figures were persuaded to follow the king by his eloquence rather than by force. The arch was also embellished with inscriptions including the king's motto, "Donec totum impleat orbem" (Till he fills the whole world), and a quatrain explaining that the estates of France follow the king of their own volition.[12] Henri II was commemorated by an arch at the Pont Notre-Dame, where he was depicted as Typhis, captain of the ship Argo, pilot of the Republic, and conqueror of the golden fleece. The navy, which became a regular symbol in royal entries, represented good fortune and stability. At another arch further on, Henri II and the duc d'Anjou were depicted as Castor and Pollux, also symbolizing pilots of the ship of state. In the inscriptions the Argonauts proclaimed Henri as their pilot. The imagery included a figure of Hermes Trismegistes who represented the young ruler, while a soaring eagle, Jupiter's bird, symbolized the ascent to heaven of the deceased king's soul. The last arch of the processional route erected on the rue Saint Antoine was designed in the form of an H to honor the king and bore the figures of Belgius, Brennus, Mars, and Dis. The inscriptions compared Henri's kindness and prudence to the virtues of the Greeks and Romans.

The artistic and musical pageantry of the Valois era reached its peak during the regency of Catherine de Medici and the reign of her son, Charles IX. Determined to preserve the monarchy for her sons and to resolve the bitter religious and political conflicts of the time, Catherine frequently used court festivals as a political weapon; she believed that portraying Charles as a god would enhance his stature and that Protestants and Catholics could work out their hostilities in dramatic, make-believe combats. In 1564 Catherine arranged an elaborate succession of fetes, jousts, tilts, and mascarades at Fontainebleau, highlighted by a musical water ballet on the pond behind the château.[13] The theme of the aquatic drama was that the religious wars had caused a moral decline and had ruined the happy life of the realm. Fauns, nymphs, and other divinities of nature had been driven into hiding by the destructive power of Circé. Charles IX, however, would expel Circé, restore the forest gods, and heal the wounds of the kingdom by reconciling Huguenot and Catholic.

A florid mascarade commemorating a royal visit to Bar-le-duc offered an even more flattering picture of the king's abilities. In the allegorical drama the four elements clashed with the four planets for the honor of serving Charles. Charles' rule of the earth was likened to Jupiter's domination of the heavens. Catherine de Medici also worked international politics into the court fetes. In 1565, while Charles was enjoying a series of mascarades at the Hôtel de Ville in Paris, Catherine held a ceremonious meeting in Bayonne with her daughter Elizabeth, the wife of King Philip of Spain. Catherine was later accused of having plotted the Saint Bartholomew's Massacre on this occasion. In addition to an allegorically presented tournament, a fanciful mascarade was performed. Knights and maidens who had been changed by sorcery into trees and rocks were miraculously restored to human form when France and Spain concluded peace.

On the eve of the Massacre, Catherine staged one of the most politically charged *spectacles* produced in the period of the Valois. Seen in retrospect, it might have chilled the blood of the spectators. The *Paradis d'amour* was performed on August 20, 1572, in the salle de Bourbon in connection with the festivities for the wedding of Marguerite of Valois and Henri, the Protestant king of Navarre. It was a fully developed dramatic ballet with sung récits and, in contrast to the processional quality of earlier court *spectacles*, had a set scene where the action took place. Although it was still linked to the old mascarades by the element of a masked joust which interrupted the drama, the *Paradis* introduced a new genre, the ballet de cour.[14] The drama, with verses by Ronsard and music by Le Jeune and Courville, depicted an assault on the nymphs of Paradise by a band of knights, representing the Huguenots, and by the bridegroom himself. The knights were defeated and dispatched to hell by characters representing Charles IX and his two brothers, the duc d'Alençon and the duc d'Anjou. In act 2, Cupid and Mercury delivered a critical harangue to the defenders of Paradise. Joined by twelve nymphs, Mercury performed a lengthy ballet whose rhythmic power delivered the naughty knights from their underworld prison. The theatrical warfare was sustained the following day by a tilting match in which the king's troop, dressed as Amazons, were opposed by Henri de Navarre's troop, dressed as Turks. Later regarded by Protestant writers as a prophecy of the Massacre, the drama was probably intended to forestall real combat by providing a substitute. But this mock warfare proved an inadequate substitute and must have contributed to the tense atmosphere in which the Massacre occurred just three days later.

The court of Charles IX enjoyed its dramatic and musical pageantry in the form of ceremonial processions and entries as well as in the more theatrical form of ballet. The musical and artistic ingredients of these processions were so similar to those of the more structured dramatic ballets that the two forms of court pageantry were nearly indistinguishable at times. For these pageants Charles employed a battery of poets and artists, and a permanent corps of twelve instrumentalists and seven singers.

In March 1571 Charles IX made a grand entry into Paris in a spirit of buoyancy and optimism: a treaty with the Huguenots had ended temporarily the civil conflicts, and France had a new queen, Elizabeth of Austria, the daughter of Maximillian II.[15] For the occasion, the whole city was dressed in the garb of an antique mascarade. A grand procession was followed by water festivals, dramas, and jousts. The poets Ronsard and Dorat handled all the details of the entry for the city officials, supplying the artists Germain Pilon and Niccolo dell'Abbate with specifications for the arches, sculpted figures, and devices, and providing the verses inscribed on the arches. The first arch at the Porte de Saint Denys was surmounted by figures of Francus and Pharamond. Ronsard explained that the kings of France descended from Francus, son of Hector; like the Romans, they were descendants of the Trojans. Since Francus' wife was a German princess, Charles IX's marriage to Elizabeth restored the ancient bond of Trojan and German. It is significant that Charles IX had consulted earlier with Ronsard during the composition of his poem *La Franciade* in order to assure himself that the poem firmly established the descent of French kings from the heroes

of ancient legend. His fixation on this special fabulous lineage
of French sovereigns was shared by most of his successors. Invented
originally by the Merovingians, the idea that French rulers were
descended from Francus the Trojan was accepted as serious
genealogy and explains in part why mythological figures were
so important in all of the artistic and musical productions of the
sixteenth and seventeenth centuries.[16]

Thus, all along the processional route, Ronsard devised a
spectacle of arches with easily interpreted symbolic figures[17]
representing Catherine de Medici as Gaul and Artemis, and
Henri II and his brother as the Trojans Castor and Pollux piloting
the ship of France to victory. Moreover, the interior walls of the
arches contained Virgilian verses heralding the union of France
and the Empire; they were lined with emblematic paintings by
dell'Abbate.

The artistry of the poets, painters, and sculptors was again
demanded to celebrate the queen's entry three weeks later, and
was applied to a richly painted banquet hall in the palace of the
bishop of Paris where the procession concluded. On the ceiling
four allegorical navies representing the four estates of the realm—
religion, justice, nobility, and commerce—were portrayed chained
to a central navy commanded by Cadmus as the king and Harmony as the queen. On the walls Dorat and dell'Abbate had
executed twenty-four tableaux, each accompanied by a Latin
distich relating Nonnos de Panopolis' legend of Cadmus' victory
through the power of music over the giant Typhée. Having
seized Jupiter's thunderbolts and prepared an attack on the
heavens, the giant was subdued by Cadmus' enchanting melodies;
Jupiter was then to regain his thunderbolts and with the stars'
help to defeat Typhée. Grateful to Cadmus for saving the harmony
of the world with his music, as Charles had preserved the harmony
of France by defeating the Huguenots, Jupiter gave Harmony,
the daughter of Mars and Venus, to Cadmus for his bride, as
Charles had taken Elizabeth for his bride. The four daughters of
Cadmus and Harmony were then represented as the four navies,
or four estates, portrayed on the ceiling. The ship holding them
together was the emblem of the city of Paris and also stood for
the French monarchy, which is thus portrayed leading the four

estates into a sea of harmony. Cadmus' conquest of the giant and restoration of harmony in the world resulted from his penetration of the secrets of ancient music. In the Panopolis version, Cadmus, who later became the musician-king of Thebes, was a suitable symbol for Charles, who had just founded the Académie de poésie et de musique for the purpose of recovering the ancient effects of music. To reinforce the symbolism, the Académie's director, Jean-Antoine de Baïf, composed two poems about the royal marriage which related the union of Charles and Elizabeth to the peace of the kingdom and to the effects of music. The banquet held in the bishop's palace after the queen's entry was accompanied by concerts and was followed by musical mascarades arranged by Baïf. It is likely that other musical *spectacles* were presented by the Académie in connection with the royal processions.[18] Although the musicians were paid by the crown, the poets and artists were financed by the échevins of Paris, who spent a total of 49,000 livres on the entries.

The final pageantry of Charles' reign celebrated the election to the crown of Poland of his brother and imminent successor, the duc d'Anjou.[19] The concluding event of the festivities, held in the Tuileries on September 14, 1573, was an allegorical production entitled the *Ballet des Polonnais*, the first piece to be called a ballet. Set to music by Orlando di Lasso, the ballet included a dialogue called "La paix et la prospérité" among characters representing France, Peace, and Prosperity. The Polish ambassadors were said to have "admired the well-disentangled confusion, the well-formed figures of the ballet, and the different musics [sic], and said that the French ball was impossible for all the kings of the earth to imitate."[20]

Despite the wars of religion and the dangers threatening the monarchy, ceremonies, festivals, and especially religious processions continued during the reign of Henri III. Indeed, Henri's determination to become a leader of the Counter Reformation led him to revive the religious confrérie who reinstituted the kinds of processions and theatrical pieces they had sponsored in the fifteenth century.[21] The ordinary confrérie consisted of pious laymen belonging to a particular art or craft who had joined together, usually to practice charitable acts. Carrying images of their particular saint, the confréries provided entertainment in French villages in the form of mystères. These religious dramas became more popular than ever when two religious orders, the Capuchins and the Minimes, began acting out walking mystery plays during their own processions, and especially when Henri III sponsored two new religious orders whose penitential processions were veritable ambulatory ballets closely resembling court entertainments. Henri founded the Ordre du Saint Esprit in 1578 for the purpose of forming a loyal nobility. An order of knights located in the Church of the Grands Augustins who held several processions each year through the streets of Paris, the Ordre included leading noble families, high-ranking clerics, and the king. Five years later, Henri inaugurated the Congrégation des Pénitents de l'Annonciation. Organized by the king's Jesuit confessor,[22] the Congrégation was a lay confrérie dedicated to charity and penitence. Led by the king and wearing white robes covering their heads and bodies, the penitents marched through the streets on the day of the Feast of the Annunciation (March 25) and on specified saints' days. Altogether, the various religious orders and confréries stimulated a "wave of processional hysteria" during Henri III's reign.[23] On occasions like the "king's procession" in 1583, confrères by the hundreds flocked to Paris from the countryside to join the king's knights and penitents in vast processions marked by Biblical allegories and chanting, acts of flagellation and of charity. Music was provided by the Confrérie de Sainte Cécile, a religious and musical association founded in 1575 that held its own processions each year on Saint Cecilia's Day. These processions became pious dramas. They passed by street stages where scenes of Biblical life, like those of the medieval mystères, and tableaux depicting Counter Reformation themes of charity and penitence were acted out. These pious entertainments were not unlike court fetes. "The King's Procession might be described as an artistically produced Counter-Reformation ballet, using some late medieval properties and costumes."[24]

The presence of the king's singers, who were officially associated with the Confrérie des Pénitents, helped to accentuate the musical and dramatic nature of the processions. The music of the procession of 1583 was entrusted to Girard de Beaulieu, who also composed music for royal ballets and was probably a member of the Académie de poésie et de musique. Penitents singing psalms followed the king's musicians throughout the procession, enhancing the over-all theatrical effect. In a procession involving the queen, city officials, priests, doctors, choir boys, orphans, and musicians, the entire entourage moved in concert, suggesting a ballet. The confréries, penitents, and courtiers were bound together in a species of musical pageantry closely resembling a secular court entertainment and pointing the way to the ballets produced by the Jesuits and the crown in the seventeenth century. The king's enemies did not overlook the sensual tone of the processions. The Protestant writer Agrippa d'Aubigné questioned Henri's religious sincerity because of the similarity between the religious processions and the secular fetes of the court. Agrippa in fact derided the processions as types of ballet, comparing the strange white robes of the penitents to the masked costumes worn in court ballets, and the eulogistic verses to the litany. Nor was Agrippa expressing a single-minded Protestant prejudice, because the king's confessor made the same comparison, though in the form of a commendation rather than a reproach.

On occasion, musical processions and productions served a specific political end, and the king's performers were able to cloak political negotiations in the garb of splendid pageantry. In fact, the last opulent *spectacle* of the Valois era was staged over a two-week period in 1584 at a time of important negotiations between France and England and in the midst of mounting criticism of the crown by the ultra-Catholic, pro-Spanish Guise faction.[25] The international situation was precarious. Supported by the duc d'Anjou, heir to the French crown and suitor to Queen Elizabeth, William of Orange was leading the resistance to the Spanish invasion of the Netherlands. The deaths in June and July of both Anjou and William, however, made it necessary for England, Holland, and France to take steps to prevent a Spanish victory. In January 1585, envoys from the Netherlands arrived in Paris for the purpose of offering the sovereignty of the United Provinces to Henri III. During their stay, an English embassy also arrived whose unofficial aim was to enjoin French cooperation in the defense of the Netherlands. Officially, however, the English emissaries were there to receive Henri III into the Order of the Garter, a decade after his actual election. The conferral of the insignia of the Garter in 1585 was to represent Anglo-French friendship, and Henri intended to receive it with a display of pomp designed to impress his internal and foreign enemies. Besides, the ceremonial events would mask the secret negotiations from the Guises, who were opposed to an alliance with Elizabeth.

On February 13, the tone of chivalrous knighthood which pervaded the festivities was struck when the English knights led by the Earl of Derby were met near Paris by 300 French nobles, thirteen of whom were knights of the king's Ordre du Saint Esprit. The fact that the English knights were Protestant and the Ordre du Saint Esprit was Catholic fitted into Catherine de Medici's policy of religious reconciliation, but it antagonized the Guises; they did not appear during the round of processions and entertainments, and they charged the king with plotting against the Catholics with Elizabeth's help. Faced with mounting Guise hostility and power, the crown was forced to cancel its plans for public *spectacles*, including tilts and aquatic pageants, in favor of more private festivities such as ballets, mascarades, and banquets. "The embassy was to be a musical, if not a visual event of the first magnitude."[26] Thus, from Sunday to Thursday of the first week of its stay, the English embassy was feted with concerts, ballets, and balls staged at the Hôtel de Longueville. On Thursday, February 18, in the presence of the knights of both orders, the Earl of Derby invested Henri with the robes and insignia of the Garter in the quarters of the provost of Paris. Accompanied by the king's trumpeters, a procession moved to the Church of the Augustins, the headquarters of Saint Esprit, where Henri, bathed in the song of the Magnificat, signed the Garter oath in the presence of the papal nuncio. The week's festivities concluded with a spectacular ballet involving 120 masked and elegantly costumed performers. Dressed as sylvans, dryads, and fruit trees, the performers executed "letter dances" which traced the names of the king and queen. The second week of fetes ended with a five-hour mascarade performed at the bishop of Paris' residence near Notre-Dame. Meanwhile behind the scenes of these glittering fetes, Henri had rejected the offer from the Dutch envoys and agreed to cooperate with England in the Netherlands. The Garter festivities indicate how the imperiled court of the Valois used musical ceremonies and entertainments for political ends.

Musical pageantry in the closely related forms of courtly entertainments and religious processions declined sharply after the assasination of Henri III in 1589 and during the civil warfare that followed. Court ballet was not revived until the turn of the century. There was no religious drama in League-dominated Paris. A few penitents continued to march, but these confrères, wearing helmets under their hoods, served the League as symbols of opposition to the crown. For that reason, Henri IV did not revive their processions.

The Académie de Poésie et de Musique

Musical productions throughout the sixteenth century served more than an entertainment function. They had a significant place in the Catholic revival, helping to temper the bitter mood of religious animosity. Above all, musicians in the company of poets and artists transformed the French court into a human Olympia, glorifying the Valois as the legendary gods of antiquity or as personifications of Christian virtues. Given the cooperative nature and the importance of their role, it was natural that the crown's poets, painters, composers, and performers should come together in an organized fashion under the monarch's aegis. They formed an academy, following the Italian example, that was guaranteed full protection by Charles IX. More than a common social function, however, was responsible for the first French academy. Poets and musicians were profoundly influenced by the humanistic and Neo-Platonic revival of the musical philosophy of antiquity. The Académie de poésie et de musique was the creation of men who, in the intellectual tradition of Plato, Augustine, Ficino, and Tyard, believed in the power of a union of poetry and music to affect human temperament and moral conduct.

The Académie was the direct descendant of the poets grouped
around Jean Dorat at the Collège de Coqueret.[27] Dorat, who
taught classical literature, in the 1540's organized at the Collège
a small academy whose membership formed the nucleus of the
Pléiade. The group included Ronsard, Tyard, Du Bellay, Baïf,
Belleau, and Jodelle. The musical thought of antiquity exerted
a strong influence on the poetic concepts of the Pléiade because
they knew how much attention the ancients had given to music
in their own idea of poetry. Ronsard in particular almost venerated music.[28] Although most of Ronsard's verses were set to
music, they fell short of a genuine rebirth of ancient poetry
because the airs by Certon, Goudimel, Janequin, and other
composers were not strictly adapted to the structure of Ronsard's
verse. In addition, although Ronsard's verses could be sung to
the lyre because of an arrangement of the strophes or couplets
and an alternation of the rhymes, they did not employ the internal
structure of ancient verse, that is, the quantitative metrics of
ancient poetry. That important step was taken, however, by the
poet Jean-Antoine de Baïf, who believed that in order to realize
fully the ancient union of poetry and music, the value of musical
notes must be made to correspond exactly to the quantity of the
syllables of French verse.

Baïf, who became the guiding figure of the Académie, was
the illegitimate son of Lazare de Baïf, an ambassador of François I
in Venice.[29] Tutored for several years in Latin and Greek by
Jacques Tousain, Baïf later became a student of Jean Dorat.
After Lazare's death in 1547, Baïf inherited his father's hôtel
in the Faubourg Saint Victor near the Abbey of Saint Victor,
a center of Neo-Platonism and Augustinian thought. His luxurious
hôtel, a few steps from Ronsard's house, became the home of
the Pléiade and later of the Académie. The publication in 1551
of a poem eulogizing the Valois launched Baïf's literary career.
It was entitled "Sur la paix avec les Anglois" and it appeared
in a collection of Latin verse called *Le tombeau de Marguerite de
Navarre*. Baïf earned popularity through two collections of love
sonnets intended to be sung, *Les amours de Méline* (1552) and
Les amours de Francine (1555). These and other poems indicate
Baïf's attachment to the ancient Greek and Latin poets, especially

Virgil and Ovid, and to Plato, Petrarch, Pietro Bembo, Ariosto, and the Florentine Neo-Platonists. Baïf attained recognition in court and ecclesiastical circles. In 1562 he accompanied the cardinal of Lorraine and several French bishops to the Council of Trent, and he remained in Italy for five years. Realizing that he needed royal and aristocratic patronage to sustain a literary career, he later returned to Paris, where he flourished by writing poems about royal births, marriages, coronations, entries, and military exploits. His poems were always dedicated to the royal family, wealthy nobles, bishops, or government officials. He was made a secretary of the king's chamber and pensioned by Charles IX and Henri III, receiving 1200 livres a year, a large sum for the period.

Around 1567, Baïf began to experiment with a form of poetry that would be so completely united to music as to revive the powerful effects of the ancients. His poetic experiments went beyond those of Ronsard in the sense that the internal structure of the poem was devised in such a way that the quantitative meters of ancient verse were employed. Rules were formulated to establish the prosodic quantity of French syllables, relating the different types of classical feet to a determined number and type of syllables.[30] He followed the primary rule that consonants following vowels make the preceding syllable long. Moreover, in order to correlate written language with speech, he invented a system of phonetic orthography that provided signs for the vowels. His orthography made precise the prosodic nature of the syllables and enabled him to reproduce the sounds of spoken language. Claiming that the Greeks and Romans had written in rhymed verse only until they had invented measured poetry, Baïf embarked on his first attempt at measured verse in a translation of the Psalter in 1567. Shortly thereafter he composed his *Chansonnettes mesurées* and resolved to rhyme no more. The fact is, however, that his verses, when separated from a musical setting failed to attract support, and Baïf abandoned measured verse in 1577. The French language simply proved unsuitable for quantification, though Baïf did succeed in getting an accentual approximation of the metrical patterns of classical verse in his French poems.[31] More important, he provided a poetic fund and instructions on measured verse (*vers mesuré*) to the Académie's composers, Thibault de Courville, Claude Le Jeune, and Jacques Maudit. Reviving ancient music was, of course, the goal in the first place.

Musique mesurée, which was an abrupt departure from traditional musical styles,[32] was accepted warmly by poets and musicians. The poets of the Pléiade lauded Baïf's efforts to restore the effects of ancient music, and most of the leading composers of the time were won over to Baïfian principles. Courville, who was a lutist for Charles IX and helped Baïf organize the Académie, was the pioneer composer of measured music. Le Jeune, a composer of the king's chamber, used Baïf's measured verse in composing his chansonnette collection, *Le printemps*, and he collaborated with Baïf on ballets and mascarades for the court. Maudit, who wrote treatises (now lost) on the theory of measured music and verse, composed settings for Baïf's measured psalms and published a collection of Baïf's measured chansonnettes.[33]

Courville, Le Jeune, Maudit, and other French composers were won over to Baïf's belief that the secret of the effects was a type of music and poetry measured together in the manner of the ancients. This necessitated the adaptation of musical rhythms to the rhythms of ancient poetry. Rhythm, rather than harmony, was the key to the effects; it was the link between poetry and music, meaning and sound. Claude Le Jeune, whose preface to *Le printemps* is one of the few surviving theoretical statements of the principles governing the compositions of Baïf's circle, explained that the ancients made a distinction between harmony and rhythm. Harmony, which they knew little about, had been developed thoroughly since antiquity, producing great effects; rhythm, which the ancients perfected, had been neglected since antiquity. Le Jeune's point was that rhythm has the greater power to animate even the dullest soul "by the sweet violence of its regulated motions."[34] Harmony is still essential as the source of the soul's ecstasy, but rhythm must be developed to balance harmony and because it can really ravish the spirit, arouse or calm the passions.

The French composers and poets never translated their theory of rhythm into a direct correlation of specific emotions and specific feet.[35] They did not try to correlate or imitate particular passions with particular musical rhythms, but only to use rhythm to provide a sense of motion and sound vaguely appropriate to the emotional content of the text. Rhythms were not to serve as images of the passions except in the most general way. And their aim was not to arouse or soften emotions through rhythm, but to use rhythm in combination with harmony to get at the mind and at the inner proportion and consonance of the soul. The path to the soul lay not through the passions but through correlating exactly musical rhythm with the mathematical proportions of the strophes and feet, because these proportions both mirrored and affected the proportions and consonances inherent in the soul. The use of mathematically measured music and poetry was the way to awaken the soul. Thus, the composers and poets created a musical rhythm, a sort of musical prosody, which, being calculated on the prosody of the syllables, could express in music the metrical structure of the verse. To establish the exact quantitative correlation of music and text—a difficult task in a language which is not quantitative—Baïf laid down the cardinal rule that syllables stressed in French should be counted as longs and that a long (–) in the text must be musically represented by a minim (d) and a short (ᴗ) by a crotchet (♩). A Maudit chansonnette follows Baïf's rule (Example 1).[36] The

Example 1

composer could vary this formula by rendering the longs or the shorts in reduced musical values. Notes of less value than those in the preceding example could be sung on a single syllable as long as their total value was equal to the length of the white or black note they replaced. Example 2 from a Le Jeune chansonnette illustrates the point.[37] As for the measures of music, the sixteenth century generally employed the two-beat binary measure represented by the symbol **C** , or by ₵ , indicating a livelier

Example 2

À l'aid, à   l'ai - d,   hé - las, hé - la   -   s! Je suis bles-sé

movement. In translating the ancient poetic meters into musical measures, the composers equated the value of a measure to that of a foot. A dactylic verse had this pattern:

Thus, the musical measure accommodated the poetic meter, except where iambic meters or verses composed of unequal feet were involved. The fact that unequal feet did not fit the musical measures, caused disputes between the musicians and the poets. The latter wanted to preserve the same prosodic value for the syllables and the measures by lengthening or shortening the syllables. In most cases, the composers of measured music (*musique mesurée*) followed the ancient poetic rhythms and used syncopations and ties to fit them into musical measures. Nevertheless, the composers made great sacrifices on the altar of the ancient effects since it was the poets who imposed their quantitative rhythm on the composers.

One of the firm rules of measured music was that each syllable of the verse must be sung simultaneously by all the vocal parts. Quantitative rhythms made it necessary that the longs and the shorts of the verse be reproduced by an ensemble rhythm in which there is a parallel movement in all parts. The contrapuntal polyphony employed in most sixteenth-century music was unacceptable to the Baïfians, who believed that it could not have been used by the ancients. In the contrapuntal style, the interlacing of the voices obscured the sense of the text and the sense of rhythmic regularity and precision so essential to achieving the effects. In order to escape this flaw, the French substituted syllabic homophony for the old style. The Baïfian circle joined the Italian humanists in the war on polyphony, but the homophonic style of the French composers was distinctly different from any other contemporary style, including Italian monody.[38] Italian theorists such as Vincenzo Galilei and Girolamo Mei were convinced that ancient music had been monodic and that the text could be clearly rendered only by a single voice with instrumental accompaniment. The French theorists, joined by the Italian Zarlino, simply believed that harmonic progress had been made since antiquity; monody was too great a departure from the polyphonic music favored by the sixteenth century; a suitable compromise capable of achieving the effects was a homophonic style in which each of the four or five parts would sing simultaneously every syllable of the text, thus preserving the metrical scheme of minims and crotchets, longs and shorts. Homophony enabled the Baïfians to retain the stress on rhythm of the ancients and the harmonic development of the moderns.

Finally, since Baïf's music was intended for court fetes and dramas based on classical themes, he worked out a form of measured dancing.[39] Traditional dances were altered so that the length of the syllables and the notes were reproduced in the steps of the dancers. For example, the gaillarde, which has six, equally valued notes, was translated into four equal steps, a jump coinciding with the pause, and a posture on the final note. Baïf achieved a union of music, poetry, and dance that he believed would enable the dramatic ballets of the Valois court to reproduce the effects of the dramas of the Greeks.

Baïf's experiments began around 1567 and culminated three years later in the founding of the Académie. "Perhaps the most thorough-going attempt ever made to translate into practice the precepts of musical humanism,"[40] the Académie was officially established by Lettres patentes and statutes issued by Charles IX in November 1570. These documents not only indicated the monarchy's full endorsement and support of the Académie, they also fixed the royal stamp of approval on the musical philosophy of antiquity. Referring to the ancient philosophers and legislators, Charles acknowledged the power of music to affect morality, and, in a passage reminiscent of Plato, he called for placing the music of the country under the laws in order to secure an orderly, disciplined society.[41] The king took note of the progress Baïf and Courville had made in creating a measured poetry and music in the ancient style. Emphasizing that these efforts had been studied closely by the queen, his brothers, and the members of his council, Charles declared:

We have freely accepted, and do accept the title of protector and first listener, because we wish and understand that all the exercises which are done there are to the honor of God, and to the growth of our State, and to the embellishment of the French people. So let us give a mandate of it to our trustworthy friends the particular citizens of our courts of Parlement, court of accounts, courts of our aides, bailiffs, seneschals and others of our justices and officers who are concerned with our present establishment, in order that they can read, publish, and register point by point that which is contained herein, allowing the said applicants, their agents and successors to play and to use. . . . Such is our pleasure.[42]

The statutes, which outlined the strict rules governing the Académie, were introduced by a preamble written by Baïf in which he underscored the effects. The perfection of ancient music, he wrote, lay in the musical representation of poetry "so as to produce the effect which the sense of the words requires, either lowering or raising or otherwise influencing the spirits." The means employed by the Greeks were measured poetry and music. "In order also that by this means the minds of the auditors, accustomed and trained to music in all its parts, may be composed so as to become capable of the highest knowledge after being purged of the remnants of barbarism, under the good pleasure of our sovereign lord the King we have agreed to form an academy."[43]

The statutes went on to stipulate that there were to be two kinds of members: the musicians, who were paid a regular salary by the king and performed two-hour concerts of measured music exclusively every Sunday in Baïf's home; and the listeners, who paid semiannual dues for the Académie's maintenance and were admitted to the concerts on presentation of a special medal that could not be loaned or sold. The musicians held daily rehearsals at Baïf's but could not copy or carry out any of the music. They had to agree to obey Baïf and Courville, as the listeners had to agree to be quiet during performances and not to touch any of the music or instruments. The directors could refuse membership applications; their permission was required if an auditor wanted to bring a guest. The Académie's purpose was not to popularize measured music, not to attract large audiences, but to develop a fixed musical style which would be closely guarded by the king and an elite circle of influential poets and musicians as Plato had suggested in the Republic. Once the musicians had been trained and the style perfected, it would be imposed on the public for their moral benefit. The Académie aimed to become "an aristocratic dictator of musical and poetic style."[44] There was little question that this aim was feasible since musicians and poets were dependent on the king for financial support, and music publishing was monopolized by the printing firm of Le Roy and Ballard, whose royal privilege could be revoked.

Although the statutes made no reference to the fact, Baïf intended the Académie to become a university specializing in music and poetry. France's future musicians would be trained in science, geography, mathematics, military exercises, and even in gardening and cooking.[45] Seeking the development of man's whole body and soul, Baïf seemed again to echo the Platonic view of music as the root of the entire encyclopedia of knowledge.

The Académie encountered immediate opposition from the Parlement and the University of Paris because of its royal support, its air of secrecy and special privilege, and its claim of exercising power over morals in education. The Parlement refused to register the Lettres in December 1570 on the grounds that the Académie might tend to "corrupt, soften, unbridle, and pervert the youth."[46] Baïf responded by petitioning the Parlement to send twelve opponents of the Académie to hear a performance of measured music at his residence and to report to the Parlement. Baïf also asked the Parlement to appoint three of its officers and the king's advocate as "Reformers of the Academy" to ensure that morality and law were upheld. Within the Parlement,

Guy du Faur de Pibrac, Charles' advocate, argued Baïf's case.
He held that the Académie should be ratified, provided that its
members would compose nothing offensive to God or the king.
After considerable discussion the Parlement issued an arrêt on
December 15, 1570, submitting the documents and the whole
matter to the University. At a full meeting of the University
on December 30, the Académie was discussed as a school of
music and poetry, but the only decisions reached were to send
the documents to the separate Faculties and to ask Baïf if he
wished to separate himself from the laws of the University. On
January 22, 1571, the University rector, Nicholas Musemble,
urged the University to oppose the Académie, promised the
support of the archbishop of Paris, and referred the question
again to the Faculties. At this point Baïf addressed appeals in
the form of sonnets to Charles and to Catherine de Medici. On
February 1 he explained to Charles in person the plans of the
Académie; he later recalled that Charles had with his baton
symbolically silenced some growling dogs under the table.
Charles IX then intervened. New Lettres were drawn up in May
forbidding further opposition to the new "school" and ordering
that any subsequent difficulties be handled by his private council
rather than by the Parlement. Both the University and the
Parlement submitted to this ultimatum, though the University
requested Cardinal de Bourbon and the archbishop of Paris
to protect the privileges of the University. The first concerts took
place immediately after the royal ultimatum, with the king in
attendance.

The "Magnificences" of 1581

Despite the king's firmness in silencing the Parlement and his
demonstrations of support for the Académie, the opposition
continued and was picked up by musicians who had been excluded
from the Académie and, thus, from the favoritism of the court.
Baïf seized the gauntlet. With uncharacteristic dramatic flourish,
he proposed in a letter to the king that a contest of musical
styles be held among all the musicians of Christendom. The
contest would be judged by a jury of musicians on the basis

of whose music produced an ethical or emotional effect on the audience. The purpose, Baïf stated, was to deal with men who are rigid in their beliefs, and "to arouse in them a desire of learning and of taking the right path in order to arrive at the same perfection of art that we are capturing, which is not to leave the spirits in hiding or to bring them to us, in the way that most men maintain today, but, as the sense of the letter requires, to create the three effects, or as many of them as would be appropriate, which are to tighten, to relax, to enlarge the spirits, impassioned and affected by the song, with the well-composed, well-sung, well-heard letter."[47] It is probable that Baïf's real motive in proposing the contest was to rally his supporters. Placing the burden of response on the listeners was a ruse on Baïf's part since he never sought a popular reaction to his music and probably never intended the contest to occur. There is no record that a contest did in fact take place. That he proposed one at all suggests either an inordinate confidence in his own music or, more probably, that he was sure of his king. Indeed, Charles remained unswerving in his support. Baïf, in turn, catered to the royal taste for ballet and musical eulogy. The Académie, which represented the first major step toward the cultivating of a national musical style, marked the beginning of the centralization of art under the French monarchy.

Unfortunately, it is not known how many of the musical *spectacles* produced at the Valois court were undertaken by the Académie. Probably there were many. It is known, however, that the musicians and poets of the Académie played an important part in the most dazzling round of entertainments ever produced for the Valois—those presented in October 1581 in celebration of the marriage of Marguerite de Lorraine, the queen's sister, to the duc de Joyeuse, the king's favorite and a financial backer of the Académie. In staging these "magnificences," Henri III's purpose was to put on a show of the prosperity and happiness which France pretended to enjoy despite the civil and religious wars that were crushing the kingdom economically and morally. The "triumphs and magnificences" of these celebrations will demonstrate, wrote Catherine de Medici, that "France is not as reduced to poverty as the foreigners estimate."[48] The festivities,

planned on a grand scale under the general direction of Baltasar
de Beaujoyeulx, a Savoyard violinist in the queen-mother's
service,[49] included an equestrian ballet for Spanish horses and
a mock combat held in the torch-lit tiltyard of the Louvre.
Triumphal arches created by Jean Dorat, Germain Pilon, and
Antoine Caron depicted the glories of Henri III. There were
banquets, mascarades, races, and even a nautical parade on the
Seine in which the king and queen, members of the royal family,
and the married couple were drawn up the river on a chariot
barge by fanciful sea horses surrounded by fireworks and concerts.[50] All these entertainments formed a rare visual spectacle,
but the greatest impression, according to an observer, was
created by "the music of the voices and instruments [which were]
the most harmonious and flowing that we have ever heard."[51]
Although the music for these events is lost, or undated, most
of it was probably composed by Claude Le Jeune.[52] For the
mock combat, he composed an appropriate air, with a text by
Baïf in pure measured music and verse, entitled "Arm, arm."
The text described the conquest and torment of Love by War,
certainly an appropriate theme for the period, especially in light
of the participation by the ducs de Guise and de Mercœur.

The week-long pageantry was crowned by the *Ballet comique
de la reine*, a landmark in the development of the ballet de cour
and of the French opera (Figure 2). In his unctuous dedication
of this work to the king, Beaujoyeulx pointed to the king's ill-
disguised political motives in sponsoring the entire festival. "Has
Your Majesty not desired to show how he could shed sweetness,
delight, and the good fragrance of peace on his people? Has he
not wanted to refresh his nobility from so many military fatigues?"[53] The *Ballet comique* is only one of the thousands of
pleasures by which you can show "to all the neighboring kings
and to all of the most distant peoples, what is his grandeur,
what is his dominion, what are the fertility and the abundance
of his kingdom." After so much trouble in the realm, the king
is able "to enliven his subjects with more splendor and magnificence than [other] monarchs would know how to create with
a long peace and tranquility." Even the strongest kings could
scarcely imitate Henri, Beaujoyeulx declared. To observe such

great affluence and so many contented individuals after all the disorders, "will serve as a true and infallible mark of the good and solid establishment of your realm." The ballet will make Henri celebrated among the great men of history, according to Beaujoyeulx, and will place him, as in the ballet itself, with Jupiter among the gods and goddesses. "Your name, Sire, will be forever perfumed with this gracious scent not only of virtuous reputation, but of agreeable delectation."[54] Beaujoyeulx added that he had been instructed to design the *Ballet comique* in such a way that the king could participate and that the work had been approved by Henri, the queen, and several ladies of the court.

Produced at an estimated cost of 400,000 écus,[55] the *Ballet comique* was lavish in its use of scenic effects concocted by the king's principal painter, Jacques Patin, and its use of an uncharacteristically large chorus and orchestra. The performance lasted from ten o'clock in the evening until four the next morning and was performed in the grand hall of the Palais du Petit-Bourbon before an unusually large audience that included ambassadors and foreign dignitaries. Although it is known that Baïf and Claude Le Jeune were among the members of the Académie who provided verses, music, and other services for Henri's "magnificences" (Baïf and Ronsard were paid 2,000 écus), the precise role of the Académie in the production of the *Ballet comique* is not known. The surviving accounts show that the author of the verse was Sieur de la Chesnaye, the king's chaplain, and that the music was composed by Jacques Salmon, a singer and lutist, and Lambert de Beaulieu, a violinist of the royal chapel. Their connection, if any, with the Académie is uncertain. Analysis of the text and score reveals, however, that the airs and choruses were composed according to the Baïfian formulae, using syllabic homophony. The instrumental pieces do not correspond to Baïf's dicta, but it is probable that the Académie influenced the over-all musical and dramatic plan of the *Ballet comique,* just as its poets and musicians had played a leading role in the other fetes of the wedding, and that Baïf's rules were bent in order to fit the requirements of a court *spectacle.*[56] It is worth noting that Claude Le Jeune, who collaborated with Baïf through-

out the fetes, believed that his music could not only produce
the effects presumably desired by the court, but also attract the
influence of the stars for the benefit of the imperiled monarchy.
Thus, behind this refulgent spectacle alluding to the magical
power of Henri III lay "the outlook of Neoplatonic occultism
as expounded by Marsilio Ficino, with its belief in the power
of rightly composed music to act as a charm in drawing down
the 'spiritus' from the stars."[57]

Indeed, if the *Ballet comique* and the accompanying entertainments had a central theme, it was the avoidance of catastrophe
in this final hour of the Valois monarchy through the miraculous
intervention of the heavens. At the Valois court, where Italian
attitudes and Ficinian Neo-Platonism were influential, the belief
in astrology was pervasive. Catherine de Medici employed magicians and carried a talisman representing Jupiter on his eagle
surrounded by magical signs; Henri III was awed by the occult
and was attacked by the Catholic League for his belief in necro-
mancy. Given the magical theme of the *Ballet comique*, Le Jeune's
insistence on the astral power of his music, the Académie's
contention that its unique music could produce the effects, and
the prevalence of astrological beliefs and Ficinian ideas among
the Valois, it is not difficult to understand why the *Ballet comique*
or the other events of the marriage celebration should be viewed
not just as entertainment but as a musical incantation.[58] Everywhere the astrological theme was apparent. Special arches with
paintings and inscriptions summoning spiritual radiation decorated the city. The largest of these was an amphitheater designed by Jean Dorat as a model of the sky, with lights representing the constellations of the zodiac and the motion of the
planets, a rainbow (Catherine's emblem), the three crowns
(Henri's emblem), and the stars of Castor and Pollux proclaiming
peace from the ship of France. The king was represented in the
scene as a *roi soleil* driving his solar chariot past the moon. Through
artistic symbolism, poetic supplication, and the special power of
music, the "magnificences" were intended to summon the astral
gods to fulfill the destiny of the Valois, eradicate the internal
conflicts of the kingdom, and restore peace and happiness to
the realm.

These themes formed the central idea of the *Ballet comique de la reine*, which dealt with the acquisition of magical power by the Valois monarchy through the defeat of the enchantress Circé. The setting of the *Ballet* accentuated the central role of the king in the drama. Henri was seated on a platform flanked by attendants and ambassadors at one end of the large hall (Figure 2). Along the side of the hall to the king's right was an oak-lined wood illuminated by silver lamps in the shape of ships. The home of the god Pan, the wood contained a grotto which concealed an organ and several musicians. On the other side of the hall to the king's left, radiant, billowing clouds gilded with stars encircled a wooden vault that supported ten groups of singers and instrumentalists. In his program for the ballet, Beaujoyeulx referred to this edifice as the *voûte dorée* and noted that it represented Plato's idea of the celestial harmony. At the far end of the hall opposite the king stood the enchanted garden of Circé, decorated with an arched trellis and lighted by a golden sun. A marble fountain was adjacent to the garden and supported sirens, tritons, and naiads carrying musical instruments in their tails. A giant star-encrusted cloud in which the gods would descend was suspended from the ceiling at the center of the hall.

Beaujoyeulx' text explained the fable of Circé in various ways. A physical interpretation based on the widely used sixteenth-century mythological manual of Natale Conti explained that Circé, the daughter of the sun and of Perseis (daughter of the ocean), represents a mixture of the elements. The fountain is an added symbol of Circé's magical blend of sun and ocean, heat and matter. The idea behind the symbolism is that, as Circé changes men to beasts, man's body is subject to the mutations of the elements. Yet, through spiritual power, man's soul can escape the physical world and realize its divine nature. In order to apply this physical interpretation more directly to the plot, Sieur Gordon, a gentleman of the king's chamber, supplied a moral rendition of Conti in the program. Heat and humidity, symbolized by Circé, can create lust in man and can lead to lasciviousness, cruelty, drunkenness, avarice, and ambition unless curbed by reason. Circé stands for these animal passions, as Ulysses stands for the rational faculty of the soul. The fabulous

Figure 2. The hall and the opening scene of the *Ballet comique de la reine.* Henri III, seated in the foreground, is greeted by a fugitive from the garden of Circé, located at the opposite end of the hall. Note at the king's left the wooden vault engulfed by clouds, known as the *voûte dorée*, which supported musicians and represented the Platonic idea of the celestial harmony. Engraving by Jacques Patin done on command of the queen; reprinted from Baltasar de Beaujoyeulx, Lambert de Beaulieu, and Jacques Salmon, *Balet comique de la royne, faict aux nopces de Monsieur le Duc de Joyeuse et Mademoiselle de Vaudemont sa sœur* (Paris, 1582), p. 5. (Photograph courtesy of the Bibliothèque Nationale, département de réserve imprimée.)

characters of the *Ballet comique*, therefore, are locked in a struggle of cosmic relevance over the rational and irrational parts of man's soul.

The action commenced as a fugitive from Circé's garden approached the king, entreating him to save the world from Circé's sorcery. Henri, whose courage was compared to the heroic feats of the gods, was praised for ending the bloodshed in France. The fugitive was interrupted by Circé, who chased him back to the garden. Her tirade was followed, however, by a choir of sirens whose song compared the French king to Jupiter:

> Jupiter n'est seul aux cieux,
> La mer loge mille Dieux;
> Un Roy seul en France habite.
> Henry, grand Roy des François,
> En peuple, en justice, en lois
> Rien aux autres Dieux ne quitte.[59]

Composed in measured music, this song was echoed by the performers from the *voûte dorée*. The sirens, who usually (in Homer and Conti) represented the temptations of the flesh, were treated (following Xenophon) in the *Ballet comique* as beneficent creatures who stimulate virtues by singing about great men. Since their song was echoed by the *voûte dorée*, the sirens were intended to represent the daughters of the Muses and the sirens who, according to Plato, conducted the music of the celestial spheres. Their harmony was the harmony of the heavens and of a well-governed kingdom.

In the next episode the mobile fountain was moved to the center of the hall. Attached to it was a balustrade supporting the queen, Louise de Lorraine, and twelve attendants, representing water nymphs and naiads. Over their heads was a tapered column of basins and dolphins which spouted scented water. A chariot was drawn by two sea horses ridden by Beaulieu, the composer, and his wife, dressed as the sea gods Glaucus and Tethys. This bizarre cortege was accompanied by eight musicians dressed as tritons, who sang eulogies to the queen. The tritons symbolized the true religion concealed before Christ's coming, and their tridents were signs of Christian preaching. Joined by

the sirens, Glaucus and Tethys sang to the king about the evils
of Circé, after which a band of the violins ushered in from behind
the fountain a troop of naiads who performed a ballet. The troop
performed thirteen measured dances which formed numbers and
geometrical figures.[60] Probably the dances reflected the awe that
the followers of Plato felt toward number. Frances Yates writes:
"The Pythagorian-Platonic core of the Academy—that all things
are related to number, both in this outer world of nature and
in the inner world of man's soul—perhaps found in the marvelous
accuracy of this measured dancing one of its most perfect expressions."[61] Enraged, Circé touched the performers with her
wand, turning them into statues. But no sooner had she worked
her sorcery than, with a clap of thunder, Mercury descended
in the cloud at the center of the hall and sang of his plan to cure
the minds of those who, like Ulysses, pursued pleasure at the
expense of virtue and reason. Sprinkling the nymphs with juice
from the moly herb, Mercury restored them to their animated
music and dancing. The pleasure was brief, however, as Circé
reappeared, immobilized Mercury, and turned the nymphs to
stone again. Mercury was powerless without Minerva: she represented wisdom, while he stood for eloquence, which is helpless
without the force of reason behind it. Circé then sang about
the meaning of her sorcery. Virtues and vices are only names
given to changes in custom; the real changes of the seasons and
the centuries are governed by the laws of destiny which she
controls. Hers is the power of natural law obliging men to decay
with the elements and of the law of time or history obliging
them to grow old with changing seasons. The nymphs who tried
to break her spell put their trust in what they believed were
the absolute, timeless values of antiquity—values such as justice—
failing to understand that they cannot defeat the inexorable
flow of time any more than they can pit moral choice against
the enslaving laws of nature. Act 1 concluded with a tableau
in Circé's garden. In front of the enchantress passed a stag, a
deer, an elephant, a dog, a lion, and a pig, all formerly human
beings whose passions have subjected them to Circé's power.

Act 2 opened in Pan's grotto, where concealed musicians were
giving a concert. Flute-playing satyrs emerged to make a tour

of the hall. Their songs of praise to the king were echoed from the *voûte dorée*. This procession was followed by the march of an oak tree bearing dryads to Pan's grotto, where organ music was being played. The dryads joined the satyrs in a song of appeal to Pan to challenge Circé. But Pan, symbolizing nature, explained that he was under the irresistible spell of Circé; that a more powerful moral and intellectual force was required.

That force was suggested at the start of act 3 when four allegorical figures of Virtue appeared, each dressed in a star-spangled blue costume and each bearing her traditional attribute: Fortitude with a pillar, Justice with a balance, Temperance with a vase, and Prudence with a snake. Echoed from the *voûte dorée*, their songs with lute accompaniment praised Henri's virtues, predicted his conquest of Circé, and called on Minerva (Pallas), the symbol of Catherine de Medici for support. The four Virtues then mounted the chariot of Minerva drawn into the hall by a dragon. Minerva carried a spear and a shield with a Gorgon's head; her chariot was encrusted with military arms, musical instruments, and books—all symbolic of the victorious triumph of virtue by the harmonious soul of man. The music complimented the visual drama as the musicians of the *voûte* sang about the blend of celestial and human music.

Promising the king that she would conquer Circé for him, Minerva invoked the aid of Jupiter, leader of the gods. Jupiter made his descent amid thunder and the song from the *voûte* about the fires of the ship of France, a reference to the gods Castor and Pollux whose appearance as stars on the rigging of ships, according to legend, was a signal to sailors that the tempest was over. Jupiter had been drawn by the power of the measured music from the *voûte* which acted "as a kind of astrological talisman in favour of the French royal house."[62] Crowned, sceptor and thunderbolt in hand, a golden eagle at his feet, Jupiter launched the successful assault on Circé, joined by Minerva, Pan, the Virtues, the satyrs and dryads. Proclaiming himself Henri's progenitor, Jupiter sang:

> Chère Pallas, fille, regarde-moy;
> Demeure icy, tu es sœur de ce Roy
> Ce Roy, mon fils, fleur du sceptre de France.

> Fay des regards de Méduse changer
> Ses ennemis et son peuple ranger
> Sous sa loy juste, humble, d'obéissance.[63]

Defeated, Circé was conducted around the hall by the gods. She was forced to surrender her wand to the king, an act which represented the transference of Circé's magic to the French monarch who would use it for virtuous purposes. A grand processional ballet followed in which forty figures were traced by the dancers. The breaking and joining of the figures symbolized the passage of the seasons and the mutation of the elements, while the figures themselves represented man's capacity through reason and moral choice and with divine help to overcome his passions and discover eternal truth. The performance concluded when Louise presented Henri with a gold medal showing a dolphin swimming in the sea, symbolizing the queen's promise of a dauphin.

In addition to all its mythological and astrological symbolism, the *Ballet comique* conveyed an unmistakable political message. The conquest of Circé after a difficult struggle represented the king's attainment of peace for the realm after the turmoil of religious warfare. Your poetic history has been related, Beaujoyeulx informed the king. The real opponents of Circé were Henri and the queen-mother, clearly identified as Minerva (Pallas). Throughout the ballet, Circé and Henri faced each other at opposite ends of the hall. All of the gods and fabulous characters solicited the help and sang the praise of the king as the ballet progressed. With Circé's constant identification of Jupiter with Henri, it was clear that the king of the gods was the king of France. Thus, the *Ballet* had at least four levels of meaning: the physical or natural one drawn from Conti, in which man struggles against the forces of time and nature; the moral one steeped in the mythological analysis of antiquity and the Middle Ages, in which man uses his will and his reason to combat his concupiscence; the Platonic and astrological one, in which man's quest for harmony and peace are answered in the celestial harmony which he attracts through measured music, poetry, and dance; and the political one, in which Henri III's triumph over the evils of civil war is dramatically depicted in the defeat of

Circé's sorcery. The *Ballet comique de la reine* and the other "magnificences" of the wedding, like all the *spectacles* of the Valois era,
were probably meant as a healing device, a means of bringing
hostile aristocratic and religious factions together in a setting
where they might act out and resolve their hostilities under the
splendor of the royal aegis. But the wedding fetes, however,
were no more successful than the *Paradis* or the Garter Embassy
had been. The deep and irreparable conflicts dividing Huguenots,
Guise, Catholics, and royalists resumed not long after the wedding;
Henri might have been likened more accurately to Mercury in
the *Ballet* than to Jupiter.

Although its political sequel was not fortuitous, the *Ballet
comique de la reine* represented at once a summing up of the musical
artistry of the Valois era and the beginning of a new aristocratic
musical genre. It brought together the processional and ceremonial quality of both the religious and secular pageantry of
the sixteenth century with the momeries, mascarades, ballets,
and other earlier forms of court entertainment. Reaching back
into Plato and Ficino, it gave form to the musical philosophy
of the Pléiade and the rules of the Académie. A union of poetry,
music, and dance was achieved within a set scene and a unified
drama. The metrical quantification of the ancients was dropped,
but the homophonic choruses, the measured songs and dances,
and the close union of text and music reveal the strong influence
of Baïf. Although they never achieved a revival of ancient Greek
drama, Baïf and the battery of musicians, poets, and artists
who created the *Ballet comique* had given a new dramatic unity
and a sense of form to the musical entertainments of the monarchy.
These changes led to the emergence of ballet de cour and eventually to opera.

Baïf's Académie could not survive the economic and political
reversals at the end of the century. Exactly when it ceased
functioning is unknown. It was weakened by unpaid subscriptions
and erratic financial support by the crown whose resources were
stretched to the limit during the sporadic periods of civil and
foreign war. Charles IX's death in 1574 deprived it of its strongest
royal supporter; although Henri III probably maintained it,
as the *Ballet comique* and the other fetes of the 1581 wedding seem

to show, his support was thinner than Charles'. Henri preferred oratorical to musical eulogy. He created a new institution with headquarters in the Louvre, the Académie du palais, which was more concerned with oratory, philosophy, and morality than with music and poetry.[64] Under the direction of Guy du Faur de Pibrac, the membership of the new academy did at least include the familiar names of Ronsard, Tyard, and Baïf. In 1584, Henri moved the new academy to Vincennes where it turned to more devotional subjects and activities. Until his death in 1589, Baïf and his friends continued to perform measured music in the privacy of Baïf's home. After Baïf's death, Maudit kept alive the values of the older academy among the circle that met at his house on the rue des Juifs.

Encouraged by the publication and popularity of several pieces of measured music at the turn of the century, Jacques Maudit laid plans to launch another academy to be called the Confrérie, Société et Académie royale de Sainte Cécile, vièrge et martyre. It was to be primarily a musical academy employing fifty singers and instrumentalists and awarding prizes for compositions. Both rhymed and measured verse would be cultivated. Nothing came of Maudit's ambitious plans, however, mainly because he received no royal support. The academic tradition of the sixteenth century found few patrons at the courts of the early Bourbons. The musical, artistic, and intellectual life of Henri IV's court must be considered rough by Valois' standards. Neither the king's personality and Protestant background nor the duc de Sully's economic austerity were conducive to an academic or artistic revival.

Ballet under the Early Bourbons

During the regency of Marie de Medici (1610-1614), David de Flurance Rivault, the chief tutor of Louis XIII, made an abortive attempt to found a new academy. Rivault published detailed plans for the academy; its chief purpose would be to hold debates on philosophy, history, poetry, ethics, and other subjects.[65] There would also be regular sermons on piety, training in oration, and lessons on the art of warfare. Music had a place only insofar as the members would sing songs after the debates. Rivault's plan, which typified the over-all utilitarian view of learning and the arts held in the seventeenth century, stressed the practical nature of the academy's work. The only link to the sixteenth-century academies, other than the encyclopedic nature of its program, was Rivault's own philosophy. In a book entitled *L'art d'embellir* (1608), he referred repeatedly to Plato, Plotinus, Augustine, Ficino, and Ronsard and he dealt extensively with musical thought in a way reminiscent of the Neo-Platonists. An academy run by Rivault might very well have been imbued with Baïfian thought adjusted to the utilitarian requirements of the Bourbon government. Without royal support, however, the academy never got off the ground.

The musical and dramatic ballet did continue as a court entertainment, and the lack of an academy did not impede the development of a musical establishment by the early Bourbon rulers. Under the Valois kings, the artists, poets, and musicians of the Académie had been supported with royal and private money. In addition, even before the Académie was formed, the king or the city of Paris employed individual performers for particular ceremonial occasions. A few were lucky enough to receive pensions and were employed as servants in the households of kings and nobles. Under the Bourbons, the size and significance of the musical establishment increased and the menial duties of the performers diminished as their musical obligations were expanded. By Louis XIII's time, a corps of composers, singers, and organists were attached to the royal chapel. Moreover, Louis XIII established the first permanent chamber ensemble, the Vingt-quatre violons du roi, which gave concerts for the court and accompanied the monarch's ballet productions. Upon the director of the violins, Louis conferred the title of king of the violins of France, with the authority to grant letters of mastery to musicians and to establish bands of violinists throughout the realm.[66] Thus, musicians became useful servants of the young Bourbon monarchy. This meant that musical style and performance would be more deeply influenced than ever by royal taste, and royal taste meant ballet. Ballet flourished as never before under Henri IV, Marie de Medici, and Louis XIII. In his conversations with the chevalier de Meré, the maréchal de Clérambaut remarked: "When I come to the court, I am persuaded that in order to be an upright man, it is necessary to know only how to dance."[67]

Two types of ballets existed side by side in the early years of the seventeenth century: the ballets-comiques, which were performed on a theater stage and retained the traditional allegorical and mythological subjects; and the ballets-mascarades, performed in the grand halls of Saint-Germain and Fontainebleau, in which the masked nobility danced entrées, mimed little farces, and performed acrobatic stunts. Frequently the two forms were mixed and were difficult to distinguish. Although no set rules or traditions governed the ballet during this period, by 1605 vocal récits superseded declaimed récits in both the dramatic ballets and the mascarades.[68] In general, the earlier vogue of dramatic ballet of the sort produced by Beaujoyeulx gave way to the ballets-mascarades, in which the connection between the drama and the dance was so loose as to turn the productions into ballet tableaux with an overriding decorative function and with increased emphasis on the music and on the symbolic meaning of the danced figures. The philosophical and moral meanings that the numbers and figures represented were explained in programs distributed at the performances.[69] The numbers used in some of the ballets were drawn from the ancient alphabet of the Druids, and in every case the numbers symbolized some human virtue or attribute such as love, ambition, courage, grandeur, fame, and the like. Each dancer held a point in the figure or number. He would be tied by ribbons to other points (dancers), permitting a constant rearrangement of number combinations. Thanks to the programs, the spectators did not have to guess at the meanings of the dances. Indeed, the value of the dance for the spectator was believed to rest mainly on the mental and spiritual inspiration he derived from contemplating the hidden, symbolic meanings expressed in the figures. Conceivably he was supposed to absorb psychologically the morality conveyed by the figures. The simple grace of the dance was itself regarded as a sign of internal grace and excellence. Thus, the ballet by its nature was an emblem of virtue. By gearing his mind to it, the spectator tunes in to "the higher order of virtuous concord" of which the dance and the music are an imitation.

The ballet scores were composed by musicians of the Musique de la chambre du roi (most were members of the Vingt-quatre violons du roi or Grande bande), who also set up the steps and the figures of the ballets. The composers included Pierre Guédron, Henri Le Jeune, Antoine Boesset, and Jean de Cambefort. The instrumental music of the ballet used standard rhythmic formulas corresponding to the dance steps and drawn from traditional, provincial, and courtly dances such as the gaillarde and gigue. Binary and ternary forms were alternated in the entrée airs, and occasionally a programmatic device relevant to the plot was inserted. Stylized musical motifs came into use to accompany stock characters like demons, gods, peasants, and Negroes. Basic dances like the branle were used for standard situations such as the village wedding. A rich variety of songs included monodic and polyphonic récits to present the subject, measured songs (*chansons mesurées*) for one or more voices to accompany the dances, and airs de cour. Choruses were also employed occasionally, either for the opening instrumental prelude, or as interludes, or to accompany the dance. The airs de cour are especially interesting since some, at least, show the influence of Baïf's measured music, whose clear regular rhythms bore a natural resemblance to the rhythms of dance tunes.[70] In many of the airs de cour the music is keyed to the textual meter, and each syllable has the value of a minim or crotchet. The airs, thus, accentuated the meter of the text as in measured music. Moreover, the airs were often composed in three, four, or five parts, in a homophonic style akin to measured music. The great variety of styles in the airs de cour and such characteristics as the unnatural use of verbal rhythm and poorly placed accents make it impossible to view the airs as a direct outgrowth of Baïf's measured music, but the similarity of certain stylistic elements suggests an influence.

The texts of the airs and récits were significant elements in the ballets. The texts of the airs were in strophic form, with four or six verses. Each strophe had a self-contained subject or meaning.

The division of strophes was further accentuated because the only bar or measure used in the airs appeared at the end of the strophe. A melody, often built on the metrical structure of the verse, was composed for the first strophe and adapted to the others by the singer, although French singers seldom used diminutions or florid techniques.[71] Words or phrases were never repeated as in the Italian airs. Accents nearly always fell on the caesura that was followed by a long note. The formulas under which the airs were composed allowed for little embellishment or variation, and the airs tended, therefore, to be stiff and monotonous. The récits, however, afforded more latitude of expression and a more natural declamation. But since the ballets de cour of the early seventeenth century were more like tableaux than dramas, the récits were still bound by a strophic form and lacked the freedom and impassioned spirit of Italian operatic recitatives. The subjects of the verses of airs and récits dealt invariably with amorous themes, mythology, and most frequently with the virtues of the royal family. Poets still found that the road to pensions and literary recognition began with the composition of poetry which flattered the king, complimented the ladies of the court, or alluded to diplomatic victories of the government. The verses frequently implied parallels between the personality and life of the noble who was dancing and the character he represented. Most important were the verses about the king which extolled his deeds in a lofty and pompous manner. Through such verses the monarchy could hold up to itself, to its subjects, and to visiting dignitaries an adulatory and felicitous image of its grandeur. More than a court entertainment, the ballet was becoming an image of the monarchy.

The ballets, which were produced under the careful supervision of Louis XIII's confidant, Albert, duc de Luynes, were important public attractions. They were performed most often in the Petit-Bourbon (Hôtel de Bourbon), which faced the Church of Saint-Germain-l'Auxerrois. Most of the spectators stood, and soldiers and archers guarded the doors in order to hold back the throngs of people anxious to glimpse the king and his court at their pleasure. Ballets were also performed in the grand halls of the Hôtel de Ville, the Louvre, and the Arsenal, as well as in the châteaux of Vincennes, Saint-Germain, Fontainebleau, and Chantilly.

In addition to the small-scale ballets given regularly in the king's chambers or in the residences of the nobility, about one major ballet was produced each year during the reign of Henri IV. These ballets were usually associated with ceremonial occasions, and nearly all were based on allegorical or patriotic subjects. In the *Ballet de chevaliers françois et béarnois*, performed on August 23, 1592, a group of knights presented a dance of loyalty to Madame (Henri IV's sister). During a mock battle to win her favor, Mercury tried to appease the knights and persuade them to direct their zeal against the foreign enemies of France; thereupon, the knights departed for war against the Spanish. In 1593 a group of ballets was performed for Henri IV on the occasion of Madame's arrival from Tours. The verses accentuated Henri's heroic virtues. The king's greatness was attributed to his bravery and magnanimity, and he was praised for having saved France from her mortal enemies.[72]

Many of the ballets from this period had humorous or exotic subjects; for example, the *Ballet des maîtres des comptes* (1604), the *Ballet des souffleurs d'alchimie* (1604), the *Ballet des coqs* (1603), the *Ballet des garçons de taverne* (1603), and the *Ballet des vieilles sorcières* (1604). A ballet of the barbers was performed in October 1598 when Henri IV lay seriously ill at Monceaux. Concocted by a group of nobles, including the duc de Gramont and the maréchal de Bassompierre, the ballet was intended to lighten the spirits of the ailing king.[73] A few days later the *Ballet du roy Henri le Grand* was performed at Saint-Germain-en-Laye to celebrate the king's recovery and the baptism of his and the duchesse de Beaufort's son. The comtes d'Auvergne, de Tourville, and de Bassompierre portrayed a troupe of Indians who came to France to pay homage to Henri le Grand. Our lands are so devastated, the Indians declared, that we are compelled to seek comfort in France, whose monarch's magnanimity is renowned.

> Quelque jour son empire esgalant son renom
> Il rendra son empire aussi grand que son nom
> Et tout le monde enfin, telle est notre espérance
> Ne sera qu'une France.[74]

Like all the ballets of this period, Henri's concluded with a grande entrée for the performers and spectators, dressed in their glittering finery and led by the king himself. These final, sumptuous dances, which were more like the ceremonial processions of the Valois than ballet entrées, made it clear that the production was given to celebrate the monarch. The music for these grand ballets was stately and pompous, befitting the occasion (Example 3).[75]

Example 3

During the later years of Henri IV and the regency of Marie de Medici, the ballet continued to be an aristocratic spectacle, adorning the Bourbon monarchy with an image of artistic brilliance, social refinement, and national well-being. Henri IV was celebrated in music, dance, and verse as the consummate peacemaker, the symbol of virtue, the epitomy of enlightenment, humility, and benevolence His wife and queen, who was not given to hesitation in matters concerning her pleasure and glorification, sponsored numerous musical entertainments that combined obsequious ceremony with the dance. In the staged productions such as the *Ballet des météores* (1613) and the *Ballet des argonautes* (1614), Marie de Medici and the members of the royal family were frequent performers. The allegorical plots dwelt on their exploits. Contemporary events such as the struggle between the regent and the nobles that culminated in the calling of the Estates General (1614) were commemorated in music and dance.[76]

Henri IV and Marie de Medici also revived the carrousels and tournaments which had played such a prominent part in the pageantry of the Valois and which resembled the ballets. The contests were always accompanied by musical performances and by exotic allegorical processions and costumed entries with mythological tableaux acted out on mobile machines. The first of the new wave of carrousels was presented in February 1605 in the Petit-Bourbon. In it the knights of Thrace battled the knights of France.[77] An open-air carrousel in 1606 in the court-yard of the Louvre included the figures of the elements, with foreigners representing fire, Juno and a flock of birds as air, sirens as water, and Mars as earth. These Italianate productions reached a climax in the carrousel of 1612 held in the recently constructed Place Royale to herald the future marriage of Louis XIII and the Spanish Infanta (Figure 3). A model palace built in the Place was decorated with symbols of the sun and other allegorical figures. The defenders of the palace, the knights of glory, were carried to the scene on a chariot drawn by giants and lions and accompanied by the lyre of Amphion, a standard symbol of the power of music. The first quadrille depicted Orpheus drawing toward him by the magic of his lyre a forest of laurel trees and the knights of the sun. The music also summoned the chariot of Apollo, a symbol of the union of the French and Spanish crowns, bearing Time, the Seasons, the Hours of the Day. A race by the knights of the lily was then held, followed by an equestrian ballet. In subsequent quadrilles mythological themes were depicted, including the legends of Amadis of Gaul and Perseus, both of which became popular thereafter in French *spectacles* and were later used in French operas. The quadrilles were laced with all the elements of ballet: récits, musical inter-mezzos, dances, and every conceivable legendary figure, from Hercules to Jason, who could be likened to the members of the royal family. After three days, the carrousel concluded with a final triumphant entry of Roman warriors, leading the captive kings of Africa and Asia mounted on elephants. The palace

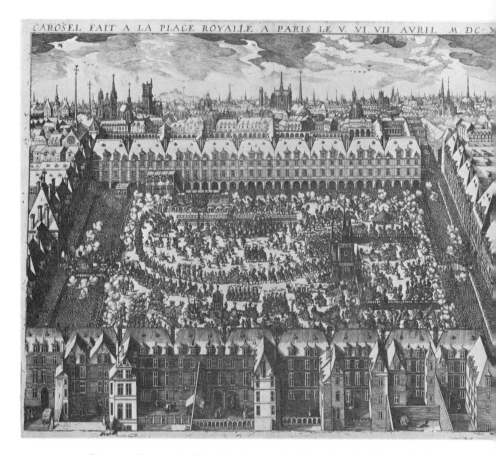

CAROSEL FAIT A LA PLACE ROYALLE A PARIS LE V. VI. VII. AVRIL. M.DC.X

Figure 3. Carrousel of April 1612 in the Place Royal (Place des Vosges) commemorating the impending marriage of Louis XIII. Engraving by Nathieu Néran; reprinted from Marc de Vulson, sieur de la Colombière, *Le vray théâtre d'honneur et de chevalerie, ou le Miroir héroïque de la noblesse* (Paris, 1648), following p. 360. (Photograph courtesy of the Bibliothèque Nationale, département de réserve imprimée.)

went up in a blaze of fireworks and a fanfare of trumpets. This was the last of the dramatic carrousels until the reign of Louis XIV, though the music, the legendary and allegorical figures, the machines and costumes, and the sun devices reappeared in the ballets of Louis XIII's reign.

During the reign of Louis XIII the ballet de cour reached its fullest development as the chief entertainment of the French court. Performed by the youthful king himself in 1617, the *Ballet d'Armide, ou La délivrance de Renaud* (based on the epic poem *Gerusalemme Liberata*, 1575, by Torquato Tasso) represented the early culmination of both the ballet-comique and the ballet-mascarade. A continuous-action plot unfolded by means of pantomime, vocal récits, danced entrées, and a final grand ballet executed by masked nobles wearing sumptuous garments and plumed turbans. As if a conscious effort were made to tie the drama to the masked ball, the stage for *La délivrance* was connected to the hall in front of it by inclined planes. The music was composed by Guédron, and Belleville directed the dances; Baïf's old partner, Jacques Maudit, conducted the sixty-four singers and an orchestra of twenty-eight violins and fourteen lutes. François Durand, a provincial controller of war and a royal adviser, found the ballet "truly royal and worthy of such majesty as his (the king)." Even the scandal-mongering persons (there were apparently some who felt the king's dignity was lowered by performing a full-length role in a ballet) have had to hold their tongues, Durand declared, when they witnessed the regal *spectacle* of sumptuous costumes, the order of the hall, the ravishing glitter of diamond-clad queens and princesses, and the "judicious conduct of the different ballets."[78]

Louis XIII, who had personally selected the subject of the ballet, performed the role of the demon of fire costumed to look as if he were bathed in flames (Figure 4). He believed that this attire could express his ardor for the queen (he married the Spanish Infanta, Anne of Austria, in 1615), his kindness to his subjects, his power over his domestic enemies, and his majesty to foreign dignitaries present.

He knew well that it is the property of fire to purify unrefined bodies and to unite homogeneous and similar things, separating gold and silver from all other less noble and less rich material, just as it is his Majesty's principal desire to remind all his subjects of their duty, and to purge them of all pretexts for disobedience. He knew well . . .

PREMIERE ENTREE

I. Le Roy en demon du feu. 3. mr. le cheualier de Vandosme 2. mr. de Luynes 1.er gentilhomme representant le demon des eaux. de la chambre faisant Renault 4. mr. de monpoullan en esprit de l'air.

Figure 4. Performers in the *Ballet d'Armide, ou La délivrance de Renaud:* (1) Louis XIII as the demon of fire, (2) the duc de Luynes in the role of Renaud, (3) the chevalier de Vendôme as the demon of water, (4) M. de Monpoullan as the spirit of air. Anonymous engraving; reprinted from *Discours au roy du Ballet dansé par le Roy le dimanche XXIXᵉ jour de janvier 1617* (12 plates). (Photograph courtesy of the Bibliothèque Nationale, département de réserve imprimée.)

that fire runs after combustible material, but consumes nothing in its natural place, and thus contributes to the support of inferior creatures and gives contentment to those who see it from a proportioned distance, just as his Majesty easily destroys those who outrage him and uses his authority only for the conservation of his peoples or the aggrandizement of those who approach him with the respect which is due him: in short, he recognizes that fire cannot be imprisoned or circumscribed except by natural limits, just as he can be limited only by divine power and by his own will, and that the spirits which are nearest to God among the celestial hierarchies, being called seraphin, signify warming fire. He must also affect a quality agreeable to God himself, since he is the nearest and the best loved by him among men. It is for all these reasons that he wanted himself covered with flames, and these flames being adorned and created by such artifice, that the fire itself is rendered more brilliant by them, when the rays of the innumerable torches of the studded hall are directed above, and that those who look at them receive his reflection.[79]

Although the title role was performed by his first gentleman of the chamber and the lieutenant general of Normandy, Albert de Luynes, the sixteen-year-old king danced the principal entrées of the ballet, and in the final act he portrayed the Christian conqueror and defender of the holy sepulcher, Godfrey of Bouillon. The performance concluded with the monotonous music of the grand ballet, danced by the king and the masked nobles of the court (Example 4).[80] Durand reported that "the majesty which seems contrary to such actions always accompanied his steps and the grace was reserved for him alone, so that those who accompanied him occasionally stepped aside in order to admire that which they could create by imitating him: but everyone sensed the power that his Majesty then had over minds."[81]

La délivrance de Rénaud was succeeded by a series of equally spectacular ballets. In 1619 two ballets, one for the king and one for the queen, were performed at the Louvre: the *Ballet de roi*, produced on Louis' order by the duc de Gramont and performed on a mobile stage, dealt with the adventure of Tancred in the enchanted forest; the *Ballet de la reine* was drawn from the fable of Psyche and cast the queen herself in the role of Juno.[82]

Example 4

As an art form, the ballet by 1620 was midway between the old mascarades and the future opera. It reflected the taste of the court. Although its function of glorifying the monarchy and entertaining the court aristocracy remained unchanged, the ballet underwent certain stylistic modifications after 1620. The dramatic unity of the earlier ballets began to loosen: the allegorical plots became more obscure; the récits became more arbitrary and less closely tied to the plot; and the songs, choruses, concerts, and dances were increasingly less justified by the drama. In short, the ballet de cour under the duc de Nemours, superintendent of royal *divertissements,* leaned more to a lyrical than a dramatic form, and, in a sense, reverted to the earlier format of a series of diverse scenes connected by a vague theme rather than by a dramatic plot.[83] The concluding grand ballets were still opulent and were usually introduced by a chorus. Frequently the prologues to these ballets contained récits praising the king. Standard backgrounds of mountains, forests, palaces, and grottoes, and exotic characters such as sorcerers, savages, and the elements and seasons appeared over and over again. The elaborate machine-operated sets of François Francine gradually gave way to simpler scenery with a single background.[84] The musicians were usually situated on a platform to the side of the stage. They performed occasional orchestral interludes, overtures (after 1640), and accompaniments for the récits and entrées. The music of the ballets de cour was as standardized, uniform, and symmetrical as the dance. The entrées were cast in binary form; alternating from major to minor, the harmony clung to a single key throughout each ballet. The music lacked contrapuntal complexities and irregular intervals, and was characterized by the parallel motion of the notes.[85] The ballets lost none of their regal sheen and were more than ever the principal showpiece of the crown. Michel de Marolles, abbé of Villeloin (1600-1655), who evinced keen interest in the development of French ballet, wrote: "The king, who loves all beautiful things, in which he succeeds admirably, has delighted in producing all kinds of ballets. I have learned from those who have been spectators of them and from the reports which I have read of them, that they have been well-planned according to the subjects; that in the serious ones, the magnificence of the machines and of the costumes was everything that could be desired."[86]

In the decade of the 1620's Louis XIII frequently treated his Parisian subjects to an elaborate, often ridiculous, ceremonial ballet in the Hôtel de Ville. On these occasions, which were regarded at court as a great honor for the city, preparations were made by the city officials weeks in advance of the *spectacle*. In anticipation of the *Ballet du roi*, planned for February 24, 1626, special chandeliers, tapestries, and paintings were placed in the amphitheater of the hôtel; machines were installed on February 23, and a battery of cooks was contracted for the collation. The king arrived at five in the afternoon of the twenty-fourth with a coterie of masked dancers, who entered the hôtel to the accompaniment of trumpets and a volley of fire from the cavalry.[87] The duc de Nemours had planned the subject of the ballet, which was the imaginary marriage of the Douairier de Bilbahout to a lady called Fanfan de Sotteville; the characters' names were appropriate according to the abbé de Marolles, because names "must have something pleasing about them, and there is an art in choosing them well." The ballet opened with an entrée for Atababpa and peoples from America and a récit that described the awe in which all peoples held the French monarchy. The entrée for the Americans was followed by dances for peoples from Asia led by Mohammed, and then an entrée for Turks. The Grand Turk boasted of his power in a récit, but concluded with homage to Louis XIII:

> Mon pouvoir imite le cours
> du lame que marche toujours
> d'un pas fatal à la contraincte :
> Mais quoy! ces titres inoüis
> Ne m'exemptent pas de la crainte
> d'accroistre quelque jour les palmes de Louis.[88]

Succeeding entrées were danced by the peoples of Greenland and Iceland (the duc de Nemours portrayed the bailiff of Greenland), the peoples of Africa, Europe, and Persia, and a *cacique* (native chief) on an elephant. Representing a Persian, Louis XIII cautioned the spectators about his dress:

> Je viens comme Persan, Docteur et Gentilhomme,
> Ne m'en croyez pas moins de la Foy protecteur,
> Un turban sur le chef du fils aisné de Rome
> Est tel qu'un mauvais livre en la main d'un Docteur.

The ballet was a successful display of royal pomp for the citizenry of Paris.

The conquest of the Huguenot stronghold of La Rochelle in 1628 and the pacification of the realm after yet another period of civil and religious upheaval provided the monarchy with an opportunity for spectacular celebration. An exotic outdoor ballet was performed with the Seine as a stage.[89] A colossal rock was placed in the river beside the Louvre. Chained to the rock was the figure of Andromède, symbolizing the Catholic religion. Around her swam a group of nymphs carrying torches and singing mournful songs. Out of the water rose a horrible flame-spitting monster, which moved toward the rock. Just as the monster reached the girl, Perseus, mounted on Pegasus, swooped down from the heights of the Tour de Nesles, which seemed to go up in flames behind him. As the monster was slain, a ballet of celebration was danced on a bridge of boats while fireworks exploded over the river and a procession of fiery-costumed characters carried banners with the king's name, the royal arms, and emblems of the sun. Of course, the monster represented the Huguenots, and Perseus was Louis XIII.

The *spectacle* of 1628 pointed up the fact that the ballets de cour of Louis XIII's reign contained more and more allusions to the events of the reign. Whereas the earlier ballets had celebrated the king's virtues and compared him with allegorical and mythological figures, the ballets produced in Cardinal Richelieu's time took on added political importance by portraying the crown's political achievements, especially its victories over its enemies. By 1630 the ballets de cour had become an essential ingredient in the life of the monarchy, not just as a form of entertainment but as a dramatic rendition of its exploits and its grandeur. In a preface to his ballet, *Le grand ballet des effets de nature* (danced by Louis on four consecutive days in December 1632 at the jeu de paume of the Petit Louvre), Guillaume Colletet expounded the current royal view of the value of ballets. "The Dance is a living image of our thoughts," he declared, "and an artificial expression of our secret thoughts."[90] Recognizing its beauty and significance, the world's greatest leaders make the dance an intimate part of both their private and public lives; "I will say that among the most respectable *divertissements* in which kings and princes derive pleasure, there are none which do not yield to dances and ballets." Princes have never spared the expense or effort necessary for the creation of new music, poetry, and machines because they realized that the ballet has the power "to content the public and for that reason to be like a pleasant panacea." Moreover, in a more general sense there is a traditional view shared by the great men of the past and the present that the dance possesses a divine quality; that the origin of dancing coincides with the genesis of the world itself; and that measured dances correspond to and perhaps reflect the perfect harmony of planetary motion. Thus, the theory of the universal harmony and the doctrine of the effects were linked to the king's entertainments.

Although Colletet's remarks must be understood in the context of the benefits he derived from royal patronage, nonetheless, he reflected the prevailing view of the purpose and meaning of music and ballet in seventeenth-century France (see Chapter 1). Indeed, in an essay similar to Colletet's that also appeared in 1632 as a preface to the printed edition of the *Ballet de l'harmonie* (danced by Louis in December), an unidentified author expressed the contemporary conception of ballet as a species of God's harmony which involves man's senses of sight and hearing equally. Man has an inner awareness of universal harmony; through ballet the human spirit can be drawn into rapport with the universe. And as the central figure of the ballet, the king was the embodiment of wordly order and the symbol of universal harmony.[91] In short, in addition to its function of diverting the court and the public from more serious matters, the ballet represented man's affinity with the cosmos. The king, of course, was the earthly symbol of universal harmony and order; through him the people had a sense of their unity within the nation and in effect within the universal scheme of things. The royal ballets could presumably help to convey this message. They put the nobility at least in direct touch with the earthly source of unity and order, just as the earth is in touch with the superior but steadfast power of the sun. Reviewing the *Ballet des triomphes* (produced at the Louvre along with the *Ballet des quatre monarchies chrétiennes* in 1635), the *Gazette de France* wrote: "It is characteristic of the force of the sun to concur with inferior bodies without descending from its sphere. It is an effect of the power of kings to familiarize themselves when they wish with their subjects, without lessening any of their sovereign authority; rather, it is through his dance or regulated movement that this king of the stars communicates to us his warmth and light; that is what fulfills his comparison with us."[92]

Still, the ballets of the 1630's also performed the less lofty but more important purpose of calling attention to the political and economic successes of the crown. From the beginning of the Regency in 1610 to the consolidation of royal authority under Cardinal Richelieu after 1630, the French nobility, especially the Huguenots, mounted several challenges to the crown and to its chief minister. Each attempt, including the nobles' revival of dueling in an effort to place themselves above the law, the revolt of the Huguenots in Languedoc and La Rochelle in 1627, the crisis of the Day of Dupes in 1630, and the attempt of the

Parlement of Paris to increase its legal jurisdiction at the crown's expense, resulted in failure and in the increase of royal power under Richelieu's administration. The ballet composers of the 1630's commemorated this outcome by references to the events and eventually by devising dramatic plots dealing specifically with the successes of the monarchy. In its review of the *Ballet de la marine* (performed at the Arsenal in 1635), the *Gazette de France* pointed to this development: "When Louis' valor and arms had smothered heresy and destroyed the schemes of forces which had been until now the cause of our civil wars, this same king, the most just of all the monarchs, assisted by the wise counsels of the greatest mind who was ever called to be the first minister of France, made plans to bring his peoples the wealth and the peace of which the intestine troubles had robbed them for too long."[93]

The *Ballet de la marine* itself treated another of the cardinal's ventures—the establishment of a French navy and the centralization of shipping and oceanic commerce. Richelieu made France a naval power by setting aside local privilege and gaining control of Le Havre, Brouage, and other coastal ports for the crown, establishing arsenals at La Rochelle and Brest, and ordering the construction of fifty ships for the royal navy. Although the cardinal was less successful in establishing a merchant marine, he did launch several new trading companies operating under government regulations and investments. The *Ballet* celebrated these achievements in a semiallegorical fashion. Récits and dances of marine gods and sea nymphs heralded the glorious revival of the French navy and proclaimed "the esteem of foreign princes who admire the wonders of the great Monarch of the world" and who send through their ambassadors "assurances of affection."[94] Ambassadors from Moscow, Persia, China, and Africa paid tribute to the naval supremacy of France, and the Moorish ambassador (portrayed by M. de Sainctot Lardenay) delivered the principal récit:

> Du rivage bruslé qu'une mer escumeuse
> de flots impétueux va sans cesse battant,
> Je viens vers ce grand Roi dont la gloire fameuse
> de climat en climat jusqu'au notre s'estend.

Je lui viens présenter tout l'or de notre Empire
pour la haute conqueste où sa valeur aspire;
Mais mon offrandre est vaine, et la source de l'or,
seroit même inutile à cet heureux monarque,
puisqu'ayant Richelieu dans sa guerrière barque,
Il possède en lui seul un immense thrésor.[95]

Even more relevant to the French political situation in the 1630's was the *Ballet de la félicité sur le sujet de l'heureuse naissance de monseigneur le dauphin,* performed at Saint-Germain in February 1639 and at the Hôtel de Richelieu in March. The ballet celebrated Louis XIV's birth the preceding September, but the principal theme was the Thirty Years' War. Seeing the war as a dynastic struggle and alarmed by the Habsburg victory over its allies in the Heilbronn League in 1634, Richelieu had brought France into direct conflict with the enemy for the first time in 1635. After a stinging defeat in 1636, in which France narrowly escaped disaster at the hands of Imperial and Spanish armies, Richelieu had mounted a successful offensive in 1637 and 1638 with the support of his Dutch, German, and Italian allies. When the ballet commemorating the dauphin's birth was performed, the French had invaded Spanish territory and had defeated a Spanish fleet off the coast of Fuenterrabiá; the Dutch had reconquered strategic positions in the Low Countries including Breda, and were preparing what would be the devastating defeat of a Spanish armada; and the armies of Marshal Turenne and Bernard of Saxe-Weimar had captured the critical city of Breisach on the Rhine, leaving Germany exposed and her princes helpless before the French. In short, France and her allies had taken the strong initiative against the Imperial and Spanish branches of the House of Habsburg and "the war degenerated altogether into a contest between the Kings of France and Spain, fought on German soil."[96] And this is the way it was treated in the *Ballet de la félicité,* except that France was portrayed as the victim of foreign ambition personified by the Spanish monarchy. The allegorical characters of Ambition and Discord revealed how they had wrecked mankind's hopes for peace by inspiring a desire for world conquest in such rulers as Alexander the Great, Julius Caesar, and Tamerlane. Imbued with the same power lust,

Philip IV of Spain was depicted as the modern personification of ambition. His nemesis was the moderate and magnanimous Louis XIII, whose only motive was to protect France and the world from Spanish aggression. This idea was projected in the first seven entrées of the ballet; in the eighth, dancers performed a mock combat between Spanish and German troops and French and Swiss soldiers. The ballet-combat was stopped by the figure of Felicity, who appeared triumphantly in a chariot, with the dauphin in her arms and Justice seated at her feet. Justice and Felicity dispersed the soldiers, carved the globe into four parts, and sang récits about the peace and harmony which the infant king would bring to the world. In subsequent entrées a Saxon emissary (the comte de Toulon) presented France with the enemy flags to mark her victory, and the Spanish danced an entrée of peace with the French around fountains of wine and jets of fire. In a drinking song Sieur Chastelet likened the wine to the blood of the gods and the Bourbons. The justice of the French cause in the war was proclaimed by the figure of Fame, who paid homage to Louis XIII:

> C'est lui dont la juste balance,
> règlant sa volonté,
> sçait peser sa bonté
> avec que sa puissance;
> c'est ce roi qui s'en fait
> par une juste guerre,
> l'arbitre de la terre.[97]

In the concluding entrées the Turks menaced Europe but were forced to retreat before the combined resistance of the major European powers, and the singers foretold that the final and enduring alliance of France and Spain would be sealed by the dauphin.

The last and most luxuriant of the political ballets of Louis XIII's reign was the *Ballet de la prospérité des armes de France*, produced by Cardinal Richelieu at his palace on February 7, 1641. Richelieu, who had always regarded ballets as useful and worthy distractions for the king and his court, brought the celebrated Italian wizard of staging, Giacomo Torelli, to Paris

En fin lors que la nui vient foulager les peines,
Les pourtraits animez des actions humaines,
Montent fur vn Theatre artiftement pare;

LE SOIR.

Il y voit de fes faits les viuantes hiftoires
Mais le feint et le vray de toutes fes victoires
Touchent egalement fon esprit moderè'.

Figure 5. Richelieu's theater in the Palais-Royal during the performance of a play in 1643. Seated (*left to right*) : Cardinal Richelieu, Louis XIII, Anne d'Autriche, the dauphin (Louis XIV); courtiers in loges. The theater later became the principal center for the production of Jean-Baptiste Lully's operas and was modified to enlarge the seating capacity and to accommodate new machinery. Copperplate engraving by M. Van Lochom, *imprimeur du roi pour les tailles-douces;* in "Grande folio: Histoire de France, 1640-1643"; set entitled "Occupations ordinaires du roi." (Photograph courtesy of the Bibliothèque Nationale, cabinet des estampes.)

for the event and installed elaborate machinery and scenery in the palace theater (Figure 5). By a system of weights and levers, the stage decorations could be shifted and changed rapidly. The lavish sets represented the fields of Arras, the plain of Casal, the snow-capped Alps, in addition to a stormy sea and scenes of hell and heaven. The performance was presided over by Bishop de Valenca (later the archbishop of Rheims), who was also in charge of the collation following the ballet. Special places were reserved for the king and queen and for Cardinal Richelieu's favorite bishops, abbés, and confessors. A preface to the printed copy of the ballet pointed out that it was to be a part of a winter-long fete to provide relaxation for the people after the summer's arduous war: "Not only the king and his great minister, who have attended and worked for the aggrandizement of the state, and all the valiant warriors who have executed his noble designs so courageously, must take repose and *divertissement*; but all the people must rejoice, who after their anxieties in the expec-tation of great successes, feel as great a pleasure from the victories of their prince as those themselves who have contributed the most toward his service and his glory."[98]

The music for the *Ballet de la prospérité* was somewhat more diversified and lively than that of earlier ballets, especially in the more descriptive string passages, where stylized tone-painting was used to depict the agitation of the furies and Jupiter's descent from the clouds. In part 1 the entrée for Victory was typical of the music in this and other ballets of the period (Example 5).[99]

The *Ballet de la prospérité* opened with the entrance of Harmony on a cloud. In a récit Harmony announced that her chords permeate the universe and that in order to rule successfully, all kings must follow her. Torelli's machinery then shifted the set to expose the bowels of hell, from which emerged the duc d'Enghien and other dancers representing six demons of pride, trickery, murder, desire, tyranny, and disorder. In subsequent entrées Pluto, Proserpine, and the Furies made their appearance and released an eagle and two lions. Part 1 concluded with the disappearance of hell and the entry on the earth of Mars, Fame, Victory, and Hercule Gaulois, danced by the comte d'Harcourt, who drove away the eagle and the lions. Appearing on a snow-

Example 5

capped mountain in the Alps in part 2, Italy appealed to the
French monarch for help against the tyrants who wanted to
conquer her:

> Vostre valeur m'a sauvée autrefois
> De la fureur d'une injuste entreprise;
> J'ay sçeu ranger l'Univers sous mes lois,
> Et maintenant je crains d'estre soumise.

> Depuis mille ans c'est aux lys que je dois
> Ce doux repos que le Ciel favorise;
> J'ay sçeu ranger l'Universe sous mes lois,
> Et maintenant je crains d'estre soumise.[100]

Summoned by the four principal rivers of Italy, the French
defeated the Spanish army in a fierce combat. Fortune entered
in the fourth entrée to carry the French arms, as the scene
shifted to Arras in Flanders near the French border, where the
French were feted by the Flemish with pots of beer and carried
through the city by Pallas (goddess of prudence) on a chariot
drawn by Spaniards.

The references to the contemporary scene in this ballet were
obvious. The mountain in the Alps from which Italy summoned
the French was in the Valtelline: the upper valley of the Adda
River which Swiss troops in the pay of France had occupied

during the war in order to cut off the principal route of the Spanish army through the Spanish-Habsburg possessions in Italy to Habsburg, Austria. Richelieu not only held the Valtelline, but by 1641 the French army under the comte d'Harcourt had defeated the Spanish in northern Italy and had occupied Turin. As for Arras, Richelieu's troops had conquered that frontier fortress in 1640 and had liberated the Flemish people from Spanish domination. The drive against the Habsburg forces included the occupation of Alsace and, by 1642, the Pyrenees' province of Roussillon. The *Ballet de la prospérité* commemorated the expertise and success of Richelieu's highly skilled army and turned his ambitious foreign policy, including an unsolicited intervention in Savoy, into a heroic defense of enslaved peoples against the hellish forces of aggression and tyranny.

The allegorical references to the events of the war continued throughout part 3 of the ballet. Sirens seated on rocks in the sea sang about the French victories and the forthcoming conclusion of hostilities: "Louis, by pushing the war aside, is going to fill the sea and the earth with his deeds." The chorus referred to the abortive attempt to begin preliminaries for a peace conference in Hamburg in 1641. The entrées, on the other hand, depicted the seizure of American treasures by the Spanish galleons and their defeat by the French navy. Part 4 opened with the descent of the nine Muses from the sky. They sang a récit to Louis XIII:

> Poursuivez, O grand Roi, d'éstonner l'Univers,
> Par tant de beaux exploits, doux sujets de nos vers;
> Nos éscrits qui vivront en depit de l'Envie;
> Ne parleront jamais d'une si belle vie.
>
> Dès l'avril de vos ans votre bras a soumis
> vos rebelles sujets et vos fiers enemis.
> Nos éscrits qui vivront en depit de l'Envie,
> Ne parleront jamais d'une si belle vie.[101]

Reverting to the theme of part 1, the ballet continued with entrées for Venus, three Graces, Mercury, Bacchus, Apollo, and troops of satyrs and troubadours. The eagle and the two lions, vague symbols of France's enemies, returned to be battled by Hercules and subsequently pacified by Jupiter, who descended from the clouds on a luminous throne.

The final part of the *Ballet de la prospérité* took place in a pastoral earth-setting of flowers and fruits. Here Concord appeared in a chariot. She called on Spain and France to revive the peaceful arts and to submit to her laws of tranquillity. The entrées were danced by the marquis de Chanvallon, de Charny, du Gast, and other nobles in the roles of Abundance, Good Cheer, Games, Pleasures, and Exercises. In the fifth entrée, sieurs Jourdain, de Lauvre, le Vacher, and Perishon represented four of the king's admirers and danced through lush pastures to display their joy. As Glory was hoisted to the sky, the curtain fell. It rose again moments later to reveal a grand ballroom ornamented with paintings and lighted by crystal chandeliers, underneath which stood the thrones of the king and queen and benches for the ladies and gentlemen of the court. From the rear of the theater a bridge was raised to permit the king and queen to pass to the hall where a collation and ball followed the ballet.[102]

Produced near the end of Cardinal Richelieu's life, the *Ballet de la prospérité des armes de la France* was a showcase of the military wares of France set to music and dance. It reflected the most exalted image which the monarchy had of itself and of its political and military victories. It was the culmination of a long association between musical *spectacles* and royalism which originated in the Middle Ages. Since the fifteenth century, if not earlier, music and dance were drafted into the royal service by the French monarchy, not only as its primary source of entertainment, but as the necessary adornment of its ceremonies and rituals. A succession of Valois and Bourbon kings found in musical *spectacles* an effective means to show off to the foreigner the wealth, energy, and happiness of the kingdom in wartime. Astute leaders such as Richelieu discovered that the ballet was a useful exercise and a time-occupying diversion for the restless nobility. And the monarchy found that the plots of these productions, spun out through entrées and récits, could convey an image of glory, benevolence, courage, and strength to the court sycophants in attendance at the Louvre and to the bedazzled bourgeoisie at the Hôtel de Ville. By the time of Louis XIV's birth, musical *spectacles* had become a state institution; the Sun King was to enlarge the scope of such *spectacles* and extend their function far beyond anything attempted by his predecessors.

*3

Music and the Monarchy during the Youth of Louis XIV

Louis XIV substantially augmented the musical legacy which he inherited. Although rulers like Charles IX and Louis XIII had brought the arts into close association with the monarchy, Louis XIV so deepened and expanded that association that many of his contemporaries viewed his reign as an era of artistic rebirth. It is debatable how tangibly and concretely Louis was responsible for the over-all cultural and scientific brilliance of his time, but his personal concern for the musical life of France is certain. He may not have "restored them [the arts] to their first dignity," as André Félibien, the king's historiographer, insisted,[1] but he did provide direction and support for music in particular which fixed a monarchical stamp on the French Baroque. In his youth Louis was content to cultivate his love of the dance and to perfect the musical practices of his ancestors. Later on, after assuming the full prerogatives of kingship, he considerably strengthened the link between music and statecraft.

Louis came by his musical interest and talent naturally. His father had often danced in the ballets de cour; he had also composed an occasional air which he sang to lute accompaniment. The young dauphin was encouraged to develop similar talents. Training in music was part of his education, and he was admonished especially to emulate his father's reputation as a dancer.[2] Louis also studied the clavecin under François-Étienne Richard, and he was taught to play the guitar by Jourdan de la Salle, whom Cardinal Mazarin brought from Spain.[3] He was reputed to be a proficient guitarist. Louis' musical discernment became so acute during his youth that he could "distinguish among a troop of musicians the one who makes a false tone, which is the reason that the music of his Chapel and of his Chamber is considered even by the foreign ambassadors as the most accomplished of all the European courts."[4] An Italian visitor to the French court, Primi Visconti, maintained that the king was as conversant with musical designs as with military strategy.[5] Louis' skill as a dancer was acknowledged by his courtiers, who had ample opportunity to observe him at his favorite recreation. Jacques Bonnet contended that "since the king knew music to perfection, he overshadowed through his grand air and good grace all the famous dancers of the court."[6] Louis XIV's youth has been characterized by many historians as a time of carefree frivolity for the young king, who whiled away his hours practicing dance steps and listening to concerts. Louis supposedly escaped from the meetings of the royal council into the dressing room, where he played the guitar and discussed the ballet with a gentleman-in-waiting. The Venetian ambassador wrote disapprovingly in 1652 that "games, dances and comedies are the King's sole pursuits."[7] Other contemporary observers found the king dull and indolent. While Mazarin, Richelieu's successor, attempted to steer the country through the perils of the Fronde (the revolution of 1648-1653), Louis "amused himself at the reviews, at the dances, at the ballets; . . . he lived as a private person without troubling himself with anything."[8]

Contemporary observers believed that Mazarin encouraged the king's amusements out of the dual motive of distracting the court from his own schemes and contributing to the brilliance of the monarchy. The cardinal "invited gaiety to approach the throne" in order "to render his power less invidious."[9] In his contemporary history of Louis' reign, Henri-Philippe de Limiers suggested that Mazarin sponsored *divertissements* in order to distract the nobility, and Nicolas Goulas, a gentleman of the chamber, asserted that the cardinal imported Italian musicians for political reasons. "He governed with sweetness," Goulas declared; "it seems that he worked for peace, and he maintained the court in union and in repose which contributed to the welfare of the state."[10] As he grew older the king probably came to understand the cardinal's purposes. While he danced his entrées and passed his harmless notes to Marie Mancini "during the performance of allegorical ballets, . . . the airs of which sufficiently expressed the nature of such missives,"[11] Louis XIV began to display an earnestness not required for such amusements. Madame Françoise de Motteville made the revealing remark: "I often noticed with astonishment that in his games and amusements the King never laughed."[12]

Around the age of thirty, Louis XIV began to realize with Mazarin-like dispassion the value and utility of music as a diversion for the nobility. In his younger days, however, the king was attracted to musical productions by the flattering feeling of superiority and grandeur which they gave him. Stimulated by Louis' vanity in the early years, music and the other arts became genuinely useful tools for projecting the more tangible glory of his later years. As a youth Louis was obsessed with visions of glory; he wallowed in the obsequiousness of his court and shared with them the musical amusements which fed his ego. The courtiers appeared to relish the royal *spectacles* as much as the king and were "delighted to see a brilliance in their princes."[13] Issac de Larrey, who was court counselor for the ruler of Prussia's ambassador, declared that Louis' attention to the arts "provides him not only with excuses, but in fact with panegyrics for his loves and wars."[14]

What better means did the young ruler have to savor his glory than the musical eulogies of the ballet de cour? The verses for the mid-century ballets by Isaac Benserade celebrated the most commonplace events in the king's life with the same serious mien and enthusiasm given to the important achievements of the reign. Louis accepted Benserade's adulatory panegyrics with the aplomb befitting the Dieu-donné ruler of France, almost as if they were punctilious homilies from the pulpit. Vanity Louis had in abundance, but vanity alone does not explain the young king's susceptibility to the flattery of his musicians and poets. He came to the realization that if his image as a glorious, wise, and beneficent monarch was projected often and vividly, it would be believed. With reference to Benserade's lyric verses, one writer expressed it this way: "A superior man appears pleased at the concert of eulogies which are perpetuated around him, and . . . he encourages the insipid enthusiasm which exalts him to the skies: *la politique* wants it; his single ambition revels in it. The flatterers serve him by making the vulgar accustomed to see him under the highest proportions. . . . He made flattery a political instrument."[15]

Although the perspicacious Louis de Rouvroi, duc de Saint-Simon, believed that Louis was poisoned by self-love, he recognized Louis' view of the function of flattery: "He loved splendor, magnificence, profusion in everything. He turned this taste into a political maxim and urged it in everything at his court."[16] The king construed luxury to signify honor and sometimes necessity. He occupied the nobles with *divertissements* that fed his pride; "the court was another intrigue of the politics of despotism."[17] Moreover, the young monarch brooked no competition in the realm of opulent display as his notorious visit in 1661 to Fouquet's château, Vaux-le-Vicomte, proved. Entertained lavishly by concerts, a ball, a ballet, musical intermezzos, and récits, Louis responded by dismissing and incarcerating the erstwhile finance minister. Of course, Fouquet had confused the state's revenue with his own and might have been ousted even if he had used his power more discreetly; but the parading of his wealth so blatantly before the monarch was the final blow.[18] The youthful Louis XIV wanted to have only himself and his court surrounded with the lavish brilliance which musical *spectacles* could provide. Beyond the obvious desire for flattery lay the conviction that glorification of the monarch was at the same time glorification of the French nation, and that display of royal splendor was a service to the state.

Mazarin and the Italian Opera

The history of music during Louis XIV's youth was dominated by three major developments: the performances of Italian opera by Italian musicians imported by Cardinal Mazarin to the French court in the 1640's; the ballets de cour of the 1650's by Isaac Benserade; and the comédie ballets by Jean-Baptiste Molière and Jean-Baptiste Lully in the 1660's. The first of these developments was encouraged by the personal taste and political calculations of the astute Mazarin. The Barberini family and their pope, Maffeo Barberini, or Urban VIII (1623-1644), had built an opera theater in their palace in Rome and had sponsored expensive productions there, many of which Mazarin had seen. The cardinal in 1632 helped stage Stefano Landi's opera *Sant Alessio*, the libretto for which was written by Giulio Rospigliosi, who was later to become Pope Clement IX. On the death of Urban VIII in 1644 the Spanish candidate, Cardinal Panfili, was elected Pope Innocent X. An enemy of the Barberinis and of France, the new pope investigated the disreputable state of the Barberinis' finances and called a halt to operatic productions. Encouraged by Mazarin, Urban VIII's three nephews (one of whom, Cardinal Antonio, later became archbishop of Rheims) fled to France with a retinue of Italian musicians. The celebrated soprano, Leonora Baroni, had already been summoned to Paris by Mazarin in 1643 and given residence in the comte de Brégy's home with a yearly salary of 1,000 pistoles;[19] she was now joined by a dozen castratos, including Atto Melani (who served the cardinal as a secret agent in 1648-1649), the composers Luigi Rossi, Marco Marazzoli, and Carlo Caproli, the master machinist Giacomo Torelli, the librettist and apostolic protonotary Francesco Buti, and several more poets and musicians formerly in the Barberinis' employ. The Italians were directed to entertain the court and to prepare operatic productions.[20]

In December 1645 the Italians offered their first production, a musical comedy entitled *La finta Pazza* (Figure 6). First performed in Venice in 1641, this three-act play had a libretto by Giulio Strozzi, machines by Torelli, and music by Sacrati. Produced in the spacious hall of the Hôtel du Petit-Bourbon, which was equipped with Torelli's machines, *La finta Pazza* emphasized exotic *divertissements* such as a ballet for monkeys and bears, a dance for ostriches, and a ceremony in which four Indians presented parrots to the hero.[21] Torelli deliberately tried to dazzle the audience with unusual lighting and stage techniques that made it possible, for example, for Jupiter's kingdom to appear in the sky through parting clouds. Aside from Torelli's machine effects, *La finta Pazza* made little impression on the

Figure 6. Scene from the prologue of the Italian musical production *La finta Pazza* (1645). The flying figures were propelled by the elaborate machinery of Giacomo Torelli. Engraving after Giacomo Torelli; reprinted from Giulio Strozzi, *Feste Theatrali per la finta Pazza Drama del Sig* (November 25, 1645). (Photograph by Pic; courtesy of the Bibliothèque de l'Opéra, Paris.)

small gathering of spectators. The queen's confidant, Madame de Motteville, wrote: "The queen had one of the musical comedies performed in the little hall of the Royal Palace where there was only the king, the queen, the cardinal and the familiar of the court. ... We were only twenty or thirty persons in this place, and we thought we would die of boredom and cold."[22] Madame's boredom notwithstanding, the Italian production was noteworthy in one important respect: France was introduced to the machine wizardry of Torelli, whose innovations made a lasting impact on

the French theater. Prior to Torelli, Italians such as Niccolo
Sabbatini (1574-1654) and Giovanni Battista Aleotti (1546-1632)
had developed an art and a technology of stagecraft which
permitted changes of scene, special effects of perspective and
illusion, and flying figures propelled by machines.[23] Sabbatini
devised various techniques for changing the back scene, including a raked stage where the scene could be changed unnoticed behind the action taking place on the forestage. He also
published a widely read manual (*Practica di fabricar scene e macchine
ne' teatri*, 1638-1639) with instructions on the operation of flying
machines whereby angels and spirits could appear miraculously,
the gods could descend on billowy clouds, and demons could
be whisked across the stage. His ideas on the uses of sound and
lighting effects, smoke, water and fire, trap doors, and other
ingenious devices of stagecraft made possible the complicated
and bizarre theater pieces of the seventeenth century. Aleotti
pioneered the art of scenic variation by inventing wings constructed of wooden frames and attached to wheels which ran
on rails beneath the stage. The scenery, which was painted on
canvases on the frames, could be wheeled back and forth on
the stage as needed. Used in the theaters of Ferrara and Parma,
Aleotti's stage technology was further developed by his pupil
Giacomo Torelli (1608-1678). Torelli, after he had worked in
Venice, Tuscany, and Rome as an operatic designer, brought
the art of Italian stagecraft with him to France. To the techniques
of Sabbatini and Aleotti, he added his own inventions, including
a rapid, one-man method of changing wings by means of rollers
and wheels. He was especially noted for his mastery of perspective,
lighting, and design, and he was largely responsible for the brief
vogue of Italian opera in the 1640's and for the théâtre des
machines of the 1650's. His successors included Giovanni Burnacini,
who staged Italian operas for the emperor in Vienna, Gaspare
Vigarani, who built the salle des machines in the Tuileries in
1662, and Gaspare's son Carlo who built several small theaters
in Paris and worked in association with Lully on the operas and
divertissements of Louis XIV. The Italian monopoly on stage design
was finally broken by Jean Berain who succeeded Vigarani as
Lully's designer and who adapted Torelli's ideas to French taste.

The art of Torelli was sufficient to sustain the interest of the French court in Italian opera following the unenthusiastic reception of *La finta Pazza*. Boosted by Mazarin's support, the Italian performers in 1646 staged the opera *Egisto* by Pier Francesco Cavalli.[24] This production drew less attention, however, than the opera *Orfeo*. *Orfeo* was composed on Mazarin's order specially for France by Luigi Rossi, the official composer for Cardinal Antonio Barberini, and the abbé Francesco Buti, an Italian doctor of laws. It was first performed under the composer's supervision on March 2, 1647, at the Palais-Royal before a large group of spectators including the young king, the queen mother, Mazarin, the court, foreign ambassadors, and members of the Parlement of Paris. The opera was sung on this occasion and in subsequent Paris performances by an Italian cast that included the castratos Atto Melani as Orfeo and Marco-Antonio Pasqualini as Aristeus, and the soprano Rosina Martini as Venus; the latter two were protégés of Mathias de Medici. Torelli assisted by Charles Errard, the future director of the French academy in Rome, designed the elegant costumes and complicated machine-propelled scenery. Gold ornaments adorned the paneled walls from which hung paintings sketched by Errard and painted in part by the sixteen-year-old Noël Coypel.[25]

The opera began with a prologue in which the French army successfully besieged an enemy city. After singing the call to assault in a triple chorus, the French soldiers stormed the crumbling city wall, and Victory descended from heaven in a chariot singing an aria to honor Louis XIV and the queen mother:

Behold me! And when, O invincible armies of Gaul, have I ever failed you? I walk with these banners; these golden lilies that flame are my own badge, and clearly say: "Let all yield to the French Monarch!" Behold me! It is I who have received your King in a bower of trophies, and who have placed a thousand palms upon his brow. It is I who make the two hemispheres tremble under his rule, and place a curb for him upon the great ocean. . . . His happy fates wish that glory may shine on you through the eyes of the noble Anne, whose beautiful hands hold the sceptre and hurl the thunderbolts.[26]

The rapid aria unfolded floridly over a firm bass (Example 6).[27] Act 1 introduced a series of colorful scenes of a forest, a palace,

Example 6

Fran - co Mo-nar-ca - o - gni   ri - pa - ro

the gardens of the Sun, and the Sun's descent in a flaming chariot adorned with gold and diamonds. The amorphous plot dealt with the love of Euridice and Orfeo (Orpheus), the musician-poet son of Apollo, but the highlight of the opera was Euridice's death and an infernal scene when scores of harpies and sundry monsters crowded the stage. While the point of Buti's vapid yarn was not altogether clear, the moral seems to have been that virtue is incompatible with earthly happiness.

Although liberally laced with French ballets, the opera was a typical representation of mid-seventeenth-century Italian musical style. Orchestral sinfonia held together an assortment of da capo arias, cavatina airs, and ariettas which, unlike the later French operas, were sharply demarcated from the recitatives that "unrolled themselves for hours like an endless ribbon upon a white road."[28] Arias were usually accompanied by a figured, often chromatic, bass and were characterized by an abundance of florid ornaments such as trills and appoggiaturas. The harmony consistently shifted abruptly, moved into remote keys, and was flavored with dissonances and chromatic alterations—all practices foreign to the French music of the time and to the French opera later in Louis XIV's reign. An aria or a recitative was frequently built around exclamations such as "Ah! Piangete!" ("Oh! Weep!"), which were occasions for dissonant chords, irregular rhythms, and elaborate vocal embellishments. Often an entire aria was made up of a series of florid variations on two or three principle themes, composed without doubt to enable the singer to show off his virtuosity. One of Orfeo's airs, for example, proceeds, after a four-bar descending figure in the bass (which repeats twice during the aria), with three four-bar phrases, each repeated in variations. The scheme of the harmonic movement was:

Section:	A	B	B′	C	C′
Key:	d	da	dF	Fa	ad

This entire plan then repeated twice, providing an over-all pattern of A, A′, A″.[29] *Orfeo* was thus a singers' opera with the added attraction of exotic staging. It differed substantially from the musical fare to which the French were accustomed, and it bore strikingly little resemblance to the French operas of Jean-Baptiste Lully that appeared thirty years later. Most significant in terms of later French opera was the Italian practice of obscuring the text and burying the plot beneath a potpourri of irrelevant episodes and characters. Italian composers such as Luigi Rossi "treated the libretto as hardly more than a conventional scaffolding for the musical structure."[30] It was precisely the importance attached to the text (a text which glorified the French monarchy) and the concomitant clear, untrammeled exposition of the vocal line that characterized the musical experiments of the sixteenth century and that distinguished the national opera in France in later years from the Roman and Venetian opera which supposedly influenced it so much.

Although Rossi's opera might have stirred controversy even if France had not been having internal difficulties, the fact that it was performed in Paris on the eve of the Fronde, as criticism of Mazarin's fiscal policies was mounting, doomed it to failure. The opera, which Mazarin had hoped would further his purposes, redounded against him. The initial criticisms of the Italians were moralistic and were directed at the queen. Just as Mazarin had planned, Anne was seduced by the musical performances of the Italians even before *Orfeo* and was enamored of some of the singers, particularly Leonora Baroni and Atto Melani. (She pleaded with Mathias de Medici to permit Melani to remain in Paris). The queen's preoccupation with her pleasures and her habit of consorting with castratos and ladies of the theater, one of whom "had the reputation of selling beauty,"[31] occasioned serious criticism of her behavior and of her Italian friends. With the help of the curé of Saint-Germain, some of Mazarin's enemies got seven doctors of the Sorbonne to sign a statement that declared the Italian productions sinful. The queen retaliated by winning the support of Hardouin de Beaumont de Péréfixe, the archbishop of Paris, who, with some fellow members of the French academy, signed a statement commending the Italian productions as lawful and good for princes. The cardinal, meanwhile, maintained his silence. One of his enemies, Nicolas Goulas, said of him: "Monsieur le Cardinal, who was implicated in this affair by the pleasure he took in Italian Comedy, thought fit to say nothing, knowing that he had enough followers and frivolous friends at court to uphold his interests in the matter. But he knew that religion could not hold him or this perpetual acting, this love of the nastiness of the theater, and the worst and most licentious practices of a court whom he invited to share his pleasures and whom he had always about him."[32]

The attacks mounted with the success of *Orfeo* and the March 1647 revival of *La finta Pazza*. The queen did refuse to permit continuous performances of *Orfeo* during Lent, and she even condescended to leave for chapel in the middle of the March 2 performance, since the following day was Shrove Sunday. Nonetheless, the moralistic criticisms leveled at Mazarin, the court, and the Italians continued. The *Gazette de France* tried to counter these attacks by pointing out the moral value of *Orfeo* itself:

Virtue is always victorious over vice in spite of the difficulties that present themselves. Orpheus and Eurydice were not only faithful in their chaste love, notwithstanding the efforts of Venus and Bacchus, the two most powerful authors of moral laxity, but Love himself opposed his mother, as he did not wish to lead Eurydice to be faithless to her husband. Shall we not also expect something beyond honest instruction in what is good, when a play is honoured by the presence of one so wise and devout as our own queen?[33]

The reaction of the Parlementarians, who were invited to the performance of *Orfeo* on March 2, portended more serious consequences for Mazarin and the court. Anxious to regain the political influence that Richelieu had denied them, the nobles and members of the Parlement of Paris intensified their constant opposition to Mazarin in 1647. In that year the unstable financial situation grew worse, and the Parlement refused to register a new tax. Mazarin, who was always disliked as a meddling Italian, drew a torrent of criticism for flooding the court with Italian musicians and spending large sums of money on the production of *Orfeo*. Estimates of the cost varied: one source observed that Mazarin "loved music and spectacle and spent over a million for the opera of *Orphée* which he produced at the Petit-Bourbon."[34] One of Mazarin's enemies, François de Paule de Clermont, marquis de Montglat, estimated the cost at 400,000 livres, and another opponent, Guy de Joly (an aide to Cardinal de Retz), set the amount at 500,000 livres. Joly said the entire matter gives everyone cause for reflection, especially the "sovereign societies who are tormented and see well by this excessive and superfluous expense, that the needs of the state are not so pressing that one could spare them easily if one wished it."[35] The French people talked of nothing else but the cost of *Orfeo*, according to Nicolas Goulas. "Each was bent upon the terrible expense of the machines and the Italian musicians who had come from Rome and elsewhere at large costs, because it was necessary to pay them to leave, to come, and to be supported in France."[36]

Estimates of the cost of Mazarin's opera may have been exaggerated (his librarian Gabriel Naudé set the figure at 30,000 écus), but the criticism that *Orfeo* engendered had very real consequences. When the Fronde commenced in June 1648, there was a veritable castrato hunt in the streets of Paris: Torelli was incarcerated; Rossi and Melani fled the country. Introduced for political reasons, Italian opera fell for political reasons. Mazarin wisely headed off the queen's plans for a new opera, and the Italians had to wait out the Fronde before staging a comeback. Their return was also to prove frustrating, however, because, although the French were dazzled by Torelli's machines, their taste did not run to singer's opera set to texts which they could not understand. Accustomed to a lively succession of ballet entrées connected by verses and a plot which, however loose, glorified their king and involved their nobility, the French court rejected Italian music. Ultimately, after Mazarin had died and the king had decided to nationalize and centralize the arts, the Italians were swept out on a tide of national feeling.

In spite of the charges against *Orfeo*, the opera stimulated a series of successful machine productions and pastoral dramas in Paris during the 1650's, which are regarded as the forerunners of French opera.[37] The day after the opening of *Orfeo* the Italian theater group, who performed at the old Hôtel de Bourgogne on rue Mauconseil, revived a play called the *Descente d'Orfée*, which emphasized machines and decorations. The tragi-comedy *Ulysse*, with songs and machines, followed in the spring of 1648, and *La naissance d'Hercule* in 1649. In response to the success of these machine plays and in part to make use of the elaborate machines which Torelli had built for *Orfeo*, the dramatist Pierre Corneille and the composer Charles d'Assoucy wrote the drama *Andromède*, at the request of Mazarin, for performance at the Petit-Bourbon in February 1650. Labeled a "tragédie représentée avec les machines," *Andromède* incorporated airs, duets, and choruses into a five-act drama with a prologue.

Music was a subsidiary element in *Andromède*; its chief function was to cover up the sounds of the machinery and to help along dramatic incidents such as the descent of Jupiter, Juno, and Neptune in the last act. Corneille took a cavalier attitude toward the music: "I have employed music only to satisfy the ear while the eyes are looking at the machines, but I have been careful to have nothing sung that is essential to the understanding of the play because the words are generally badly understood in music."[38] The most interesting feature of Corneille's production in terms of later developments was the prologue, in which Melpomène, the Muse of tragedy, sang with the Sun about the glory of Louis XIV. Reaching to the clouds in the center of the stage was a mountain through the center of which a grotto and the sea could be seen. Melpomène emerged on the moutain top to greet the Sun, which advanced in a horse-drawn chariot (Figure 7). Asked by the Muse to cease his orbiting in order to admire the country of France, the Sun protested that he must continue his course over the entire universe. Melpomène replied:

> Je dis plus, tu le dois en faveur du spectacle
> Qu'au Monarque des Lys je prépare aujourd'hui;
> Le Ciel n'a fait que miracles en lui
> Lui voudrois-tu refuser un miracle?[39]

Figure 7. Scene from the prologue of *Andromède* by d'Assoucy and Corneille, showing Melpomène advancing toward the Sun's chariot. Engraving by François Chauveau; reprinted from Charles d'Assoucy, *Andromède, tragédie représentée avec les machines sur le Théâtre royale de Bourbon,* text by Pierre Corneille (Rouen, 1651). (Photograph courtesy of the Bibliothèque Nationale, département de réserve imprimée.)

The Sun agreed to the proposal and admonished Melpomène to "divert him well" while he waited for the future when his destiny would be fulfilled. Together the Muse and the Sun praised Louis as the greatest of the Bourbons and a rival of Caesar, Pompey, and Alexander. The Sun sang: "We will proclaim that he is the youngest and the greatest of kings." A duet followed which was taken up by the chorus:

> La Majesté qui défia l'environne
> charme tous ses François,

> Il est lui seul digne de sa Couronne,
> Et quand mesme le ciel l'auroit mise à leur choix,
> Il seroit le plus jeune et le plus grand des Rois.

Although *Andromède* was an unimpressive attempt at music drama, the prologue carried on the French tradition of flattering the monarchy in musical *spectacles*.

Concurrent with the modish machine plays were the pastoral dramas of the 1650's and 1660's. These plays used settings of forests, mountains, and rivers; their plots dealt with the love of shepherds and nymphs. Little development in the music or in the drama was necessary to depict these sterotyped situations. Bucolic settings had been common in the ballets; in the 1650's pastorals seemed the obvious vehicle for combining drama and music. The early pastorals, for example, d'Assoucy's *Les amours d'Apollon et de Daphné* (1650), alternated spoken and sung passages, after the fashion of the earlier ballets. As in the machine play *Andromède*, *Les amours* contained a brief prologue praising the king. Louis' brilliance was again compared to the sun's: "Beautiful God, leave to Louis the care of the light, the years, and the seasons."[40] D'Assoucy accompanied his piece with a dedication to Louis XIV in which he observed that in order to be loved, it was not necessary to be perfect like the sun, but rather to have virtues like those of a king such as Louis. The first entirely sung pastoral was *Le triomphe de l'amour*, by Charles de Beys and Michel de La Guerre, performed before Mazarin in the Louvre on January 22, 1655.[41] The most notable of the pastorals from this period was the *Pastorale d'Issy*, by Pierre Perrin and Robert Cambert, which marked the real beginning of opera in France (see Chapter 4).

In 1654, with the suppression of the Fronde, some of the Italian musicians returned to Paris and produced Carlo Caproli's opera, *Le nozze di Peleo e di Teti*. Again, the main attraction was Giacomo Torelli's machinery which hurled the hero in a chariot through the air, unleashed a tempest, sent Jupiter flying in on an eagle's back, and enabled various deities to descend from the heavens on a cloud. *Le nozze* culminated in a spectacular rustic wedding, which was attended by Juno, Hymen, and the Intelli-

gences. Simultaneously cupids performed a ballet in heaven
(Figure 8). The French court enjoyed the opera even though
most of the nobles could not understand the Italian text.

Figure 8. The rustic wedding and the celestial ballet of the cupids from
Carlo Caproli's opera (machinery by Torelli) *Le nozze di Peleo e di Teti.*
Engraving by Israël Silvestre; reprinted from Beringhen Collection, no. 94,
"Decorations et machines aprestées aux Nopces de Tetis, ballet royal; repré-
sentée en la salle du petit Bourbon par Jacques Torelli, inventeur, dédiées au
Cardinal Mazarin," p. 91. (Photograph courtesy of the Bibliothèque Nationale,
cabinet des estampes.)

The highlight of *Le nozze* was the ballet inserted in the middle
of the opera by Isaac Benserade and the duc de Saint-Aignan.
When Jean Loret wrote in his journal that the production won

"the admiration of many a foreign agent and ambassador," he was referring to this ballet danced by Louis XIV, his brother, thirty nobles, and thirty professional dancers. Loret declared:

> Louis, the marvel of Kings,
> The glory and the honor of France,
> Danced his ballet of consequence
> With such high demeanor
> That there has never been a parallel.[42]

Louis danced six roles—Apollo, a Fury, a dryad, an academician, a courtier, and War. For each role Benserade wrote accompanying verses in which accusations against Spain and allusions to the Fronde were given. As Apollo, Louis declared:

> Plus brillant & mieux fait que tous les Dieux ensemble,
> La Terre ni le Ciel n'ont rien qui me ressemble;
> De rayons immortels mon front est couronné :
> Amoureux des beautez de la seule Victoire
>   Je cours sans cesse après la Gloire,
>   Et ne cours point après Daphné.

> J'ai vaincu ce Python qui desoloit le Monde,
> Ce terrible Serpent, que l'Enfer & la Fronde,
> D'un venin dangereux avoient assaisonné :
> La Revolte, en un mot, ne me sçauroit plus nuire;
>   Et j'ai mieux aimé la détruire,
>   Que de courir après Daphné.[43]

In portraying the role of War in the tenth entrée, Louis proclaimed:

> Nous l'aurons, cette Paix tant de fois désirée,
> Qui depuis si long-temps s'est au Ciel retirée,
> Et la *Guerre* à la fin va combler nos souhaits :
> Cent Oracles fameux ont prédit à la Terre,
>   Pour avoir une bonne Paix,
>   Qu'il faloit une bonne *Guerre*.[44]

The favorable reaction to *Le nozze* was doubtless a response to verses such as these and to the glamour of the ballet itself. The Italians tried to capitalize on the established success of the

French machine productions, pastorals, and ballets, but they failed to regain their former position in Paris.

Some of the Italian musicians remained at the court, however, and formed a little singing group under Caproli to entertain the king. Lully used their talents in his *Dialogue italien de la guerre avec la paix* (1655) and in his *Ballet de Psyché* (1656). During the carnival season in 1656 Mazarin asked Lully to entertain the king at dinner one evening with his *Ballet de la galanterie du temps* in which all the airs were Italian. In January 1657 Lully again mixed Italian and French ingredients in his *Ballet de l'amour*, which in effect was a small Italian opera (Atto Melani sang the role of Love) coupled with a French ballet. The most popular entrée, however, contained a French air quite unlike the aria style of Caproli or Rossi. In the *Ballet de la raillerie* (1659) Lully included a humorous dialogue between Italian music and French music in which he contrasted "the simple syllabic style of the Italian canzonetta with the subtle turns of the French air."[45] The text portrayed the dispute:

La musique françoise. Le trop de liberté que tu prends dans tes chants,
Les rend parfois extravagans.

La musique italienne. Toy, par tes notes languissantes,
Tu pleures plus que tu ne chantes.

La musique françoise. Et toy, penses-tu faire mieux
Avec tes fredons ennuyeux?

La musique italienne. Mais ton orgueil aussi ne doit pas se promettre,
Qu'à ton seul jugement je me vueille soumettre.

La musique françoise. Je composeray comme toy,
Si tu veux chanter comme moy. . . .

Toutes deux. Cessons donc de nous contredire,
Puisque dans l'amoureux empire,
Où se confond incessamment
Le plaisir avec le tourment,
Le cœur qui chante et celui qui soupire
Peuvent s'accorder aysément.[46]

Even Lully, who had been born in Italy, was beginning to pull away from the Italians and their music. Disgusted with the Italian style of violin playing practiced by the king's Grande bande which emphasized constant improvisation and multiple ornaments and broderies on the written note, Lully organized his own Petits violons (sixteen players) and taught them techniques of precision bowing and unembellished playing. The king supported the group out of the funds of the Menus plaisirs, and they played for him at dinner and on retiring.[47] Lully's playful alternating between the Italians and the French finally ceased when Mazarin died. Shortly afterward he became the champion of a national French style of music.

The Italians' abortive conquest of the French musical scene climaxed in the early 1660's. On November 22, 1660, Francesco Cavalli's opera *Xerxes* (first performed in Venice in 1654) was performed in the grand gallery of the Louvre to celebrate Louis XIV's marriage to the Spanish infanta Maria Theresa. A special ballet for the occasion was composed by Lully and danced by the king and his bride.[48] The prologue commemorated the conclusion of the war between France and Spain in 1659; nymphs from the two countries sang:

> Depuis enfin les deux plus grands rois de la terre
> ont terminée la guerre par un mariage joyeux,
> et que touchez des maux, par leurs peuples soufferts,
> Ils ont fait retirer la Discorde aux Enfers;
> Que d'harmonieux sons et de cries d'allégresse
> L'air doucement troublé retentisse sans cesse,
> Et que par cent chansons leurs sujets réjoüis,
> Exaltent les vertus de Thérèse et Louis.[49]

Xerxes was performed several more times in November and December and drew large crowds. The main attraction, however, was the ballet; aside from the scenery and costumes, the opera had little appeal to the French audience. In his poetical journal, Jean Loret stressed the superbly constructed theater, the decorations, and the royal splendor. He found the opera itself objectionable because it was Italian, and excessively long.[50] The final performance was given on January 11, 1661, in Cardinal Mazarin's quarters, just two months before he died.

A second opera by Cavalli, *Ercole amante*, was prepared on Mazarin's orders for the marriage celebrations, but because of delay in the construction of the salle neuve (théâtre des machines) in the Tuileries where *Ercole* was to be given, the opera was not presented until February 7, 1662.[51] As a result of the cool reception given *Xerxes*, Cavalli made certain concessions to French taste: he restored choruses, which he had not used since 1642; he added little symphonies before each act; he composed an elaborate prologue in praise of the French monarch; and he left ample room for a ballet composed by Lully and Benserade. Moreover, the recitatives were less freely composed and less elaborate, and dance rhythms were introduced in the songs.[52] Nevertheless, the production was still "too Italian" for the French who, as in the case of *Xerxes*, were attracted mainly by Gaspare Vigarani's machines and Lully's dances. Loret, who devoted two hundred lines to the ballet and only four to the opera in his journal, complained that he could not understand the Italian. He extolled Benserade's verses, the royal pomp, the symphonies, decorations, and the ballet entrées.[53]

The ballet again solemnized the Peace of the Pyrenees and the marriage of Louis and Marie, who portrayed the Houses of Bourbon and Habsburg. Members of the court—including Monsieur (Louis' brother), mesdemoiselles de Rohan, d'Alençon, and de Valois, the duchesses de Sully and de Luynes, and the comtesse de Guiche—represented imperial families and paid homage in dance and verse to the royal houses. Special entrées were created for the king, enabling him to appear as Pluto, Mars, and finally in his proper role as the Sun.

The prologue to *Ercole* also eulogized the French monarch. Allegorical figures representing the moon and fourteen rivers under French domination hailed the king as a benevolent peace-maker. He was commended for his "hard labors," dedication to France's welfare, and accessibility to his "least subjects."[54] More important, Louis was represented as a king who always worked for peace but would not allow other kings to infringe on the "rights" of the French throne. The prologue thus served the functions of exalting the king's virtues, justifying the recent diplomatic and military policies of the crown, and holding up the flattering mirror of royal absolutism to itself. Such prologues later became the most important feature of the French national opera.

Except for Paolo Lorenzani's pastoral opera *Nicandro* (produced at Fontainebleau in 1681), *Ercole* was the last Italian opera performed in Paris for sixty-seven years. The Italians left France in 1666 at the behest of the king. "The king has dismissed his Italian music fifteen days ago," wrote Robert Ouvrard, "and they will return thus to their country."[55] France was the only European country after 1670 which was able to resist the competition of Italian music. The Italians failed for two principal reasons. The French found the Italian language, the arid recitatives, and the florid arias disorderly, unbalanced, and boring; they disdained what they regarded as the irrational absurdities in the opera dramas. Conversely, they were proud of their own uncontaminated classical drama and their rich ballet heritage. "The lucid rationalism of the French classical tradition," Manfred Bukofzer has written, "prevented French music from succumbing to the turbulent affections unleashed by the Italian baroque."[56] The king himself scarcely bothered to listen to the Italian operas. Moreover, Louis XIV wanted the French to challenge Italian supremacy in the arts. Who could agree with Louis more than his own musicians, whose economic security was threatened by the Italians? Musicians were valuable export articles for Italy, and they drew salaries twice as large as native performers.

Stimulated by the Italian example, the French created their own national opera after 1670.[57] The Italians stole the show in the 1640's, but the decades of the fifties and sixties brought the long tradition of French ballet de cour to its fullest development; then, concurrently with the Italian productions and their stepchildren, the machine plays, came the celebrated ballets of Isaac Benserade and his collaborators. And although Italian opera was probably a weapon in Mazarin's political arsenal, the French ballet of Louis' youth became a full-fledged institution of the crown.

Benserade's Court Ballets

The dramatist Isaac Benserade (1613-1691) was the key figure in the ballets de cour of the 1650's.[58] His polished poetry and unified plots turned ballet into a literary form. A successful playwright in the 1630's and 1640's, Benserade (who was from a noble family) had wisely supported Mazarin during the Fronde and had gone to Saint-Germain with the court in 1649. Louis pensioned him for his loyalty, and he maintained intimate relations with the courtiers throughout his lifetime. He wrote many poems and a set of rondos praising the king, and in 1664 he was elected to the French Academy. Beginning in 1651, he created ballets for the carnival season or for special occasions such as marriages, military victories, and the signing of treaties.

Benserade's ballet verses were designed to flatter the king and to poke fun at the amorous foibles of the court. The verses, which were frequently declaimed, dealt not only with the roles represented, but with the persons representing them as well. He freely mixed historical, mythical, and allegorical characters. He introduced female dancers into his ballets and employed instrumentalists on the stage to lead the dancers or to participate in the action when the drama called for it. The official programs and verses for his ballets were printed and distributed to the audience.

The music for Benserade's ballets was written by several composers and included airs, dialogues, choruses, symphonies, and récits. Jean-Baptiste Lully contributed to some of the ballets, including the *Ballet des bienvenus* (1655), *Amour malade* (1657), and the *Ballet de raillerie* (1659). Some instrumental music for the entrées was written by members of Louis' Grande bande, among others, Louis de Mollier, Michel Mazuel, and Guillaume Du Manoir; and the music for the récits was composed by musicians of Louis' Chambre including Jean de Cambefort and Antoine Boesset.

Benserade's first ballet, *Cassandre*, was danced at the Palais-Royal on February 26, 1651; it was on this occasion that the young monarch made his first appearance as a character in a ballet.[59] The *Gazette de France* announced the ballet and attacked the critics of the court's musical amusements and "those who would seek out other reasons for this activity and draw from it other consequences than the King's pleasure." Ballet, according to the *Gazette*, reflects the joy of France and the dignity of the king. The *Gazette* predicted that the young ruler would "dance one day against his enemies some armed dances à la *Pyrrichienne;* let us let him play, meanwhile, among his other royal exercises, these innocent delights of his age, before the burdens of his crown . . . prevent him from them or at least diminish the pleasures." Madame Madeleine de Scudéry took a slightly different view of the king's pleasure, however: Louis has danced a wicked ballet, she wrote, which "makes me remember those little birds who sing so well and who are enjoyed, while imprisoned in their cages; because, after all, this poor young king is presently more prisoner than they."[60] Indeed, there was probably more behind the production of this and other ballets than just the routine entertainment of the young king. Mazarin wanted to shield Louis from the Fronde, and in a very real sense he was "caged" during these years. Pleasure and flattery seem to have kept him occupied; Benserade eulogized the monarch in his verses just as Corneille had done in *Andromède* the preceding year.[61]

Although the threatening attacks by the Frondeurs forced Mazarin temporarily into exile, the young monarch continued to dance at the court, with apparent indifference to the turmoil. Following his success in *Cassandre*, Louis appeared in the *Ballet du Roy des Festes de Bacchus* on May 2, 1651. The king's performances in the roles of Apollo (Figure 9), an augur, a bacchante, an icicle, a titan, and a Muse were so popular with the court that the ballet was repeated on May 4, 7, 9, and 12.[62]

Mazarin's final victory over the Frondeurs was the occasion for a gala ballet on February 23, 1653, at the Petit-Bourbon. The crowd fought for three hours to get into the palace to see their king dance. Loret wrote angrily in his poetical journal that he tried desperately to obtain entrance, and when he did succeed, he had to sit in a seat at the side:

> Thus, sad, vexed, confused,
> for thirteen hours I was
> like a true spectator of chaff,
> the most badly placed in the room.[63]

He learned enough about the performance, however, to write a glowing account of the decorations by Torelli, the costumes for sorcerers, Turks, monkeys, dragons, the verses by Benserade, and the "ravishing airs." Special praise was accorded Louis XIV, who appeared as a

Figure 9. Louis XIV as Apollo in the *Ballet du Roy des Festes de Bacchus* (1651). Drawing by an unknown artist, watercolor with highlights of gold and silver; reprinted from *Ballet du Roy des Festes de Bacchus dansé par Sa Majesty au Palais-Royal le 2 jour de May 1651* (Paris, 1651), fol. 104. (Photograph courtesy of the Bibliothèque Nationale, cabinet des estampes, réserve.)

> Sun brilliant with light,
> whose singular beauty
> could be called rightly,
> the ornament of the entire horizon.

Louis danced six different roles in the *Ballet de la nuit*. Benserade wrote verses for each; they glorified the monarch as lover and warrior, alluded to the defeat of the revolutionaries, and predicted future victories over Islam for the king:

> Je ne suis point à moi, je suis à l'Univers, . . .
> Et l'ordre ne veut pas que mon plaisir m'arreste . . .
> Quand j'aurai dissipé les Ombres de la France
>   [the Frondeurs],
> Vers les Climats lointains, ma clarté paroissant,
> Ira, victorieuse, au milieu de *Byzance*
>   Effacer le Croissant.[64]

Many of Benserade's récits referred to the Fronde; Aurora sang:

> La Troupe des Astres s'enfuit
> Dés que ce grand Astre s'avance;
> Les foibles clartez de la Nuit,
> Qui triomphoient en son absence,
> N'osent soûtenir sa presence:
> Tous ces volages feux s'en vont évanouïs,
> Le Soleil qui me suit c'est le jeune LOUIS.

One of the highlights of the ballet was Venus' récit to the youthful king (Example 7).[65] An interesting sidelight of the ballet was the appearance among the dancers of the English dukes of Buckingham and York, for whom Benserade had written verses that complimented them but condemned the execution of their monarch.

Benserade's ballets of the mid-1650's reflected the relaxed and sportive atmosphere of a court that had weathered revolution and a kingdom that was enjoying success in war. Louis savored the unctuous attention of the court nobility and reveled in the obsequious verses. "Inundated with joy," Paris was treated to a series of balls, concerts, and ballets in which the king's graceful carriage and ravishing appearance were on constant parade.[66] Love and pleasure were the principal themes of court life and of

Example 7

Jeu-ne Lou-is   Jeu-ne Lou-is Le Plus Grand des Mo - nar - ques, dans

quel-que temps.   Vous por-te - rez des   mar - ques   de ce

Dieu   dont ja - mais   on n'é - vi - te les coups.

the musical festivities. Benserade amused the courtiers with many references to their amorous quests. Verging on mockery and satire at times, he stressed the free-wheeling pursuit of sexual conquest that was condoned by the teenage king and his admirers. His *Ballet des plaisirs* (1655), which included verses for the king's brother, expressed the mood of the court:

> Beau, jeune, de bonne Maison,
> Si je prétens gagner les cœurs les plus rebelles,
> Est-il à la Cour quelques Belles
> Qui ne pense que j'ay raison?
>
> Il est vray le sexe me plaist,
> Et je ne rougis point de brusler de ces flames,
> Quand j'aymerois toutes les femmes
> Je sçay bien que la Gloire l'est.

Je suis souple, adroit, circonspect,
Aussi quoy qu'un flatteur à nos oreilles prosne,
Tant plus on est proche du Throsne,
Tant plus on luy doit de respect.[67]

Louis XIV danced in this ballet as an Egyptian and as a debauchee.

Toward the end of the decade, the court ballets became more operatic and more dramatically involved; Benserade's domination was coming to an end, and Lully was rising to prominence as the foremost composer of the entrées. In his efforts to amuse the frisky king and his self-satisfied court, Lully concocted an Italianate opera-ballet entitled *Amour malade*. In this farcical, exotic composition, which portended the later works of Lully and Molière, the young Italian scullion (Lully was employed as a cook's helper) prepared a musical salmagundi of entrées depicting a hail storm, alchemical experiments, a parody of academic examinations, and the divinitions of astrology. Traditional dances such as the gaillarde and gigue were performed by Louis and the nobles in the concluding scene of a village wedding. Loret reported that the audience, which included the duc de Modena and Cardinal Mazarin, was dazzled by the unusual characters in the ballet, the king's performance, and the "angelic" music.[68]

Following the success of *Amour malade*, Lully and Benserade again combined talents in a prodigious production entitled the *Ballet d'Alcidiane*. Performed as a celebration of the king's twentieth birthday, the ballet was danced by eighteen nobles and forty-seven professionals, accompanied by several vocalists and a twenty-nine piece orchestra. Louis was cast in the roles of Hatred, the wind god Aeolus, a demon, and a Moor. The overture and the orchestral interludes, which "formed a celestial mélange," were the highlights of the ballet and drew attention to the man who composed his way out of the kitchen. Loret wrote:

This great number of symphonies,
Admirably well-united,
Created an effect without equal;
And certainly, with regard to the musical art,
I would be a frank atheist,
If I did not believe that Baptiste,

Notwithstanding the old songs,
Is one of the most celebrated servants
Of the rare and grand harmony
Which Auzonie [Italy] has ever produced,
Since it is he who, truly,
In order to please Louis of Bourbon,
Ingeniously assembles
So many different efforts together.[69]

The foreign ambassadors were invited to the second performance of *Alcidiane* on February 17, and on February 24 Queen Christine of Sweden, who had arrived in France in September 1656, was the honored guest. The ambassadors were unanimously pleased with the ballet, according to Loret, and "strongly praised the King's dance." Queen Christine reacted similarly and recognized that "without doubt the French court is the first of the universe in pomp and diverse charms."[70]

The Apex of French Ballet under Jean-Baptiste Lully

The decade of the 1660's brought important changes in the musical life of the French court: the Italians left Paris as a policy of artistic national self-sufficiency took root; Louis sponsored the first of the large-scale *divertissements* which were given periodically during his reign (see Chapter 4); the foundations of the Académie royale de musique were laid; and Lully continued working with Benserade on court ballets, while at the same time producing with Molière a new kind of comédie-ballet. In many ways the decade belonged to Lully, whose success as a ballet composer was merely a prelude to his dominance of French musical life during Louis XIV's reign.

Known as "the Florentine," Lully was born in Florence on November 29, 1632. He was brought to Paris in 1646 by Roger de Lorraine, the chevalier de Guise, and placed in the domestic service of the chevalier's cousin, Mademoiselle de Montpensier. When Mademoiselle joined the Frondeurs, he left her and became a servant of the king. He received a salary of 150 livres a year as a garçon de la chambre, and, although he performed the duties of a cook's boy, he continued his musical education, which had begun in Italy. Michel Lambert, a composer of the king's chamber, taught him to play the violin and to compose airs de cour; three of Louis' organists, Nicolas Gigault, Nicolas Roberday, and Nicolas Métru, gave him harpsichord and organ lessons and instructed him in the principles of composition. He rose rapidly in music circles, becoming compositeur de la musique instrumentale in 1653. His efforts with the Petit violons and his successful collaboration with other musicians at the court in composing music for Benserade's ballets in the 1650's led to his appointment as superintendent of music in May 1661. In the same year Lully became a naturalized Frenchman and in the following year he married Michel Lambert's daughter Madeleine in the Church of Saint-Eustache. His marriage produced six children.[71]

Having mastered the stylistic elements of French ballet music, Lully became the foremost composer of the royal ballets of the 1660's. In collaboration with Benserade, Lully presented his first important ballet (*Ballet de l'impatience*) at the Louvre in February 1660 for the two queens (Anne of Austria and Marie Thérèse), foreign ambassadors, and the court. Lully and Benserade celebrated the conclusion of the war with Spain and stressed the king's prowess as warrior, peacemaker, and lover. Through the verses, the comtes d'Armagnac, de Saint-Aignan, de Beaufort, and de Guiche testified to their happiness as subjects of the Bourbon crown. Benserade's verse for Louis, who danced the role of "a great lover," projected his heroic image:

> L'Univers a tremblé de bruit de mon Tonnerre,
> Et la posterité ne s'en taira jamais :
> Avec beaucoup d'éclat j'ay par tout fait la Guerre,
> J'ay bien plus fait encor, mesme j'ay fait la Paix.[72]

Lully's music was appropriately pompous, but its clarity and precision drew praise from the dramatist Jean Racine: "What really delights me here is Lully's music; it is natural, grand, with simplicity; it is on the path of the heart."[73]

The success of the *Ballet de l'impatience* resulted in the fruitful collaboration of Lully and Benserade on several more productions of this sort.[74] Using allegorical and mythological figures, composer and poet created an idealized image of the kingdom's contentment. Louis was cast in the role of the benevolent shepherd whose only concern was the peace of Europe and the prosperity of his subjects. Whereas ballets such as *Impatience* had glorified war and the virtues of bravery and loyalty, the later ones revealed the mood of tranquillity and well-being which the king wished to communicate. Henceforth, as the political winds shifted during the reign, Louis' musical *spectacles* reflected the changing "party line" of the royal absolutism.

In 1664, Lully began his collaboration with Molière. In a series of productions beginning with *Le mariage forcé* in January 1664, and continuing with *Princesse d'Élide, Amour médecin, Pastorale comique, Monsieur de Pourceaugnac,* and *Le bourgeois gentilhomme,* Lully created ballet entrées which were interspersed among the scenes of Molière's comedies. The comedies were self-contained works which scarcely needed musical accompaniment, however, and which did not incorporate the kind of glorification of the monarch that had characterized the early ballets. Musically, Lully's work on the comédie-ballets was important for his development of a French style of recitative and more elaborate choral and orchestral forms. Lully's use of recitatives to connect ballet scenes, in the manner of Italian opera, differed from the previous practice of composing unconnected, individual récits in the fixed form of the air. It is important to remember that in spite of this thrust toward an operatic style, the comédie-ballets offered only the coexistence of music, ballet, and drama, not their integration into a consistent and developed plot. The ballet did not further the action; it simply embellished it.

Lully and Molière also collaborated on a more traditional musical *spectacle,* the *Ballet royal des amours désguisez.* Performed at the Palais-Royal in February 1664, this colorful piece mingled historical characters such as Antony and Cleopatra with the gods Venus and Mercury and made use of machinery to present a spectacular naval battle. The king, who had spared no expense for this production, was hailed in the prologue as the arbiter of the earth. Loret observed that the king "in the flower of his age, is as charming as he is sage."[75]

By the fourth year of the Sun King's personal rule, the court aristocracy had come to expect a long and prodigious carnival season. The year 1665 witnessed probably the most profuse musical entertainments yet presented. Three new comédie-ballets were introduced: *Le favory*, performed at Versailles in June in honor of the queen; *L'amour médecin*, also given at Versailles in September; and the *Ballet de la naissance de Vénus* produced at the Palais-Royal in January to honor Monsieur's marriage to Princess Henrietta of England. Paris was full of the pleasures and gaiety accompanying the endless succession of celebrations, balls, collations, and ballets. For the performance of *La naissance de Vénus*, the Palais-Royal held a glittering array of countesses, marquis, duchesses, and the most distinguished nobles of the court. They were treated to an equally opulent ballet, about which Loret wrote:

> I have seen thirty ballets in France,
> But among those of the greatest importance,
> (May I die if I do not tell you the truth),
> I have seen none
> More rich, superb, and smart. . . .
> Beyond the majesty of the king [in the role of Alexander]
> Who danced the best, believe me,
> And Monsieur, his only brother,
> On whom the just heavens confer
> All the beautiful virtues
> Which are desired in princedoms;
> A prince of the best French blood [the Duke of Orleans],
> Also appeared in this dance,
> And several dukes, counts, marquis,
> All seigneurs of refined talent,
> Permitted themselves to be joined in the said ballet,
> By citizens of lesser quality.[76]

Loret praised Lully's music, calling particular attention to the "angelic chorus," and he lauded the choice of subject. The verses were written by Benserade, whom Loret dubbed the "great doctor of Parnassus." The summer and autumn festivities at Versailles, which included the two comédie-ballets by Lully and Molière, were merely a continuation of the kind of entertainments given in Paris during the carnival seasons. Louis' ambassadors to the foreign courts, including the ambassador to the Hague, comte d'Estrade, were guests at the ballet performances. It is only at the court of France, wrote Charles Robinet, that "very select citizens can create a ballet."[77]

After a performance of the mascarade *Le triomphe de Bacchus dans les Indes* in January 1666,[78] the court was idle because of the death of the queen mother. Perdou de Subligny lamented that the nobles had almost forgotten how to dance.[79] Subligny noted, however, that news had reached him concerning preparations for a new ballet to be given at Saint-Germain. When the *Ballet des muses* was produced, all the official sentiments of mourning had evaporated. Subligny wrote:

> Do you dancers not create marvels?
> Are your ears not enchanted by the new ballet airs? . . .
> Dance, seigneur, dance; lead a happy life,
> While you have the money and the time.
> When you will have lived a hundred years,
> You will contract, if it is necessary, melancholy.[80]

The *Ballet des muses*, which glorified Louis as a patron of the arts, was performed several times between December 1666 and February 1667 and constituted the principal entertainment, along with three comedies by Molière which accompanied it, of the *divertissements* given to the court at Saint-Germain by Louis XIV (see Chapter 6).

In the following year Lully and Benserade prepared a royal mascarade entitled *Le carnaval* to honor the king's return from the military campaign in Flanders in January. The central theme was the duty of the court, the musicians, and the poets to provide entertainment for the conquering hero. The ballet entrées were danced by nobles and professionals in the roles of the pleasures, the gamblers, the gourmets, and the dancing masters, all of whom facilitated Louis' cavorting in the role of a pleasure. Benserade's verses alluded not only to Louis' campaign against the Spanish, but also to his plans for an invasion of Franche-Comté:

> A ce Plaisir se mêle un travail assidu,
> > La Gloire en est, tout se rassemble,
> > Et s'unit tellement ensemble,
> Qu'il n'est rien de mieux confondu.

Ce Plaisir a dequoi combler nostre desir,
  Et cette derniere Campagne
  A fait avouer à l'Espagne,
  Que c'est un terrible Plaisir.

Elle doit cet Hyver détourner ses malheurs,
  Si non au retour du Zephire,
  Je crains qu'elle n'ait lieu de dire,
  Pour un plaisir mille douleurs.

S'il flate nostre goust, pour elle quant & quant,
  Il est d'une amertume insigne,
  Et selon qu'on s'en trouve digne
  C'est un Plaisir doux & piquant.[81]

In 1669 Isaac Benserade collaborated with Lully for the last time in a ballet de cour in which the king danced his next-to-last performance. Lully and Benserade wrote an unusually large number of vocal récits for the *Ballet royal de Flore*, and they were cast in every form from solos, duets, and trios to grand choruses. Benserade seemed at the limit of his ability to eulogize the king:

Soleil, de qui la gloire accompagne le cours,
  Et qu'on m'a vû loüer toujours
Avec assez d'éclat quand vostre éclat fut moindre :
  L'Art ne peut plus traiter ce sujet comme il faut,
  Et vous estes monté si haut,
  Que l'Eloge, & l'Encens ne vous sçauroient plus joindre.

Vous marchez d'un grand air sur la Teste des Rois,
  Et de vos rayons autrefois,
L'atteinte n'estoit pas si ferme & si profonde;
Maintenant je les voy d'un tel feu s'allumer,
  Qu'en ne sçauroit en exprimer,
Non plus qu'en soustenir la force sans seconde.[82]

Produced several times in 1669, the *Ballet de Flore* drew plaudits from the poet-journalists. Mayolas stated that the affective performance of the king must garner all the accolades usually reserved for professional dancers. The princes and princesses, seigneurs and ladies, envoys and ambassadors were ravished by

Louis' brilliance.[83] Charles Robinet observed that Louis does everything with an éclat which is "much less human than celestial." In peace and in war, Robinet contended, Louis has no parallel except the sun itself and few means to project his brilliance as well as this spectacle.[84] In his journal entry for March 10, following a performance of *Flore* the preceding day, Mayolas addressed himself directly to Louis:

> Sire, in whatever you are able to do,
> You are extraordinary,
> And in your innocent pleasures,
> Your deeds are always ravishing.[85]

Whatever your costume, Mayolas continued, your subjects can recognize your divine person and kingly character.

In the fall of 1669 Louis took several of his nobles on a hunting trip to Chambord. They were accompanied by Lully, Molière, and some comedians and musicians who, on October 6, 1669, performed the comédie-ballet *Monsieur de Pourceaugnac*. Lully adorned Molière's play with a ballet whose whimsical plot concerned two lovers' escape from parental authority. He employed a rich mixture of serenades, dialogues, airs, and a dainty combat ballet, and he introduced musical buffoon scenes, including the lament of a melancholy hypochondriac who suffers from a case of polygamy. *Pourceaugnac* was a delightful romp whose central theme, reflecting the amorous tone of Louis' court during his youth, was expressed in an air for an Egyptian:

> Aimons, aimons jusqu'au trépas
> La raison nous y convie
> Hélas! si l'on n'aimait pas,
> que serait-ce de la vie.[86]

The court returned to Chambord the following year for another hunt and was again diverted with a comédie-ballet by Lully and Molière—*Le bourgeois gentilhomme*. The idea of a ballet (the French considered *Le bourgeois* first a ballet and secondarily a play) with a Turkish motif grew out of Louis' and the court's general interest in things Turkish and was prompted by the return from the Porte of Louis' ambassador Laurent d'Arvieux. D'Arvieux has written:

Long having wanted to take a trip to Chambord in order to enjoy the *divertissement* of the chase, the king wished to give his court a ballet; and because of the *idée des Turcs* which has been quite recently seen in Paris, he felt that it would be appropriate to have them appear on the scene. His majesty ordered me to join with messieurs Molière and Lully in order to compose a piece for the theater in which something of the dress and manners of the Turks could be introduced.[87]

D'Arvieux worked for several days on the costumes and consulted with Molière at his home in Auteuil on the drama. Louis approved the finished product and ordered it performed at Chambord on October 13. Subsequent performances took place at Saint-Germain in November and at the Palais-Royal before the Guinean ambassador, Don Metheo Lopez, on November 23. The high point of each performance was of course the Turkish ceremony in which Lully himself played the mufti.[88]

Louis XIV danced his last ballet at Saint-Germain in February 1670. *Les amants magnifiques* was also one of the last of the comédie-ballets by Molière and Lully which had delighted the court so much in the 1660's. The king appeared twice in the ballet: first as Neptune in a dance of sea gods and fisherman; then in the familiar role of Apollo. Crowned with laurels, Louis accepted a golden symbol of the sun from his people, and the ballet concluded with a chorus and the words, "Let us all open our eyes to the supreme light which sparkles in these places."[89]

Although Louis XIV had danced his last step before the sycophants of the court, he kept his interest in the musical productions, which not only gave him pleasure and relaxation, but which were useful in keeping before the court, the Parisian populace, and foreign visitors an image of the heroism, benevolence, and brilliance of the monarchy. The musical productions of the 1650's and 1660's fed the young king's vanity; they exalted Louis as a lover, soldier, patron of the arts, and finally as a peacemaker. The royal theme and function of the musical productions changed little during the king's early years, but their form and style underwent considerable development. Mazarin brought Italian musicians and opera to Paris with the hope of occupying the queen and distracting the potentially dangerous nobility. His costly maneuver backfired and he discovered that French taste ran counter to his own. The Italians came and went, but French ballet de cour, with a long tradition of success at court, remained and flourished under the direction of Benserade and Lully. Gradually, but perceptibly, the elements of dance, drama, song, scenery, and concert were drawn into an integral association which resulted in a uniquely French opera. Patronized by the king, Jean-Baptiste Lully, who by 1670 was already a man of wealth and property,[90] created and nurtured the new genre and put it in the service of the king.

✤4

The Centralization of Music[1]

Colbert and the Artistic Academies

After Cardinal Mazarin's death in 1661, Louis XIV embarked
on a policy of centralizing political, religious, and economic
power which carried the royal absolutism to its zenith. Convinced
by the record of the past that the arts contributed to a prince's
esteem and glory, Louis extended the policy of centralization to
the fine arts. He placed them under his personal protection and
supervision and coordinated their activities through a group of
academies. He earnestly wanted his reign to be famous for its
artistic brilliance, and he believed that his artists, if properly
directed, could ensure his immortality. Such desires, even coming
from a king obsessed with his image, do not, however, reveal
the basis of Louis' artistic policies. The keystone of his political
system was monarchical centralization and control for the
purpose of establishing France's independence and her supremacy
in Europe. In this total, rationally conceived policy the arts
played an essential role. The king had to control the arts and
supervise them with the same care he devoted to other state
matters, because the arts performed the vital function of creating
an image of power and glory for both foreign and domestic
consumption and because in combination they provided the
setting for his deliberately ceremonial life-style and the entertainments with which he fed the helpless court nobility. Moreover,
supremacy in Europe entailed self-sufficiency and leadership in
the arts. The Italian domination of European culture must be
ended; France must set the artistic standards for Europe and
export, rather than import, her culture. The *Mercure galant*

understated the matter when it wrote: "The establishment of academies is a very serious affair because of the utility which the state can derive from them."[2]

The politics underlying the artistic academies were those of mercantilism. Centralization, regulation, self-sufficiency, French preponderance—these were the bywords of mercantilism. Its chief practitioner in the age of royal absolutism was Jean-Baptiste Colbert, the controller-general of finances after 1662 and the guiding figure of the artistic academies.

There is little doubt that Colbert conceived of the academic and artistic system put together by the crown in the 1660's as a piece of mercantilism. Although he was quite willing to employ a foreigner here or there in order to accelerate France's artistic progress, he stressed the development of native talent and aimed for the exportation of French art. In 1683 he called on the intendants to search the provinces for persons showing ability in literature, art, and science.[3] Opposed to the importation of foreign goods, Colbert sought to produce in France what the foreigner had to offer. This policy was extended even to the Roman branch of the French academy. "Just as it was considered desirable that French workers should be enabled to produce on French soil for French consumption Venetian glass, Venetian lace, English cloth, German lead and brass so that no capital was lured out of the country, Roman antiquity and Renaissance were also to be made available to the people of Paris by the work of the Rome scholars."[4] In short, Colbert wanted to make France so superior in the arts that other countries would eventually send their artists to study French models.

Colbert's personal attention to the work of the academies was everywhere in evidence. Not content with setting the rules of these institutions, he placed himself in the role of protector and busied himself with the details of their business. The Académie des inscriptions took its orders directly from Colbert at their regular meetings in his library. He wrote the rules for the Académie de peinture, often dictated the themes of their compositions, chose the subjects and dates of their lectures, and insisted that their conferences conclude with a reading of the precepts of the Académie. Indeed, he personally attended to the royal collection of art and negotiated the purchase of works by the Italian artists Titian and Veronese.[5] In his capacity as superintendent of buildings Colbert was particularly concerned with architecture, and he became the protector of the Académie d'architecture after 1671. He commissioned French and Italian architects to draft sketches for the Louvre, and he brought Lorenzo Bernini to Paris in 1665 to present his proposals.[6] Colbert issued his own instructions to the celebrated Italian architect, including an admonition to "observe everything necessary in order to place the music well and preserve the voices."[7] Colbert ordered that a grand ballroom and a hall for festins be constructed beyond the salle des gardes in such a way that the music would be audible to everyone. Such concern for detail was characteristic of Colbert and reveals his knowledge of the king's will.

For all his endeavors on behalf of the academies, Colbert was no lover of the arts; nor was he noted for financial generosity; nor was he merely the obedient servant of the king's fancies. Too frequently Colbert has been portrayed as the frustrated servant of a prodigal king bent on pursuing his *gloire*. In contrast to the vainglorious monarch, the efficient finance minister has been described sympathetically as a well-intentioned liberal who was prevented from carrying out his reforms and forced to replenish the treasury for the king's wars and pleasures. The distinction between king and minister is exaggerated in some respects, and wrong in others. If Colbert was unhappy with the financial drain caused by Louis' military adventures, he administered with enthusiasm the expenditures aimed at the artistic embellishment of the king's image. His role in promoting the arts was central to his administration not just because he was an effective minister, but because he shared the king's belief that there was wisdom in spending for royal grandeur and that whatever promoted the king's illustrious image enhanced the prestige and strength of the nation. The historical medals, the allegorical paintings, the operas and festivals, the grand edifices of Versailles, the Louvre, the Invalides, and the triumphal gates of Saint-Denis and Saint Martin—all these in Colbert's mind lent prestige and strength to the nation and rendered Louis' reign immortal. The arts must be cultivated even in time of war, he wrote, because "they will help to perpetuate his grand and glorious deeds."[8] In short, for Colbert, as for Louis, the artistic projection of royal grandeur was a costly necessity of state. "If one cannot understand this attitude," Victor-L. Tapié has written, "this longing for grandeur and prestige, one cannot really understand Colbert."[9]

Appropriately, the first academy established by the crown was the Académie royale de danse. The Académie was created on the king's order by his personal dancing master (who, earning 2,000 livres a year, was one of the highest paid among Louis' servants) and several professional dancers and choreographers who participated in the royal ballets of the 1650's. The Académie de danse had a special function to perform and operated according to rules laid down by the king. In the Lettres patentes of March 31, 1661, which established the Académie, Louis XIV stressed the utility of the dance: "The art of the dance has always been recognized as one of the most respectable and most necessary to train the body and to give it the first and the most natural dispositions to every kind of exercise, to that of the arms among others; consequently, it is one of the most advantageous and useful to our nobility and to others who have the honor of approaching us, not just in war times in our armies but even in times of peace in the *divertissement* of our ballets."[10] The dance must be extricated, Louis continued, from the abuses it suffered under unskilled hands during the disorders of the recent wars. Qualified instruction in dance must be given to citizens of quality, and they must demonstrate their serious dedication to its mastery.

The Lettres patentes were accompanied by ordinances outlining the rules of the Académie. Louis named thirteen directors and instructors, including Jean Renault, the duc d'Orléans' dancing master, Sieur Galand du Desert, the queen's master, and several prominent dancers at court. He specified that these thirteen men alone could teach dancing in the realm and directed them to assemble once a month in order to confer on the dance, advise and deliberate on how to perfect it and correct its faults "following and conforming to the said statutes and rules so attached under the counter-seal of our chancellery." Louis granted the members of the Académie the same privileges given to other officers of the royal household and freed them from the need to obtain letters of mastery from any other source.[11] The king himself was designated protector; Sieur du Desert officiated as the Académie's chancellor. Not long after its foundation, the Académie took up residence in the Palais-Royal. By 1668 its members were assembling one day each week to create new dance steps and airs for the king's ballets, as well as to provide instruction for aspiring performers and teachers. Those who passed the requirements of the Académie were permitted to teach dance in Paris and to enjoy the privileges given the Académie by the king.[12] The directors worked on many of the king's ballets during the 1660's and later performed in the ballet sequences in Lully's operas. Occasionally, the members of the Académie presented Louis with a special gift such as Jean Lorin's collection of contradanses. Lorin, a director of the Académie, included in the collection a set of instructions for executing contradanses, and he praised Louis for cultivating the art of dance. "The dance has always been regarded as an art necessary for exercise and the perfection of the body; it is for that reason that people have taken pleasure in learning it, because it renders one's bearing free and easy and gives one the good air; that is why it is in use in all the courts of the world."[13]

The Lettres patentes for the Académie de danse were duly registered by the Parlement of Paris in March 1662, but the entire matter provoked considerable controversy. Long before Louis ascended the throne, a musicians' guild known as ménestriers or maîtres de danse et joueurs d'instruments had held the exclusive right to teach and award letters of mastery to aspiring instrumentalists and dancers. Their privileges had been spelled out in a decree and a Lettre du privilège issued by Henri III in 1575, and Louis XIII had subsequently dubbed the head of their society roi du violon. The society chose Julian as a patron saint and became known as the Confrérie de Saint-Julien des ménestriers. When in 1661 Louis XIV gave the Académie the exclusive right to teach dancing and certify mastery, he thereby not only severed the traditional link between music and dance, but abrogated the privilege of the ménestriers. Guillaume Du Manoir, the roi du violon in 1661, responded with a supplication to the king, protesting the creation of the Académie and referring to the privileges granted to his society in former times. Du Manoir also addressed to Louis a treatise on the subject in which he condemned the Académie for daring to call itself royal and for imposing unwarranted restrictions and burdens on musicians. He charged that the thirteen directors had wormed their way into the king's graces and offended the king by their pretensions. Pointing to his long association with dancers, Du Manoir accused the Académie of severing the ancient bond of music and dancing. Citing the musical theories of Pythagoras and Plato, Du Manoir asserted that the art of dancing is tied inextricably to music as a reflection of the motion and harmony of the heavens. But whereas dancing is merely a physical imitation of music, music is the source of all knowledge and the image of the celestial harmony. Therefore, to remove dancing from the control of violinists, who represent music in its totality, is to reduce the significance of the dance and to rob music of its full power. Du Manoir concluded that the Académie should be forced to disband and to recognize that "the dance and the violin have only one master, form only one body," and have been instructed properly by only one organization whose authority was provided by the kings of France.[14] Du Manoir carried his argument to the Parlement of Paris, requesting that body to refuse registration of Louis' Lettres patentes. Responding to the king's will, the Parlement denied Du Manoir's appeal in an arrêt issued on August 3, 1662.[15] The crown had made its position clear. The thrust of Colbertian politics was to impose centralization, order, and regulation on all aspects of French life. This meant undercutting the freedom and independence of the guilds. Colbert knew that the authority of the crown could not be fully exerted over dancers and musicians enjoying guild status, anymore than manufacturing and trade could be easily controlled through the old guilds.

The members of the Académie, meanwhile, defended their privilege in a discourse which asserted the independence of the dance from the violinists. The movement to establish an Académie independent of the ménestriers has had the full support of the king, the discourse contended. "Whatever is the judgment of the most enlightened and most absolute of all kings must be sufficient to the Dance in order to persuade it that all reasonable persons will consider it from the outset as independent of the instruments of Music and as a body which can easily subsist without being animated by their harmony."[16] Directing the discourse to "the satisfaction of his Majesty," the authors emphasized the accepted view of the utility of the dance as an exercise for war and good practice for marching soldiers, as well as an aid in correcting poor bodily posture. Some men have made their fortune in the military because their dancing ability has enabled them to advance rapidly in the ranks, the authors contended. In short, the dance makes men "more able to serve their prince in battles and to please him in *divertissements.*" The violin is necessary to set the steps and cadences for the dancers, the discourse went on, in the way that drums and trumpets animate soldiers to fight; but just as the trumpets do not show men the manner in which they must fight and do not sound commands which the officers do not wish, the violins must not dictate to the dancers. Moreover, while the violin makes no lasting impression on the body or the mind, the dance not only gives pleasure to both, but advances the cultivation of the nation and provides a sign of high birth and good education. The greatest proof of the dance's importance, the discourse concluded, is that the king has perfected it and has become protector of an Académie dedicated to its cultivation.

The fruitless protests of Du Manoir and the ménestriers and their continued interference provoked Louis to issue two edicts against them. The edicts, promulgated in his Council of State at Versailles in 1682, recognized the Académie's legitimate complaint against Du Manoir's persistence in granting letters of mastery in dancing. Louis' edicts also revoked all the old Lettres patentes that gave the confrérie the right to teach dancing; he forbade all persons from interfering with the functions and privileges of the Académie on penalty of a 500 livre fine.[17] The ménestriers continued to train instrumentalists, however, and in 1691 Louis created a four-man directory for the confrérie, whose positions were hereditary, and he provided that oboists be included among the musicians over whom the society exercised the right to issue letters of mastery. Clavecinists were included later, but organists retained their independence.

The 1660's opened with the founding of the Académie de danse and closed with the creation of the Académie royale de musique. Meanwhile, the other fine arts were institutionalized by the crown. The king established the Académie des inscriptions, médailles, et belles-lettres in 1663 and the Académie de l'architecture in 1671. In addition, the Académie de peinture et sculpture was reorganized in 1663.

Louis XIV regarded the Académie des inscriptions as "an advantage for the nation," according to Paul Tallemant, who published a history of the Académie in 1717.[18] The original members were selected from the Académie française (founded in 1635). Charged with a variety of tasks, the Académie first undertook to devise subjects for Louis' tapestries and to make insignia for the vouchers of the royal treasury. Moreover, the members were instructed to strike medals portraying the great events of the reign. The king and his artists clearly believed that the allegorical imagery of these medals, which suggested Louis' virtues, talents, and heroic deeds, was politically persuasive. In 1702 all the intendants and the presidents of the Parlements were ordered to keep on their desks a copy of Menestrier's book, *Histoire du Roy Louis le Grand par les médailles, emblèmes, devises.*[19] The work of the Académie des inscriptions soon expanded to include the creation of designs for paintings, sculptures, and fountain ornaments, as well as decorations for apartments and gardens. After 1672, Philippe Quinault was required to consult the Académie on the subjects, scenery, and *divertissements* of the operas and to inform Louis of the Académie's recommendations. The members of the Académie were greatly interested in ancient history and mythology, so that poets and painters alike relied on them to provide suitable subjects drawn from ancient legends which could be used to glorify the monarch. Thus, the Académie dabbled in almost every aspect of art that could contribute to the nation's luster; Jacques de la Cassagne, one of the founders and guiding lights of the Académie, wrote to Colbert: "I know that it is your intention that no significant event be allowed to go by without operating for the king's glory."[20] Colbert served as the protector of the Académie, and upon Cassagne's departure the poet Charles Perrault stepped in as its chief director. Perrault was probably Colbert's top official in the fine arts and, particularly after

Colbert's death, "occupied himself only with everything which could help the growth of the fine arts and make them flourish according to the king's intention."[21] At the Académie des inscriptions Perrault was concerned mainly with reviewing and revising the numerous eulogies to the king, whether in verse or in prose, which were submitted to the Académie for inspection. In addition, all official writings on the reign such as histories or accounts of royal ceremonies and *divertissements* were placed under Perrault's supervision. Perrault and his colleagues were granted pensions by the king in addition to special sums for their works. Louis himself laid down the rules for the Académie, the first of which stated that it "will always remain under the king's protection and will receive his orders."[22] Louis approved all new members, appointed its officers, honorary members, and pensioners, and submitted projects to the Académie. In a message to the Académie des inscriptions, he wrote: "You can judge, Messieurs, the very special esteem that I have for you, since I confide in you the matter in the world that is the most dear to me, which is my glory; I am certain that you will perform wonders; for my part, I will furnish you with the material which is worthy of being placed in a work by citizens as capable as you."[23]

The Académie de peinture et de sculpture, like the literary Académie française, antedated the Colbertian academic system. It had originated as a rebellion of French artists against the medieval guilds, whose rules and restrictions had governed painters since the thirteenth century.[24] In the sixteenth century a distinction had developed between the guild artists and those Italian and French artists employed by the crown who were independent of the guilds. The cleavage grew wider under Henri IV, who accused the artists' guilds of obstructing the embellishment of Paris. Nevertheless, the privileges and the rules of the guilds were upheld by the crown in 1622 and by the Parlement of Paris in 1639. In 1646, when the masters demanded that the Parlement limit the number and the freedom of royal *brevetaires*, a group of court artists, including the painter Joost van Egmont, the sculptor Jacques Sarazin, and the young Charles Le Brun, called on the crown to establish an academy which would distinguish the noble arts from the mechanical arts, guarantee the freedom of royal artists from guild regulations, and provide a program of artistic instruction. The request was granted, and the Académie held its first meeting on February 1, 1648. A constitution governing membership, artistic instruction, and financial administration was drawn up. The events of the Fronde, however, enabled the guildsmen, led by the painter Simon Vouet, to block the Académie's development. It was not until June 1652 that the Parlement of Paris registered the privilège accorded to the artists by the crown in 1648, thereby assuring the Académie's ascendancy over the guilds. Moreover, in 1655 the Parlement registered a new set of rules, and Louis XIV promised the members 1,000 livres a year and rooms in the Louvre. The king also gave the Académie a monopoly over life-drawing and the same privileges enjoyed by the Académie française. In 1661 the Académie was transferred to the Palais-Royal, and Colbert was installed as vice-protector. In addition, the king appointed four rectors, placed the jurisdiction of the institution under his Council of State, and created a pension fund for its officers and members. Charles Le Brun was made chancellor, with the title of premier peintre du roi and a salary of 3,200 livres a year. He was empowered to arbitrate disputes and to establish rules and models for instructing students in painting and sculpture.

The Académie de peinture et de sculpture developed subsequently as a full-fledged institution of the crown, fitting comfortably into the mercantilistic policies of Colbert's economic and artistic system. Colbert used the academic revolt against guild regulations as a weapon in his own struggle against guild independence and particularism. The regulatory spirit of mercantilism was then imposed on painters, sculptors, and architects, who bent the arts to suit the purposes of the crown. Colbert completed the centralization of the Académie in December 1663, when a new constitution was issued by a royal decree. The royal grant was also increased to 4,000 livres. Registered by the Parlement in May 1664, the constitution established a hierarchy of members descending from the protector, vice-protector, and director through the echelon of four rectors at a salary of 300 livres each, twelve professors at a salary of 100 livres each, four counselors, an unlimited number of academicians, and eight benefactors. Each professor was responsible during one month of the year for setting the models, supplying the drawings, and supervising the students' work. The Académie functioned mainly as a school of art. Its curriculum was divided into a lower class in which the students copied their professors' drawings and an upper class in which they drew from live models and from casts of classical sculpture. The students were also supplied with paintings from the royal collection, whose reserves since the time of François I had grown to over two thousand paintings.[25] For their instruction, the students at first paid the Académie five sous per week, but in 1683 Louvois, Colbert's successor as protector, abolished the fees. Royal scholarships were available for the poor. The Académie attracted so many students, perhaps in part because its students were exempted from military service, that monthly examinations were begun in 1689 to weed out the untalented.

In addition to the drawing classes, the students attended regular lectures on anatomy, geometry, and perspective and, along with the members of the Académie, heard Le Brun and other artists deliver discourses on what Colbert termed the "préceptes positifs" of art. In a famous discourse on Nicolas Poussin's painting *Eliézér et Rébecca* in December 1670, the celebrated portraitist Philippe de Champaigne accused Poussin of plagiarizing the ancients and of distorting the subject by omitting the camels which had led Eliézer's caravan. Le Brun was obliged to defend Poussin on the grounds that he had followed the proportions of the ancients and had left out the camels for the sake of clarity.[26] In an interesting digression, Le Brun noted Poussin's adherence to the ancient conception of musical harmony, in which clashing modes were never mixed. Believing in the law of harmonic unity, Poussin refused to introduce something comical into a grave subject, as the ancients would not have mixed the phrygian mode with the dorian. Le Brun could have added that Poussin, like Félibien and other members of the Académie, not only believed in the power of music to arouse the emotions, but in the similarity of the effects of music and painting. Using colors as if they were musical tones, Poussin apparently felt that he could induce sadness, joy, and other emotions.[27] Likening the affective power of music to that of painting (Ronsard and Mersenne had previously drawn the comparison) doubtless aided the Académie's importance.

The discourses of the painters, together with published treatises by Fréart de Chambray, André Félibien, and others, usually contained analyses of paintings based on Le Brun's categories of invention, proportion, color, expression, and composition. These discourses attempted to establish precise rules for each category. Considerable attention was paid to the subject of a painting. Believing that all proper paintings should be didactic, the academicians stressed the analysis of historical and allegorical subjects,[28] and Félibien even established a value scale of subjects ranging from still-lifes at the bottom to historical scenes at the top. Under the category of expression, Le Brun presented a precise discourse correlating different bodily movements, especially facial expression, with the entire panoply of human emotions.[29] Each inward passion of man's being was assigned an exact physical representation, thus demonstrating the rapport of man's psychological and physical sides and providing the artist with a precise definition of how to render all forms of human expression.

For those students who were adept at following the rules of artistic expression, the rewards were great. Every year a pyramid of competitions was held in which the students were gradually eliminated and a winner emerged. Awards accompanied achievement at each level, and the final winner was granted a four-year scholarship at the Roman branch of the academy established by Colbert in 1666. There the student joined other young French artists engaged in copying the great works of Italian art. The last award awaiting the prize-winning student was selection by the protector as an academician. Upon entering the august ranks of the Académie, where he could rise into its officialdom, the artist submitted a reception painting, usually a topical allegory such as Louis XIV's suppression of the Huguenots. This symbolized his admission to the ranks of the king's artistic servants. Henceforth, his creative talents were trained on the single objective of advancing the monarch's image. His mission was to join other painters and sculptors in proving to the world and to posterity that "this great Monarch had no less a passion for the progress of the sciences and the arts, than for the glory of arms."[30]

It was said of Louis XIV that "in order to please him it was necessary that painting deify him in compositions borrowed from mythology."[31] Indeed, he expected the same from all the arts: in sculpture, tapestry, medals, engraving, and canvas, the Sun King was presented in the garb of the gods and most often as Apollo. The artists of his academies usually accompanied the mythological representations with scenes of Louis' military campaigns and with allegorical figures suggesting the king's moral attributes. Legend, history, and allegory were the artistic tools by which Louis' image was created. What strikes the historian of music is the ease with which these visual images were transferred to the musical and literary media of ballet and opera. The king, who was taught mythology in childhood by means of a card game, favored music over the other arts, perhaps because opera combined all the arts in a *spectacle* designed to appeal as much to the eye as to the ear. In the ballets and operas, all the creatures of Le Brun's paintings or Girardon's sculptures sprang to life on the stage. Opera was a visual medium created at a time when thoughts and words were more closely associated with visual experience than possibly at any other time in European history. It was an age which fused intellect and sense, an age when men had to see their thoughts, ideals, and standards of conduct cast in images.

The importance of the arts, including opera and ballet, as visual media can be appreciated fully only if the philosophical tradition behind artistic allegory and mythology is understood.[32] Just as the musical theory of the seventeenth century was rooted in Neo-Platonism, so too was the age's conception of visual imagery and symbolism planted in a Neo-Platonic soil. Visual symbols, according to the Neo-Platonists of both late antiquity and the Renaissance, were reflections of the invisible, incorporeal world and a form of divine revelation. They could be disguised as creatures of nature—the pelican, for example, was a prefiguration in nature of Christ's charity; or they could appear in ancient poetic myths and fables, where profound ideas and truths equivalent to those of the Scriptures were concealed. The poets hid these truths in myth and imagery to keep them from being profaned. "All mythology," the Neo-Platonists believed, is nothing more—or pretends to be nothing more—than a system of ideas in disguise, a "secret philosophy."[33] Moreover, those ancient ideas and truths could still be perceived through intuition, which the Neo-Platonists regarded as a more direct route to knowledge than reason. Images and symbols containing hidden truths are more accessible to sudden flashes of intuition than to the reasoning faculties of the mind. Thus, by studying and contemplating the symbols of the ancient poets, philosophers, Church Fathers, even those of the Egyptian priests and Eastern esoteric sources, knowledge of ultimate truths or abstract ideas such as time and beauty can be gained.

The assumptions of Neo-Platonism help to explain the significance attached to visual imagery throughout the early modern period of European history. They account for the popularity of emblems and devices with symbolic meanings and of allegorical representations of ideas such as justice, and moral attributes such as courage, in all modes of painting, drama, and court pageantry. The point is that to a man of the sixteenth or seventeenth century "a truth condensed into a visual image was somehow nearer the realm of absolute truth than one explained in words."[34] This was the message of the many manuals of iconography and emblem books that artists of the sixteenth and seventeenth centuries consulted for information on allegorical and mythological subjects:[35] visual images forcefully and directly impress ideas on the mind which otherwise would elude it. Though written mainly by Italians, these manuals were translated into French and used as commonly as dictionaries. In addition, France had her own mythologist, Jean Le Maire, whose *Illustrations des Gaules et singularités de Troie* gave a full range of the historical, moral, and physical meaning of fables. These manuals explained how all the ancient gods could be represented, presenting moral interpretations side-by-side with physical and philosophical interpretations. The attributes of each fabulous figure were explained in detail so that he could be represented accurately and recognized. Jupiter, for example, must always be represented with his sceptor, his eagle, and his thunderbolts. The important thing for the artist was to represent in symbols and images the idea embodied in the painting—to give the idea a visual form.

By the time of Louis XIV, under the impact of Cartesian

thought, the Neo-Platonist conception of the power of visual imagery and symbolism probably no longer carried the metaphysical weight it had enjoyed in the fifteenth and sixteenth centuries. Few court painters or academic officials believed, like Ficino, that symbols embody supranatural essences or contain hidden revelations of God or possess the actual quality of what they represent. Nevertheless, the court artist still used the iconographic and pedagogical manuals which were laced with Neo-Platonism: he still used the symbolic language of Neo-Platonism. The importance attached by artists and public alike to the expressive power of symbolic figures was part of a Neo-Platonic outlook. The popular portrayal of the king as Hercules or Apollo, surrounded and eulogized by figures representing justice, courage, wisdom, prudence, and so forth, and by Mercury, Jupiter, and other deities from the ancient pantheon, was still based, perhaps subconsciously, on the Neo-Platonist idea that a figure magically appropriates the powers and other attributes of what it represents and that an abstract concept can enter our understanding when it is given a visible shape. Though they may have used allegorical images more and more because they were conventional and decorative, the painters, poets, and musicians of Louis XIV's reign operated on the assumption that allegorical images penetrate the mind in a flash and direct the emotions toward the ideas represented. Above all, both artists and public relished representations of virtues and vices in the form of legendary personages.

Louis' favorite mythological image was Apollo, and his artists, poets, and musicians made the most of it. Apollo was actually a very old image of the harmony of the cosmos. He had been represented by pagans and early Christians in the dual role of leader of the Muses and ruler of the planets. The Neo-Platonists had used the image of the sun, or Apollo, to represent god. He was attended by the three pagan Graces which the Neo-Platonists converted to the Trinity or to the three Christian Virtues (faith, hope, and charity).[36] Apollo was also the god of music, especially in the Platonic sense of music as the imitation of universal harmony and as the foundation of all knowledge. In this sense, Apollo was a unified symbol of universal order, music, and knowledge.

The Graces, who nearly always accompanied representations of Apollo and who were originally deities of fertility, also came to be associated with music and were usually shown dancing. In addition, the Muses were musical symbols; since Pythagoras they had been treated as celestial musicians, creating harmony in the spheres. They were closely identified with the dance in both antiquity and the Renaissance. An engraving illustrating a musical treatise (*Practica musica*, 1496) by Franchino Gafurio shows Apollo as an image of cosmic musical tonality; seated atop the heavens, he looks down on the earthly elements and leads the Muses, who set into motion the planets, each of which represents a musical mode. Thus, the sun god is the center of the universal harmony.[37] This kind of imagery remained popular in the seventeenth century. The association of the sun with a monarch was, of course, easily achieved. What better analogy could there be than that of a king at the center of a political order and the sun at the center of a celestial order?

In fact, the sun had been regarded as the protective god of monarchs in ancient Egypt, and the Roman Emperors had been represented as Apollo. The earliest use of the sun emblem by the kings of France did not come, however, until the fourteenth century, when Charles V adopted it along with other emblems as a symbol of power. But the emblem was not reserved for French kings until the reign of Charles VI, who adopted the sun as his devise.[38] It was subsequently employed by Charles VII, Louis XI, Charles VIII, and Louis XII as an emblem of the monarchy in the decorations of royal entries and pageants.

The sixteenth-century monarchs turned to other gods, however, and Apollo appeared only as the god of music at the court of François I and Henri II. The popularity of Apollo as a royal symbol was restored thanks to the spread of Copernican ideas and the vogue of astrology. In the seventeenth century, the interest in astrology reinforced Ovid's description of Apollo as the sun god surrounded by the days, hours, months, seasons, years, and centuries. Apollo was linked inextricably to the signs of the zodiac and to astrological influences. It also became customary in the art and fetes of the Renaissance, especially in Italy, to depict Apollo in a horse-drawn chariot surrounded by allegorical figures. Italian astrological engravers were apparently responsible for interpreting the sun god as a ruler: in representing the planets, they usually placed a crown on the sun. The first clear representation of the Sun King occurred in connection with Charles IX's entry at Lyons. He was greeted by figures portraying the legendary kings of Gaul (Francus, Hercules, Rhemus, and Belgius) and the figure of an illuminated king mounted on a chariot bearing the inscription "Soli Carolo." Thereafter, the figure of the *roi soleil* was repeatedly associated with French kings, especially after the Bourbon rule began. But although Henri IV and Louis XIII were often likened to Apollo and the sun emblem was used along with other symbols to represent their virtues and deeds, Apollo did not become the unique, personal symbol of a French king until Louis XIV adopted it.

Thanks to the artists, writers, and musicians of his academies, no king in the history of Europe has ever been so totally identified with a mythological figure as Louis was with Apollo. Even before his birth, Louis was portrayed as the Sun King. A medal was struck in 1638 showing the still unborn ruler riding a chariot led by Victory with the image of the *soleil levant*. The image first appeared prominently in 1651 when he danced as the figure of the sun, dressed in a costume of flames, in the *Ballet du Roy des Festes de Bacchus* (see Figure 9). The emblem reappeared during the festivities of Louis' wedding and again at the carrousel of 1662, when Louis wore a sun costume, apparently inspired by the monarchical image described by the translator of Ripa's *Iconologia*. The sun was proclaimed Louis' official emblem in 1663 by the Académie des inscriptions, which announced that as the sun enlightens the earth and several celestial globes, Louis is fit to govern France and several kingdoms. It appeared often thereafter in the artistic productions of the academies as well as in the ceremonies, pageants, and musical productions of the court.

All of Versailles was designed, of course, as a mammoth shrine to the sun god. In his description of the palace, André Félibien wrote: "It is good to remark at first that as the Sun is the motto of the king, and the poets make no distinction between the Sun and Apollo, there is nothing in this superb house which does not have a bearing on this divinity; also all the figures and the ornaments which one sees there are not placed haphazardly; they have relation either to the Sun or to the particular places from which they were taken."[39] The theme of Apollo appears through the entire east-west axis of the park, extending from the parterre overlooking the bassin de Latone to the bassin d'Apollon, where the god is represented charging on his chariot out of the surging water toward the palace. He symbolizes the king springing to life to enlighten the world. Surrounding this axis are figures of the seasons, the temperaments, lesser divinities such as Bacchus and Circe, all basking in the Sun's radiance. Apollo is present everywhere: on a balcony of the king's chamber overlooking the cour de marbre, there is a figure of the god's lyre intertwined through a double "L"; the escalier des ambassadeurs, crowded with allegorical figures, contains the figures of Apollo conquering a serpent and the sun above the king's bust with the motto "Nec pluribus impar." Beyond the staircase lies the salon d'Apollon, where ambassadors were received, the ceiling of which displays Apollo with his lyre. Louis' emblem also richly adorned other royal residences; there were Mignard's decorations in the Tuileries, Le Brun's gallery of Apollo in the Louvre, and the entire layout of the pavilions at Marly, depicting the sun surrounded by the signs of the zodiac and the months of the year. All of these representations would have been dwarfed, however, if the Temple of Apollo planned by Nicodème Tessin had been built. This bronze and white marble palace would have been situated either at the end of the grand canal or of the lac des Suisses, where Bernini's transfigured equestrian statue of Louis now stands, and would have served as a museum for the royal art collection. It would have been decorated with many allegorical devices and images of the sun. A colossal globe over the cupola surmounted by Apollo and surrounded by the ring of the zodiac was planned for the domed roof, while the interior was to be illuminated by an artificial sun made of crystal lamps whose light would be reflected in the glass-paneled walls. This magnificent edifice was not conceived until 1712. The plans, along with what was done at Versailles, do indicate the extensive and opulent use made of a legendary image by Louis XIV's artists.

All of the king's academies participated in the mythologization and allegorization of the monarch, but the Académie de peinture played the leading role in the early years of the reign. More than anyone else, Charles Le Brun, who was the director of the Gobelins, the king's first painter, and the guiding figure of the Académie de peinture, was responsible for turning visual allegory and mythology into a principal weapon of Louis' artistic arsenal. The subjects of his paintings and designs point up the striking parallel of the visual arts and the musical *spectacles*. Le Brun's characters were seen nightly at the opera, where they were anticipated and easily identified. Le Brun's paintings even formed a perfect complement to the physical setting of Lully's operas. For example, at the château of Saint-Germain-en-Laye, Louis' birthplace and the scene (the salle du bal) of many operas and ballets, Le Brun painted allegorical figures of Music and Dance. The twin themes of love and glory which figured in nearly all of the royal operas were everywhere represented in the decorations of the château, along with the gods and goddesses of the music dramas—Juno, Daphiné, Venus, Apollo, and Neptune.[40] At Marly, where the king's musical diet was no less rich despite the absence of the formal ceremonial atmosphere that prevailed at Versailles, Le Brun achieved a satisfying blend of legend and allegory. Twelve satellite pavilions, each named after a god or a symbolic figure, each ornamented with trophies, cameo tableaux, and bas-reliefs of fabulous subjects, flanked the central Palais du Soleil, whose four sides were painted with scenes depicting the celestial journey of Apollo.

For their allegorical evocations of Louis' virtue and strength, both Le Brun and Lully drew their inspiration from the military escapades of the king. In April 1677 Louis took Le Brun, André Le Nôtre, and Van der Meulen on a tour of the sites of Condé's recent sieges at Cambrai and Valenciennes. These scenes were in Le Brun's mind when he planned the salons of War and Peace and the grand gallery of Versailles. The ceiling of War is dominated by the image of France wearing an impenetrable breast plate with the picture of Louis XIV. Surrounded by the Victories, France receives the homage of Spain. Holland is submerged in water, while Germany kneels, blindfolded and disgraced. Flanking the other side of the gallery, the salon of Peace shows France riding a chariot led by Louis XIV and pulled by doves from whose necks dangle the arms of Savoy, Castille, and Bavaria, Louis' allies. Thus, Louis' success at diplomacy and his image as a peacemaker balance the conquests represented in the salon of War. Between the two salons, Le Brun crowned the gallery of mirrors with thirty tableaux which tell the story of Louis' success in war and peace. Filled with the heroes of mythology and the allegories of virtue, the vast chronicle unfolds: Louis' determination to govern without a first minister; his independence of the papacy; his relief of his famine-stricken subjects; his reestablishment of oceanic commerce; his support of the academies. These scenes balance those of military triumph, in which the figures of France, Justice, Victory, and Fame join Mercury, Mars, Minerva, and the Muses in hailing Louis, the personification of France.[41]

One is struck by the almost monotonous recurrence of these same themes and figures in the musical dramas, and by the fact that Le Brun fulfilled the same role as Lully, that of a historian and eulogist. Painting and opera were almost interchangeable media. The operas played up the visual effects and employed the same allegorical figures and legendary subjects as the paintings. Each painting was in turn like an operatic prologue down to the last detail. How often Louis in the operas crushed Discord, received the laurel crown from Glory, and basked in the accolades of the Graces, Talents, Games, and Muses, as he does in Le Brun's *Le roi gouverne par lui-même!* How often the countries of Europe came to life on the stage to sing their obeisance to France, as they do on the ceiling of the grand gallery! Through sheer volume of production, the king's image was guaranteed, for as Lully's musical eulogies were not limited to the opera stage but were performed at church, on parade, at the table, on a simple walk in a garden, Le Brun mythologized and allegorized his royal patron in paintings, arches, tapestries, and medals strewn throughout the royal residences, the theaters, hôtels, and churches of France. The impact of Louis' image was massive. All the artists of all Louis' academies were engaged in the same task of glorification as Le Brun.

The Academy of Music and the Origins of French Opera

According to the philosophy of Plato, which was still the intellectual underpinning of seventeenth-century aesthetics, music was more important than any other art to a well-governed society because it so affected the passions and temperament of man as to influence moral conduct. That, at least, would be the impact of a form of music in which harmony, rhythm, verse, and dance were united. Opera seemed to some writers to be the fulfillment of the Platonic ideal. Created in Florence at the end of the sixteenth century by the humanists, opera had proved to be an exportable item of Italy's culture. But in France it fell into political hot water and succumbed to the courtly preference for the dance. The visual *spectacle* was pleasing to the French, however, and if molded to French taste and encouraged by the crown, it seemed that opera might have a future in France.

During the 1650's and 1660's, several steps were in fact taken toward the creation of a national opera. In these years the Italians still living in Paris stimulated the production of machine plays and pastoral dramas which frequently included musical scenes; Benserade's ballets offered many of the literary and scenic ingredients necessary for opera; and Lully's airs, dialogues, and symphonies approached an operatic style of composition. A cohesive plot in which the drama was carried by recitatives was still missing, however. Lully himself refrained from taking the step; he believed that the French language was unsuitable for music drama and feared that the cool reception given Cavalli's operas meant that French taste would reject music drama. Clearly, if opera was to succeed in France, it would not be Italian, it would have to be an art form made up of recognizably French ingredients, and it must have the support of the French monarchy.

The first self-proclaimed creators of a national operatic style were Pierre Perrin and Robert Cambert. In 1659 they produced what was labeled the "Première comédie française en musique réprésentée en France." Cambert, born in Paris in 1627, was known primarily for his motets and chansons. In 1660 he became organist of the church of Saint-Honoré and superintendent of music to Anne of Austria, the queen mother. Although Cambert had a short-lived success collaborating with Perrin in music drama and helping to found an academy of music, he was not a distinguished composer. When Lully took over the Académie in 1672, Cambert went to England, where he died five years later.[42] Cambert's more important colleague, Pierre Perrin, was an egotistical and ambitious poet who hoped to profit by the trend toward establishing academies for each of the fine arts during the 1660's. Born in Lyons in 1620, Perrin at the age of twenty-three married a sixty-one year old dowager whose money enabled him to buy an appointment as introducer of ambassadors and foreign princes for Gaston d'Orléans. Perrin's wife quickly abandoned her spendthrift husband, however, and for the rest of his days, the poet was plagued by financial troubles that landed him in jail more than once. He wrote dozens of undistinguished poems and verses for airs de cour before his death in 1675, but he achieved renown as the founder of the Académie royale de musique.[43]

In April 1659 Cambert and Perrin produced a musical comedy known as the *Pastorale d'Issy* at the home of M. de la Haye, the queen mother's maître d'hôtel. Perrin, possessing somewhat clearer vision of the court's musical needs than Lully, hailed his own work as a triumph for "our poetry and our music over a foreign language, poetry, and music." In a letter, dated April 30, 1659, to his friend Cardinal de la Rovera, archbishop of Turin and formerly apostolic nuncio to France,[44] Perrin contended that, unlike other Frenchmen, he had not despaired of creating opera in the French language. Perrin dedicated himself to "eradicating the faults of the Italians" and to creating a form that has "the ability to express the passions in a more touching manner" than ordinary drama. In a ringing denunciation of Italian art, Perrin referred to their music as "plain chant and cloister airs, which we call songs of the hurdy-gurdy or of the ricochet—a music of the gutter." Mistakenly viewing opera as a recent (twenty or thirty years) development in Italy, Perrin lampooned the ridiculous plots, rambling recitatives, excessively florid, repetitious arias, and stilted sentiments of the Italians. In comparison, Perrin claimed that his *Pastorale* offered a wide range of emotions affectively expressed; every scene, he argued, is natural to sing, not just a dull excuse for the singer to display his virtuosity. The French like brevity and diversity, Perrin explained, and the *Pastorale* is scarcely one and one half hours long and contains a variegated assortment of vocal and instrumental selections. Perrin was especially critical of the poetry in the Italian operas; he called it obscure and criticized the forced metaphoric expressions. French poetry has abandoned antique expressions and has acquired an unparalleled clarity and an appropriate rhythm for the natural expression of the passions. Alexandrian verse has been replaced by short, lyrical verses with caesuras and rhymes appropriate for singing. And finally, Perrin added, we have dispensed with those singers (the castrati) who are "the horror of women and the laughter of men." Insisting that he had created a new national musical genre, Perrin concluded his letter to the archbishop with this statement: "I have the distinction of having opened and smoothed the path, of having discovered and cleared this new earth, and furnished to my nation a model of French comedy in music."

In the libretto, copies of which were distributed at the performances of the *Pastorale d'Issy*, Cambert and Perrin wrote an introduction in which they tried to reply to the critics of music drama, who contended that the emotions could not be treated as powerfully through music as through pure drama. Perrin and Cambert argued that if the composer has a good knowledge of the language as well as of his native musical style, he can create a satisfying work. The opera can touch the heart more strongly than words alone, they asserted. The numerous devices available to music to convey meaning can "uplift the whole man, . . . charm the eyes with the sight of magnificent costumes, superb scenery, admirable mechanical devices, and agreeable ballets; the ear by the excellence of the song, the accompaniment and the symphonies; the mind by beautiful designs, and the heart by depicting the passions in the most vivid and touching manner, which uplifts and transports them."[45] Above all, Perrin and Cambert insisted that the French language was quite suitable for musical expression.

In spite of all the claims made for it by the authors, the *Pastorale d'Issy* (the music for which is not extant) was not an especially original work. In form, subject matter, and verse, it greatly resembled the pastoral *Le Triomphe de l'amour* (1655) by Charles de Beys and Michel de La Guerre (see Chapter 3). The five acts of the *Pastorale* were essentially a series of vaguely related short tableaux in which arias, recitatives, and dialogues were sung by sylvan deities and shepherds. The sets depicted a fanciful rustic world where happy creatures sang to each other about the joy and sadness of love. Although the *Pastorale* was not performed initially before the king of France, references were made in the final act to the recent conclusion of hostilities between France and Spain. The concluding récit was directed to Louis XIV:

> Grand Roi, secondez nos désirs;
> Suivez l'Amour, quittez les armes,
> Vous trouvez dans ses plaisirs
> Autant d'honneur et plus de charmes :
>
> Vous pouvez sans doute acquérir
> Beaucoup de gloire par la guerre;
> Mais donner la paix à la terre
> C'est plus que de la conquérir.
>
> Par tout où marchent nos guerriers
> La victoire les accompagne :
> Déjà des moissons de Lauriers
> Vous attendent à la campagne,
> Vous allez sans doute.[46]

A sizable crowd of courtiers were attracted to Issy in the spring of 1659 for the performance of the *Pastorale*. The overflow had to stand in the garden. Loret estimated the throng at 300 and stated that it included many members of the bourgeoisie. Perrin and Cambert received everyone's approbation, according to Loret, who, speaking for himself, wrote: "I went, I saw, I heard, and with a delicate pleasure, I enjoyed."[47] News of the piece reached the king, and Perrin was invited to give a performance of the *Pastorale* in May at Vincennes for Louis XIV, the queen, Mazarin, and the court. The final verses were sung by a shepherdess

> With sweetness and solemnity,
> Before His Majesty,
> Who, fixing her in his gaze,
> Listened to them with great spirit.[48]

In his letter to the archbishop of Turin, Perrin noted the pleasure of the king and particularly that of Mazarin, who "confessed his surprise at its success and indicated to M. Cambert his intention of undertaking similar pieces for him."[49] At Mazarin's request, Perrin and Cambert began work on a new pastoral called *Ariane* or *Le Mariage de Bacchus*. They were deprived, however, of their most influential protectors by Gaston d'Orléans' death in 1660 and Mazarin's in 1661.

Perrin had visions of success for *Ariane* and for his new tragedy *Le mort d'Adonis*, and he continued working on both pieces in spite of his imprisonment for debt in 1659. He also took pleasure in the inimical reaction to Cavalli's opera, *Ercole*, while delighting in Lully's continued success with ballets during the 1660's. He wrote:

> We hail these little maids of flying feet,
> There's nothing quite so sweet or quite so neat;
> But not these grandiose concerts of old *Laures*, of *Signores*,
> And these *non-sunt* who chant their *libra*
> In memory of their *et cetera*.[50]

Released from jail in 1666, Perrin had already completed a collection of poems intended for musical settings, which he dedicated and sent to Colbert. The collection included the verses for *Ariane* and the drama *Le mort d'Adonis*. In the dedication Perrin wrote: "Since I know monseigneur that in working principally for the glory and the grandeur of our monarch, you do not neglect that which can contribute to his pleasures, I thought that upon reading this Collection you could perhaps take up the plan of giving him the *divertissement* of hearing a few of these novelties executed in music; in order to allow you the liberty of so doing, before having this work printed and making the words public, I offer them to you in manuscript."[51] In light of the glory of the king and of France in so many areas, Perrin continued, it is unthinkable that "a nation everywhere victorious be conquered by foreigners in the knowledge of these two fine arts, poetry and music." Perrin admitted that the Italians had held the upper hand in recent years, but he assured Colbert that the French language and poetry "are capable of the same beauties as theirs and . . . have the same advantages for music." France must prove to all of Europe that she can surpass them. The poet assured Colbert that he had only the glory of the French nation in mind and not his own ambitions; but he reminded the French minister that fame attends any stateman who promotes "the greatest pleasures and the ornament of the court." Although his dedication does not mention the matter, Perrin may have suggested also the establishment of an academy of music to Colbert. In any event the idea evidently took root in the minister's mind during this period.

Perrin, meanwhile, made Cambert his partner and, with a group of hired musicians, they presented the comedy in music *Ariane* at the Hôtel de Nevers in 1669. There is no evidence that Colbert or the king were present, but Perrin, nonetheless, took the occasion to pen a flattering prologue to the king:

> Monarch of the French, oh how the gods are crazy
> For having given birth to such a great king as you;
> Already your merit and your various exploits
> Have filled the universe in the flower of your years.
> You are youthful, handsome, rich, valiant and wise,
> And the censor of the gods, for whom everything is poorly done,
> Who can blame the most perfect work,
> Finds you entirely perfect.[52]

Although *Ariane* was not a great success, Perrin's ten-year campaign to attain recognition for a national music drama was rewarded when Louis XIV granted him Lettres patentes calling for the establishment of "Académies d'opéra ou représentations en musique en langue française sur le pied de celles d'Italie."

The Lettres patentes, signed by Louis and Colbert on June 28, 1669, and distributed to the king's counselors and the Parlement of Paris, called attention to the production of operas in Italy under the sponsorship of the Pope, Italian princes, and members of noble families. The king called for the production of similar pieces in the French language. Louis expressed the hope that such entertainments might encourage his French subjects to cultivate the noble art of music. The Lettres granted Perrin permission to establish academies in Paris and other cities in France for the purpose of "producing and singing public operas and performances in music and French verse." Recognizing the large expenditures necessary for the theaters, machines, decorations, and costumes, Louis permitted Perrin to charge the public whatever admission fee he deemed appropriate and accorded him the right to place guards at the doors of the theater to preserve order. No one else would undertake similar productions without Perrin's consent, and failure to comply with this ruling would result in a fine of 10,000 livres. Furthermore, the Lettres granted ladies and members of the nobility the right to participate in the performances without detracting from their noble station. In creating the Académie royale de musique, Louis affirmed his purpose of "desiring to contribute to the advancement of the arts in our kingdom and to treat favorably the said exponent [Perrin] as much out of consideration for the services he has rendered lately to our very dear and well-loved uncle the duc d'Orléans as of those that he has rendered us for several years in the composition of words for music which is sung both in our chapel and in our chamber."[53]

In spite of the king's support, Perrin needed financial backing, and he received it from two rogues, the marquis Alexandre de Rieux de Sourdéac and Laurens Bersac de Champeron.[54] Sourdéac, who was an amateur machinist, offered to support Perrin in return for a share in the profits of the Académie. Champeron also contributed funds and acted as business manager. Cambert was jockeyed out of a real partnership but continued his job as Perrin's composer. The contract between these men was entirely verbal. The debt-ridden poet and his troupe of musicians were obliged to rely on the promises of financial backing by Sourdéac and Champeron, but neither the singers nor Cambert, who was to receive a monthly salary of 250 livres, were ever paid. What little money Champeron and Sourdéac had was soon spent on the rental of a theater, which the police promptly closed. However, with the help of Henri Guichard, intendant of buildings and gardens for the duc d'Orléans, they installed a theater on the site of a tennis court on the rue Mazarine, facing the rue Guénégaud. On March 3, 1671, the theater opened with the first of a long series of performances of the "opéra, ou représentation en musique" *Pomone*, by Perrin and Cambert.[55]

Varying little from the musical pastorals of the period, *Pomone*, nonetheless, was an effort to adapt the music of the recitatives to the meter of French verse.[56] The airs closely resemble those of the ballet de cour; unlike their Italian counterparts, they are short, unpretentious, and have no dramatic significance. Cambert's harmony, compared with that of the Italians, is very conservative. The "Prologue to the praise of the king" is a recitative-dialogue between the Nymph of the Seine and Vertumne. Snatches of imitation and an occasional florid passage enliven things, but on the whole Cambert's music is more prosaic than either Lully's or that of Italian composers such as Cavalli. The setting for the prologue was the Louvre, and Perrin's text was directed to the king. When asked what she thinks of France in comparison with all the parts of the earth which she has seen, Vertumne responds: "Your greatest marvel is the pompous majesty of the king who commands there. In the august Louis I find a new Mars. In his superb city a new Rome. Never, never was such a great man seated on the throne of the Caesars."[57]

Pomone was an enormous success: crowds flocked to the performances, which continued for eight months. The duc d'Orléans and many other persons from the king's court came. Public enthusiasm was so great that the police in May issued an ordinance aimed at restraining the crowds.[58] A popular song heralded the opera's success and taunted Jean-Baptiste Lully:

> Quand l'opéra tant vanté par la Grille [one of the king's
>   musicians]
> Aujour paroîtra
> Toute la cour l'admira
> Baptiste [Lully] rentrera dans sa coquille.[59]

Although *Pomone* was financially successful, Perrin, Cambert, and the musicians failed to profit from it. Champeron and Sourdéac controlled the box office, pocketed the earnings, and allowed Perrin for the second time to be imprisoned in June for indebtedness. In an effort to strike back at his two dishonest partners and recoup some of his losses, Perrin sold an interest in the Académie in November 1671 to Henri Guichard and Jean Granouillet de la Sablières, intendant of music for the duc d'Orléans. Champeron and Sourdéac claimed that Perrin's action was illegal. No one was really sure, however, who was the beneficiary of the Lettres patentes, who was to direct the Académie, and how the profits were to be divided. Amid this confusion, Cambert composed a new opera, or "pastorale héroïque," on a text by Gabriel Gilbert, and it was produced at the theater on rue Mazarine in February 1672.[60]

The pastorale *Les peines et les plaisirs de l'amour* was a further step toward a national French opera. More varied rhythmically and harmonically than *Pomone*, *Les peines* offered somewhat more elaborate recitatives, and the prologue to the king, which had become a fixture in productions of this sort, was lengthier. The harmony modulated more freely and cadences were likely to occur on a fourth or a sixth. Cambert also employed orchestral tone-symbolism (later used extensively by Lully and his successors). For instance, a dotted figure in the bass depicted the descent of Venus and Fame (Example 8) in a chariot.[61] Moreover,

Example 8

Cambert employed certain musical techniques to project more emphatically particular phrases or ideas in the text: The phrase— "charmed by his bravery, / we come to these places in order to divert this king to peace, / this victorious king"—was sung first by a four-part chorus, then as a solo, and finally in a contrapuntal trio.[62] Elsewhere Venus sings: "Louis is the greatest of kings"; the phrase was not only repeated for emphasis, but was embellished in its repetition as well (Example 9).[63] Throughout the prologue, Cambert developed the idea that Louis' reputation and domain extended over all the earth. Fame predicted that one day Louis would rule India, and Venus declared that some day the universe would be only one court. When Fame sang "Already the inhabitants of the Nile and the Tagus and the most remote from the French Empire, the savages without laws, are coming

Example 9

Lou - is est   le   Plus Gra - nd   des Rois

to pay him homage," a chorus of Africans, Moors, Egyptians, and Spaniards appeared on stage, dancing and singing about Louis' exploits.

While reserving the prologue for Louis, Gilbert adroitly dedicated *Les peines* to Colbert. Referring to Perrin and Cambert, he wrote: "If these ingenious spirits have deserved general esteem, it is to you, monseigneur, that the principal glory is due for it, since you have deemed it well to encourage them, and they have undertaken nothing without the assurance of your protection."[64] Gilbert praised Colbert's efforts on behalf of the academies of science, painting, and architecture, and he lauded Colbert for undertaking so many projects without ostentation. The new Académie de musique, he added, has the advantage over the other arts "of exercising a nearly absolute sway over the passions of men." He continued:

An old king of Greece, being unable to pacify the fierce spirits of his subjects through his laws or to confine them to their duty, invited the most excellent musicians to come to the cities of Greece, and, through the charms of their art, made a civil and obedient people out of this rude and savage nation. Perhaps, Monseigneur, this history, which Polybius relates, has given birth in you to the thought of establishing the Academy of the Opera, not in order to pacify the spirit of the French, but in order to preserve them in the beautiful sentiments in which they were born, and in order to achieve this beautiful science which Nature has begun so well. If the establishment of the French Academy . . . has given so much glory to Cardinal

Richelieu, this Academy of Music, whose purpose is to pacify and refine manners [mœurs], will be no less glorious to its protector.

The Greeks were the originators of music drama, Gilbert stated. They concluded every act of their plays with musical choruses. Our production simply extends that practice, he continued, by integrating music with the parts of the poem itself. Doubtless Colbert was impressed, for he soon took action to free the Académie from its administrative and financial predicaments.

Lully and the Académie Royale de Musique

In the meantime, Jean-Baptiste Lully, who had played no part in the founding of the Académie, continued to produce his royal ballets for the court. While Perrin and Cambert prepared *Pomone,* Lully presented his ballet *Psyché* at the Tuileries on January 17, 1671 for the king, the queen, and the dauphin. Subsequent performances were given for the papal nuncio and the Venetian ambassador. The ballet ran at the Palais-Royal from July to October. A sumptuous production with many changes of scene, *Psyché* came close to being a full-fledged opera. The prologue continued the tradition of praising the king and foreshadowed the opulent prologues of Lully's operas. Flore, the goddess of flowers, hailed Louis XIV for concluding the recent War of Devolution for control of the Spanish Netherlands:

> Ce n'est plus le temps de la guerre;
> Le plus puissant des rois
> Interrompt ses exploits,
> Pour donner la paix à la terre.
>
> . . . . .
>
> Nous goûtons une paix profonde;
> Les plus doux jeux sont ici-bas.
> On doit ce repos plein d'appas
> Au plus grand roi du monde.[65]

Although Lully was pleased with the favorable reception accorded *Psyché*, he was amazed and disturbed by the success which Perrin and Cambert were having with *Pomone*. When *Les peines et les plaisirs* elicited even more enthusiasm than *Pomone*, Lully began having second thoughts about his earlier rejection of the feasibility of a French opera, and he settled on a determined effort to take over the financially mismanaged Académie royale de musique. Whether Lully approached the king and Colbert on the matter first or they sought him out is uncertain. There is no question, however, that Lully had royal backing when he visited the imprisoned Perrin in the Conciergerie and persuaded the poet to sell him all the rights to the Académie, much to the consternation of Champeron, Sourdéac, Guichard, and Sablières. In an effort to explain how Lully received royal support, Charles Perrault later claimed that Lully, having noted the financial gains of the Académie, asked the king directly "for the privilege of creating the operas alone and getting the profit from them."[66] Perrault maintained further that Colbert opposed this move and "found no justice in dispossessing the inventors, or, at any rate, the restorers of this *divertissement*." Colbert's objection was not sustained, however, according to Perrault: "Lully demanded this favor from the king with so much force and daring, that the king, fearing that out of anger, he might quit everything, told Colbert that he could not do without this man in his *divertissements*, and that it was necessary that he be granted whatever he requested." A few days after Lully received the privilège of the opera, Perrault overheard some of the courtiers declare to Colbert that one man alone should not be given an enterprise which was bound to be enormously remunerative. Loyal to the king's decision, Colbert reportedly told the courters that if Lully made a fortune from the opera, it would set a good example for other musicians and motivate them "to exert all their best efforts in order to attain the same station as he."

Perrault may have been mistaken about Colbert's initial objection to awarding the privilège to Lully. In a letter to Colbert dated June 1672, Lully wrote: "You know, monseigneur, that I have taken no other course in this matter than the one which you have prescribed for me."[67] Whatever Colbert's initial feelings had been he quickly got behind Lully. Madame de Montespan may also have interceded on Lully's behalf and conceivably provided Lully with the money to buy out Perrin.[68] The *Mercure galant* pondered the reasons for the transfer of the

Académie from Sourdéac and his associates to Lully and concluded: "One must never penetrate into the secrets of kings and
one must believe always that they are right."[69] Louis XIV
himself perhaps provided the best general explanation. In his
Mémoires, he wrote that the principal function of the ruler "is to put
each particular person in the post in which he can be useful to
the public. One certainly knows that we cannot do everything,
but we must give orders so that everything will be done well,
and this choice depends mainly on the choice of those whom we
employ. In a great state there are always appropriate citizens
for everything, and the only problem is to recognize them and
put them in their place."[70]

On March 13, 1672, a few days after Lully had negotiated
with Perrin for control of the Académie, Louis XIV issued new
Lettres patentes. The sciences and the arts are "the most notable
ornaments of states," Louis began.[71] He observed that, since
giving peace to his subjects, he has taken pleasure in rewarding
and encouraging talented artists. Louis referred to the Lettres
patentes of 1669 permitting Pierre Perrin to establish an academy
of music, but he stated that since certain difficulties have prevented Perrin from being able to "support fully our purpose and to
raise music to the point that we have promised, we have been
persuaded that in order to make it succeed better, it would be
appropriate to give the leadership to a person whose experience
and capability have come to our attention."[72] Louis acknowledged
his familiarity with the great talent of "our dear and beloved
Jean-Baptiste Lulli," who for years has given daily proof of his
ability in the royal service. Lully will be permitted, therefore,
"by these present signatures of our hand, to establish a Royal
Academy of Music in our good city of Paris to be composed of
such a number and quality of persons whom he will advise to be
worth, [and] we will choose and check on the report that he will
make to us in order to perform some productions before us, when
it pleases us, of pieces of music which will be composed as much in
French verse as in foreign languages." In the event of Lully's
death, the king provided that one of the composer's children
would succeed to the charge. In order that Lully might recoup
the costs of costumes, machinery, and decorations, the king

granted him permission to produce for the public the same pieces that he presented for the king. Lully was instructed to set his own prices and to charge admission to persons of title and officers of the royal household. The document prohibited all persons from "singing any piece entirely in music, either in French verse or other languages, without the permission in writing of the said Sieur Lully, in penalty of 10,000 livres fine and confiscation of theaters, machines, decorations, costumes and other items." The king permitted all ladies and gentlemen to sing in Lully's productions without being censured or losing titles and honors. Finally Louis ordered the document sent to the Parlement of Paris and to his counselors to be read, published, and registered, and he declared all previous privilèges null and void.

Lully's accession to power elicited sharp criticisms from Sourdéac and Champeron, who were obliged to close the theater on the rue Mazarine. Indeed, one suspects that a legal crisis was in the making, since Colbert, acting with unusual dispatch, sent a letter on March 24 to Achille de Harlay, procureur général of the Parlement, urging that the Lettres patentes be registered at once. Colbert told Harlay that Lully had informed the king about the complaints of Sourdéac, Champeron, Sablières, and Guichard, and about their efforts to prevent the registration of Lully's privilège. Colbert assured Harlay that Sourdéac and Champeron had only a letter drawn up between them and Perrin which had no legal validity in giving them any right to Perrin's privilège. Moreover, all claims were annulled by the king's recent action, according to Colbert. The king was persuaded that if Lully managed the Académie, "His Majesty and the public will be able to have the benefit of it," and he "has ordered me to inform you that he wants this matter settled as soon as possible and that you give him favorable conclusions as far as justice is able to permit you."[73]

A few days later, the king sent a letter to M. de la Reynie, lieutenant of police, ordering him to close the theater on the rue Mazarine on April 1 "in order to put a stop to the performances of the said opera which have continued to be given."[74] On April 14, Louis issued an arrêt reaffirming Lully's privilège, and on the twenty-fourth Colbert sent another letter to Harlay stating that "His Majesty wishes that you give to the said Lully all the assistance and protection which belongs to the authority of your post."[75] Colbert added that Louis believed that there was no room for doubt that Lully "will handle these works better than all those who have worked there until now." Royal ordinances consistent with Lully's privilège were also issued in April. They limited to six the number of musicians that Molière's players, who performed in the Palais-Royal, were permitted to use.[76]

In spite of the king's firmness, Sourdéac and Champeron sent a formal petition to the Parlement of Paris on May 30 protesting Lully's privilège. They reminded the Parlement that since 1669 they had labored at great risk and expense to make the Académie a success. Sourdéac and Champeron accused Lully of greedily seeking to capitalize on their efforts and to defraud them of their profits. They argued that Lully won the king's support by spreading the false rumor that the Académie was going to fail unless it was handed over to him. They appealed to the Parlement not to register Lully's patente.[77] Alarmed by their boldness, Lully wrote to Colbert charging his opponents with chicanery and falsehood.[78] He questioned the legality of their deal with Perrin and denied that he had duped the king. He reminded Colbert that he had followed the line of action suggested to him by the finance minister himself. Sourdéac and Champeron have not submitted themselves to your judgment, Lully charged, because they knew that you would not tolerate the deception which they had used with the Parlement. Lully added that he scarcely had time to fight calumny and work on the king's operas at the same time. He also requested Colbert to persuade Louis to let him have the hall of the Louvre for the productions of the Académie and invited Colbert to examine his projects for the return of the king, who at that time was in Holland. Lully must have pressed Colbert to get the Louvre even before this letter, for in a letter to Louis XIV dated May 29, Colbert wrote: "Sieur Lully asks me often if Your Majesty has agreed that he use the hall of the Louvre in order to begin the performances of the operas."[79] From his camp near Rheinberg, the king replied on June 4: "It seems to me that the Louvre is inappropriate for public performances."[80] Lully's request was denied probably because the king either did not want the crowds tramping through the Louvre or because he figured that a public theater would draw more people to these productions which eulogized his great deeds.

Lully's fears about the petition of Sourdéac and Champeron were unfounded. He was probably unaware of Colbert's letters to the procureur général which clearly indicated the resolve of the king and his minister to support him. The Parlement recognized the monarch's determination and was not prepared to make an issue of the matter. Consequently, on June 27, 1672, the Lettres patentes were registered by an arrêt of the Parlement. The arrêt recognized Lully's exclusive rights to the Académie and ordered Sourdéac and Champeron to indemnify Perrin, Cambert, and the singers of the opera. Soon afterward, Cambert went to London in the service of Charles II, and Perrin died three years later. Lully, meanwhile, opened a theater on the rue Vaugirard opposite the Palais du Luxembourg in the fall of 1672 and signed a contract with the machinest Carlo Vigarani, who helped finance the venture and for the first few years received one-third of the profits. While they prepared their first production, the king issued another privilège reconfirming Lully's position. Addressed to "our friends and fellow counselors, the citizens of our Parlementary Courts, Masters ... of our lodgings and of the Palace, bailiffs, seneschals, provosts, lieutenants, and all other judges and officers to whom it may concern," the privilège stated that the music which Lully had already composed, the pieces which he offered daily "by our orders," and the operas which "he will be obliged to compose in the future" for the Académie, are of "such a quality that the least change or omission would cause them to lose their natural grace."[81] Since Lully alone creates and produces this music, Louis continued, he alone should reap the profits from any public distribution or printing of his works. Louis ordered, therefore, that no copies of Lully's music should be made without his consent and that the composer should determine the size, character, plates, figures, and designs of such editions. Violation of this order would result in a fine of 10,000 livres.

Lully, who enjoyed the king's confidence and possessed probably more personal power than any composer before him, was determined to make the Académie royale de musique a success. He rushed the composition of his first piece, however, with the result that it was little more than a pastiche culled from his earlier ballets with a desultory text by Philippe Quinault, Jean-Baptiste Molière, and Isaac de Benserade.[82] Nonetheless, *Les fêtes de l'amour et de Bacchus*, presented at the Vaugirard theater on November 15, 1672, appealed to the audience because of its colorful scenery, its celebration of idyllic love, and its animated dances. The production was also very well timed. In March 1672 Louis had begun his second major war and had left Paris on March 27 with Louvois and Pomponne to march with his victorious armies through Holland. He had earlier obtained treaties with England and Sweden and had neutralized some German territories along the Rhine (Münster and Cologne) by subsidy treaties, so that his march through the United Provinces was a glorious success. On June 12 he had watched his troops cross the Rhine. The French easily occupied Yssel and Utrecht, but the Dutch prevented a total rout by opening the sluices and inundating their territory. Nonetheless, Louis returned to Paris as the conquering hero, and Lully was ready to celebrate the occasion. In an introduction to the libretto, which was distributed to the spectators at the opera, Lully noted that the king had conquered distant lands and secured the glory and happiness of the nation. Louis' glory does not end with military conquests, however, Lully continued:

At the same time that he overthrows the states of his enemies and astounds the entire earth, he neglects nothing which could render France the most flourishing empire that ever was. The art of war, which he exercises with an heroic passion and in which he makes such surprising progress, is not at all capable of filling the vast scope of his untiring diligence; he still finds some attention to reserve for the most beautiful of arts, and there is nothing which is worthy of some esteem that he does not favor with a special indulgence. It is that which his Royal Academy of Music has the good fortune of attempting under his endowment.[83]

Lully added that his pastorale for the Paris public was modeled on productions given at Versailles for royalty and should "not fail to please the whole world" since similar productions were "able to delight an infinitely enlightened monarch." *Les fêtes* is just the beginning, Lully concluded, because "this Academy works without relaxing" to live up to the honors bestowed on it by the king.

The prologue of *Les fêtes* comprised two elaborate entrées in a great hall adorned with paintings, behind which was a palace in the middle of a garden. The production opened with a comic scene in which the attempts of a hawker to sell librettos to the audience were interrupted by the jeers of singers whom Lully had stationed in the balcony. In the first entrée Polymnie, the Muse of sacred music and dance, appeared inside a mechanical cloud which opened to reveal her in the midst of objets d'art. She interrupted the comedy and sang:

> Élevez vos concerts
> Au-dessus du chant ordinaire;
> Songez que vous avez à plaire
> Au plus grand Roi de l'univers,
> Le grand titre de Roi n'est que sa moindre gloire;
> Il est encor plus grand par ses travaux guerriers,
> Et sa propre valeur a cueilli les lauriers
> Dont il est couronné des mains de la Victoire.[84]

The Muses of tragedy and pastoral harmony, Melpomène and Euterpe, advanced on two more clouds which opened to display trophies of war, festoons, and crowns of flowers. At this point Lully presented an ingenious combat between two symphonies— one strong and vigorous, the other placid and sweet. The two Muses beseeched Polymnie to help them prepare *divertissements*, and she replied: "I seek to please the most august king who deserves to rule forever over everything illuminated by the sun." Melpomène and Euterpe contested the right to celebrate the king's exploits. Lully playfully composed Euterpe's passages in the florid style of an Italian aria and Melpomène's in the traditional unembellished style of a French air. Polymnie invited both Muses to contribute in their own way, but she acknowledged Melpomène's greater power: "I reserve for you my greatest works." Lully, thereby, cleverly suggested the monarchical decision to champion a national musical style, or at least a style that was labeled French. The entrée concluded with the prepara-

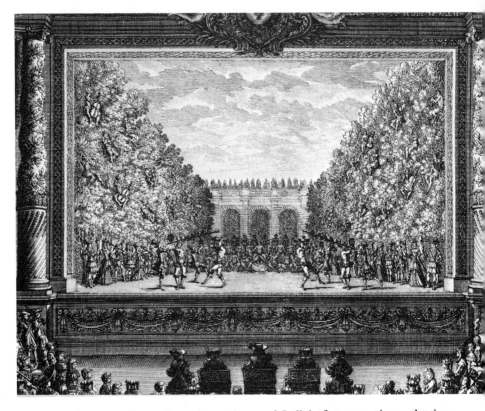

Figure 10. Scene from the prologue of Lully's first operatic production, *Les fêtes de l'amour et de Bacchus.* After an opening performance in Paris in November 1672, the piece was repeated for the king's *divertissement* of July 1674 in an outdoor theater at Versailles (shown here). Engraving by Antoine Le Pautre; reprinted from *Fêtes de l'amour et de Bacchus* (Paris, 1678), p. 115. (Photograph courtesy of the Bibliothèque Nationale, cabinet des estampes.)

tions for a *spectacle* by troops of artisans, heroes, and shepherds (Figure 10). The second entrée was a series of trios for the three Muses, intermingled with choruses praising Louis XIV: "Let us sing about the glory of his arms; let us sing about the sweetness of his laws," they chanted. The pastorale itself was the usual celebration of innocent love intoned by shepherds, maidens, goblins, sirens, and sundry rustics. The piece was received enthusiastically in Paris, and at one of the first performances attended by Louis XIV, several gentlemen of the court joined the professional dancers on stage.

Les fêtes was an auspicious beginning for Lully's Académie royale de musique. As a musical potpourri, *Les fêtes* indicated the kind of production that appealed to the French. Musically and dramatically, however, it was more similar to the traditional pastorales and ballets than to Lully's operas. In 1709 Durey de Noinville defined opera as "a theater piece in verse put to music and in songs, accompanied by dances, machines, and decorations. It is a universal *spectacle*, in which each finds something to amuse himself, in the genre which is the most suitable to him."[85] French national opera was thus a unification of the fine arts, an appeal to the eye as well as to the ear. Lully's first production in this new genre, which he called a tragédie-lyrique, came in 1673.

Louis XIV was present for the opening performance of *Cadmus et Hermione* on April 27, 1673, and subsequent performances were attended by the duc d'Orléans, the dukes of Villeroi and Gramont, and the English ambassador. The favorable reaction to *Cadmus* and its long run assured Lully's success as head of the Académie. In December 1673, Madame Marie de Sévigné wrote: "The king said the other day that if he were in Paris when the opera was being played, he would go every day. This word will be worth 100,000 francs to Baptiste."[86] Sévigné herself was quite overcome with *Cadmus;* after one performance she wrote that "there are some spots in the music which have already made me cry; I am not the only one who cannot withhold them [tears]."[87] The success of *Cadmus* also guaranteed the position of Lully's librettist, Philippe Quinault. The king "would accept no author other than Monsieur Quinault," according to Charles Perrault.[88]

Quinault took the text of *Cadmus* from Ovid but altered and cut the original to suit his needs, keeping only the central part of the fable and adding a love intrigue. Moreover, he used every opportunity afforded by the drama to insert *divertissements* and *spectacle* scenes such as the celebration of Africans in act 1, the ballet for statues in act 2, and the sacrifice to Mars in act 3.[89] Many of the elements of the comédie-ballet were retained in *Cadmus*, and the airs greatly resembled Cambert's pastorale tunes. And like the pastorales and ballets, *Cadmus* included comedy scenes that were blended into the over-all tragic character of the opera. *Cadmus* was distinguished from earlier pieces in being a music drama with a cohesive, developed plot carried by the recitatives. Moreover, the prologue was considerably more elaborate; it not only eulogized the king, but allegorically referred to his military activities. In short, the prologue of *Cadmus* was a musical-dramatic report to the French people of the latest glories of the monarch.

Drawn from the first book of Ovid's *Metamorphoses*, the subject of the prologue is the birth of the serpent Python in the warm mud of the earth after the Deluge, and his death at the hands of the Sun.[90] The scene opens in a country field in the middle of which is a marsh; dawn breaks and the sun rises as the overture is played. Palès, goddess of the shepherds, and Mélisse, divinity of forests and mountains, enter with their rustic followers to sing in duet and with the chorus about the brilliant light which they behold in the fields. In scene 2, Pan, god of the shepherds, joins the nymphs with his singers and dancers in a feast to honor the gods. Musically, the first part of scene 2 comprises a rondo air for fauns in B♭ major, an air in the same key for Pan, and the rondeau air for the fauns repeated. A new section, still in B♭, for chorus and orchestra, introduces a lively fanfare motif and a change of mood. Singing "what sudden disorder," the chorus of rustics scatters as the stage darkens and subterranean voices are heard. The contrapuntal style is intended to indicate confusion and consternation, as the chorus chants: "The day grows pale, the sky is troubled; let us flee, save us." In scene 3 Envy emerges from the darkness to unleash the monstrous serpent Python, who, springing from the marsh, spits flames while Envy releases the Winds to stir up a storm. In a recitative in C major Envy challenges the Sun's power and summons her monsters to "fill the land with horror so that nature is confounded." The Winds then dance an entrée around her as she distributes serpents to them. Lully's musical accompaniment of rapid sixteenth notes suggests the whirlwind of the storm, but he fails to use harmony for a similar purpose. The AAB framework of this passage firmly encompasses a harmonic pattern that seldom wanders further away from the tonic, C major, than a fourth. At Envy's importunity, Python rises from the marsh, and the chorus sings defiance of the Sun. Suddenly, flaming bolts of light pierce the storm and strike Python, who flounders and sinks back into the ooze. Envy and her Winds are extinguished in a rain of fire from the sky. In a final recitative she sings: "You triumph, Sun; everything surrenders to your power. . . . Oh what rage! What despair!" Filled with the Sun's rays, the stage is now a scene of joy and triumph as the rustic spirits return to celebrate the Sun's victory and dance a concluding gavotte.

Scene 4 is a lively trio sung by Pan, Mélisse, and Palès, which alternates with a chorus. They sing about the Sun's conquest of Envy and Python and their preparations to receive him and proclaim his glory "to the end of the universe." The Sun appears in a chariot in scene 5 and sings a recitative punctuated by orchestral ritornelli: "It is not for a pompous sacrifice that I am pleased to see my efforts rewarded. . . . I make the sweetest of my vows in order to render the whole world happy." Inviting the Muses to provide songs and games, the Sun returns to his orbit as the chorus sings his praises (Figure 11). The trio of gods resumes singing about the return of love to the earth, and Archas, a forest deity, sings: "Love is content, its pain enchants; love is content, all is well. . . . In the beautiful days of our life the pleasures are in their season; and the little follies of love, are often worth more than reason." An orchestral minuet concludes this prologue, which is a veritable opera within an opera.

The meaning of the prologue was apparent to French audiences. In the summer of 1672 Louis had temporarily abandoned the war against the Dutch, who had foiled his advance by opening the sluices. In Lully's prologue the United Provinces are the marsh and the Dutch are Envy and her Winds. The many-headed serpent was symbolic of the Dutch threat. Victory does not come easily when your successful march through a country is countered by the opening of the dikes; or when after one head of the serpent is cut off, several more pop up for battle. Assisted by Sweden, Louis opened peace negotiations with William of Orange in April 1673, but, to show his strength at the same time, he joined Vauban and the French army for a successful attack on the city of

Figure 11. Scene from the prologue of Lully's opera *Cadmus et Hermione.* Apollo, after slaying the serpent Python, returns to his orbit; he invites the Muses to provide songs and games. Copperplate engraving by François Chauveau; reprinted from Jean-Baptiste Lully, *Cadmus et Hermione, tragédie représentée par l'Académie royale de musique* (Paris, 1673), frontispiece. (Photograph courtesy of the Bibliothèque Nationale, département de réserve imprimée.)

Maestricht in June 1673, and the war resumed. Thus, in Lully's prologue, the Sun, obviously meaning Louis, cut through the storm and defeated Python and Envy. The rustic creatures, who sing Louis' praises, were the French people. And Quinault cleverly provided the Sun with a final verse expressing Louis' claim that he fought to secure his subjects' happiness and not just to satisfy his own pride. Thus, the prologue to *Cadmus* eulogized the monarch and interpolated a synopsis of the king's war for the French nation. It was thinly veiled allegorical propaganda which, presented through the attractive means of music drama, was bound to affect those who saw and heard it.

The dedication to the king that Lully wrote for his opera was included in some of the manuscript copies sold at the door of the theater. Lully's position with the king must have been very secure, for the composer was less joyful about Louis' war in his dedication than he had been in his prologue. He wrote:

> Grand Roy, dont la Valeur estonne l'Univers,
> J'ai préparé pour Vous mes plus charmans Concers;
> Mais je vien vainement Vous en offrir les charmes,
> Vous ne tournez les yeux que du costé des Armes;
> Vous suivez une Voix plus aimable pour Vous
> Que les foibles appas de mes Chants les plus doux,
> Vous courez ou la Gloire aujourd'hui Vous appelle,
> Et dès qu'elle a parlé, Vous n'escoutez plus qu'Elle.[91]

Lully lauded Louis for providing diversions for his subjects, but chided him for running out on them in search of conquest. Louis gives the pleasures of peace to his estates, Lully declared, but he does not realize that his country is restless with fear for its ruler's safety. France finds enough grandeur in having you for its king, Lully continued, without seeking to enlarge its boundaries. And he concluded:

> Et l'Univers tremblant Vous demander la Paix.
> Qu'un Peuple dont l'orgueil attira la Tempeste
> Par son abaissement l'escarte de sa teste,
> Et quand il n'est plus rien qui puisse résister,
> Que la Foudre en Vos Mains desdaigne d'esclatter.

Lully may have spoken for France more realistically in this dedication than through the rustic peoples of his prologue; but the prologue gave the official view and reflected monarchical policy. The five acts of *Cadmus et Hermione* contained no reference to the king, but the plot was designed to appeal to royal taste. Hermione, the daughter of Mars, is promised to the terrible giant Draco and wooed by the fearless Cadmus. To save her from a terrible fate and win her for himself, Cadmus must slay a dragon and fight an entire army. Aided by the goddess of love, Cadmus is successful, Palès turns Draco to stone, and the happy marriage is concluded in the palace of the gods. While Italian elements can be found in the plot, the drama cannot be dismissed as a mere setting for the arias as it was in Italy during the seventeenth century. Quinault's scenes are logically connected and even the *divertissement* scenes are dramatically justified. Musically, Lully's melodic ideas hark back to Cambert and Boesset rather than to Cavalli or Rossi. Lully's most original achievement was the recitative, which carefully follows the meter and the meaning of Quinault's verse and carries the drama along its course. Lully varied his tempo and his harmony to coincide with the expressions of the text. The drama, so insignificant in Italian opera of the second half of the seventeenth century, was paramount for Lully. Moreover, Lully seldom used the vocal ornaments employed by the Italians with abandon. Embellishments were used when the text seemed to call for them. Even the orchestral tone-painting and grandiose fanfares employed in *Cadmus* were justified by the drama. And finally, Lully used his harmony discreetly and reservedly, again with the text in mind. He seldom strove for striking effects unless the drama warranted it. He modulated frequently, but cautiously; he used parallel motion excessively, but he avoided other harmonic clichés.[92]

Louis XIV was delighted with Lully's first opera. He left the initial performance "extraordinarily pleased with this superb spectacle," according to the *Gazette de France*.[93] *Cadmus* ran throughout the summer of 1673, and in July 1674 a special performance was given in the park at Versailles with the courtiers participating. Subsequent revivals were offered at Saint-Germain-en-Laye in July 1678 and at Paris in October 1679, December 1690, September 1703, and August 1711. It was also performed at Amsterdam in 1687.[94]

While Lully was preparing the first performance of *Cadmus*, he continued to press Colbert for a change of residence for the Académie royale de musique. Failing to obtain use of the Louvre, Lully requested the theater in the Palais-Royal which Molière's comedy troop was using. (Molière himself died in February 1673.) Jacques le Mercier designed the original theater of the Palais-Royal for Cardinal Richelieu in 1640 (Figure 5). It was a rectangular room with an open arcade above the main floor. Molière had made some alterations, including a new ceiling and a tier of boxes on a level with the stage, and the theater was still equipped with the machinery installed by Torelli in 1647. It was the perfect place for Lully to present his musical *spectacles*. Thus, he approached Charles Perrault to help him persuade Colbert to ask the king for the theater. Perrault was favorably disposed and later wrote in his *Mémoires:*

I submitted the proposition to this minister, who listened to me favorably. I recall telling him that one of the things which the Roman emperors had observed carefully was to give games and spectacles to the people, and that nothing had contributed any more to maintain them in peace and tranquillity; that today it was no longer the custom for princes to be so concerned, but that certainly it was very agreeable to the Parisian at least to be able to receive these kinds of *divertissements* in the palace of his prince. "You are eloquent," Colbert replied to me smiling: "I will think about it." He spoke of it to the king, who was very glad to grant this favor to Lully.[95]

The king reached his decision the day after he saw Lully's opera *Cadmus*. Lully, therefore, transferred the Académie to the Palais-Royal and displaced Molière's players.

Lully promptly made a few modifications to increase the seating capacity. A second tier of boxes was added, but the spacious gallery above it, where the seats were not separated by partitions and where the spectators could roam about freely, was kept. To the rear of the hall behind the boxes a parterre and an amphitheater provided additional space for the large audiences. The performances could be heard but not seen from the amphitheater. Although the amphitheater was dark, candles were provided for those who wished to read the libretto.[96] Later in the summer of 1673 Lully petitioned Colbert to ask the king to allow the Académie to utilize the part of the Palais-Royal directly above the theater. Lully wanted to enlarge the theater and to remove some large supporting beams in order to install new machines. The composer also requested the government to pay the costs of redecoration and said that its decision would determine whether he could produce a new opera before winter. A note written by Colbert in the margin of Lully's requête seems to have granted the composer's petition.[97]

Lully enjoyed such favor with the king that he was able to rule the Académie like a musical despot, with no restraints or restrictions on his authority whatsoever. He personally composed and supervised all aspects of the productions. Brooking no competition from rivals or interference from outsiders, he produced two or three of his own operas each year at the Palais-Royal and set the performances in a regular weekly sequence of Tuesdays, Fridays, and Sundays. He fixed the prices of the tickets, often collecting the money himself at the box office, and he sold librettos at the door for thirty sous. The seats sold uniformly for seven livres, ten sous for the first boxes, four livres for the second boxes, two livres for the parterre, and thirty sous for the gallery. In addition, for thirty or forty pistoles, one could attend every performance with the right of sitting anywhere in the theater.[98] These regular patrons saw the same opera as often as thirty or forty times a year. Of all the seats in the theater, the most sought after were probably the worst from the standpoint of seeing the production. The proscenium was joined to the auditorium by a narrow balcony. The nobles got into the habit of sitting along this balcony and on the stage itself—a privilege for which they paid double the cost of a first box seat—because there they could be seen by nearly everyone and could also flirt with the actresses. Lully was not happy with this innovation. He had always insisted on a disciplined audience that was forbidden from entering the orchestra or the stage. But in order to ensure the continued popularity and financial success of the opera, he bent the rules in 1680 and gave in to the whims of his wealthiest clientele. Nicholas du Tralage explained the situation in the following way:

The rules have been relaxed from greed of gain, and when M. le Dauphin visited the opera and was at a loss to find room for the overflow of his suite and the courtiers who came to exhibit themselves and their long-skirted coats, they filled every available place, and what began as a mere accident with no thought of ulterior consequences finally became a custom. To hinder the occupation of these places, M. Lully doubled their price, but the sole effect of this was to make these gentry doubly desirous of exhibiting themselves there and having the pleasure of holding tender discourse with those actresses who were most to their liking.[99]

The range in ticket prices and the enormous popularity of the opera provided Lully with a full house at nearly every performance. The narrow, badly lighted entrance to the theater was jammed with people at performance time; long lines formed at the box office, and the street (now the rue Saint-Honoré) was clogged with carriages. In order to see the start of a performance, it was necessary to arrive at the Palais-Royal at 4:00 P.M., one hour before the opera began, just to get through the crowds at the entrance. Jean de La Fontaine has evoked the scene:

Les jours de l'opéra, de l'un à l'autre bout
Saint-Honoré rempli de carosses partout
Voit malgré la misère à tous états commune
Que l'opéra tout seul fait leur bonne fortune.[100]

Indeed, the opera drew its audiences from all social elements. Although the aristocracy who attended in large numbers formed the hard corps of the audience, enthusiasm for the opera was not limited to the upper class. A mixed group of serious fans of the opera who went to hear the music and follow the text stood in the dark recesses of the amphitheater, while the inexpensive places in the gallery were filled by military officers, clerks, shopkeepers, artisans, and other bourgeois elements. The audience in the upper gallery was indeed a social mélange and included many persons who attended more in search of adventure and to make liaisons with the prostitutes who mixed freely with the crowd than to hear the music. The gallery became a place of intrigue and sexual play, exposing the opera to strong censure by moralistic writers such as Boileau, who saw a relationship between Lully's sensuous music drama and the licentious behavior of the gallery crowd. Lully's music and the spectacle on the stage of amorous adventure among anthropomorphic deities and legendary heroes, whose likeness to Louis XIV was unmistakeable, apparently stirred the emotions of the opera audiences at the Palais-Royal. Reports of the gasps, swoons, and tears of the listeners are numerous.[101] Thus, the opera seemed a natural accompaniment to the pleasurable pursuits of both courtiers and cooks. Moreover, it became stylish not only to make pick-ups at the opera, but for a young nobleman to have a singer as a mistress. "A seigneur of the court and a rich partisan make a merit out of having a girl from the opera as a mistress; that is fashionable, it is the vogue: those who did not have a lover would be regarded as wretched persons."[102]

Instances of pregnancy among the singers provided problems for Lully. In a rage he dismissed Loyson Moreau, one of his principal performers, for getting pregnant, but he was later persuaded to take her back by his own mistress, Mademoiselle Certain. He had to cater to the sport of the nobles, who were the mainstay of his business, and to the riff-raff in the gallery, who could swell the size of an evening's purse. He was greatly flattered that the common people of the Pont Neuf sang and whistled his music, and as a former scullion he was doubtless proud that every cook in Paris reportedly knew the air "Amour que veux-tu de moi" from the opera *Amadis* (Example 10).[103] In order to hold

Example 10

his audiences of aristocrats, bourgeois, and commoners, the Florentine was obliged to soften his natural authoritarian ways and to relax the rules over performers and public alike.

Lully could afford to be lenient with the crowd—they made him a very wealthy man. The revenues from the opera and from his monopoly over France's musical life enabled him to live elegantly in his residences on the rue Sainte Anne and the rue de la Madeleine. Although there are unfortunately no records of the receipts and expenditures of the Académie during the seventeenth century, it is estimated that the opera frequently took in 4500 livres a day.[104] The earliest precise accounts that have survived are those for 1702, when the receipts for the opera totaled 26,531 livres for the year. A breakdown for the year 1706 indicates that the peak month was December, when the amount taken in was 5,095 livres, and the low month was July at 1,248, livres. The total figure for 1706 was 30,726 livres.[105] One can assume that Lully's earnings were considerably higher than these figures because, whereas his operas played to packed houses, the Académie suffered in attendance and had severe financial problems in the first decade or so of the eighteenth century. Lully did not pay rent for the theater in the Palais-Royal, and he could probably afford to pay his performers well. Vigarani, the machinist who had invested in the Académie, reaped one-third of the profits during the early years; thereafter, he probably received about 1,000 écus a year.[106] Quinault, a baker's son, received a handsome remuneration of 4,000 livres per opera. In addition, he received a pension of 2,000 livres from the king. Quinault's marriage to the wealthy widow Madame Bonnet brought him the sum of 100,000 écus, enabling him to buy the office of auditor of accounts.[107] Aside from Quinault, the principal poets and musicians of the Académie were paid at the fixed rate of 100 livres each for each of the first ten performances of an opera, and fifty livres for each of the next twenty performances.[108] Although it is not known how much Lully paid his singers, dancers, and the other personnel of the opera, the financial records of the Académie for the year 1713, when the king placed the administration under the Secrétariat de l'État of the Maison du Roi, provide an approximation of the salaries for operatic performers in Lully's time. The Académie employed three high basses and three high counter-tenors at salaries of 1,000, 1,200, and 1,500 livres in each category.[109] Two regular tenors received 600 livres each, while six actresses were paid salaries ranging from 1,500 livres to 700 livres. The twenty male members of the chorus got 400 livres each, and the twelve female members were given the same rate. Since each opera included lengthy ballet interludes, Lully employed a permanent corps of about twenty-four dancers. In 1713 their salaries ran from a figure of 1,000 livres for the two principal dancers to a base salary of 400 livres. In addition, a dancing master was employed for 500 livres. There were about thirty-eight instrumentalists in the opera orchestra, each receiving 400 livres each. The conductor earned 1,000 livres. Finally, a stage designer received 1,200 livres, two machinists earned 600 livres each, a master tailor was given a salary of 800 livres. The total sum spent on salaries by the Académie in 1713 was 67,050 livres. It should be added that nearly all of the musicians received pensions from the crown in addition to their salaries. These ranged from 300 to 1,000 livres for the singers, dancers, and musicians, and from 1,000 to 6,000 livres for directors, composers, and poets.

The popularity of Lully's operas made him probably the wealthiest composer in history, and his influence with Louis XIV made him unquestionably the most powerful musician of modern times. He used his influence throughout his career to increase his hold over France's musical establishment. Indeed, no sooner had he ousted Molière's players from the Palais-Royal than he persuaded the king to reduce their musical forces. After having moved into Lully's old theater on rue Vaugirard, they were directed to employ no more than two singers and six violinists. The king's ordinance stated that the previous number of six singers and twelve instrumentalists allotted to Molière's troupe constituted "a considerable detriment to the execution of the theatrical works of S. Baptiste Lully, Superintendent of the Chamber Music of His Majesty, from which the public already has derived much satisfaction."[110] The reduction in the number of musicians employed by Molière's players was necessary to give Lully every advantage to perfect his productions, the ordinance concluded. A subsequent statute in 1675 reduced the number still further, and in 1684 an ordinance prevented the troupe from using professional singers and denied any person the right to perform operas in the kingdom without Lully's permission.[111] The king's action had the effect of curbing interest in the productions of Molière's company, because French audiences had been attracted by the musical interludes.[112] It also caused the players to join the ranks of the growing number of opponents to Lully and his privileged collaborators.

Many were disaffected as a result of Lully's sudden attainment of power and influence: dramatists suffered because of the new vogue in opera; musicians found no employment except through Lully's sanction; poets and writers were jealous of Quinault;[113] Jansenists regarded the operas as immoral; Sourdéac, Champeron, Guichard, and Sablières felt cheated; and Molière's troupe suffered a decline of their audience. Several of these persons formed a cabal and set out to irritate Lully and lampoon his operas (see Chapter 5). The actors inserted parodies of the opera *Cadmus* in their productions. They satirized Lully's nymphs and gods in their songs.[114] Sablières, who had lost all his rights to the Académie, wrote a pamphlet attacking Lully for perfidy in securing exclusive rights to the opera. Not only has Lully duped the king, Sablières wrote, he has greedily pursued his own self-interest to the public's disadvantage by preventing other musicians from performing operas. Sablières charged Lully with cheating Perrin, Guichard, and himself, posing falsely as the inventor of French opera, and making musicians slaves by denying the actors the right to employ them. Lully "prefers his interest to serving the king, the public's satisfaction, and the nation's glory," and we know, Sablières declared, "that his foreign birth prevents him from having the sentiments which inspire love of country."[115]

The most nearly successful of Lully's attackers was Henri Guichard, who spread malicious rumors about Lully's morals. Guichard also stole Lully's thunder in 1674; Lully's plans to set off fireworks in front of his hôtel to celebrate the king's victory in Franche-Comté misfired, but Guichard's comparable spectacle succeeded, with the result that Louis granted Guichard's request to establish an Académie des spectacles. A brevet from Louis in August 1674 gave the Académie, specifically Guichard, the right to supervise the production of carrousels, tournaments, games, matches, and fireworks. Guichard was permitted to construct amphitheaters in Paris for these events, but he could not use musicians.[116] Guichard's fortunes fell as quickly as they had risen, however, with the outbreak of a scandal in 1675. Guichard deserted his mistress, the opera singer Marie Aubry, and she, wishing to strike back, told Lully that Guichard had hired her brother Sebastien to poison Lully. The composer complained to the king and filed suit against Guichard on May 12. Guichard denied the charge and accused Lully of jealousy and debauchery.[117] Witnesses were heard, and on May 22 Guichard was incarcerated in the Grand-Châtelet. The trial was swift because Colbert wrote the procureur général that the king wanted the matter promptly settled. Moreover, on June 14, 1678, Colbert informed Harlay that the king did not want the brevet issued to Guichard in 1674 to be registered; consequently, it was withdrawn.[118] Guichard promptly fled to Spain; he was later exonerated in the matter of poisoning Lully, but his challenge to Lully's supremacy had failed, and he had lost his Académie des spectacles.

Although his opponents' criticism did not abate, Lully weathered the attacks and piloted the Académie royale de musique to further successes. For many years Lully had been skeptical of the possibility of creating operas that were distinctively French. He learned from the methods of Perrin and Cambert, however, and subsequently forged a music drama that was not only intrinsically French, but which served the king's interests and was useful in magnifying the policies of the crown. After having sponsored several academies in the 1660's in order to stimulate and centralize the arts and sciences in France, Louis XIV saw the value of an academy of music and gave his chief composer absolute authority to operate it. Lully was so successful that the king granted him the right to make the Académie hereditary in his family. On Lully's death in 1678, the king issued an ordinance giving control of the Académie to Lully's son-in-law Jean-Nicolas de Francine for three years, and in March 1689 Louis extended Francine's privilege for ten years on condition that he pay Lully's widow 10,000 livres a year and other sums to her children. Financial difficulties forced Francine to take on a partner, and when the privilège was extended in 1698, it was accorded jointly to Francine and Hyacinthe Goureault du Mont, commandant of the dauphin's stable.[119] The Académie was never as successful after Lully's death. Under the Florentine, however, it had flourished. The French people were given the same operas that the court enjoyed at Versailles and Fontainebleau. Both court and citizenry were treated to the spectacle of the opulence and grandeur that were the hallmark of the royal absolutism under Louis XIV.

✤ 5

The Operas of Lully

Elements of Style

Jean-Baptiste Lully controlled every aspect of operatic composition and production in Louis XIV's France (Figure 12). He
was aided in this stupendous task by many individuals and groups:
the king, Philippe Quinault, the Académie des inscriptions et
belles-lettres, the composer's assistants Jean-François Lalouette
and Pascal Colasse, the ballet master Pierre Beauchamps, the
machinist Carlo Vigarani, and others. Quinault took the initial
step in the production of an opera by selecting several subjects
and submitting them to Louis XIV for consideration. The
monarch made the final choice of subject. After Quinault had
sketched a general design for the piece, Lully arranged the
sequence of acts and conceived the special *divertissements*, dances,
and spectacular scenes which he later worked into the operas.
Quinault then composed the text. Acting on the king's instructions, Quinault submitted each finished scene to the "petite
Académie" (Académie des inscriptions). Although the final libretto was chiefly Quinault's, the poet was obliged to adopt
textual revisions made by Charles Perrault and other members
of the Académie. After having incorporated these modifications,
Quinault turned the text over to Lully, who always had the last
word. Lully was free to accept or reject the changes recommended
by the Académie and to alter Quinault's score to suit his musical
and dramatic requirements. It was common practice for Lully
to return the libretto to Quinault for additional, often extensive,
revisions. Indeed, Quinault was forced to work through twenty
revisions of certain scenes from the opera *Phaéton* in order to

Figure 12. Jean-Baptiste Lully, a lithograph after the portrait by Pierre Mignard. (Photograph courtesy of the Bibliothèque Nationale, département de la musique.)

make the hero less merciless and brutal than he appeared in Quinault's first draught. Thus, despite the importance of the text in the tragédie lyrique, the composer's will prevailed over the poet's. "The musician," wrote Viéville, "had the patience and the talent to lead the poet by the hand."[1]

Once the text had been shaped to his taste, Lully committed it to memory and then composed the score. Seated at his clavecin, he worked day and night until each air and recitative was firmly fixed in his mind. He then called in one of his secretaries, to whom he dictated the score. During the three months that he usually devoted to the composition, Lully worked assiduously, seldom leaving his house, never seeking the opinion of others on his music, and rarely playing portions of the score for visitors. Although he was criticized for refusing out of vanity the assistance of other composers and dramatists, Lully carefully guarded his score from all eyes but the king's. "He had a kind of justification for excusing himself when he did not consult anyone on the operas which he was going to bring to light; it is that the king paid him the honor of being anxious to be the first to have it: the king would not tolerate anyone seeing them [the operas] before him."[2]

Lully always tried to maintain the same rigid standards and personal control over the performance of his operas that he exercised during their composition. He was a relentless drill-master with his orchestra. Listening to a rehearsal from the back of the theater, he could quickly identify any violinist who played a wrong note or was careless in his execution. He demanded precision and accuracy from his musicians and would not allow the violinists to embellish the score with agréments of their own invention. It was not uncommon for Lully to punish a stubborn or forgetful player by smashing his instrument. The result of Lully's authoritarianism and musicianship, however, was that his orchestra attained European renown, especially for precision bowing and sharp attack.

Lully was no less the strict disciplinarian with his singers than with his instrumentalists. Weeks before the general rehearsals began Lully worked individually with the actors, carefully directing their every gesture and drilling them in the inflections, the accents, and the declamatory style of delivery which he had studied at the Comédie-Française. He controlled the musical expression of his singers by forbidding the florid vocalizing common in Italian opera. An enemy of individuality, Lully would not permit the singers to embellish their parts. Nor would he tolerate prima donnas. Lully tried to forestall the popularity of an individual singer; he treated all as equals, playing no favorites and sternly suppressing jealous rivalries among his performers.

Despite Lully's preeminence, the backbone of his operas was the libretto. Unlike the dramatic anarchy of Italian opera, in which a loosely knit, often incoherent plot was casually devised to provide a setting for a string of florid arias, French opera was primarily a drama to which the embellishments of music and ballet were added. One author has written: "The essentially French conception of the opera as a literary form stood in direct opposition to the Italian attitude which rejected all literary implications in the art."[3] Although he was criticized for corrupting traditional classical drama, Quinault openly emulated Pierre Corneille and Jean Racine. In spite of the numerous diversion scenes, which interrupted the flow of the drama, and the miraculous intervention of celestial deities in the plot, Quinault's dramas unfolded with amazing clarity, unity, and logic. He avoided unnecessary complications; he excluded buffoonery after his second opera, Alceste; and he aimed for the order, simplicity, and coherence of the classical theater. Even the ballets and spectacles were woven smoothly into the drama; they were logically justified by the action and fitted the context of the plot. Quinault also copied the meter and retained the Alexandrian couplets of classical tragedy. He was careful, however, to endow his verse with rhythmic accents appropriate to musical expression. He composed free verse for the recitatives to enable Lully to vary the flow of the verse according to his musical design. Moreover, Quinault used many of the same classical sources that the dramatists had employed. From the writings of the Roman poet, Ovid, Quinault drew the subjects for Cadmus, Thésée, Atys, Isis, Proserpine, Persée, and Phaéton; from the Greek dramatist, Euripides, he took Alceste. Renaissance poets, Lodovico Ariosto and Torquato Tasso, provided Quinault with the subjects for Roland and

Armide. Of course, Quinault altered the original texts considerably and added his own material, but he did preserve the essential character of Ovid's ancient tales. His sources provided a necessary sense of the marvelous: they lent themselves naturally to the spectacular scenes in which a *deus ex machina* was employed.

Quinault's principal themes were glory and love, and he doubtless agreed with Madame Madeleine de Scudéry that there was a "marvelous rapport" between these two themes; after all, Scudéry asked, does one not speak about conquests, slaves, and crowns, when one refers to love?[4] Quinault used Ovid primarily because the Roman poet's verses provided numerous opportunities for glorious scenes of combat, sacrifice, and celebration, in which the heroic virtues of courage, pride, gallantry, and magnanimity could be portrayed. These were the virtues attributed to the Sun King. In nearly every opera, the hero confronts insurmountable obstacles: he triumphs over gods and tyrants; he foils the evil powers of sorcery; he slays dragons and monsters; he crosses mountains and oceans. Despite the torment he is forced to endure, the hero is always charitable to his enemies. His reward is the love of a woman. Bold in the face of danger, the hero is tender, chivalrous, and faithful to his lover. Quinault's characters were unfettered by complex or ambiguous motives; they express clear, undiluted emotions. Love dominates the hero's behavior, and, conforming less to the realities of seventeenth-century conduct than to its aspirations, the hero personifies fidelity. He confronts the rivalries and jealousies of love, and he falls victim, occasionally, to human frailty; in the end, however, he is loyal, and he recommends constancy to the audience. "The tragédie lyrique is not content to celebrate the tenderness and to sing about the joy of love," according to Quinault's biographer, Étienne Gros. "It gives the rules of conduct; it counsels, directs, decrees the laws."[5] The hero's love is seldom passionate or profound; it is delicate and discreet, in keeping with the play of manners in vogue at Louis' court.

Quinault's operas began with prologues that were transparent allegorical tales acted out by gods, nymphs, and demons, in which the "official history" of Louis XIV's reign unfolded. The prologues constituted perhaps the most important element of the libretto. Although some prologues (*Roland* and *Atys*) served as introductions to the main part of the opera, most were self-contained little dramas, whose subjects were unrelated to the tragedy that followed. In the operas *Thésée* and *Armide*, the prologues were direct, unencumbered encomiums to the monarch; in other operas, *Cadmus*, for example, praise of the king was handled allegorically, and characters representing the Sun, Glory, and Victory mingled with human characters. The prologues usually alluded to Louis' latest military exploits and interpreted the events of the reign for the audience. Quinault emphasized Louis' heroic virtues, but he did not confine himself to the king's bellicosity and bravery. Jean-François Marmontel, an eighteenth-century author, has observed: "One can see that of all the flatterers of Louis XIV, Quinault has been the least culpable, since in praising excessively the glory of his arms, he has not hesitated to place magnanimity, clemency, justice, and love of peace above this same glory, and while attributing these to him as his favorite virtues, he was indeed recommending them to him."[6] Louis was delighted with this unctuous musical and dramatic characterization of himself and his exploits. The duc de Saint-Simon observed that, although the king possessed dubious vocal ability, he liked to sing to himself "the parts of the opera prologues that were the most laudatory," and that during the large banquets for the court, "he would sing these same praises between his teeth when the airs which accompanied them were played."[7]

Quinault's free, elastic verse and his own experience as a composer of ballets enabled Lully to compose diversified scores.[8] His music lacked the harmonic audacity of the Italians: he avoided startling modulations, dissonant chords, and abrupt rhythmic shifts, and he employed standard musical ingredients in every opera; nevertheless, he blended his formula with a sufficiently variegated assortment of solo airs, choruses, duets, ballets, and concerts to insure variety. He also kept his audience interested by using a variety of machines, decorations, and fancy costumes, and by contriving spectacular combats and awesome sacrifices. Lully knew the taste of his king and audience well, and he catered to their predilection for grandiose effects. He created the kind

Example 11

of opera that a contemporary dictionary described as a "public *spectacle*, a magnificent production on the stage of some dramatic work in which the verses are sung and are accompanied by a large symphony, dances, ballets, costumes, and superb decorations, and extraordinary machines."[9]

Lully likewise used a rich assortment of musical forms and techniques to give his operas color and variety. He introduced stylized fanfares and marches to accompany the battles, sacrifices, and infernal scenes. Scored for trumpets in four parts and drums in two parts, the *Marche pour le combat de la barrière* from act 1 of *Amadis*, which accompanied a ballet for contestants in a mock battle, was typical of Lully's diversion music (Example 11).[10] In addition to his orchestrally brillant military scenes, Lully composed descriptive instrumental passages designed to imitate thunder, winter wind, breaking waves, chirping birds, and other natural sounds. Occasionally, Lully used the orchestra to suggest mood or atmosphere. In an extraordinary scene from act 3 of *Amadis*, he composed a passage which was to suggest the resurrection of a ghost (Example 12).[11] The orchestral pièces de

Example 12

résistance of the tragédie-lyrique were the chaconnes, usually inserted toward the end of an opera as an introduction to the choral apotheosis. Composed for a five-part ensemble of strings and winds, Lully's chaconnes were variations on a rhythmic pattern over a bass that was freely varied. They were majestic instrumental edifices that heralded the optimistic resolution of the drama.

Lully's choruses were no less massive. Eschewing contrapuntal textures, the composer constructed four-part tonal blocks, which moved energetically, chord by chord, to a clear resolution. Lully was especially fond of antiphonal effects and often used large and small choruses in juxtaposition. In act 3, scene 1 of *Amadis*, for example, he achieved a remarkable musical and dramatic contrast by alternating a chorus of jailers with one of prisoners. The mood of the scene was established in an orchestral prelude, in which Lully used chromatic harmony (a rare practice for him) and the suggestion of a contrapuntal texture to provide a grief motif. The music modulated from an introduction in c minor to the relative major (E♭); it touched on the key of G major, and returned to the initial c minor for the entrance of the chorus. The passages for the prisoners were marked "doux," and the hymn-like music moved by whole and half notes; many tones were successively repeated. The prisoners sang: "Ciel! finissez nos peines." In a distinctly different style, in which the music moved by eighth notes and was marked "fort," the jailers sang: "Vos clameurs seront vaines." The prisoners responded: "Ciel! Ô Ciel! quel supplice! hélas! Ciel!" Shifting into the relative major for this supplication, Lully employed an affective appoggiatura on "Ô Ciel," and a diminished seventh chord on "supplice." The jailers completed this short but poignant passage in c minor: "Le ciel ne nous écoute pas."[12] Lully's choruses usually participated in the drama, as they did in *Amadis*, but the composer also used them occasionally to comment on the action, in the manner of a Greek chorus. Their most important function, however, was to interrupt the tiresome string of recitatives without disturbing the unity of the drama.

Although the public and the court were doubtless drawn to the opera primarily by the *spectacle*, the fundamental ingredient of the tragédie-lyrique was the recitative. It was the recitative that welded music and drama into a unified composition. Lully's paramount artistic aim was to project the text lucidly and directly. His great achievement was creating a style of musical declamation that, tailored to the French language, clothed the verse without smothering it. The first law of Lully's recitative style, which was reminiscent of Baïf's, was that the music must conform to the rhythm of the verse: he, therefore, observed strictly syllabic diction and accentuation on the rhyme and on the caesura. The phrasing of the vocal line, the melodic curve, the inaudible shifts in meter—all were regulated by the rhythm of the verse, or, at times, by the emotions expressed in the text. In other words, the Italian practice of allowing the melodic curve to govern the verse, leaving important aspects of the rhythm to the singer, was simply reversed in French opera.

Moreover, Lully abandoned clear demarcations between recitative and aria, a characteristic of Italian opera. The seed of a Lully air was planted within the recitative and germinated imperceptibly from it. The composer created this musical metamorphosis when the text called for emotional climax. And the air which it yielded was very different from the species grown in Italian operatic gardens: its coloratura was pruned and it was sprayed to resist chromatic blight. Lully reserved agréments, dissonances, abrupt key changes, and appoggiaturas for especially affective moments in the drama, and his sparing use of these devices made them all the more striking when they did appear. Lully's harmony was, thus, basically conservative: he used cross relations and parallel motion repeatedly; his chords were mainly consonant, and his frequent and clear cadences were usually in the tonic. Generally, the airs were either standard binary or da capo form, and they were accompanied. Most were enclosed by orchestral ritornelli. Removed from the context of the drama and divested of the interruptions of *spectacle* scenes, both the recitatives and the airs of Lully's operas seem dull and lifeless. The harmonies lacked richness and musical interest and his rhythms were stereotyped. The absence of counterpoint and the frequency of cadences gave his music a listless, static quality.[13] Yet, Lully's prolix recitatives and airs were the heart and soul of the tragédie-lyrique; they carried the opera and differentiated it from both the classical drama and the court ballet. The important fact is that the tragédie-lyrique was, indeed, a drama, and Lully's music was dramatic music, not concert music.

Historical Perspective

Produced in April 1673, Lully's first opera, *Cadmus*, was a success at court and in Paris (see Chapter 4), and the composer followed it quickly with a new opera, *Alceste*. The king attended the first performance of *Alceste* at Versailles in November 1673, and, according to Madame de Sévigné, he went to subsequent performances in Paris.[14] The opera was very well received by the courtiers and by the *Mercure*.

Reactions from other quarters were less favorable. Lully had many enemies, and there was a literary clique led by Jean Racine and Nicolas Boileau-Despréaux which, partly out of jealousy, criticized Quinault for his feeble verse and boring subjects. During the performances of *Alceste* in January, a sonnet ridiculing the opera was circulated in Paris:

> Dieux! le bel opéra, rien n'est plus pitoyable.
> Cerbère y vient japer d'un aboy lamentable,
> O quelle musique de chien.[15]
> Chaque Démon d'une Joye effroyable
> Y fait aussi le musicien.
> O quelle musique de Diable.
> Les ombres, les esprits par de tristes clameurs
> Versent en musique des pleurs.
> O la musique déplorable.
> Par trois fois répétons—le bien,
> O la musique déplorable.
> O quelle musique de chien,
> O quelle musique de Diable.[16]

One literary figure, Pierre Perrault, however, came to the defense of the opera. In Perrault's imaginary dialogue between Cléon and Aristippe, Cléon suggests that the only persons disliking opera are the musicans who do not perform in it, the poets who write for the theater, and the friends of the marquis de Sourdéac.

Cléon also points out the approbation which the opera won at court.[17]

In disputes of this type, it was Louis' verdict that really counted. The king indicated his approval of *Alceste* by coming to Paris for performances and by ordering that it be produced at Versailles for the festival celebrating the conquest of Franche-Comté in July, 1673 (see Chapter 6). Years later, on the occasion of the first edition of the printed score of *Alceste* (1708), Lully's second son, Jean-Baptiste, wrote that of all his father's works, *Alceste* "belonged more particularly than the others to Your Majesty." While the public wavered in its judgment, "Your Majesty's taste was its law and led to the praises that this work always received afterwards."[18]

The drama concerns the love affair of Admète, king of Thessaly, and Alceste, princess of Yolcos. King Lycomède of Scyros also loves Alceste and carries her off in his ship during a water festival. In act 2, Admète and Hercules (who also loves the young maiden) pursue Lycomède and lay siege to Scyros. Alceste is freed by Hercules, but Admète, having been wounded mortally, appeals to Apollo, who agrees to spare the hero if someone is sacrificed. Alceste herself fulfills the bargain, but, after an elaborate funeral scene, Hercules agrees to enter the underworld in search of Alceste, if Admète will relinquish her to him. In act 4, Charon transports Hercules across the river Styx and delivers him to Pluto. After having found Alceste, Hercules returns with her in act 5. Moved by the sorrow of the farewells between Alceste and Admète, Hercules releases Admète from their bargain and grants to Alceste her true love. Although Quinault's libretto offered a theme and several colorful scenes that were bound to please French taste, it is somewhat surprising that Louis and his court, who liked proud, courageous, and honorable heroes, would relish the rather weak and cautious Admète. In many of Lully's operas, the heroes are greatly assisted by gods and goddesses, but only after the heroes have overcome overwhelming obstacles and have defeated superhuman demons and jealous deities. In *Alceste*, however, the god Hercules is the only male character throughout the opera who displays the human virtues of bravery, honor, and compassion. It seems probable that the audience was expected to associate Louis XIV with Hercules, who for years had served in artistic and musical compositions as a symbol of the French monarchy.

The libretto of *Alceste* provided Lully with many opportunities to employ diverse musical effects. The recitatives, which had first become the identifying characteristic of Lully's operatic style in *Cadmus*, were employed effectively in *Alceste*. Lycomède's d minor recitative in act 1, scene 5 contains bold melodic leaps and intervals of the fourth, fifth, and octave; it moves rapidly into a bright air for voice and two violins but clings to the somber d minor key.[19] In act 2 Lully effectively contrasted Alceste's lament in A major with Lycomède's harsh declamatory air in d minor. Quinault's libretto also enabled Lully to compose several *spectacles:* in act 1, scene 7 the nymphs of the sea joined sailors and fishermen for a marine festival. During the scene, Cephise (confidante of Alceste), dressed as a sea nymph, expressed an attitude toward love that was quite congenial to the spirit of Louis' court:

> Jeunes cœurs, laissez-vous prendre,
> Le Péril est grand d'attendre,
> Vous perdez d'heureux moments
> En cherchant à vous défendre;
> Si l'amour a des tourments
> C'est la faute des amants.[20]

The conclusion of act 1 gave Lully the chance to compose a pictorial storm scene: Hercules prepares to pursue Lycomède, as clusters of sixteenth notes played imitatively and in quick alternation by the strings suggested gusts of wind from the north.

Lully also took advantage of the siege of Scyros to insert a long combat scene; indeed, most of act 2 is devoted to the siege. Preceded by a soldiers' chorus, the combat in scene 2 is accompanied by trumpets, violins, and kettledrums. During the combat, choruses of soldiers sing: "Aux armes, aux armes, à l'assaut, à l'assaut." *Alceste* marked the beginning of Lully's musical formula for military scenes: he made a great deal out of them, especially when an opera was performed during or following one of Louis' successful campaigns, as *Alceste* was. He employed large double and triple choruses, instruments used in the battlefield (trumpets and field drums), fanfare and martial motifs, and, occasionally, a contrapuntal texture in the orchestral passages. *Alceste*, like Lully's other operas, concluded with a pompous apotheosis in which the heavens open up, the gods of Olympus appear, and dances of celebration are performed.

The prologue to *Alceste* lauded the king and alluded to the war against the Dutch, which Louis had begun in 1672. The setting was the palace and gardens of the Tuileries. Resting on an urn, the Nymph of the Seine (representative of the French people) laments the absence of heroes due to return from battle; she asks: "Serai-je toujours languissante, / Dans une si cruelle attente?" The mood shifts abruptly as the key changes from a minor to C major, and a fanfare of trumpets announces the entrance of Glory, who descends "to the noise of a warlike harmony."[21] Glory assures the Nymph that her sorrow is recompensed, because the hero for whom she waits is accomplishing wonderful deeds. He causes the whole world to tremble, but he will soon return and must be greeted cheerfully. (Louis was with his army on the Rhine in the summer of 1673 when the libretto was written.) Impressed with Glory's admonition, the Nymph beckons rustic gods and nymphs to echo his remarks. A chorus of nymphs sings: "Qu'il est doux d'accorder ensemble / La Gloire et les Plaisirs." The Nymph of the Marne joins the gathering and a ballet of river gods ensues. The prologue concludes as the nymphs call for the restoration of entertainment and pleasure.

In his dedication of *Alceste*, Lully entreats the king, who had exposed himself to enemy fire, to turn away from the "horrors of war" and to enjoy the concerts which have been prepared for him. He lauds the king's numerous victories, undertaken in spite of the cold of winter, and praises especially the celebrated crossing of the Rhine, which had occurred in June 1672:

Ses flots n'ont opposé qu'une foible barrière
À la rapidité de vostre Ardeur guerrière.
Le Batave interdit, après le Rhein dompté
A dans son désespoir cherché la sécurité.[22]

The Dutch have been compelled to open their territory to the sea in order to stop the advance of your army. You can now prepare new campaigns while enjoying your leisure.

Louis relaxed at Versailles in the summer of 1674, but his armies were not idle. Condé's successful maneuvers against the Dutch at the battle of Seneff in August were matched by Turenne's defeat of the Imperial army near Heidelberg. Subsequently, Turenne marched through the Palatinate and pursued the enemy into Upper Alsace, where in a winter campaign he forced the Imperial troops to evacuate the left bank of the Rhine in January 1675. The war was temporarily concluded with the French having the upper hand. Once again, Lully could commemorate the success of French arms and the cessation of hostilities. His third opera, *Thésée*, was first performed for Louis and the court at the château of Saint-Germain-en-Laye on January 12, 1675.

Lully and Quinault devised an effective dramatic contrast for the prologue, which was set in the gardens of Versailles. The mournful songs of the Loves, Graces, Pleasures, and Games, who lamented the king's absence from Versailles were juxtaposed with the militant chants of Mars, who hailed the triumphant victories of Louis' armies.[23] The text alluded to the brief period of anxiety at the French court when Turenne was forced into a temporary retreat by the armies of the emperor and the Elector of Brandenburg. The conflict between Venus, representing the call to pleasure, and Mars, representing the call to war, was resolved in a blend of songs of love and songs of victory. The compatibility of glory and love formed the principal theme in the remainder of the opera.

This theme also runs through Lully's opera *Atys*, which was performed for the king at Saint-Germain on January 10, 1676. The winter campaign against the Dutch and the Imperial forces had brought tragedy to the French—the death of Henri de la Tour, vicomte Turenne. In January, Louis waited restlessly for the spring thaw in order again to take command of his troops for an invasion of Flanders. In the prologue to *Atys*, Time and a chorus of Hours complain about the ice and cold of the winter season, but a Zephyr laments the approach of spring and the fresh campaigns it necessitates: "Spring is sometimes less sweet than it seems; its beautiful days are too dear: it comes in order to dispel the Games and the Loves, and it is winter which brings them together again."²⁴ The concluding lines of the prologue suggested the king's disposition: "The time for games and rest helps him to think about new conquests."

Louis XIV was so fond of *Atys* that he ordered it repeated in his chambers and at Saint-Germain in 1678 and 1682; it became known as "the king's opera." Elsewhere, judgments of *Atys* were qualified: Madame de Sévigné commended the decorations and costumes, but found Lully's symphonies soporific and Quinault's characters weak.²⁵ In Paris, *Atys* was received with indifference, especially in comparison to the furor aroused by Lully's next opera, *Isis*.

When *Isis* was first performed in January 1677, the court was occupied with gossip about Louis' newest amour. Madame de Montespan, who had been the king's mistress for ten years, was temporarily replaced by Madame de Ludres. Montespan's jealousy was common knowledge. Accustomed to the allusions to contemporary persons and events in Lully's operas, the courtiers detected a striking similarity between the character of Isis (also called Io) and Madame de Ludres, and between Juno and Montespan. Madame de Sévigné referred to Ludres as "the beautiful Isis," and on June 15, 1677, she reported to Madame de Grignan that "Io was at Mass."²⁶

The cause of the court's amusement and of Montespan's anger was that Isis, or Io, was the sympathetic heroine of the opera, while Juno was the jealous and spiteful villainess. In the first act, Io, the nymph of the river Inachus, rebuffs the affections of her lover Hiérax and confesses her passion for the god Jupiter. Descending from the heavens, Mercury assures Io that Jupiter shares her feelings and is coming to greet her. In a pompous concluding scene, Jupiter, whose likeness to Louis is indisputable, arrives in the company of the gods and announces his intention to protect the innocent, defeat tyrants, and bring peace to the earth. Enveloped in clouds that hide them from the jealous eye of Juno, Jupiter and Io profess their love.²⁷ Mercury warns them, however, that Juno and her friend Iris have arrived on the earth and are seeking vengeance. Undaunted by Iris' failure to find the lovers, the suspicious goddess finally pierces Jupiter's clouds. She conceals her wrath, however, and invites Io to accompany the gods on their return to the heavens. Io realizes too late that she has been tricked, as Juno and the Furies of hell carry the nymph to the icy, northern lands of the savage Scythians. Tormented by the fiends of War, Sickness, Famine, Fire, and Flood, Io cries out: "Is it so great a crime to love what the entire universe adores?" This question in particular was proof to the French court that Quinault was referring to the love triangle involving Louis XIV. In act 5, Jupiter rescues Io from the river where the Furies have finally thrown her, but he opines that fate and Juno's inflexibility render him helpless to do anything further (an interesting commentary on Montespan's hold upon the king). Satisfied with her victory, Juno now offers to free Io and to establish her in heaven as the goddess Isis, on the condition that Jupiter vows never to look at another woman. The god agrees but chides Juno for her inability to rise above jealousy. Juno replies that Jupiter is the master of everything except his own heart.[28]

Irritated by the audacious representation of herself as Juno, Madame de Montespan complained to the king and demanded the dismissal of Philippe Quinault as Lully's librettist. She had made previous attempts to have the poet replaced by her protégé, the fabulist Jean de la Fontaine, and she probably suspected that Quinault was treating her to his own brand of revenge. The poet professed complete innocence in the matter, however, and claimed that no comparison between Montespan and Juno was intended. Nevertheless, Louis XIV dismissed Quinault from further service at the court. *Isis* was not performed again in Paris until 1704. Lully, who was as culpable as Quinault, came away from the affair unscathed. The verse of a popular song of the time implied that the king had made Quinault the scapegoat:

> Il faudroit en conservant Baptiste,
> Qu'il prit le soin de nous oster Quinault.[29]

In order to demonstrate his continued support of Lully, the king ordered a baptism ceremony for the composer's thirteen-year-old son, in which Louis became the boy's godfather.

Though *Isis* fell into disrepute, the prologue contained the usual transparent flattery of the king, with references to the efforts of "so many kings" to challenge his power. Louis' kingdom was likened to Neptune's aquatic kingdom, and the king of the sea joined Fame, Apollo, the Muses and the Arts to warn "the enemies of peace" against the power of a conqueror whose navy equaled the strength of his army.[30] Neptune referred to the French engagement of the Dutch and Spanish fleets in the Mediterranean in the spring of 1676. Equipped with a fleet which was comparable to any navy in Europe, Admiral Abraham Duquesne had obtained possession of Messina in Sicily after defeating the Dutch and Spanish navies. Louis received the welcome news during his march through Flanders, and Quinault, who was working on *Isis* at the time, commemorated the event in his prologue. The poet's flattery, however, did not keep *Isis* from being frowned upon by the court.

Deprived of Quinault's services and suffering from illness, Lully did not provide his royal benefactor with an opera in 1678. With the literary assistance of Thomas Corneille and Bernard de Fontenelle, however, Lully began composing a new opera, *Bellérophon*, which was ready for its Paris premiere in January 1679. Meanwhile, in the summer of 1678, Louis XIV concluded the war against Holland and Spain (Treaties of Nimwegen) and was close to signing a treaty with the emperor (signed in February 1679). In his dedication of the new opera, Lully announced his intention to celebrate the return of peace. "I place *Bellérophon* at his feet," Lully wrote; Bellérophon, too, was a hero "who crowned his great deeds by defeating a monster of three different species;" he, too, gave repose to "a considerable part of the earth."[31]

The legend of Bellérophon had been used before Lully's time by French poets chiefly as an example of how a moral truth could be concealed in a fable. In subjugating the chimaera of a lion, dragon, and a goat, Bellérophon was symbolically subjugating and controlling his passions. Thus, in Lully's opera as in the poetic imagery of Ronsard, La Primaudaye, and others, Bellérophon represents temperance and self-control.[32] Lully, Corneille, and Fontenelle intended, of course, that Louis XIV's virtues, especially his restraint and moderation in dealing with his enemies, were the same as Bellérophon's. And, as Bellérophon had defeated the three monsters in the form of one, Louis subdued the Dutch, the Spanish, and the emperor. The conquest in the opera was performed before a throng of people (for whom Lully composed music to tremble by) who chanted a final accolade: "The greatest of heroes gives calm to the earth; he stops the horrors of war."[33]

Bellérophon was an unqualified success. It ran for nine months at the Palais-Royal. Contending that everyone in Paris saw the opera, the *Mercure* considered it to be Lully's masterpiece and claimed that many people called it a miracle. Special performances were given during the spring and summer for the dauphin, the bishop of Strasbourg, and the duchess of Hanover. The king ordered new decorations and costumes for the performances at Saint-Germain in October and again in January 1680. Louis was so pleased with the opera that he interrupted it on several occasions to have choice sections repeated.[34]

As a result of the good feeling aroused by the peace, the extraordinary success of *Bellérophon*, the solicitations of the Florentine, and the fading influence of Montespan, Quinault was restored to his post by the king in October 1679. The last bars of *Bellérophon* had scarcely faded at Saint-Germain in January, when Lully and Quinault introduced the fresh airs of *Proserpine* on February 3. The new opera was received enthusiastically both at Saint-Germain and in Paris, where it opened in November. The *Mercure* reserved special praise for the scenery, which was the handiwork of Lully's new machinist, Jean Berain.[35]

Peace was again the dominant theme of *Proserpine*. In the prologue, Discord chains Peace, Felicity, Abundance, the Games, and the Pleasures to the walls of her den. As Peace entreats the "heroes of the universe" to deliver her from bondage, a chorus of Hatred, Rage, Jealousy, Grief, Despair, and Discord sing about the sweetness of enslaving Peace. Pointing to her success in enticing conquered nations to new, rash aggressions, Discord chants that Louis' indomitable bravery and thirst for glory are unquenchable. Suddenly, the sound of trumpets and drums interrupts Discord to herald the descent of Victory and her heroes from the sky. Joining Peace, Victory now enchains Discord. Enraged, Discord reminds Victory that she will win no further honors without her, but Victory retorts that conquered peoples offer no challenge and that "it is beautiful to give Peace to the universe."[36] Discord laments the irony that the king's courageous exploits have led to her discouraging defeat: "Did he have to leave nothing for my rage to devour except my own heart?" she asks. Her cries are smothered, however, as Victory opens an abyss in the earth which engulfs her. Lully's contrasting choral groups and shifting modes signal the triumph of Peace and the defeat of Discord (Example 13).[37] Victory and Peace join in a final duet: "The conqueror is covered with glory; people must admire him forever: he has served himself with Victory in order to enable Peace to triumph."

Quinault and Lully retained the allegorical theme of the prologue in the first act of *Proserpine*. The scene is the palace of Ceres in Sicily. The goddess entreats everyone to celebrate Jupiter's victory over the army of giants which has sought to destroy the gods' repose. She relates that Jupiter has buried the chief of the giants beneath a burning mountain (Mount Etna). Mercury enters with the news that Jupiter is nearby, but Ceres, refusing to believe Mercury, declares that Jupiter is too occupied with his new glory to think about her. Mercury reminds the goddess, however, of Jupiter's admiration for her and tells her that Jupiter requests her help in extending benevolence to the Phrygians. Unsatisfied, Ceres complains that admiration is poor recompense for years of love. Mercury protests that Jupiter is too busy caring for a great empire to become occupied with amours; but Ceres recalls a time, not long past, when Jupiter found the energy to govern and to love. Mercury replies that Jupiter is afraid to show his love, because there are jealous eyes observing him in the heavens. Ceres finds Mercury's excuses weak, however, and questions: "Of what Gods is he not the master? Does he not make all of them tremble?"[38] Ceres, nevertheless, agrees to travel to Phrygia as Jupiter requests, and she leaves her followers and her daughter Proserpine to celebrate the victory of "the most powerful of the Gods." The earth shakes and the final eruption of Mount Etna is visible in the distance

Example 13

as the act concludes. The rest of the opera concerns the amorous affair of Proserpine and Pluto and the expulsion of Discord from Pluto's kingdom.

Louis XIV is clearly represented in the opera by Jupiter, and his recent victories over the Dutch, Spanish, and the emperor are suggested by Jupiter's triumph over the giants. Jupiter's visit to Phrygia probably refers to Louis' trip with Montespan and the court through the conquered places of Flanders in 1679. The character of Ceres seemed strikingly transparent to the court. Louis had not only begun confiding in Madame de Maintenon, he had transferred his affections to a new mistress, Mademoiselle de Fontanges, in 1679. The court saw Montespan, therefore, as the jealous goddess, Ceres. Louis' growing indifference to Montespan seemed to be suggested in the dialogue between Ceres and Mercury. If it was intentional, it was a bold stroke by Quinault, who had been only recently exonerated. The poet suffered no reprisals this time, however; Madame de Sévigné wrote: "There is a scene between Ceres and Mercury which is not very difficult to interpret: it must have been approved, since it is performed."[39]

Louis was probably amused by the poet's portrayal of the women in his life. In any case, Lully's influence would doubtless have been sufficient to dissuade the king from censuring the poet. Louis bathed his composer with compliments and took great pleasure in Lully's ballet Le triomphe de l'amour, performed at Versailles in January 1681. The Florentine cleverly parlayed the monarch's approbation into a prize which he had long coveted. In December 1681, during a revival of Le bourgeois gentilhomme at Saint-Germain, Lully caused a sensation by dancing the role of the mufti. The king, who had been charmed by Lully's first protrayal of this hilarious character, praised the Florentine warmly after the performance,[40] whereupon Lully reportedly replied: "But, Sire, . . . I would aim to be secretary of the king."[41] Louis quickly granted the request, which raised Lully to the highest echelon of the court. He sent the composer to Chancellor François Michel le Tellier, marquis de Louvois, who, in spite of his own angry opposition, acceded to Louis' command. Agreeing to pay 60,000 livres for the charge, Lully signed the document which conferred on him the title of counselor-secretary of the king on December 29, 1681.[42] As part of his official reception into the ranks of the nobility, Lully gave a banquet and a special performance of his ballet, *Le triomphe*, for a select gathering of nobles. A contemporary observer described the occasion: "This evening there were twenty-five or thirty who, by right, had the best seats: in order that the chancellors could be seen in a body, two or three lines of solemn citizens, wearing evening dress and great beaver hats, were seated in the first rows of the amphitheater and listened with an admirable seriousness to the minuets and the gavottes of their colleague, the musician."[43] Many of the nobles who disliked Lully and were irritated at his sudden elevation were won over by the composer's flattery, generosity, and ingratiating manner. Before long, even Louvois began calling him confrère. The former scullion had gone far beyond the rather frozen social perimeter into which his fellow musicians were thrust. Lully's talent had catapulted him into the station of the rich and the respected. The *Mercure* hailed the promotion and declared that "when one possesses a beautiful art, . . . there are no ranks to which one cannot be elevated, especially when one, like M. de Lully, earns the admiration of nearly every refined nation."[44] In rewarding Lully, however, the king did more than recognize a skillful and meritorious musician who contributed to his diversion; Louis compensated service to the state.

Lully and Quinault were already preparing a new opera when the composer received his elevation to the peerage in December 1681. *Persée* was completed during the winter of 1682, but the king was too busy with other matters to arrange a performance. Through the dubious legality of the Chambers of Reunion, Louis had acquired territory in the Rhineland and had obtained some guarantee of his encroachments by a treaty with the Elector of Brandenburg in January 1682. He had to face, however, the counter-alliance of Sweden and Holland, which the emperor joined in February. The Turks had meanwhile begun the campaign in the winter of 1682 that would carry them to Vienna, and Louis was pondering on how best to capitalize on the emperor's plight. Ordinarily, Lully's operas were previewed by the king and the court but Lully, seeing the monarch's preoccupation, "was not able to resist the impatience of the public who wanted so passionately to see this opera."[45] *Persée* opened at the Palais-Royal, therefore, on April 18, 1682.

The king, eulogized as a gallant warrior, a charming lover, and a benevolent peacemaker in earlier operatic prologues, was represented as the man of consumate virtue in the prologue to *Persée*. What relevance this characterization had to his private or public life is unclear, unless the encroachments in Germany, the promulgation of the Gallican Liberties (Mar. 1682), or the replacement of Montespan with Maintenon can be considered virtuous. Nevertheless, in Lully's prologue, Fortune bows to Virtue in the contest for influence on Louis XIV. Fortune acknowledges that Louis alone could conquer his (Fortune's) dislike of Virtue. By following me, the king "could have had everything, but you, Virtue, have stopped him," Fortune declares. "His grand heart enables him to know better" and to extend generosity, Virtue replies; "the Gods have sent him only for the happiness of the world."[46] Conceivably, Lully and Quinault were commending Louis for relinquishing the blockade of Luxemburg and suspending operations in the Low Countries, which enabled the Spanish Habsburgs to succor the emperor. This exhibition of probity was expunged, however, when Louis reinvaded the Spanish Netherlands a few months later, during the high tide of the Turkish invasion of eastern Europe.

Although the king was unable to attend the initial production of *Persée*, he had, at least, chosen the subject of the opera. In his dedication, Lully wrote: "You yourself, Sire, have even consented to make the choice, and as soon as I cast my eyes on it, I discovered the Image of Your Majesty."[47] Persée is a faultless hero, Lully asserted: his divine birth places him above other men; the sword which he obtains from the god of thunder symbolizes his courage; Pallas' shield represents his prudence; and Pluto's cape suggests his invincibility. The composer continued: "I understand that in describing the favorable Gifts which Persée has received from the Gods and the astonishing enterprises which he has achieved so gloriously, I am tracing a Portrait of the heroic qualities and the wonderful deeds of Your Majesty."

The tragedy was based on the Greek legend of Perseus, who,

aided by Mercury, Pallas, and other gods, decapitates the snaky-haired Gorgon, Medusa. In Quinault's story, Persée rescues his lover, Andromède, from the monsters, and together they are lifted to heaven by Venus. Lully composed many impressive symphonic and choral passages to support Quinault's unusually militant plot. To contrast the hero with the weaker characters of the opera, Lully provided Persée with harmonies in the major mode, decisive cadences, and strong melodic lines.

Persée was first performed for Louis in July 1682 at Versailles. "What has occurred on this occasion is considered a marvel," the *Mercure* wrote.[48] Louis had promised to notify Berain and the engineers several days before he wished to see the opera; instead, because the king decided the dauphine should see the performance before her child was born, he gave only twenty-four hours notice. Moreover, bad weather hampered construction of the outdoor theater, so that operations were moved to the riding stable, where *Persée* was finally performed after just eight and a half hours work on an improvised theater. The *Mercure* noted that amazing feats could be accomplished to satisfy the king's pleasure, and the journal pointed out that the same skill and energy which caused fortified towns to spring from the earth were applied in the production of *Persée*. The opera was eminently successful: the king allegedly told Lully that "he had never seen a piece whose music was more uniformly beautiful than this opera."[49] *Persée* was repeated at Versailles on August 6, 1682, to honor the birth of the duc de Bourgogne. Lully used a wine fountain during this performance. The *Mercure* also reported that Prince Dietrichstein from the emperor's court danced in a performance of *Persée* at the Académie royale on July 19.

Quinault reintroduced the jealous Juno as the principal villainess in *Persée*. Conceivably, Madame de Montespan again felt that she was being mocked, for she persuaded Louis to employ the dramatist, Jean Racine, for the next opera. Racine had always been unenthusiastic about mixing drama and music; nevertheless, he accepted the charge and invited one of Quinault's sharpest critics, Nicolas Boileau-Despréaux, to write the prologue. Fearing reprisals from the king if he refused, Boileau grudgingly agreed. According to Boileau, both he and Racine found the task loathsome. Contemptuously, the poet composed a short prologue in which Poetry rebukes Music for pretending to be capable of expressing the vivid feelings suggested in verse. The project for an opera by Lully, Racine, and Boileau never reached fruition, however; according to Boileau, Quinault "presented himself to the king with tears in his eyes" and "demonstrated to him the affront which he would harbour if he could not work on the diversions of His Majesty."[50] "Touched with compassion," the king told Montespan that he could not "inflict this discomfort" on Quinault. The probability is that Lully intervened on his partner's behalf.

The new opera, *Phaéton*, was finally performed for Louis at Versailles on January 9, 1683, and four months later for the public in Paris. Because of spectacular scenes like that in which Neptune rises out of the sea and turns into a lion, *Phaéton* was very popular and became known as the *opéra du peuple*. Designed by Berain, the costumes for dancing troops of Egyptians, Indians, and Ethiopians were very colorful. The prologue, which depicted the gardens and palace of the goddess Astrée, was subtitled, "The return of the Golden Age." Lionizing "a hero who deserves immortal glory,"[51] the deiform characters proclaimed a new golden age of peace and justice.

Phaéton was performed throughout the spring and summer of 1683 in Paris; it was produced in Avignon in 1687 and in Lyons in 1688, the first opera ever given in these cities. Commenting on the successful institution of the opera in Lyons, one observer declared: "This establishment seems so solid that there is no reason to doubt that it will always subsist." He predicted that "the foreigners who enter by way of Lyon will be surprised and will be able to judge the grandeur of France by the magnificence of this spectacle."[52]

Although Lully's opera *Amadis* was composed in 1683, it was not performed for the king until March 1685, because Louis abstained from pleasures for a year after the queen's death (July 1683). The king had chosen the subject of the new opera, however, and he permitted performances for the public in January 1684. The *Mercure* observed: "Never have we seen anything more magnificent, more listenable, or more suitable to the subject."[53] *Amadis* marked a shift in the "party line" of the monarchy. Since *Bellérophon* in 1679, Quinault's texts had exalted Louis for granting peace to Europe and had stressed the ruler's benevolence and pacific virtues. In the fall of 1683, however, Louis renewed his campaign along the northeastern frontier. His armies moved into the Netherlands and laid siege to Courtray in November. Catalonia was subsequently invaded and the duc de Créqui captured Luxemburg. It was again time, therefore, to depict Louis as the glorious warrior and his enemies as envious brutes. In his dedication to the king, Lully wrote: "As soon as it became necessary to present a nation's hero, to the glory and the entertainment of which I have dedicated all my nightly hours, I became more aware of enthusiasm and divine passion. . . . The name of AMADIS inspired in me a new ardor," the composer wrote. Ordinarily, in dedicatory letters like this one, Lully continued, I would praise you and contend that the most extraordinary demonstrations of Amadis' courage were commonplace beside yours; "but, Sire, whatever praise I am able to give you would be as much beneath V. M. as beyond me."[54]

In the prologue, the celebrated enchantress Urgande and her husband Alquif lie bewitched in a quiet pavilion. A flash of lightning and a burst of thunder pierce the charm. Granting freedom to the spirits who have watched over them, Alquif, Urgande, and their followers celebrate the release by singing and dancing. Urgande explains that when the great hero Amadis died, she and Alquif fell under a spell which has been broken by the appearance of a new hero in the world. "This hero triumphs so that everything will be peaceful," she sings. "In vain, thousands of the envious arm themselves on all sides. With one word, with one of his glances, he knows how to bend their useless fury to his will. It is for him to teach the great Art of war to the Masters of the Earth. It is for him to teach the great Art of ruling."[55] Urgande beckons the earth to accept a new destiny and to witness the hero's immortal glory. With Alquif, she sings: "The whole universe admires his exploits; let us go to live happily under his laws." *Volez, volez,* she cries to the Pleasures and Games; fly to the support of Amadis.

Quinault's text, with its unmistakable insinuation of the parallel between Amadis and Louis XIV, enabled Lully to concoct a rich musical sauce. Employing every device at his command to project and embellish this text, which trenchantly endorsed the king's conduct, Lully was indeed putting the raw materials of the composer's craft into the service of the royal absolutism. The prologue's introduction, which is pervaded by a somber atmosphere in keeping with the spell and the absence of a hero, is in the minor mode (g); after the spell breaks, however, the duet of Urgande and Alquif moves to the relative major (B) and then into the key of G major on the word *liberté*. Lully has employed, thus, conventional changes of mode for textual rather than for purely musical reasons. Other techniques are even more transparent: in the phrase "It is for him to teach the great Art of ruling," Lully emphasizes the word *régner* by sustaining it for two and three-quarters measures on the dominant (D) in the soprano line, while the tenor sings a rhetorical phrase consisting of eighth and quarter notes, moving downward from the dominant to the tonic. One measure later, the two parts simply shift roles to stress the word *enseigner*. In order to accentuate the entire phrase, the chorus repeats it with embellishments for forty-six bars, during which each recurrence of *régner* is sustained. The style is noncontrapuntal. Elsewhere, the same technique of repetition and embellishment is used for the phrase "Let us go to bear witness of the immortal glory of a King who elicits the astonishment of kings." In Example 14, the tenor prolongs *immortelle* while the strings play an eighth-note counter figure that concludes with an agrément on the final syllable.[56] The tenor joins the soprano for the next phrase—"The whole universe admires his exploits." After a brief duet, the chorus sings the phrase, which is further underscored by alternating the choral repetitions with vigorous orchestral ritornelli. What began as a simple accompanied air culminates in a majestic statement of the phrase by full chorus and orchestra. Finally, Lully introduces imitative sequences and a pseudo-contrapuntal texture to project the line, *Volez tendres amours*. The upward arch of the notes suggests the flight (Example 15).[57] None of Lully's techniques in the prologue to *Amadis* was new or bold; indeed, the composer

Example 14

gloire im - mor - tel   le   d'un   Roi

Example 15

himself had used them repeatedly. What is striking and unique in Lully's scores, however, is the extensive deployment of musical resources for the elucidation and adornment of the characters, events, ideas, and moods of the text. This is the king whom we are celebrating, he seemed to be saying. *Faites attention!*

Glory and love are the inseparable themes of *Amadis*. In love
with Oriane, the daughter of the British king, Lisnart, Amadis
is tormented by anxiety about Oriane's fidelity. She is betrothed
to the Roman emperor. Amadis is determined to pursue glory
and to demonstrate his valor. Florestan, Amadis' brother, loves
Corisande, the ruler of Gravesande, but he too refuses the serenity
of amorous repose and insists that one must attain glory before
tasting love! Oriane, on the other hand, has proof of Amadis'
infidelity but is powerless to suffocate her love for him. The
villains of the piece are the knight Arcalaus and his sister Arcabonne, who is disillusioned with love and seeks to spread terror
and fear in the world. She swears vengeance on the hero, who
has taken her virginity and has killed her other brother, Ardan
Canile. The villains imprison Florestan and Corisande and then,
with the help of demons and monsters, put Amadis under a spell.
Preparing to execute Florestan and Corisande, Arcabonne is
visited by the ghost of her dead brother who reproaches her for
her jealous wrath. Unshaken, Arcabonne prepares to murder
Amadis, but the sight of him restores her sanity, and she liberates
her captives. In the meantime, Arcalaus has imprisoned Oriane,
and now Arcabonne and Arcalaus prepare to kill her to punish
Amadis. Amadis appears, exhausted and near death, but before
the villains can consummate their vengeance, the enchantress
Urgande descends in a ship from the sky and works her magic
to obliterate their jealous anger. Urgande transports the lovers
to her enchanted palace where their own jealousy disappears.

Lully's most effective instrument in his support of Quinault's
text was harmony. In the first scene of the opera, a lengthy
recitative dialogue, the meter is alternately 2/3, 3/4, 4/4, and 3/2,
according to the rhythm of the text; but the more important
movement is the harmonic. The dialogue commences in g minor
over a chromatic base. Amadis sings of his unrequited love, but
as Florestan consoles him by pointing to his courageous exploits,
the music shifts to the relative major (B) on the word *victoire*.
Amadis returns in g minor, however; while emphasizing the
torment of love, he, nevertheless, acknowledges its charm, and
as he does, the major mode is touched again. Then Amadis
suggests that he could take Oriane away from the emperor by

force. In this brief passage (13 bars), the music shifts into 6/8 time. A rapid, lightly syncopated bass line which provides a counterpoint to the voice part suggests the idea of a struggle. Ultimately, Amadis becomes reconciled to his dilemma and asks proudly: "Was there ever a lover more faithful than I?" This segment is in the bright key of G major, but the scene concludes with nagging thoughts of infidelity and the return of the g minor key.

There were numerous instances of harmonic underscoring in the text of *Amadis*. In act 1, scene 3, Oriane bemoans Amadis' subterfuges, vanity, and insincerity. The harmony runs the gambit of minor modes and occasionally rests on a diminished seventh; but when Florestan defends the hero, with the violins reinforcing his pleas, Oriane becomes momentarily hopeful, and the key of C major is used to depict her optimism. A similar shift in harmonies occurs in act 3, scene 4, when Arcabonne, after excoriating Amadis and brandishing a dagger to kill him, is suddenly and helplessly consumed with love at the sight of him. Here, the composer not only changes modes, he includes an orchestral ritornello to delineate this sentient conversion. Finally, in the reconciliation of Amadis and Oriane in the second scene of the last act, Lully presents one of his most effective passages. The scene begins in the very dark key of f minor as Oriane prepares to abandon her lover forever. A brief pause in F major, however, indicates a faint optimism, and as the dialogue of the lovers develops, the music modulates gradually from f minor through its relative major (A), to the slightly brighter c minor, on to g minor, and finally cadences in the emphatically bright key of C major. Throughout the scene, the harmony follows the lovers' reconciliation.

Amadis represents Lully at the height of his powers. He had perfected a musical style that was eminently successful in projecting the dramas with which the king presented him. He was the absolute master of the French musical world, and he was accepted at court as a peer and as the king's confidant. Not even his sexual deviation could shake the monarch's support. Lully had debauched a young court page named Brunet but, whereas Brunet was sent to the prison of Saint-Lazare, Lully escaped with a mild reprimand from Louis.[58] The Florentine had also accumulated considerable wealth. Revenues from the Académie totaled more than thirty thousand livres a year, and Lully derived additional funds from the publication of his scores and from the sale of privileges to other musicians to produce operas in cities such as Marseilles and Lyons. The composer lived comfortably in his sumptuous residences on the rue Sainte Anne and the rue de la Madeleine in Paris, and in his summer homes at Sèvres and Puteaux.

In the fall of 1684, before he had yet seen *Amadis*, Louis XIV gave his chief composer the subject for a new opera. It was produced at Versailles in January 1685. Customarily a new opera was performed three times a week, but *Roland* was performed only once a week because "the King declared that these kinds of *spectacles* bore him when he sees them performed so often."[59] The Siamese ambassadors attended a performance of *Roland* at Versailles, and envoys from Russia saw the opera at the Académie in June.[60]

Like *Amadis*, the new opera portrayed the king as the heroic defender of the nation's security against envious warmongers. Since you provided me with the subject of *Roland*, Lully declared in his dedication to the king, you have had to leave France in order to prosecute the war. The enemy has once again been forced to lay down his arms in order to restore the tranquillity of Europe, and the event must be celebrated in song.[61] The composer doubtless referred to the Truce of Ratisbon, which had been concluded with the Habsburgs in August 1684. In the prologue to *Roland*, Démogorgon, the king of the fairies, enjoins his subjects to dispel their fears and trust the great conqueror of the earth: "Ruthless war will never ravage your happy retreats."[62]

Quinault worked two contemporary events into the text of the opera. The Siamese had arrived in France in October 1684. The poet made the queen of Cathay his heroine and created scenes for "oriental natives." Moreover, Quinault kept abreast of current affairs by making Médor, the secondary hero, a "follower of one of the African kings." The French navy under Admiral Duquesne had conducted a campaign against Barbary pirates off the coast of Tripoli and had bombarded Algiers in the autumn of 1684. The main plot of the opera revolved around Roland's indecision between his desire for love and his sense of military duty. He is eventually convinced by Fame and Glory that he has a more important mission than love; that he must deliver his country from its enemies. Thus, Lully and Quinault not only renewed Louis' military image, they divorced the formerly inseparable themes of love and glory. In line with Louis' latest bellicosities and as a preliminary to his clash with the League of Augsburg, Lully and his librettist boldly proclaimed that glory was the foremost goal of heroes.

Lully and Quinault returned to a dual theme in their next opera, *Armide*, but love was replaced by wisdom in the partnership with glory. The prologue consisted entirely of a dialogue between Glory and Wisdom in which both claim the king's allegiance. Perhaps referring to Louis' revocation of the Edict of Nantes, wisdom sings that in the midst of peace, the monarch has struck down a monster (Protestant heresy) "who for such a long time was thought to be indestructible."[63] To the composer's dismay, *Armide* was not performed initially at court for Louis XIV but at the Palais-Royal for the Parisian public. The reception was as enthusiastic as any Lully had ever received in Paris. Viéville observed that the audiences watched and listened in breathless suspense until the final violin air, after which there was "a reverberant hum of joy and admiration."[64] Lully was distressed, however, because the king, who had selected the subject and had prodded the composer to finish the opera in time for the carnival season, did not order its performance at court when the season came. Lully was forced, therefore, to begin performances in Paris on February 15, 1686. In the dedication that accompanied the published score, Lully acknowledged the enormous popular success of *Armide* but added that he was less happy with it than with any other opera, because "it has had no opportunity to appear before Your Majesty."[65] Lully reminded the king that he had worked vigorously on the composition at the monarch's request. "But what does it serve me, Sire, to have made such great efforts in order to rush to offer you these concerts?" he asked. "Your Majesty has not found an occasion to hear them." The composer may have suspected that, under the influence of

Madame de Maintenon, who evinced pious disinterest in music drama, the king was making a gesture against Lully and opera. His suspicions were probably groundless. Louis had simply observed that Lully was periodically sick during the fall and early winter of 1685, and he was afraid that *Armide* would not be ready by the first of the year. He asked the composer Michel de Lalande, therefore, to present his *Ballet de jeunesse* at Versailles in January 1686.[66] Lully was angry at being preempted. In addition, Louis was cutting down on his expenses during this period, and Lalande's work had the advantage of costing less to produce. Moreover, Louis' illness in January and February prevented the monarch not only from seeing *Armide*, but also from participating in any of the entertainments provided for the court. Lully's suspicion and rancor were not justified but were understandable in light of his habit of expecting preferential treatment from the king.

Lully lost the services of his collaborator Philippe Quinault in the spring of 1686. The poet had been ill, but it was apparently for religious reasons that he retired. Philippe de Courcillon, the marquis de Dangeau, wrote: "Quinault has requested the King to excuse him from writing operas. During his last illness, some scruples occurred to him: his Majesty has acquiesced in his wish."[67] Lully selected the minor poet Jean Galbert de Campistron to compose the text for his last opera, *Acis et Galathée*. The opera was commissioned by the duc de Vendôme for performance at a festival honoring the dauphin at the château of Anet in September 1686. Dangeau estimated that the production cost the duke four to five thousand pistoles. The pastoral opera was also performed at the Académie in September, and it was the first non-German opera produced in Hamburg (December 1689). The publication of the score carried Lully's customary "Au Roy." "You have had the kindness to tell me," he stated, "that by working for Monseigneur the Dauphin, I would be working, in a certain sense, for Your Majesty himself, since the tenderness with which you honor him causes you to be strongly interested in everything which pertains to him."[68] In the prologue to *Acis*, Lully and Campistron eulogized the dauphin as the remarkable son of the most powerful monarch on earth. Apollo admonishes the dauphin to study his father's glorious victories over his enemies and to imitate the example of his virtues. *Acis et Galathée* was a success, and Lully immediately began composing a new opera with Campistron. Death interrupted his labors, however.

Death and Judgment

On January 8, 1687, Lully conducted a Te Deum, which he had composed to celebrate the king's recovery from an illness, at the church of the Feuillants (now the Église de l'Assomption) on the rue Saint-Honoré. During the performance, he accidentally stabbed himself in the foot with his baton. An abscess developed, which, despite medical treatment, became gangrenous. When Lully was near death, his Jansenist confessor persuaded him to destroy the manuscript of his unfinished opera *Achille et Polixène*. In a flamboyant gesture of moral exorcism, Lully hurled the score into the fire. The act was pure japery, however, because the Florentine had carefully preserved a copy. Lully expired on March 22, 1687; his body was entombed in the Église des Petits-Pères (now Notre-Dame des Victoires).[69] The ornate tomb, which was adorned in 1702 with a bronze bust of the composer by Gaspard Collignon, bears an inscription, which reads in part: "Here rests Jean B. de Lully, . . . superintendent of the music of His Majesty's Chamber, famous for the high degree of perfection he has shown in his beautiful songs and symphonies, who has won the good will of Louis Le Grand and the praises of all of Europe. God, who endowed him with these talents over all men of his century, gave him as a reward for the inimitable hymns which he has composed to his praise a truly Christian patience during the acute pains of the illness from which he died on 22 March 1687 in the fifty-fourth year of his life after having received all the sacraments with a resignation and an edifying piety."[70]

Lully died a wealthy man. Thirty-seven thousand louis d'or and twenty thousand crowns in specie were found in his home.[71] His total fortune, including real estate, paintings, tapestries, diamonds, and money, has been estimated at 800,000 livres. In his will, he allocated several thousand livres to religious groups

such as the Catholic daughters of Sainte-Anne. He designated
his wife Madeleine as the executor of his estate; he also willed
to her and to his son Jean-Louis the directorship of the Académie
royale de musique, providing they retain his performers and accept
the counsel of his secretary Pascal Colasse.

Lully's death elicited diverse responses from his contemporaries.
Several epitaphs, like Viéville's, revered his memory:

> Celui que ces Muses en larmes
> Pleurent ici de tous leurs yeux,
> Né pour elles, conduit pour elles en ces lieux,
> Y fit dans ses Concerts triompher tous leurs charmes
> Son art, de la raison vainqueur,
> Fut l'amour de siècle où nous sommes :
> Et ses chants, ses doux chants, tant qu'il sera des hommes,
> Sçauront charmer l'oreille et pénétrer le cœur. [72]

The verse of a popular air suggested that Lully's death portended
a gloomy future for French opera:

> Quelle pitié que l'opéra
> Depuis qu'on a perdu Baptiste.
> Aigrissement on publiera
> Personne de longtems n'ira
> Sans paroître tout à fait triste
> Quelle pitié que l'opéra
> Depuis qu'on a perdu Baptiste. [73]

A few writers presented less complimentary, satirical accounts
of Lully's arrival in Heaven. In François de Callière's version,
an Italian musician tries to convince Orpheus to bar Lully from
Parnassus. The Italian contends that the French are no better
than animals, because they pay to see the same opera over and
over again, and he charges that the entire French nation glorifies
the opera only because it is fashionable. The French obediently
renounce their inner feelings in order to admire everything given
them by Lully. The poorly constructed *spectacles* are pieced together by long, dull recitatives, the Italian declares. Above all,
he charges, Lully's sole motive is financial gain, which explains
his rushed, shoddy work. Lully now arrives in Parnassus and
states that he has heard a rumor that Orpheus plays the lyre.

Dismissing the charges against him as inconsequential prattle, Lully proposes that Orpheus join him in creating "an opera that will be worth money to us." He suggests that the Greeks are duped just as easily as the French in musical matters. Apollo can provide a theater and the Muses can perform the music. Lully offers to depict Apollo's descent in a luminous chariot to the Palais-Royal. The composer concludes: "I declare quite frankly . . . that I have worked usefully for the corruption of my century, but they [the French people] are no less deserving of the glory, because they have followed the composer's intentions."[74] Orpheus expresses admiration for every aspect of Lully's proposal; he suggests, however, that Apollo likes glory more than money. This angers Lully, who walks out in a huff.

A more sympathetic depiction of Lully's arrival in heaven appeared in a work entitled *Le triomphe de Lulli aux Champs Élysées.* In this account, Mercury conducts Lully to Charon, who ferries him across the Styx. He is met by a group of jealous French musicians who criticize his music and his debauchery before a tribunal. The Muse Polymnie defends Lully against every charge and lauds him as the creator of Louis' pleasures. Having won an affirmative verdict from the judges, Lully enters Apollo's temple, where a great celebration is held in which all of the heroes of Lully's operas appear and the composer is crowned with laurel. Finally, Apollo unveils a bust of the composer and delivers a flattering verse:

> Ce buste est de Lulli la vive ressemblance.
> Son mérite le fait triumpher en ces lieux;
> Après avoir charmé le monarque de France,
> Il va charmer celui des cieux.[75]

To the accompaniment of trumpet fanfares, Lully leaves for Parnassus. Antoine Bauderon de Sénecé, formerly a valet of the queen's chamber, wrote a similar hypothetical account, in which Lully is required to conduct his compositions before an assembly of the great musicians of the past.[76] During the performance, Lully smacks a violinist for playing *broderies* in the Italian style. The composer then mounts a throne and relates his life history to the gods, who in spite of damaging testimony from Pierre

Perrin, Robert Cambert, and Molière, declare Lully an excellent musician and erect a monument in his honor.

During his lifetime, Lully had been accused of manifold iniquities from many different quarters. In the early years of his direction of the Académie, Lully was attacked by Guichard, Sablières, and others, who felt cheated out of the privilège. The composer had had many jealous rivals, but there were also those who simply opposed the concentration of the control of musical affairs in the hands of one man and the stifling, consequently, of other talents. Even the *Mercure galant*, which seldom swerved from its praise of Lully, complained about the Florentine's musical absolutism. Deploring the constant repetitions of old operas, the *Mercure* contended that a city as artistically rich as Paris "should never be reduced to having only one opera every year."[77] The *Mercure* pointed out that at least a dozen new productions were presented every year in Venice. Implying that France had a reservoir of untapped talent, the journal criticized Lully for forcing too many composers to work for him. Lully would garner new and greater accolades if he would permit his pupils to create their own works. The *Mercure* predicted a dismal future for the opera after Lully's death if the younger composers were denied the opportunity to present their own works.

Lully was impervious to such criticism. He cared little about the future of French music and he was certainly not interested in enriching the nation's musical diet during his lifetime, especially if it meant risking competition. In fact, he dismissed his assistant Jean de Lalouette in 1677 for claiming to have composed the best music for the opera *Isis*. With the king's unconditional support, Lully had little to fear from rival composers or from ambitious challengers such as Guichard. Lully was vulnerable, however, to a different kind of censure—the musical parodies and satirical chansons which were presented by troupes of Italian performers at the Hôtel de Bourgogne.[78]

Seventeenth-century parodies took different forms: in some, Quinault's text was parodied without the music; others parodied parts of the text and retained the music. Occasionally, a parody kept a section of an opera intact, but placed it in the context of a burlesque situation. The popular songs, on the other hand, were original pieces whose verses mocked Quinault's fanciful plots or derided Lully's morals. Every aspect of Lully's life and work was fair game. The whole process of combining music and drama was ridiculed; the monotony of Lully's recitatives was especially disparaged, and the Italian players delighted in lampooning a hero's vacillation between love and glory, or a god's descent from the stratosphere. Even the regal pomposity of the sacrosanct prologues was burlesqued. If Lully was bothered by these productions, he did not show it. The king was also unconcerned. It is hard to believe, however, that Lully did not wince occasionally, particularly at some of the satirical songs which reviled him. Lully's toleration of the immoral behavior of his opera singers was exposed in songs like "Baptiste est le Dieu de Bordel," which was composed to an air from *Alceste*.[79] The verse of this song suggested that Lully was being treated for syphilis by a surgeon named Jeannot. Lully's sexual deviation, especially his relationship with the page, Brunet, was the subject of dozens of songs.[80] During a brief period, when Lully shifted his affections to the duchesse de la Ferté, the following song appeared:

> Aimable la Ferté
> Aimable la Ferté
> Qui vous voit un moment est pour jamais charmé
> Moi, qui suis Florentin, j'ai changé de costé.[81]

More formidable and less vituperative castigations were meted out by a few of the leading literary sages. In 1685 Lully incurred the hostility of Jean de la Fontaine, when the composer refused to accept his text for an opera entitled *Daphné*. The fabulist retaliated with a satirical poem, *Le Florentin*:

> Le Florentin
> Montre à la fin
> Ce qu'il sait faire:
> Il ressemble à ces loups qu'on nourrit, et fait bien;
> Car un loup doit toujours garder son caractère,
> Comme un mouton garde le sien.
> J'en étois averti; l'on me dit, Prenez garde;

Quiconque s'associe avec lui, se hasarde:
Vous ne connoissez avec lui, se hasarde:
Vous ne connoissez pas encore le Florentin;
C'est un paillard, c'est un mâtin
Qui tout devoré,
Happe tout, serre tout: il a triple gosier,
Donnez-lui, fourrez-lui, le glou demande encore:
Le roi même auroit peine à le rassasier.
Malgré tous ces avis, il me fit travailler.[82]

La Fontaine asserted that Lully was mercenary and deceitful, and he declared that the composer's wife, children, and all of humanity would be glad to be rid of the Florentine. In the poem *Épître à M. de Niert sur l'opéra*, La Fontaine expanded his attack to include French opera as well as its composer. He ridiculed the machine-driven scenery, the representation of gods, and the trumpet accompaniments of vocal passages. Recognizing that Lully's grandiosity was geared to the king's taste, La Fontaine asserted that Louis

Veut voir si, comme il est le plus puissant des rois,
En joignant, comme il fait, mille plaisirs de même,
Il en peut avoir un dans le degré suprême.[83]

The era of amorous shepherds, pastoral sentiments, and sweet sounds has been replaced by the inept verses, crude voices, and absurd machines of *Alceste* and *Thésée*, La Fontaine declared. The French love it, nevertheless, he continued; carriages are lined from one end of rue Saint-Honoré to the other on the days when Lully presents his operas:

Il a l'or de l'abbé, du brave, du commis;
La coquette s'y fait mener par ses amis;
L'officier, le marchand, tout son rôti retranche
Pour y pouvoir porter tout son gain le dimanche.
On ne va plus au bal, on ne va plus au cours:
Hiver, été, printemps, bref, opéra toujours.

La Fontaine predicted, however, that a time would come when opera would be forgotten and men would give more time to religious devotion than to pleasure.

La Fontaine's criticisms were echoed by three other prominent writers: Nicolas Boileau-Despréaux, Jean de la Bruyère, and Charles Marguetel de Saint-Denys de Saint-Évremond. Although he aimed his sharpest barbs at Quinault, Boileau called Lully an "odious buffoon" and he vilified the composer for outlandish sexual behavior. In his view, opera was a revolting orgy which violated all the rational principles of classical drama.[84] La Bruyère concurred, but his main complaint was that opera was simply boring. He did maintain, however, that different critical standards were needed for opera, because it was more like a *spectacle* than a drama.[85] Saint-Évremond agreed that the main appeal of opera was in the *spectacle*, which he found exciting. His initial thrill, however, soon lapsed into boredom: "I must also confess that these wonders are very boring, because when the mind has so little to occupy it, it is inevitable that our senses start to languish after the first pleasure that the surprise gives us; our eyes are fixed and then grow tired at the prolonged attachment to the objects."[86] Saint-Évremond complained that the music turned into "confused noise." The listener becomes exhausted after hearing the endless recitatives that have "neither the charm of a song nor the pleasing force of the words," and eventually he begins to daydream and long for the end of the music so that he can leave. In general, French music drama made no sense to Saint-Évremond. It taxed his imagination to accept characters singing about both the serious and the mundane problems of life; to believe that political deliberations could be sung; to conceive of soldiers killing each other "melodiously." Thus, Saint-Évremond's verdict on French opera was harsh. The *spectacles* were simply a violation of reason, deserving scorn not praise.

The most effective presentation of Saint-Évremond's views on Lully, French opera, and the popular reaction to the king's musical *spectacles* was his play, *Les opéra*. The plot concerns the efforts of a bourgeois, M. Crisard, to cure his daughter Crisotine of an excessive fixation with Lully's operas. Crisotine converses in song, sings operatic arias repeatedly, and chants such alarming ideas as:

Père, Baptiste, opéra, ma naissance
Me faudra-t-il décider entre nous?[87]

Exasperated by his daughter's condition, M. Crisard summons an eminent theologian to examine her, but the implacable Crisotine reveals that her religion is exemplified in Lully's sacrificial scenes and that her gods are Apollo and Mars. Crisard then calls a doctor, who explains that the girl's illness results from her inability to resist the combined onslaught of songs, dances, machines, dragons, heroes, gods, and demons. Attempting to defend herself against her father's reproaches, Crisotine states that at court and in Paris, opera is the only subject of conversation. The doctor supports her contention: "Je vous dirai bien que les femmes et les jeunes gens savent les opéra par cœur; et il n'y a presque pas une maison où l'on n'en chante des scènes entières. On ne parloit d'autre chose que de Cadmus, d'Alceste, de Thésée, d'Atys."

In the final act of Saint-Évremond's spoof, Crisotine meets her lover, Tirsolet, a young man from Lyons. They begin to imagine that they are Cadmus and Hermione. Failing to break the spell, the doctor proposes sending the lovers to the opera to stay for six months. He reasons that the endless repetitions will shatter the enchantment. Reassuring Crisotine's parents, the doctor adds: "Le Roi a donné ordre, madame; on peut être de l'opéra, sans faire tort à sa noblesse. Les plus grands Seigneurs du royaume y peuvent danser, avec l'approbation de tout le monde." Tirsolet and Crisotine exit, singing:

Finissons, finissons nos plaintes,
Voici la fin de nos contraintes :
Allons à l'opéra, pour chanter chaque jour
Des succès de guerre et d'amour.

Le grand Lulli nous donne deux machines,
Qui nous transporteront où nous devons aller.
Là, nous serons assis en personnes divines,
Et par les airs on nous verra voler.

After Lully's death, criticism of the Florentine and of opera in general became more intense. The Jansenist view of opera in particular won adherents and was publicly aired (see Chapter 8). The controversy over the merits and faults of Lully's operas merged with the broader polemic of Italian versus French music, and ancients versus moderns. Writers such as Charles Perrault and Jean Terrasson vigorously defended the modern blend of music, drama, and *spectacle*.[88] Perrault upheld repetitions in the texts as appropriate to the opera genre, and Terrasson supported the employment of machines for imaginative effects. French opera's most ardent advocate was the essayist Lecerf de la Viéville, whose treatise comparing Italian and French music was an effective reply to a similar work by Charles Raguenet. While he acknowledged French superiority in choruses and ballets, Raguenet exalted the beauty of Italian vocal art. He contended that the Italian language was better suited to musical expression and that Italian harmony conveyed more passion than French harmony.[89] Viéville's reply was in the form of six dialogues between fictitious persons who have met after a performance of André Campra's opera *Tancrède* (see Chapter 8) to discuss the merits of Lully's operas vis-à-vis the Italian productions. In the first dialogue, Viéville charged that the Italian language is less distinct than French and that Italian texts contain an unnatural progression of words. He denied Saint-Évremond's contention that French characters and plots are nonsensical; on the contrary, he argued, it is the florid vocalizing of the Italians that is unnatural. While criticizing the mannerisms of Lully's successors (Pascal Colasse, André Campra, and André Destouches), Viéville extolled every element of Lully's style in the second dialogue. The secret of Lully's success, he wrote, was his moderation, balance, and simplicity, as contrasted with the "corrupt spirit" of the Italians. Italian music reached its perfection years ago, he argued; its present condition reflects the inevitable decline of artistic standards and practices. In contrast, he held that French music attained perfection under Lully. Finally, Viéville appealed to expert opinion to resolve the controversy over the merits of Italian versus French music. Viéville's authority was Louis XIV: "The king, I say, is on our side. I do not want to lean on this name, however great it is, to uphold what he decides. Let us separate from the person of the king all the luster that is associated with his rank and his crown, and let us look only at a private person of his kingdom. One renders to him only a justice that one would not refuse to a *disgracié* Minister, in saying that he is one of the men of Europe born with the greatest judgment and the most correct and just spirit. He loves music and he understands it."[90] Proof of the monarch's appreciation of the value of music, Viéville continued, is seen in his participation in ballets, his support of Lully and other musicians, and the use that he has made of music in his own realm. His loyalty is unshakable, Viéville insisted. In order to verify his point, Viéville recalled an incident in which a young French violinist, who had just completed his training with the Italian composer Arcangelo Corelli, exhibited his talent for the king. After listening attentively, Louis summoned one of his own violinists to play an air from Lully's *Cadmus*. The monarch then said: "Voilà mon goût, à moi: voilà mon goût."

It was, of course, the king's taste that really counted. The biting parodies and excoriating songs probably rankled with Lully, and the measured expostulations of Boileau and others were doubtless annoying; but the Florentine could bear his lot with composure, securely confident always of royal favor. With Louis' aid and encouragement, he became the absolute ruler of the musical world; he got rich from the profits of the Académie, and he rose to the lofty rank of secrétaire du roi. Louis treated the composer like a crown official—a role which fitted him admirably. His compositions served the monarchy by presenting attractive explanations of the king's motives for waging war and by representing the king as he wished to appear to his subjects—a peaceful, amorous, benevolent, indestructible hero. For having portrayed the king's virtues and chronicled his military adventures, Lully merits the title of "musical historiographer."[91] He projected the aura of pride and grandeur of the royal absolutism through the massive choruses, majestic trumpet fanfares, solemn processions, and spectacular scenery of his operas. Finally, Lully gave his royal patron a music drama that was distinctively French, and he made music a part of the general policy of national self-sufficiency. Under the aegis of the Sun King and the direction of the Florentine, music was established as an institution of the state.

⚜6

Divertissements

Although Lully's operas were the principal musical entertainments of the royal absolutism, they were neither appropriate for all social occasions nor numerous enough to satisfy an active and opulent court. At best, Lully could compose one new opera a year, and the productions were costly. Consequently, Louis XIV sponsored a variety of other entertainments. During the carnival season, which lasted from January until Lent each year, he gave gargantuan banquets, lavish balls, fireworks demonstrations, collations, and multifarious recreations. Throughout the year, the court moved from the royal residences at Versailles and Fontainebleau to the châteaux of Saint-Germain-en-Laye, Chantilly, and Marly. The courtiers accompanied him in his hunts through the forest at Fontainebleau and on boat rides on the canal at Versailles; they attended vocal and instrumental concerts in his chambers, and they participated in carrousels to win his praise. Seventeenth-century journals such as the *Mercure galant* refer to these various social activities as *divertissements*. Defined in Antoine Furetière's *Dictionaire universel* as "réjouissance, plaisir, récréation," the divertissements were nearly always either musical in nature or accompanied by music.[1]

In part for political reasons, Louis XIV took his *divertissements* quite seriously. If they existed to satisfy the king's vanity and love of pleasure, their greater importance was to project the mystique of kingship so necessary to Louis' style of governing and to keep the nobles of the court harmlessly occupied. In the well-known instructions the king wrote for his son, he alluded to the importance of these entertainments: "Among the different

occupations of which I have spoken . . . , I do not neglect opportunities for *divertissement*."[2]

Because of the importance he attached to them, Louis supervised the presentation of his *divertissements* personally. He selected
his musicians, engineers, and architects carefully; he determined
their rank and salary and imposed his musical judgment on them.
The musicians who performed in his apartments, during his
promenades, or at his table, and who directed the activities of
his chapel, chamber, and stable, were officers of the crown.[3]
When they prepared special entertainments for the ruler and his
court, Louis directed their work as he did that of other officials.
In his diary, Colbert noted the king's interest in furnishing the
apartments of Versailles in 1663 and his efforts to provide the
two queens, the duc d'Orléans, and Madame (the duchesse
d'Orléans) with *divertissements* such as balls, comedies, concerts,
and hunts in October of that year. The dispatch with which
Louis' orders for festivities were executed frequently astonished
observers. André Félibien, an artistic adviser of the king, commented on the miraculous speed with which Louis' engineers
constructed temporary theaters and ornamented groves with
fountains and sculptured figures.[4] Louis' acumen in using the
divertissements "for his own advantage" exceeded that of all other
rulers, according to the contemporary historian Louis Le Gendre.
More than any prince, past or present, Louis understood how
"to make the luster of the throne appear more glorious in the
eyes of the people."[5]

That the monarchy derived considerable benefit from its
divertissements was seldom questioned until the last years of the
reign. The *divertissements* enabled the king to mingle with his
subjects; he liked them to compete for his affection. He made
them feel honored to have the privilege of participating in his
pleasures and wanted them to believe that, under his leadership,
France was the most flourishing state in the world. The "age
authorizes" *divertissements*, the *Mercure galant* contended, because
in the absence of "this necessary pleasure" the youth of the court
would turn to less permissible activities.[6] Stating it more strongly,
the contemporary historian Henri-Philippe de Limiers noted that
the monarchy sponsored *divertissements* in order to "spoil the

courtiers" and "make them more submissive." "Everything which would draw them together to waste their well-being on superfluous sumptuosity" was encouraged.[7]

Louis was especially concerned with displaying France's wealth, security, and contentment during wartime. Throughout the later years of the reign, when the French economy was being severely drained by the costs of war, the *Mercure* carefully pointed out that "everything is calm in this realm, . . . and the *divertissements* are taken in season at Paris and at Versailles in the same manner as always."[8] Most states must curtail support of the arts and sciences during a war, the *Mercure* contended; but under Louis' extraordinary leadership, France is able to continue supporting its entertainments and sustaining its artistic life. What must the enemies of France think of us now, the *Mercure* asked in 1690: "All their armaments and all their threats have not caused the least alteration in France."[9] Reporting on the *divertissements* of the carnival season of 1708, the *Mercure* stated that money was plentiful, that industry was productive, and that, in spite of recent military reverses, the balls given by Louis, the duchesse de Bourgogne, and the king of England (James II) were unusually extravagant. The *Mercure* concluded that "the foreigners who are here . . . have been surprised to see what things have occurred in a manner quite contrary to what is published in their countries about the situation in which France finds herself."[10] Thus, the *divertissements* were useful beyond their obvious purpose; they kept the nobility occupied, passive, and even submissive, and they offered a constant show of the affluence of the realm even, and perhaps especially, in time of war. In an age of wars of attrition, the regular presentation of costly *divertissements* was a useful psychological weapon which could be justified by reason of state.

The musicians who performed for Louis' *divertissements* came from the Académie royale de musique, the Chambre, the Chapelle, and the Grande Écurie. The instrumentalists of the king's stable performed for hunts, open-air festivals at Versailles, and ceremonial processions (see Chapter 7). The chapel musicians, who included organists and singers, performed when the king attended mass and on religious holidays. Louis' chamber musicians, comprising the Vingt-quatre violons du roi and numerous virtuosi of the violin, clavecin, lute, and guitar, provided music for promenades, boating, collations, and balls. In addition, the chamber musicians played daily for the king when he rose in the morning and retired at night, and when he took his meals or relaxed in his apartment. When the king traveled, he always took along a retinue of musicians, frequently at considerable expense.[11]

The music of the king's chamber was under the direction of two superintendents of music and two masters of the chamber, each of whom was chosen directly by the monarch. Prominent in these positions were C. J. B. Boesset, Jean-Louis Lully (Baptiste's son), Michel de Lalande, Pascal Colasse, and Michel Lambert.[12] The court musician who performed for Louis' *divertissements* and who did not hold the rank of master or superintendent of music was usually known as an ordinaire of his majesty's music. He came from the lower-middle class (often from a family of musicians like the Boessets or Philidors) and his income was modest. Most of the musicians performed their duties at the court for a quarter of the year, for which they received a fixed salary in addition to supplementary sums for maintenance and for special performances at ceremonies or fetes. A musician's salary depended on his rank, tenure, and the instrument that he played. For his services at the court in March 1658, the organist Joseph de la Barre received 125 livres for "wages, food, and maintenance," whereas the violinist Henri Joubert received 91 livres for his work during April of the same year.[13] The standard quarterly salary for a musician of the chamber was about 400 livres, although a lutist like Nicolas Martineau de Bignons received as little as 50 livres a quarter for entertaining the dauphin. During Louis XIV's reign, the members of the Vingt-quatre violons du roi received 365 livres each.[14] Regular salaries and special stipends for the chamber musicians were paid chiefly from the funds of the Menus plaisirs.[15]

After three months at court, many musicians went to Paris to give lessons and to play in the homes of the bourgeoisie. The best composers and performers received pensions from the king, but the average musician was often strained financially and commonly sought other means to augment his income. Musicians often petitioned the king's secretaries, requesting permission to engage in a business venture or to market a product. In April 1685, de Rosay, a master of the theorbo and the guitar, requested authorization to manufacture and sell catgut for musical instruments.[16] An organist of the king's chapel named Nivers petitioned in 1685 for the privilege of marketing firewood in the vicinity of Paris, and a certain Sieur Berard, ordinaire of the king's music, claimed to have discovered a liquid to remove stains from clothing and tapestry. He requested a royal patent. Inventing new musical instruments also led to rewards. Enterprising musician-inventors sometimes obtained an audience with the king to present their inventions, or, at least, were mentioned in the *Mercure*. Sieur des Hayes, master of the dance, for example, was recognized for his invention of a machine that would direct the bodily motions of children in such a way as to insure grace and balance. In general, a court musician lived like any other servant in the king's household. He could aspire to be a Lully, but the number of those who actually attained high status musically or socially was hardly legion.

The Petits Divertissements

Although *divertissements* were given throughout the year, they were emphasized during the carnival season at the beginning of the new year. Theatrical troupes in Paris introduced new plays at this time; concerts were performed in the homes of the nobility; Lully's new opera was the center of attention; and lavish masked balls were sponsored by the king, members of the royal family, and the nobility. Carnival season was the time of year when the young French aristocrats, if not, indeed, all Frenchmen, made a special display of their galanterie and danced through the night with their bejeweled lady friends. France is a unique nation, wrote the *Mercure galant* in 1677, because "the nobles who experienced the violence and bloodshed of war yesterday can forget the carnage today, adopt the polite and gallant air, and enjoy the leisure of the carnival." Many spectators, drawn by "the noise of the ball and of a large number of violins," come to admire this remarkable transformation in our French chevaliers.[17]

The masked balls, which were the leading attractions of the carnival season, were spectacular, punctilious affairs. Tracing their origin to the ancient Greeks, Charles Compan, in his *Dictionnaire de danse* (1787), noted the ceremonial function of gala dances in the history of the French monarchy. Great dignity was observed and only the princes and princesses of the blood, dukes and duchesses, and the nobles of the court were admitted. When the grand balls were held at Versailles, the gallery was divided into three parts: there were two balustrades, which were decorated with Gobelin tapestries, and a center area for dancing. Louis and the queen usually sat on a stage, flanked by ambassadors and princes. A small amphitheater held the orchestra, which included two dozen violins and half a dozen each of oboes and flutes. The ball commenced on a signal from the king; each person, according to rank, fell in behind the monarch. The order in performing the dances was fixed: the branle was first, followed by a gavotte and a minuet, after which the king received the greetings of the nobles.[18] The courtiers almost always appeared in costume and tried to outdo each other in exoticism. At a ball given by the dauphin in 1683, the princesse de Conti came as the queen of Egypt, and she was accompanied by servants dressed as slaves. Jean-Baptiste Lully, who conducted the music on this occasion, also dressed as an Egyptian, and Louis XIV, watching the proceedings from a throne, ordered his dancers to perform "*à la mode Égyptienne.*"[19]

Despite the high costs involved, the balls became more elaborate as the century wore on. The journals continued to maintain that France alone among the great powers could afford such affluence. Typical of these balls were the ones held in January 1700. On the twentieth, the masked ball included a children's ballet in which the characters of Arlequin and Polichinelle were represented. On the twenty-first a ball was held at Marly at which the entire court dressed as Amazons. A Moorish dancer rode in on a camel and brought with him a chorus of Amazons. A mock combat was staged among gladiators on wooden horses. The king presented a grand ball in his apartment at Versailles on the twenty-seventh. Special platforms for the violinists and oboists were constructed in both the inner and outer chambers. The ball lasted all night and the duchesse de Bourgogne changed costumes three times. The duchesse was the honored guest at a particularly lavish ball several days later. On this occasion, Swiss guards lined the street and an amphitheater was built for fifty oboes and violins of the king's chamber, all of whom wore masks, costumes, and plumed hats. Another orchestra entertained the guests in a reception hall. In an adjacent room, decorated as a chemistry laboratory, animals were placed on platforms, and a comedy about a doctor and his remedies, a ballet, and a concert were performed. During the collation, which was held about one in the morning, a choir, dressed in the costumes of different nations, sang music by Pascal Colasse. The entertainments continued on February 13, when the duc d'Orléans sponsored a ball at Versailles. A special tribune was constructed over the door to his apartment for the musicians, and a throne was built "in the style of the Chinese kings." Chinese decorations provided the theme for Monsieur's ball.[20]

Louis XIV was the center of attention at most of these affairs. Seated on a throne in the center of the ball or dancing with the ladies of the court, he presented a deliberately conspicuous spectacle of splendor, wealth, and contentment (Figure 13). He frequently went out of his way to share the *divertissements* with his court. In January 1673, the *Gazette d'Amsterdam* snidely remarked: "The king is coming back from Compiègne and is enjoying the *divertissements* of the season at S. Germain, which do not permit him to push his conquests further."[21] Occasionally, Louis gave orders for special balls to entertain foreign visitors, such as the one on May 19, 1685 for the Muscovite ambassadors and the doge of Venice.[22] Foreign ambassadors enjoyed these affairs, at least according to the journals. Reporting on a ball on January 23, 1671, the *Gazette de France* related that the numerous ambassadors "were treated in a manner worthy of our monarch" and that "they could not admire enough this diversity of pleasures, so singular, so gallant, and so superb."[23] The king did not want to leave the impression, however, that he neglected more important duties during the carnival season. Most journals discreetly

Figure 13. The king at one of his favorite pleasures—a royal ball, probably held at Versailles. Engraving by A. Trouvain, in "Réjouissance de l'heureux retour de leurs majestés," *Almanach royal* (Paris, 1682). (Photograph courtesy of the Bibliothèque Nationale, cabinet des estampes.)

noted Louis' attention to affairs of state. In 1669 La Gravette de Mayolas recorded:

> Le passe-temps du Carnaval
> masquerade, balet, n'y bal,
> n'empêchent point votre prudence
> et votre juste vigilance
> de travailler avec éclat
> à ce qui regarde l'état,
> et de bien régler les affaires,
> glorieuses et nécessaires,
> dont vous venez si à bout
> que vous trouvez du temps pour tout.[24]

The *Mercure* noticed that Louis often denied himself the pleasures which he allowed his court. Describing the balls held in 1683, the *Mercure* observed that "the king has always been without mask" and that, throughout the carnival season, he has worked unremittingly: "He has not stayed up one moment later than custom, and . . . he has taken part in the *divertissements* in order to honor those who give them by his presence, and in order to oblige his court to relish the happy repose which his attentions have procured for it."[25]

Among the entertainments at other times of the year were the jours d'appartements, when Louis opened his apartments at Versailles for the recreation of the courtiers (Figure 14). These festive receptions were usually held on Mondays, Wednesdays, and Fridays over a period of several weeks. Elizabeth-Charlotte of Bavaria, wife of the duc d'Orléans, described a typical jour d'appartements in a letter to her sister.[26] After gathering in the king's drawing room at six in the evening, the ladies and gentlemen of the court proceeded into a large chamber "where there are violins playing for those who wish to dance." The king's throne was in the next room, where there "is every kind of music, including concertos and choral singing."[27] Card games were played in the bedroom. There was an antechamber for billiards and a room for wines, tarts, and other foods. The appartements concluded with a banquet served at ten for the guests.

The nobility seldom saw the king in a more relaxed, yet dignified, atmosphere. One always feels "surrounded by light

Figure 14. A musical entertainment in the king's apartments for the duc de Bourgogne; the duc de Chartres and his wife, the duchesse; the duchesse du Maine; and other courtiers. Engraving by A. Trouvain, in "Grande folio : Histoire de France, 1676-1689," set entitled "Chambre des appartements." (Photograph courtesy of the Bibliothèque Nationale, cabinet des estampes.)

and magnificence" in the appartements, wrote Madeleine de Scudéry; the king "unites every heart in admiration and love for him by his presence."[28] All the magnificent *divertissements* of the French monarchy are gathered in one place, she continued, and "the king has discovered the art of drawing to himself all the pleasures, since it is principally his presence which makes the appartement, and without which the rest of the world would be nothing in comparison." The magnificence that Louis displayed at these affairs was necessary, not for his own vanity, but for the pleasure of all, according to Madame de Scudéry; after all, she wrote, Louis looked more to his public and to posterity than to himself. Speaking freely and easily to his subjects, the king busied himself only with the music. An unidentified author has described Louis' behavior at an appartement in the following way:

I was astonished that he was seated there without ceremony; he would turn to the right or to the left in order to direct the dance and the music, often speaking to Madame the Dauphine, who replied agreeably to him without complaisance. I saw him dance and very well; he was one of the best dancers in the entire assembly. I admired the airs which His Majesty commanded to be sung; they were well-chosen, expressive, and beautifully composed. His Majesty took pleasure in this and indicated his satisfaction when everyone was content, speaking familiarly to those around him. I thought what a contrast there was in seeing him at the head of his formidable armies, where he is the fiercest of the fierce. Whereas here, among his people, surrounded by a thousand distinguished persons, he is accessible to everybody. Yet, the bystanders are happy to look at, to laugh and to speak with a great King who, withdrawn into his Cabinet, is the terror of the Universe.[29]

That Louis regarded the appartements as a way of keeping the nobles out of mischief seems certain. His intention was verified by the *Mercure*, which stated that if the nobles of the court were not entertained three nights a week by the king's *divertissements* "it is certain . . . they would seek some pleasures during this period which could ruin them or hurt their reputations." Doubtless reflecting the king's own view of the utility of his *divertissements*, the *Mercure* insisted that the nobles were kept from dangerous temptations by amusing themselves in the royal palace where Louis could watch them. In addition, the crown reaped a further advantage from the appartements. Louis' entertainments were reported throughout Europe; indeed, they were often attended by foreigners who could see how luxuriant the daily life of the French court was and how much more magnificent France was than other nations. Louis impressed the foreign visitors who "have redoubled their admiration for him."

They observe his grandeur, and through it, they glimpse his benevolence, the *Mercure* declared. They can see that "there is no prince on earth who is able to give similar *divertissements* to his court."[30] Although the *Mercure* probably exaggerated the effectiveness of Louis' strong support of entertainments, the motives and purposes of a king who needed to overwhelm ally and enemy alike and who had grown up in the midst of aristocratic conspiracy and revolution were clearly conveyed.

In addition to the jours d'appartements, the favorite daily recreations of the king and his court were promenades and boating on the canals. The *Mercure* held that the king preferred "the innocent *divertissement* of the promenade to all other pleasures."[31] Louis' "walks" were not just ordinary strolls. He had the ingenuity to turn the most mundane pleasures into surprisingly regal events. In July 1685, Louis took some of the courtiers on a walk through the gardens at Sceaux. Approaching the cascade, the group heard the music of several oboes that were hidden behind the palisade. Several times in the course of the promenade, the same "invisible melody" was heard from different spots in the gardens.[32] At Versailles, a promenade was likely to be even more eventful. Reporting on one promenade in May 1690, following a special banquet for the dauphine, the *Mercure* described the musical entertainments encountered by the strollers. Louis and his guests were greeted by a trumpet fanfare at the entrance to the marais and then by a concert of oboes hidden behind the trees that surrounded the marais. On their arrival at the outdoor theater, they heard several violins playing from behind a palisade. After another oboe serenade in one of the wooded alleys, the group entered the salle de conseil (a small park) for another trumpet fanfare. Proceeding to the encelade, they were greeted by the music of violins and oboes from behind the arbor. Then, after another concert at the fontaine de renomée, they went boating on the grand canal, accompanied by barges of oboists and violinists. Greeted at the Grand Trianon by equestrian trumpeters, they entered the palace for supper, during which a chamber concert was given.[33] Seldom has walking been fraught with greater delights—at least for music lovers—than in the time of Louis XIV.

Boating on the canals near Louis' châteaux was a popular recreation nearly always done to the accompaniment of music. On July 23, 1685, the engagement of the duc de Bourbon was celebrated at Versailles by a promenade, fireworks, and a boat ride. The guests were accompanied on the canal by a yacht bearing trumpeters.[34] In October 1714, the son of the king of Poland, the Elector of Saxony, and the papal nuncio were given a gondola ride at Fontainebleau to the accompaniment of violins, bassoons, trumpets, drums, and a chorus. On this occasion a regal procession was held on the canal and a special amphitheater was built between two gondolas for the musicians.[35] Occasionally, Louis and his court simply paraded around the canal at Fontainebleau on horseback. In September 1681, there was an equestrian promenade of this sort. Five or six thousand lights glistened on the rocks in the water and musicians performed from a boat.

The grand canal at Versailles always held an unusual attraction for the court. It was celebrated in a ballet, *Le canal de Versailles*, which was performed for the king on July 16, 1687, shortly after his return from the initial hostilities of the War of the League of Augsburg. The nymph Amphitres sang about the worries caused by Louis' absence and the charms of his presence (Example 16).[36]

With his fondness for war, it is not surprising that Louis XIV greatly enjoyed the carrousels that were revived during his reign. Like those of the Valois court, the carrousels were usually organized around a central theme; they gave Louis a chance to watch his nobles competing in tilting matches, mock combats, and courses de bague.[37] Very early in his reign (1662), the king sponsored a carrousel honoring his new wife (Figure 15). In a lengthy account of the event, Charles Perrault noted that, although these "images de la guerre" seemed like mere *divertissements* they were really valuable exercises providing useful instruction and inducing military discipline.[38] The carrousels may have had some military utility, but their main value to the monarchy was as another opulent display of royal pomp. Louis liked imitating the Romans, and when he ordered Henri Guichard to set up an Académie de spectacles to plan carrousels (see Chapter 4), he doubtless imagined himself wearing a toga and driving a chariot.

Example 16

L'ab - sen - ce de Lou - is   nos cau - soit   mil - le al - larmes

mais   il est   de re - tour   en   ces ai - ma - bles   lieux.

Nous   re - voy - ons   ce hé - ros   glo - ri -

eux.   Ah!   que sa pré - sence   a   de char -

me   Nous   re - voy - ons   ce hé - ros   glo - ri - eux.

Ah!   que sa pré - sen - ce   a   char   -   mes.

Figure 15. Equestrian drummer and trumpeter from America parading before the king and his bride in the carrousel of 1662. Engraving by François Chauveau; reprinted from *Testes de Bagues* (Paris, 1662), p. 54. (Photograph courtesy of the Bibliothèque Nationale, cabinet des estampes.)

The carrousel held in March 1685 at Versailles was typical of such events.[39] The central theme was the civil wars in Granada. The two participating quadrilles (cavalry units) were headed by the dauphin and the duc de Bourbon, who on the first day marched around the château in a cavalcade accompanied by two trumpets from the Grande Écurie. Groups of pages followed the quadrilles, and the duc de Saint-Aignan, the marshal of the general camp of the carrousel, rode separately and was announced by trumpets and drums. The cavalcade entered the tiltyard and passed in review before the king to the sound of trumpet fanfares. On the following day, the king and the court assembled at three o'clock for the contests. Representing the Christians and dressed in gold and black, the dauphin's troop paraded past the king. They were followed by the duc d'Angeau, who represented Charlemagne and served as the judge, and then by the second troop which was dressed in gold and green. At the beginning and end of each race the trumpets and drums sounded fanfares. The prince de Turenne won the grand prize—a golden sword.

Although Louis personally provided most of the *divertissements* for his court, he was himself entertained occasionally by others. Jean-Baptiste Colbert regaled the king at his home in Sceaux in July 1677. The *Mercure* lauded Colbert for keeping the affair orderly, calm, and natural. Louis was taken on a promenade through the garden, which was interrupted by a performance of the prologue from Lully's opera *Cadmus*. Resuming the walk, they heard "voices on one side and instruments on the other; everything was brief, agreeable, given at the right time and without being anticipated."[40] After a banquet, the king was led to a theater for performances of operatic arias and Racine's play *Phèdre*. Finally, Colbert invited the residents of Sceaux to dance for the king. The *Mercure* wrote that "the oboes were heard amid the cries of *Vive le roi*, and the violins seemed to furnish an echo to all these cries of joy." The *divertissements* were sumptuous, but "without display and . . . without anything superfluous." Similar festivities were given for Louis by his other ministers, including one at Meudon by the marquis de Louvois in 1685.

Louis XIV encouraged the members of his family and the nobles of his court to pursue their pleasures independently.

In 1678 he wrote to the duc de Montausier that he was delighted to hear about the *divertissements* which his brother and his son enjoyed in Paris, and that he approved "the opera and the other honorable diversions" in which the dauphin was interested.[41] The dauphin was indeed fond of his pleasures, especially music. Louis' Jesuit confessor, Père de la Chaise, wrote special verses for a composition entitled *Mars et les muses* (1678), which glorified the dauphin. In it, the Muses contested with Mars for the young prince's attentions. Mars finally gave in and sang: "This prince has always lived in your service; through you his enlightened spirit has gained astonishing wisdom. The son of the Great Louis entertains all of the fine arts; must he ignore only the art of Mars?"[42] Jupiter assured Mars, however, that he would have his turn in the course of time. Jupiter prognosticated correctly. Late in September 1688, the dauphin participated in the siege of Philippsburg in the war against the League of Augsburg.

The dauphin's appearance in the campaign was undistinguished. Indeed, it would appear that its sole purpose was to enable the poets and musicians to create a heroic role for him in the *divertissements*. Even before his arrival at Philippsburg, monseigneur was feted with such an orgy of musical recreation that it is a wonder he ever made it to the siege. The duc d'Orléans and the prince de Conti turned the forest of Chantilly into a vast musical fairyland where for several days the dauphin was subjected to militant trumpet fanfares and warlike concerts relieved only by the rustic dances of sylvans, fauns, and satyrs through the woods.[43] Before he even smelled the smoke of battle, monseigneur was informed by a character in the opera *Orontée* (composed for the Chantilly fetes by Paolo Lorenzani, formerly the queen's chapel master) that your "incredible history will pass to posterity as the fable of a god." In its account of the fetes the *Mercure* hailed the dauphin's virtues and predicted that historians would speak for years about the wonders of Chantilly. No sooner had his brief appearance at Philippsburg concluded than the young prince was back at Versailles hearing Neptune sing about his heroism in *Les plaisirs de chalendre en réjouissance en l'heureux retour de Monseigneur* :

Sans lui, sans son ardent courage,
Nos champs, nos moissons et nos fruitz,
Deviendroient bientost le partage de nos plus cruels ennemis.[44]

This historian who does indeed reflect on the "wonders" of festivities such as those at Chantilly and Versailles in 1688 must
recognize that while the royal *divertissements* had utility for
the state, they also created a dangerous fantasy world for the new
generation of Bourbons. Was there not something ominous about
the words of the *Mercure* in February 1706? "Everything continues
on an even keel; nothing is disturbed; the pleasures reign in their
season, and to see the sovereign's calmness, one would not believe
that he must fight nearly all the forces of Europe, and if suddenly
some stranger found himself in the midst of the court, after
emerging from another world without knowing anything about
what is happening in this one, he would believe that France is in
a deep peace; and that it is occupied only in the enjoyment of its
pleasures."[45]

The Grands Divertissements

During the first twenty-five years of his reign, Louis XIV
entertained his court on three occasions with *divertissements* of
such magnitude that the contemporary journals, as recent
historians have, referred to them as *Les grands divertissements*. In
addition to these three presented in 1664, 1668, and 1674,
divertissements were given in 1671 and 1685 which were sufficiently
elaborate or unusual to warrant the word "grand". Unlike the
regular series of entertainments during the year, the *grands
divertissements* were usually organized around a central theme and
were given in honor of a particular individual or to celebrate
a special event. The *grands divertissements* often required extensive
preparations and usually lasted for several days.

In 1664 Louis ordered the duc de Saint-Aignan, first gentleman
of his chamber, to organize a festival at Versailles in May.
Presented ostensibly to honor the two queens, Anne of Austria
and Marie-Thérèse, the festival "was without doubt to be an
apotheosis of Louis XIV in his youth and glory."[46] The title of
the festival was *Les plaisirs de l'île enchantée*, and the theme for the

three-day series of *divertissements* was Lodovico Ariosto's tale (in Cantos VI and VII of *Orlando Furioso*) of the imprisonment of the knight Roger and his companions by the sorceress Alcine. The first *divertissement* was a carrousel. Held near the fountain of Latone, the carrousel commenced with a fanfare and a colorful procession. Nobles dressed as paladins were followed by musicians and persons representing Apollo, the Centuries, the Twelve Hours, and the Twelve Signs of the Zodiac. The king himself, in the role of Roger the knight, led a quadrille (Figure 16). Riding up to the

Figure 16. The opening march of the *grand divertissement* held at Versailles in May 1664. Louis XIV as Roger the knight leads the nobles of the court and the king's musicians to the carrousel that introduced the three-day dramatic *spectacle* known as *Les plaisirs de l'île enchantée.* Engraving by Israël Silvestre; reprinted from Beringhen Collection, no. 94, "Les plaisirs de l'isle enchantée ou les festes et divertissements du Roy, à Versailles en 1664," p. 134. (Photograph courtesy of the Bibliothèque Nationale, cabinet des estampes.)

queen on a golden chariot decorated with sea monsters, Apollo delivered several flattering verses, sonnets, and madrigals by Isaac Benserade, one of which indicated Louis XIV's intention of laying claim to the Spanish crown as the lawful inheritance of his wife.[47] Louis thus used the flamboyant setting of the carrousel to proclaim his intention of expanding Bourbon power over Habsburg Spain and its territories. In addition, a contemporary account of the festival relates that Louis' purpose in promoting the carrousel of 1664 was to prevent his nobility from forgetting "the exercises of Mars" during peacetime.[48] Louis has brought repose and prosperity to his peoples, but he wanted to stage *divertissements* in the form of contests "in order to prevent the idleness which ordinarily accompanies peace." Games which have the characteristics of combat, the account continued, and whose subject is the escape of fearless, heroic knights from captivity, help to augment the glorious image of Louis' court.

The carrousel concluded with the approach of darkness, but the courtiers remained encamped in the same spot. A crowd of people from Paris were permitted to watch the *spectacle* from the terrace of the château as hundreds of candles were lit and tapestries were hung for the purpose of protecting the gathering from the wind. Dressed as Orpheus, Jean-Baptiste Lully marched in with a band of thirty-four musicians, who played for the queens. They were followed by dancers representing the four seasons, each of whom was mounted on a different animal: Spring on a Spanish horse, Summer on an elephant, Autumn on a camel, and Winter on a bear. Gardeners, reapers, and grape-gatherers distributed refreshments to the guests. As Lully directed a concert of oboes and flutes, a group of artificial trees, operated by a machine, lifted dancers representing Pan and Diane into the air. A ballet was performed by the Twelve Hours and the Twelve Signs of the Zodiac, during which the controllers of the king's household, representing Abundance, Joy, Propriety, and Good Cheer, brought in a table shaped like a *croissant*, laden with flowers and food. In his account of these activities, Jacques Charpentier de Marigny wrote: "At this moment, the eyes and the ears were filled with the satisfaction which nature, art, and harmony were capable of giving them; . . . never has anything had the air of an enchantment so much as [that which] has been seen in this place, where hundreds of different objects occupied the imagination of the spectators."[49]

On the second day of Louis' *grand divertissement* at Versailles, Molière's play *La princesse d'Élide* was performed in a theater constructed in the park by Lully's machinist Carlo Vigarani. Lully's music was the main attraction of this *divertissement*. He composed elaborate intermezzos, each a miniature opera, with récits and ballets which were performed after each act of Molière's play. Lully adapted his piece skillfully to Molière's humor. In the third intermezzo a satyr attempts to teach the jester Moron how to sing, in order to enable him to have success with women. Lully mocked florid Italian singing by providing the satyr with a thickly embroidered vocal line, which Moron, who is ironically Molière's spokesman for reason and naturalness, rejects for its lack of feeling.[50] *La princesse* concluded in a grand manner with a sextet of shepherds and a final chorus which expressed the central idea of the play: "A heart begins to live only on the day that it knows love." During the singing, a machine-operated tree, bearing sixteen fauns, emerged from beneath the stage. As the tree moved forward, "under the spell of Alcine," the fauns played flutes and their song was answered by the clavecins, theorboes, and violins of the orchestra. Marigny observed that the *divertissement* was performed so expertly that everyone declared that Lully, "who was the creator of all this harmony," was "a hundred times more the Devil than the She-Devil, Alcine, herself."[51] And he added that the production had enabled the ladies of the court to discover "the true means of restoring themselves to reason."

On the third and final day, the court assembled in the evening around the basin of Apollo in the center of which Vigarani had constructed the palace of Alcine. Seated on a dais facing the basin, Louis and the queen heard a concert by Lully's musicians and watched as the palace became illuminated on the water. Standing on rocks in the basin, trumpeters announced the entrance of Alcine and her nymphs, who appeared in the water riding mechanical sea monsters. Arriving on the bank, Alcine and her followers concluded this nautical spectacle with a récit for the king. Returning to the enchanted island, Alcine and the nymphs defended their palace against invaders. Lully depicted the struggle in a sequence of ballet entrées for dwarfs, giants, and Moors, culminating in a combat between monsters and knights. Lully was able to communicate the mood of the struggle by employing a jerky, dotted rhythm and shifting from G major for the knights to g minor for the monsters.[52] Although demons leaping about in various gymnastic contortions came to the aid of Alcine, she was unable to resist Roger and his knights; they conquered the island and broke the spell of her sorcery with the help of a magic ring. The palace disappeared in a blaze of lightning, thunder, and fireworks (Figure 17).

> On finit toutes ces délices
> Par des Feux, par des artifices
> Allumez sur de claires eaux,
> Si radieux et si nouveaux,
> Que si les bruits sont véritables
> On n'en vid jamais de semblables.[53]

Commending *Les plaisirs de l'île enchantée*, the *Mercure* maintained that nothing as magnificent had been seen anywhere for several centuries. Colbert was credited with planning "these *divertissements* worthy of the great prince," and of the illustrious court of France.[54] In his account of *Les plaisirs*, the comte de Rabutin declared: "I was filled with such great esteem for the king, and I found him so perfect in everything, that I excused him for all the injustices done to me at court."[55] Marigny noted that the king applied himself so assiduously to his *divertissements* that some *"Duppes"* may be fooled into believing that he relegates important business to someone else. Instead, Marigny concluded, the king of France is a man of many talents who pays attention to all "the matters important to the glory and to the welfare of the state." Although each of these accounts was meant to be laudatory, the authors were correct to link the *grand divertissement* of 1664 to Louis XIV's conception of the glory of the state. In the years ahead, extravagant musical *spectacles* dictated by Louis' conception of the necessity of state became an essential part of life at Versailles.

In the spring of 1667, without a formal declaration of war against Spain, Louis XIV started the War of Devolution by

Figure 17. The spectacular eruption of the palace of the sorceress Alcine on the enchanted island, concluding the *divertissement* of 1664. Engraving by Israël Silvestre; reprinted from Beringhen Collection, no. 94, *Les plaisirs de l'isle enchantée ou les festes et divertissements du Roy, à Versailles en 1664,* p. 135. (Photograph courtesy of the Bibliothèque Nationale, cabinet des estampes.)

advancing into the Spanish Netherlands. The French campaign was so successful that England and Holland, formerly enemies, felt threatened enough to conclude an alliance against France, an alliance which Sweden joined in January 1668. The allies pressed France and Spain to come to terms. Louis pursued his conquests, however, and a French army overran Franche-Comté in February. Meanwhile, the allied powers (England, Holland, and Sweden) had worked out a peace settlement favorable to the French, which led to a treaty in the spring of 1668.

In spite of the war, Louis XIV encouraged his court to enjoy all the *divertissements* to which they were accustomed. After the campaign in Flanders in October 1667, Louis ordered special balls and a revival of Lully's *Ballet des muses*[56] in order to honor the return of "our valiant knights." Charles Robinet described the mood of the occasion :

> La Scène est pompeuse et brilliante,
> plus que n'est la sphère roulante
> d'où chaque jour naît la clarté,
> et votre auguste majesté
> Guerrière comme un Dieu de Thrace,
> des pas de souverain y trace,
> parmi ceux de ses courtisans
> de compliments grands artisans.[57]

Three months later, as the Triple Alliance was formed to halt Louis' aggressions and as the duc de Condé prepared his invasion of France-Comté, the French court carried on with their usual sequence of *divertissements*. While the rest of Europe is in turmoil, Robinet wrote, Louis' court summons "laughter, dance, and banquets full of opulence."[58] On January 14, Robinet mentioned a concert "filled with marvels" in the grotto at Versailles. And on January 21, he described a ball given by the duc d'Orléans in the Palais-Royal, at which the king appeared, dressed in a diamond vest.

Although there were no signs of the problems attending war at the court throughout the year 1667 and in the early months of 1668, the conclusion of hostilities was the occasion for a special festival. Before ordering the second of his *grands divertissements* at Versailles, however, Louis instructed his ambassador to Mainz, the abbé de Gravel, to supervise the production of a special musical drama on the subject of the recent peace, for the entertainment of the Elector of Mainz and several German princes. (The peace of Aix-la-Chapelle had not erased any of Louis' designs for futher conquest, and in the spring of 1669 he had begun already to detach German electors and bishops from the new alliance which was forming against him.) Louis may have conceived of the musical entertainment at Mainz as part of a diplomatic maneuver. According to Claude Menestrier, the Germans were responsible for the overture and the French for the drama itself. The *Drama musicale ob pacem inter Christianissimum regem et regem Catholicum Nuperrime Factam* began with a song by Mars about war. Mars was interrupted, however, by Fame, who proclaimed the new peace and hailed Louis XIV as its author. Fame admitted Mars' insistence that Louis loved war, but added that the French king was, nonetheless, the author of the peace. Mars reasoned that troubles at home must have motivated Louis to turn to peace, but Fame responded with the following récit: "There is peace in his estates; the princes are united to him; his subjects are faithful to him; there is nothing to fear from the Fate of which he is himself the arbiter; it is the piety, the peoples' love, the desire of the common father of the church, and the requests of the princes, his allies, which oblige him to give peace and to preserve the repose of all of Europe."[59] Mars then retired and Peace watched triumphantly as the Graces paraded the Elector's coat of arms.

Louis' *grand divertissement* to celebrate the peace of Aix-la-Chapelle was held on July 18, 1668, and was entitled *Fête de Versailles*. In his description of the event, Robinet wrote:

On veid, Lundi, ce que les yeux
ne peuvent voir que chez les Dieux,
ou chez Louis, qui les égale
dedans la pompe d'un Régale.[60]

The royal apartments were decorated lavishly; the nobles, progressing, from room to room, encountered games, collations, concerts, and balls, and they noted, according to Robinet, that their king, who had made the world conscious of his glory in war; was still "the greatest Prince on Earth" in time of peace. The honored guest of the *Fête* was Madame de Montespan. Louis entrusted the arrangements to several persons: the duc de Créqui was in charge of the comedy; the maréchal de Bellefond supervised the conferring of new titles and arranged the table service; Carlo Vigarani constructed a theater in the park; and the architect Louis le Vau made arrangements for the ball. Colbert handled the fireworks display. He gave orders for the preparation of twelve-hundred powder kegs and several dozen rockets of various types.[61] The fact that Louis made such elaborate preparations for a festival that lasted only one day was proof, according to the *Mercure*, that the king spared neither effort nor money to ensure the grandeur of his court.[62]

After amusing themselves for several hours, the courtiers gathered at a theater in the park, which was bounded by illuminated jets of water. Placed among the trees on both sides of the theater, a group of musicians performed a concert for the king and his guests.[63] The principal *divertissement* of the evening was a comédie-ballet by Lully and Molière entitled *Georges Dandin*. Molière's comedy was an impromptu, pieced together quickly for the occasion, and Lully's pastoral ballet had only the most tenuous connection to the play.[64] Nonetheless, André Félibien reported that the court was highly entertained. "One can say," he added, "that in this work, Sieur Lully has found the secret of satisfying and charming the world; because never has there been anything so beautiful nor better created."[65] The music expressed all the passions perfectly, according to Félibien, and ravished "the spirit of the listeners."

The peace of Aix-la-Chapelle (1668) marked the temporary cessation of Louis XIV's drive to secure the French frontiers. By the terms of the peace, France relinquished Franche-Comté but retained several fortified towns in Flanders, including Lille and Tournai. Louis' goal after 1668 was the conquest of Holland, and toward this end he again took possession of Lorraine and secured a treaty with Charles II of England in 1670; he also negotiated for a foothold in some of the principalities of the Rhine in order to establish magazines near the scene of war. Louis rebuffed conciliatory efforts by the Dutch and pursued his aims openly and with disdain for his opponents. The preparations for war seemed to provide Louis and his court with fresh opportunities for *divertissement*. In May 1670, the queen, Madame de Montespan, and several courtiers accompanied the king on an expedition through Mons, Brussels, Namur, and other towns in Flanders where, on Louis' order, musicians were stationed to provide entertainment for the entourage. All along the route they were feted with banquets, concerts, and fireworks. The procession terminated at the fortifications of Dunkirk in May 1671.

For three weeks during the spring of 1671, Louis' engineers

worked to make Dunkirk an impregnable fortress; five bastions had been reduced to three; six fortified ramparts were erected; trenches were dug which were two-thirds larger than before; and the counterscarps were enlarged. The king supervised the labor and "inspired the arms of 30,000 men" by his presence.[66] The *Gazette de France* reported that the king was so delighted with the new fortifications that he wanted his court to share his exuberance; he decided, therefore, to have an encampment and to produce a "truly heroic *galanterie* in this frontier spot in view of the 30,000 armed men." His engineers constructed a "theater to his grandeur" on one of the bastions for the performance of a "fête belliqueuse." The *grand divertissement* began with a collation, during which Lully and a group of violinists performed inside a tent to the left of the theater. Meanwhile, seven hundred drums were posted on the counterscarp and an orchestra of fifes, oboes, and trumpets was arranged on a large heap of fagots in one of the trenches beside the ramparts. Eighty cannons were prepared on another bastion. The scene resembled a combat as much as a fete, according to the *Gazette*: "Where have the instruments of war, serving the pleasures and the celebrations of peace, ever before been seen? And what Potentate has ever diverted himself like this Great Monarch, who relaxes from his glorious labors with things which only carry further the image of punishment and of war, thus causing all the other Powers to tremble as he plays with eighty pieces of cannon?"

After making a tour of the fortifications with the duc d'Orléans, Louis joined the court on the bastion to watch a performance of Lully's ballet *Psyché* (see Chapter 4). He signaled the drums on the counterscarp and commanded the violins, who were still inside the tent, to begin the prelude. During the prologue, when Flore sang that Louis interrupted his conquests in order to give peace to the earth, the king signaled his troops to cease working on the fortifications and ordered his servants to provide refreshments for them. During Venus' descent from the sky, toward the end of the prologue, Marie-Thérèse and several ladies of the court made a pompous entrance into the theater. They possessed an "air of conquest," the *Gazette* asserted, which made them seem like a group of "imperious Amazons who were preparing . . . a day of

triumph out of this one which was planned for their *divertissement.*"
Louis, on the other hand, having relinquished the bellicose
demeanor which he displayed while leading his troops, walked
among the ladies with "the majesty that Heaven and Nature have
imprinted on his face."

During the subsequent entrées of the ballet, Mars appeared on
the stage and sang about the glories of war. His entrance was
accompanied by trumpets, drums, and oboes, which were heard
from the counterscarp. As the music echoed through the fortifications, a salvo of cannon shot was heard from the top of the
bastion. Such a species of harmony had seldom been heard,
according to the *Gazette,* and the effect, one of "pleasure mixed
with fear," caused everyone "to admire the king's grandeur as well
as his magnificence." During the din of music and gunfire, the
courtiers advanced to a platform from which they observed the
vast spectacle of the sea. The tranquillity of the water seemed to
suggest that it wished "to submit itself to the laws of this great
monarch," the *Gazette* declared. A third salvo from the cannons
rang out and the trumpets and drums sounded retreat, after which
the court dispersed with "a deep admiration for that which it
came to see and to hear."

Once he had secured his defense perimeter and had concluded
treaties with England, Sweden, Cologne, and Münster, Louis XIV
launched his new offensive against the Dutch in March 1672.
He swiftly conquered southern Holland and crossed the Rhine
with his army in June. The Dutch saved themselves from complete
occupation, however, by opening the sluices. They were also
able to bring Brandenburg, the emperor, and Spain into the war
on the Dutch side, and in 1674 to secure peace with England.
In the campaigns of 1673 and 1674 the French suffered reverses in
the Spanish Netherlands and in the Rhineland. Early in 1674,
however, Louis XIV led his armies in a new siege of the fortresses
of Franche-Comté. In four months that province was again in
French hands. Meanwhile, French armies under Condé and
Turenne had been successful in the Netherlands and on the upper
Rhine. In the summer of 1674, therefore, the French court had
something to celebrate, and Louis, who had personally undertaken the conquest of Franche-Comté, gave orders for a *grand*

divertissement at Versailles, "in order to give to the whole court some moments of pleasure and repose from the long fatigues of a trip which the season rendered very laborious."[67] For the opening day of the festival (July 4), Louis called for a performance of Lully's opera *Alceste*. "His orders were executed so diligently," André Félibien wrote, "that there is no one who does not believe that everything was accomplished by a miracle." A theater was erected in the marble court and nearby groves were ornamented "almost instantaneously" with fountains and statuary.

Before the performance of *Alceste*, Louis took a promenade with the courtiers to the marais. Seated near a pond, in the middle of which was a large artificial tree whose branches spouted water, the king and his court enjoyed a collation and listened to the falling water, which "harmonized nicely with the sound of violins and oboes."[68] At eight in the evening, the company returned to the marble court where a theater had been prepared for the opera. The sides of the theater were elegantly ornamented with orange trees, marble pedestals, and porcelain vases. Special marble columns had been erected along the façade of the château, which formed the back of the theater; in the center, a fountain, surrounded by candles and vases of flowers, sprayed water noiselessly onto flower petals, so that the music could be heard. The king seated himself ceremoniously in front of the theater and watched as the musicians of the Académie royale de musique performed Lully's opera. He had seen the opera several times before (see Chapter 5), but, flushed with the recent victory in Franche-Comté, he must have found the prologue, which lauded his military exploits, unusually timely and appealing.

On July 11, the second official day of the festival, Louis took the court to the Trianon palace. Behind the palace garden in a small wood, which had been closed off from the park by a grill, a green, octagonally shaped *salon* had been prepared for a performance of Lully's musical pastoral, *Églogue de Versailles*. Three porticoes supported amphitheaters for the musicians; a dome over the salon opened to the sky. Through one of the two doors that led into the salon, a long alley bordered by flower-lined arcades could be seen. A fountain basin at the end of the alley was surrounded by orange trees. Above the basin, a semicircular palisade contained five niches supporting figures of musical satyrs in white marble. Facing the alley, Louis and his court listened to the *Églogue*. In this little drama, rustic shepherds sang about the king's return from his victories and hailed his pursuit of love instead of glory.[69] After the *Églogue*, Louis promenaded to the salle du conseil, where he dined and listened to a concert of violins and oboes.

On July 19, Louis accompanied the court to the ménagerie of Versailles to see his collection of rare birds and animals. Here he also gave a collation and conferred titles on the ladies; he returned to the château by means of a gondola on the grand canal. He remained on the canal about an hour in order "to relish the freshness of the evening and to hear the pleasant concerts of voices and instruments which alone interrupted the silence of the night."[70] The king's day of pleasure concluded in the grotto of the gardens, where he saw a performance of Molière's *Le malade imaginaire*.[71]

On the fourth day of the festival (July 28), Louis conferred titles on the courtiers in one of the wooded areas in the park and attended a performance of Lully's *Les fêtes de l'amour et de Bacchus* (see Chapter 4) in a theater constructed in the "alley of the dragon" near the grotto (Figure 10). The setting was unusually opulent: a Corinthian arch formed the façade of the theater, and the entrance was ornamented with a large cornice, supported on either side by two solid masses which formed a semicircle whose extremities extended to the sides of the orchestra. Two bronze statues of Justice and Felicity on pedestals were placed in niches in the mass. A shepherds' choir entertained the guests from a portico to the side of the theater. After the performance of *Les fêtes*, fireworks and an oboe and violin concert were presented on the grand canal.

A display of fireworks was also given on August 18, the fifth day of the festival. In addition, a promenade of thirty coaches, a collation, a concert, and Racine's play *Iphigénie* were presented. During the day, Louis was presented with one hundred and seven flags taken from the enemy at the battle of Senef by the prince de Condé.

The entertainments concluded on August 31 with a lavish

fireworks display on the canal. Carlo Vigarani had placed multi-colored lights and illuminated figures around the canal, and all of the fountains of Versailles were turned on. Drifting up the canal on gondolas, the courtiers were entertained by an orchestra performing on a vessel behind the king's. André Félibien wrote that "the sound of these instruments seemed to give life to all the figures," while the lights cast reflections on the water giving "the symphony a special charm that it would never have had in complete obscurity." The entire *spectacle* seemed to transcend the bounds of human endeavor and to transport the court to a magic world, according to Félibien: "It seems that the nymphs of the canals and of the fountains of Versailles assembled in order to receive the king and to honor his return with a pompous and triumphal display; and that in decorating these canals, they had constructed there some edifices and other monuments of an entirely singular structure and conforming to the nature and to the condition of the gods who preside over the waters."[72]

The *grand divertissement* of 1674 commemorated the victories of the French army. Subsequent years, however, brought greater glories to the crown. Success on the Mediterranean against the Dutch and the Spanish in 1676 and victories at Ghent and Ypres in 1678 led to the Treaties of Nimwegen between France and her adversaries. Although Louis agreed to restore Dutch territory, he was ceded Franche-Comté and considerable land on the north-eastern frontier by Spain. Moreover, in 1680, he inaugurated the notorious Chambers of Reunion, through whose pseudo-legality he claimed all the lands which at any time in the past had belonged to the territories that had been ceded to him in the recent peace treaties. He thereby claimed and occupied Luxemburg, Saarbrucken, and Strasbourg. Furthermore, in 1683, he again invaded the Spanish Netherlands and he seized Lorraine. In all of his ventures, Louis met with very little opposition. Plagued by Turkish invasions, the emperor was forced to conclude a twenty-year truce with Louis in August 1684, in which he recognized French possession of territories acquired by the Chambers of Reunion. Louis also added to his glories by conducting naval campaigns in the Mediterranean against pirates from Tripoli. His navy bombarded Algiers and forced the liberation of all Christian slaves there. Thus, by 1685, Louis XIV stood at the zenith of his power. France dominated Europe, and the Sun King boasted about granting peace to the world.

Celebration of Louis as the all-powerful peacemaker was the theme of most of the *divertissements* which the court enjoyed throughout the year 1685. On July 16, 1685 the marquis de Seignelay sponsored a *divertissement* for Louis and the court at his château in Sceaux. The guests promenaded through the gardens and heard a concert of oboes and flutes near the cascade. In the evening, vocalists from the Académie performed the pastoral *Idylle sur la paix*, by Racine and Lully.[73] Given in a specially constructed theater in the orangerie, the *Idylle* comprised a series of choruses, orchestral pieces, and recitatives in which war was condemned and Louis was hailed for vanquishing his jealous enemies:

> Qu'ont-ils gagné ces esprits orgueilleux,
> Qui menassoient d'armer la terre entière?
> Ils ont veu de nouveau resserrer leur frontière.
> Ils ont veu ce Roc sourcilleux.
> De leur orgueil l'espérance derrière,
> De nos champs fortunez deviner la barrière.[74]

Louis liked the *Idylle* so much that he ordered a substantial part of it repeated. The *divertissements* of Sceaux concluded with a concert and supper in the illuminated gardens.

The theme of peace prevailed during the court's *divertissements* at Fontainebleau in October. For several days the courtiers were feted with hunts, games, balls, promenades, concerts, and comedies; but the main attraction was Lully's new dramatic ballet *Le temple de la paix*, which was first produced on October 15, three days before Louis revoked the Edict of Nantes. Several performances were given at Fontainebleau, and subsequently, at Versailles and Paris. In February 1686, several months after the initial performance of *Le temple*, the *Mercure* stated that Lully had succeeded so well that "not only was there no other *divertissement* at Fontainebleau, but this same ballet was danced again several times at Versailles at the beginning of this winter."[75]

In his dedication of *Le temple*, Lully wrote that "the Peace which Your Majesty has given so generously to his conquered enemies is the subject of this ballet."[76] Lully described his piece as a *"diver-tissement* ordered by a prince [and] animated by your august blood." He praised Louis for neglecting his brave deeds in order "to gratify the happiness of France," and he explained that the composition was designed, in turn, to reveal the happiness and gratitude of the French people. *Le temple* followed the pattern of Lully's previous ballets in every respect except that the vocal numbers were more diversified, the récits more numerous, and the dances and orchestral pieces better integrated into the drama. In other words, the influence of Lully's operatic work was now felt in the ballet.

The exoticism which for so long had characterized French ballets was expressed in *Le temple* by groups of dancers from distant lands paying homage to the French crown. Americans extolled the king's reputation as a peacemaker and expressed gratitude for being included in Louis' empire. Their verses referred to the expedition of Ferdinand de la Salle, who explored the Mississippi River Valley in 1682 and claimed the region, which he called Louisiana, for Louis XIV. Since parts of North Africa had also fallen under Louis' influence as a result of naval engagements near Tripoli, Africans were represented in the ballet, praising the king for his clemency.

One of Louis XIV's primary activities was the maintaining of his subjects, at least those of his court, in a constant state of repose. To this end, he sponsored the endless parade of *diver-tissements* that occupied and delighted the nobility from morning until night, year after year. Occasionally assuming grand and spectacular proportions, the *divertissements* kept the court under the monarch's attentive eye. They enabled the king to mingle with his court and to receive their flattery. The French historian Roland Mousnier has written: "In a series of marvelous, fairylike festivals, the king appeared attired as the Olympian god, with the courtiers as lesser divinities or heroes. In this way, they were able to transmute their vain dream of power and greatness in this imitation of the life of the immortals, exalted above the common humanity, and, if they must obey, they would at least obey the Lord Jupiter, the King-god. Etiquette habituated them to seeing a superhuman being in the king."[77]

♣ 7

Ceremony and Celebration

Ceremony was as much a part of life at the French court as devotion to duty was at the Prussian court. In his book on the court of Louis XIV, Abbé François Duffo contended that the ceremonies of the monarchy must be regarded as "an echo and a prolongation of the actions and deeds accomplished in the kingdom."[1] For centuries the French monarchy had celebrated royal births, baptisms, marriages, and deaths with pompous processions and rituals; special ceremonies had also evolved for coronations, royal entrances, dedications, and monarchical acts such as the lit de justice; and, during the Valois era and the reigns of Henri IV and Louis XIII, military victories, the conclusion of peace treaties, and the visits of foreign ambassadors were occasions for elaborate ceremony and celebration. It was under Louis XIV, however, that the grand tradition of regal ceremony reached an apex: all of the customary ceremonies were enacted with tumid pageantry and new ones were contrived on the slightest pretext. Louis' awesome ceremonies were intended to dazzle his subjects and to make them respectful. Even when the fortunes of the crown were at a low ebb, Louis, by staging a ceremony, was able to direct attention to the majesty and grandeur of the crown. Referring to French military defeats in 1704, the marquis de Surville (aide-de-camp to Maréchal Tallard) pointed out that Louis diverted the public's attention by ordering a Te Deum to celebrate a recent naval victory: "This pompous ceremony imposes upon the people, who think that nothing but truth can come from the king's mouth. In addition, this piece of policy serves to inspire awe in the people and keeps them in obeisance."[2] Such ceremonies, according to the marquis, are an "old remedy," administered for the purpose of intoxicating the people "with the conceit of the king's good fortune."

The basic ingredients of Louis' ceremonies were spectacle and sound. Several composers, including Lully, Henri Desmarets, and Michel de Lalande, provided martial airs for oboes and fifes, trumpet fanfares, and other appropriate pieces for state ceremonies. Ceremonial music was seldom composed specifically for one particular event and then set aside; instead, composers such as Lully supplied the king's musicians with several types of compositions which were appropriate for the numerous, standard ceremonies that were held repeatedly during the reign of Louis XIV. Desmaret's march for oboes was typical of the kind of music that was played during the commemoration of a monument or the proclamation of a peace treaty (Example 17).[3] Many of the

Example 17

trumpet calls and drum signals used in royal parades were the same pieces that the army employed for military maneuvers. Lully composed the following *batterie de tambours* for the Garde Françoise (Example 18).[4]

Example 18

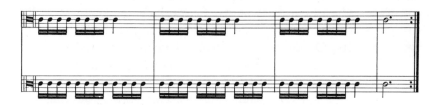

How indispensable music was to the impact and success of a royal ceremony can be gleaned from Jean Loret's description of a victory rite in Notre-Dame cathedral in 1656:

> Là, se trouve grande aflüence
> De Gens assemblée en ce Lieu
> Pour en rendre graces à Dieu.
> De Paris, le Sénat illustre,
> Y parut en son plus beau lustre. . . .
> Les gros Canons de l'Arsenal
> Ne répondirent point trop mal
> Aux réjouissances publiques
> Par leurs organes métaliques.
> O que j'oyois, d'un cœur riant,
> Ce bruit, encore qu'efroyant
> J'aime plus qu'argent, n'y pistoles,
> Les violons et les violes,
> Les clavessins, les luts charmans,
> Bref, toutes sortes d'instrumans,

Jusqu'aux tambours, jusqu'aux trompettes:
Mais quand un grand nombre de boëtes
Après le Te Deum chanté
Rétentissent, par la Cité,
Quand les canons, à large bouche,
Quoi que d'un ton un peu farouche,
Pronent les victoires du Roi,
O quelle Musique pour moi![5]

The musicians who performed for Louis XIV's ceremonies belonged to the Grande Écurie, whose membership included officers of the royal household, riding masters, heralds of arms, and sword bearers.[6] The staff of the Écurie accompanied the king on trips, military reviews, and hunts; they participated in the celebrations of marriages, receptions, contests, and proclamations of peace. The instruments of the Écurie included oboes, horns, musettes, fifes, and drums, but the position of honor belonged to the trumpets. Of the Écurie's twelve trumpets, four were also trompettes ordinaires of the King's Chapel; they had special duties and prerogatives at the Écurie, including the privilege of announcing foreign ambassadors and of accompanying the king on military campaigns.[7] Competition among the trumpeters was intense, especially when four trumpet players from the king's personal guard, known as the "trompettes des Menus plaisirs," were added to the Écurie toward the end of the century. Each group of trumpeters was very jealous of its special privileges and duties. Appointments to the Écurie were made by the king, usually on the recommendation of the king's riding master. Frequently a particular group of instrumentalists came predominantly from a certain region of France—Auvergne, for example, produced many trumpeters for the Écurie—and families such as the Rhodes sent several generations of trumpeters to the royal service. One of the privileges accorded trumpet players was the right to transfer their positions to their children.

The Écurie musicians enjoyed high prestige among the king's servants: they possessed the right of *commensaux* (meal companions of the king); they held special rank and position in public ceremonies; they were exempted from taxes such as the taille and franc-fief, from obligations to church-wardens and mayors, from tolls on food products, and from quartering soldiers in wartime. Their food and clothing were purchased for them, and they earned a regular salary of either 180 or 120 livres a year, depending on their instrument. Their incomes were augmented substantially by stipends for participation in special ceremonies such as processions on religious holidays, transporting enemy flags to Notre-Dame after a military victory, and performing for the king's entrance at a lit de justice. On September 6, 1689, for example, Louis ordered Nicolas de Fromont of the Royal Treasury to pay the trumpet players of the Écurie the sum of 360 livres for their assistance in the Te Deums sung for the dauphin at Philippsburg, Mannheim, and Frankenthal.[8] The contingent of seven drums and fifes was granted 270 livres, about 38 livres a piece, for their participation in the same ceremonies.[9] In general, the musicians of the Grande Écurie lived comfortably and were doubtless envied by their peers.

Since France was almost constantly at war during Louis' reign, it is not surprising that victory celebrations were the most numerous and pompous of all the ceremonies. At the conclusion of each successful battle, and even after some whose outcome was in doubt, Louis ordered Te Deums sung in the cathedrals of France. Officials of the crown, members of the nobility, and members of the Parlement of Paris were expected to attend these services, which were frequently accompanied by stately processions. After an especially important engagement, the ceremony was usually held in Notre-Dame for the presentation and display of the enemy's flags and trophies of war (Figure 18). These ceremonies were always preceded by a parade of the king, the musicians of the Écurie, the Swiss Guards, and other officials of the kingdom. The proclamation of peace treaties was an occasion for the most elaborate of all the royal rodomontades.

The celebrations carried out during the war against Holland in the 1670's show the character of Louis XIV's victory ceremonies. In the summer of 1672, after French armies had crossed the Rhine and the king himself had led the conquest of southern Holland, Louis XIV returned to Paris and ordered a Te Deum at Notre-Dame on August 14. The following day Sieur de Sainctot, the king's master of ceremonies, conducted a procession from the

Figure 18. A musical procession in October 1664, led by Monsieur de Sainctot, bearing captured flags to the cathedral of Notre-Dame de Paris. Anonymous engraving, in "Grande folio: Histoire de France, 1660-1676." (Photograph courtesy of the Bibliothèque Nationale, cabinet des estampes.)

Tuileries to Notre-Dame. Bearing guidons taken from the Dutch at Nimwegen, Gravelines, and elsewhere, the Swiss Guards marched to the accompaniment of fanfares, played by the trumpets and fifes of the Grande Écurie. The flags were received by the archbishop of Paris, who placed them at the foot of the altar, while an instrumental concert was presented by the musicians. Louis arrived from Saint-Germain-en-Laye at three in the afternoon, with the queen, the dauphin, and other members of the royal family. He proceeded to the church, where he took his place on the high dais in the choir. After vespers, the musicians accompanied the sisters, chaplains, and singers of Notre-Dame, the Swiss Guards, the king and queen, and the dauphin in a procession through the cathedral. The apostolic nuncio, the ambassadors from Spain, Venice, and Savoy, and the members of the Parlement of Paris witnessed the ceremony, which concluded with a Te Deum and cannon fire from the Bastille. Outside the cathedral the king received the acclamations of the crowd and the salute of trumpets and drums. The royal entourage returned for a fireworks display at the Tuileries, the windows of which contained luminous tableaux depicting the scenes of Louis' conquests.[10]

The conquest of Franche-Comté in 1674, which was commemorated at Versailles by a *grand divertissement* (see Chapter 6), prompted an orotund celebration in Paris staged on the king's orders by the officers and musicians of the Écurie. A triumphal arch was erected in the Place du Palais-Royal and an equestrian figure of the king, being crowned by Victory, was constructed on a pedestal beside it. The figures of force, justice, prudence, and magnanimity adorned the four sides of the pedestal and an inscription read: *Pugnanti, Vincenti, Triumphanti.* Military trophies were placed in the shrubbery surrounding the arch. At the sides of the arch, columns in the shape of a half-moon supported an artificial mountain. In this setting, a small-scale music drama was performed. Representing nations who volunteered to submit to Louis' authority, dancers entered in the company of Felicity, Abundance, and the Pleasures, and turned on fountains of wine. Victory delivered laudatory verses to the king, and choruses proclaimed his military accomplishments. A series of dances, concerts, and songs led to a spectacular fireworks display that concluded the celebration.

Several days later, on July 5, another turgescent fete was held at the Palais-Royal.[11] This time the principal decoration represented Mount Parnassus, where Apollo and the Muses, with appropriately garbed followers, listened to concerts of trumpets, drums, violins, and oboes. Assembled in order to praise Louis for supporting the fine arts, the Muses delivered encomiastic Latin verses interspersed with musical selections. In contrast to the earlier celebration at the Palais-Royal, in which "the idea of a military triumph" was the main theme, the July fete "proclaims only a peaceful triumph." The shift from Louis the hawk of war to Louis the dove of peace, however, apparently created problems: "The Muses of song and symphony harmonize their instruments in order to sound the praises of the king, but they find in him so many different qualities, that they do not know how to blend the tones suitable for praising a conqueror with the sweet and amorous tones which are suitable to his pacific virtues."[12] The singers in this miniature opera concluded that the gamut of Louis' diverse talents, ranging from love to law, from gentility to militancy, must be euphoniously proclaimed.

The conclusion of the Dutch war was sealed when France signed a series of treaties with Holland (August 1678), Spain (September 1678), the emperor (February 1679), and Denmark (September 1679). The Treaties of Nimwegen prompted celebrations all over France, with special ceremonies in Paris (Figure 19).[13] In September 1678, the officers of the army, the hussars, and three hundred archers marched through Paris to celebrate the treaty with the Dutch. The *Mercure* commented that "the trumpets, drums, and oboes of the Grande Écurie du roi were heard throughout the march, but they made much less noise than the acclamations of *Vive le roi*."[14] Fireworks displays were held for the public in front of the Hôtel de Ville during the month of October, while members of the nobility celebrated with banquets, concerts, and plays at a château on the banks of the Marne near Paris.[15] The official proclamation of the treaty took place in January 1679. The peace was read publicly by the king's officials during a parade through Paris. The officers of the Châtelet, troops and archers of the city corps, and the fifes, oboes, drums, and trumpets of the Écurie comprised the main body of the procession. Before and after each reading of the peace, the trumpets played fanfares. A few days later, a Te Deum was performed at Notre-Dame and a temporary temple, which highlighted figures representing commercial prosperity and the fine arts, was constructed in front of the Hôtel de Ville. The Dutch ambassadors were also received in January at the home of the president of the Parlement, where they heard a concert of forty oboes, violins, and flutes.[16]

The rest of France celebrated the peace with ceremonial pomp equal to that of Paris. At Le Havre, Chartres, and Caen, statues were erected, fountains gushed wine, and concerts, fanfares, and musical dramas commemorated the conclusion of the war. The people of Abbéville constructed a theater on the banks of the Somme River where they staged a mock combat beneath a portrait of Louis XIV to the accompaniment of trumpet fanfares. An abbreviated opera on the subject of the recent peace and

Figure 19. The royal almanac of 1679 shows musicians helping to commemorate the Peace of Nimwegen between France and Holland. Engraving by Lemoien de la Paux, in "Acord des nations," *Almanach royal* (Paris, 1679). (Photograph courtesy of the Bibliothèque Nationale, cabinet des estampes.)

Louis' benevolence toward his enemies was performed at Montpellier. A similar production was given at Bourges after France concluded a treaty with the emperor. In this piece, a Dutchman, a Spaniard, and a German sang about Louis' irresistible conquests. "The Rhine is red with our blood," intoned the German. The French assured the foreigners, however, that Louis pardons his enemies and seeks happiness and prosperity for all who submit to his laws.[17]

Meanwhile, Paris continued to celebrate the Treaties of Nimwegen in the spring and summer of 1679. The new peace with the emperor was solemnized by a procession of heralds and trumpeters and a Te Deum. A motet was sung at the Church of the Grands Augustins, the verses of which (composed by M. Marets, professor of the Sorbonne) exhorted the world to rejoice in the peace.[18] After the treaty with Denmark in September, Louis gave orders for the final ceremony in commemoration of the peace. In his account of the proceedings, Henri de Montjoye, roi d'armes, stated that, at nine in the morning on November 22, six heralds of arms gathered at the Hôtel de Ville for the procession. At eight, the drums, trumpets, and fifes of the Écurie had marched from Montjoye's hôtel on the rue Saint-Honoré to the Hôtel de Ville, where toasts were drunk to the king and queen, while the trumpets played fanfares. The procession continued to the Louvre, where the peace was proclaimed, fanfares were played, and "a grand acclamation from the people, to the noise of the drums and fifes of the said Grande Écurie of His Majesty," was heard. The ceremony, according to Montjoye, "has maintained the glory of the king, his great merit, the good success of his arms, and the well-being which France will derive from these two peaces."[19]

During the Dutch war, French power was approaching its crest, and there was a great deal to commemorate. What strikes the historian and reinforces the conviction that ceremony was politically motivated, however, is that none of the sheen disappeared from royal ceremony in the later years of the reign when there was little to celebrate. Indeed, it was doubtless more necessary after the Grand Coalition was mounted against Louis than in the earlier part of his reign to maintain the façade of splendor and well-being. Thus, the ceremonies at the conclusion of the War of the League of Augsburg were no less spectacular than those of the 1670's.²⁰ The grand processions through the streets of Paris, the concerts of Lully's music in the hôtel courtyards, and the brassy blare of trumpets, fifes, and drums announcing fireworks rekindled the embers of the recent past, when imperious merry-making was, perhaps, warranted. Even during the final, war-ridden years of Louis XIV's reign, the pretense of glory was maintained by official France. Te Deums were sung and victory celebrations were given when there was no real victory to cele-brate. By 1714, however, not even the drums of the Écurie could roll away defeat. The sound of the fife had indeed become windy.²¹

Throughout Louis XIV's fifty-four-year reign, a variety of ceremonies of state, in addition to those celebrating military victories, were held regularly. The performers of the Écurie turned these events into veritable musical and dramatic *spectacles*, which were necessary to project the mystique of the monarchy's grandeur and power. The king's own marriage celebration (August 26, 1660) set the tone for these pompous celebrations. Surely one of the most ostentatious parades in French history, the procession moved from the royal residences at Vincennes, through what became known as the Place du Trône (now the Place de la Nation), and on to Paris. At the Place du Trône, the royal couple, seated on a specially constructed dais, were saluted with grandiloquent speeches by representatives of the clergy, the merchants' guilds, the University of Paris, doctors of law, medi-cine, and theology, the Parlement of Paris, the Mint, and the corporations. By two o'clock in the afternoon a new procession had been formed which resumed the march toward Paris. The royal couple were joined by the officials of the Écurie and the royal household, along with Chancellor Séguier and his attendants, the musketeers, the cavalry, officers of the crown, the princes of the blood, and numerous nobles.

On its way to the Louvre, the procession passed through several triumphal arches reminiscent of those built for entries of the Valois kings. Standing in the Faubourg Saint-Antoine, the first edifice, which was Roman in appearance, was composed of three arches flanked by Doric columns and decorated with a frieze and entablature welcoming the royal pair to Paris. Statues representing faithfulness, obedience, joy, gratitude, concord, and constancy crowned the arches.[22] These allegorical figures were familiar to Parisians and served to link the visual arts and Louis' dramatic *spectacles*, for they appeared regularly along with mythological figures in the operas and ballets of the period. Eighteen oboists were placed on top of the arch and greeted the procession with a concert that was echoed by the trumpeters of the Écurie. Further along the route, Louis' entourage passed through a second arch, which was a reconstruction of Henri II's arch at the Porte Saint-Antoine. The stone arch was richly decorated with statues by Van Obstal and François Anguier and a bust of Louis XIV based on a sketch by Nicolas Poussin. The inscription on the entablature commemorated the recent peace secured by the king and Cardinal Mazarin. The arch, which was consecrated by the merchants' guilds and the town counselors of Paris, was crowned with a sculptured ensemble of figures representing France and Spain linking arms and Hymen holding a flaming torch. After a concert at the arch by a band of violinists, the procession moved down the rue Saint-Antoine and turned into a side street (now the rue François-Miron) in order to pass the hôtel of Madame de Beauvais, where the king and his bride were saluted from the balcony by the Queen Mother, Cardinal Mazarin, Cardinal Antonis Barberini, and Marshal Turenne. At the nearby church of Saint-Gervais, the procession stopped in front of a third arch, which represented the Temple of the Muses (Figure 20). Rising forty feet in the air over a grotto, this elaborate floral arch was encrusted with figures representing virtue, Eros the god of love, angels, and a group of famous writers. At the summit, a wooded Parnassus supported the figures of Thalia and the seven Muses, Apollo playing the violin, Calliope and Clio. Upon arriving, the royal entourage was greeted by a choral rendition of a hymn by Henry de Thier du Mont, a musician of the royal chapel. The verse, composed by the abbé de Boisrobert, hailed Marie Thérèse for giving up her title of Infanta and winning the hearts of her new subjects. Continuing to the Île de la Cité, the parade moved past Notre-Dame, where a concert of bagpipes was heard, before passing the

Figure 20. Floral arch supporting the Temple of the Muses on Mount Parnassus crowned by the figure of Apollo. The arch encompassing a grotto was constructed near the Church of Saint-Gervais for Louis XIV's marriage procession into Paris in August, 1660. Anonymous engraving; reprinted from *L'entrée triomphante de leurs Majestés Louis XIV, roi de France et Navarre, et Marie-Thérèse d'Autriche, son épouse, dans la ville des rois, capitale de leur royaume, en retour de la signature de la paix générale et leur heureux mariage* (Paris, 1662), following p. 8. (Photograph courtesy of the Bibliothèque Nationale, cabinet des estampes.)

fourth arch at the end of the bridge leading to the Cité. The allegorical figures on the arch symbolized conjugal fidelity and the triumph of Cupid over Mars.

Finally, the long procession reached the last of the magnificent arches constructed for Louis' ceremonious peregrination from Vincennes to Paris. Situated in the Place Dauphine, which "had been turned into a vast amphitheater,"[23] the grandiose, elaborately decorated arch had been designed by the king's chief artist, Charles le Brun. Le Brun had constructed the arch so that the equestrian statue of Henri IV, the Pont-Neuf, and the Louvre could be seen in the distance. A towering obelisk representing the king's power was constructed over the arch, which was meant to signify the French people. Le Brun's decorations were intended to symbolize the grand reconciliation between the elements of fire and water, air and earth, the harmony between man and the elements, and the grandeur of the French monarchy in comparison with that of antiquity. Several figures and inscriptions on the arch and the obelisk represented the genius of Mazarin (under the figure of Atlas), the piety of the queen, the bravery of the king, and the royal marriage bearing the fruit of peace. Before leaving the resplendent surroundings of the Place Dauphine, the monarch and his bride heard a concert by the Vingt-quatre violons and orations by officials of the Parlement and the University of Paris, after which the procession moved on to the Louvre, where the royal couple watched fireworks and water games on the Seine. The day's procession was an appropriate prelude on a grand scale to the ceremonial pomp that in later years filled the daily life of the Sun King. Victor-L. Tapié has conveyed what seems to me to be an accurate impression of the meaning of the procession: "It gave an idea of the situation of the country at that particular time, of what was fashionable in Paris, and also shows us how great were the intellectual and artistic resources of France. . . . It was an expression of one of the most powerful States in Europe, and of a people who in spite of the sufferings of a long war and of an attempted revolution, were now rejoicing in the future. It was not a court function. In Paris this fete reflected the national feeling. Its gaiety and spontaneity could only have come from a mature civilization; one could think of no other European city that could have staged such a demonstration."[24]

Although the procession celebrating Louis XIV's marriage was a unique event in the history of the reign, it established the flamboyant, imperious mode characteristic of the ceremonies produced for the king by the Grande Écurie and other groups of the royal household. The king's calendar (see Figure 13 and 19) was a sustained chronicle of ceremonies commemorating royal births, baptisms, weddings, and deaths—all deemed necessary in order to preserve Louis' image of grandeur and to inspire public awe.

The spectacular ceremonies consecrating the births and baptisms of Louis' children and grandchildren were always highlighted by sonorous musical flourishes. The birth of the king's first son in 1661 occasioned a public celebration at the Hôtel de Ville, with a wine fountain and a concert of oboes and cromornes.[25] For the dauphin's baptism in 1668 at the chapel of Saint-Germain, special decorations were provided by Le Brun, and a patriotic motet, *Plaude, Laetare, Gallia*, was conducted by Lully. The ceremony possessed all the brilliance of a *spectacle*, according to Charles Robinet.[26] Celebrations for the duc de Bourgogne's birth on August 6, 1682, were even more ostentatious. Te Deums, fanfares, and fireworks greeted the birth, and Lully gave a special free performance of his opera *Persée* at the Palais-Royal. The crowd entered the theater through a triumphal arch which, following the performance, appeared to go up in flames as a figure of the Sun was lifted into the air and a fountain of wine was turned on. Elsewhere, Charles Le Brun staged a fireworks display at the Gobelins. Describing the jubilation of Paris, the *Mercure* wrote: "The drums, trumpets, violins, oboes were heard everywhere, and their sound mingled with the rockets, the firearms, the bustle, the public acclamations, and the cries of *Vive le Roi*, . . . creating a concert which can be heard in no other city in the world.[27] Sumptuous religious services added to the pageantry of the occasion: a Te Deum which employed sixty voices, clavecins, theorboes, bass viols, and bassoons, was performed at the royal abbey of Saint-Victor, while outside the church a corps of twenty-four drums and fifes accompanied a musket salute. The Jesuits and Capuchins held similar ceremonies. In the city of Lyons, the

Jesuits spent 2,000 écus honoring the duke's birth. On October 25, the Collège de la Trinité sponsored a carrousel in which Turks, Persians, Romans, Greeks, and Frenchmen, each with a retinue of musicians, engaged in five quadrilles, followed by fanfares and fireworks. The next day brought a concert of flutes, oboes, drums, and trumpets at the Collège de Notre-Dame and a grand march through the city, featuring allegorical symbols of marriage and peace. In another carrousel, a chariot, bearing cromornes, oboes, flutes, and drums, introduced characters representing Clovis, Pépin, Hugh Capet, and Hercules (Louis XIV).[28] Other cities such as Toulon, Metz, Geneva, Avignon, and Poitiers held celebrations similar to those in Lyons throughout the winter and spring of 1683. At Toulouse in February 1683, the Jesuits presented a "comedy ornamented with an allegory in the form of an opera" entitled *La naissance de Mercure*. As late as June, the *Mercure* was still reporting festivities. The merrymaking had scarcely run its course when the dauphine gave birth to her second son, the duc d'Anjou, in December 1683, and the celebrations began again.

The last major commemoration of a royal birth occurred in June 1704, when the duchesse de Bourgogne gave birth to a son, the duc de Bretagne. The event guaranteed a new successor to the throne and prompted the *Mercure* to deride those foreigners who wished the worst for France. The celebrating began on June 25 during the duchesse's labor. All of the lights at Versailles were turned on and crowds of people gathered outside to hear the drums, trumpets, and "other sweeter instruments." Following the birth on June 26, Louis ordered a Te Deum and advised the officials of the chambre des comptes and the cour des aides to be present. At two in the afternoon, on June 27, three hundred archers from Paris, the drums, trumpets, and oboes of the Écurie, the prévôt des marchands, the procureur du roi, and the con- seilleurs of the city (dressed in silk robes) marched to Notre-Dame. During the Te Deum, which the Vingt-quatre violons performed, cannons were fired from the Bastille. The musicians of the Écurie performed during the banquet for a thousand persons at the Hôtel de Ville and during the fireworks that followed. A ball at the Hôtel lasted most of the night. On June 28, the king's musicians entertained the residents of Paris with a public concert at the

Tuileries, and on the 29th bread and wine were distributed. Nearly everyone in Paris participated in the celebrations: fireworks displays were given all over the city, and the Hôtels de Bouillon, de Créqui, and others were illuminated; the Jesuits, "who are always ready to give marks of their zeal when the glory and welfare of France are at stake,"[29] presented fireworks and music every evening at the Collège de Louis-le-Grand. The Feuillants of the Monastère-Royal on the rue Saint-Honoré draped their church in tapestries and held a procession around the church to the accompaniment of artillery fire. At seven in the evening on June 29, trumpets, drums, and oboes played fanfares from a balcony in the church, while outside a fountain of wine was started and bread was distributed. This was followed by another procession in the churchyard, during which the Exaudiat was sung, incense burned, and orations to the king declaimed.

The birth was also celebrated by the people on the rue Saint-Jacques; the street was lined with candles and emblems of the king, and the artisans of the district gave out free wine. The people "sang several songs, whose words and airs they had composed, to the glory of the king."[30] Comparable festivities were held near the Palais-Royal and in other districts of the city. The papal nuncio M. Fieschi provided a feast and a concert at his hôtel, as did many of the foreign ambassadors in Paris. One of the most unusual celebrations took place at the Collège Mazarin, where the teachers first distributed money to the poor of the parish of Saint-Sulpice and then celebrated a Mass. After the service, a hundred vessels were put in the Seine and the citizens of Paris were permitted to boat on the river while a symphony of trumpets, drums, and oboes performed in the Place du Collège. The event turned into a *spectacle* when the pavilions, cornices, balustrades, pedestals, and the dome of the Collège were illuminated, and figures of the sun appeared above each window. Fires were lighted on the high balustrade, rockets were shot from the dome, and "trumpets, drums, and oboes were heard while the illumination lasted."[31]

The most dazzling of all the celebrations for the duc de Bretagne's birth was given at Versailles on July 26. Organized by M. Bontemps, the first valet of the king's chamber, the *spectacle* commenced when cannon shots summoned the courtiers at nine in the evening. Proceeding to the grand porch of the château, the nobles watched an illuminated chariot appear "like a globe of fire" in the darkness. Emerging from the chariot was the figure of Mars, who, on his return from the scene of French conquests (according to the *Mercure*), learned of the duke's birth and came to pay his respects and to bring news of victories in Italy. Mars mounted a throne near the chariot which was covered with fleurs-de-lys and precious stones bearing inscriptions of the names of cities conquered by Louis' armies. Bellone and Pallas sat amid the war trophies and drums at Mars' feet. The god was also accompanied by two trumpeters who announced his entry and whose music "blended with the sound of drums and fifes, creating a military and very pleasing harmony."[32] Twelve French officers dressed as Romans completed Mars' entourage. The chariot moved beneath Louis' apartments as cannons fired from the front of the château. The bellicose music of the trumpets and drums suddenly blended with the harmonies of musettes and oboes as Louis appeared on a balcony. Mars announced his obedience to the king's laws and proclaimed victory for French arms on the Po River. As he concluded, the musicians played a new concert, suns appeared in the night from various points in the garden, and rockets were fired.

Aside from a scattering of celebrations in the provinces, the events commemorating the birth of the duc de Bretagne concluded with the *spectacle* at Versailles in July. Nine months later, on April 13, 1705, at seven o'clock in the evening, the infant duke died.

For obvious reasons, the child received an unusually sedate burial. Ordinarily, however, funerals of royalty or of government officials were pompous state occasions. The French were as determined to surpass the Italians in funeral rites as in other areas where spectacle, ceremony, and the fine arts were involved. Father Menestrier, who was chiefly responsible for establishing the French standards for funeral pomp, decoration, and symbolism, called for self-sufficiency and progress in this field.

The arts flourish among us. Good taste in painting, sculpture, and architecture has been introduced. Our language has attained perfection. The queen's *Entrée* and the king's *Carrousel* have revived in our time the pomp and magnificence of ancient triumphs. Our theatre is more serious, more solemn, and more polished than that of other Nations. Our music need not be envious any longer of that of Italy. People come to France from all parts to admire its wonders. The magnificence of the court, the splendid buildings, the gardens, the fountains, the commercial prosperity, the scholars, the academies, the military maneuvers, the fervour, the courage, the experience and the discipline of our soldiers, among whom the least important officers are qualified to command, to guide, and to lead are admired by foreigners. It is not proper that funeral decorations remain the only thing which is not performed with the same intelligence that is found in everything else. It is easy to do it if we are willing to give the direction of them to wise persons with a little experience. If we wish, we cannot only succeed as well as the Italians, who are such skillful decorators, but greatly surpass them, because we have the most magnificent prince who ever lived, and more excellent workmen than can be found in Italy.[33]

Several years after Menestrier's book appeared, however, the *Mercure* was able to view proudly France's superiority in funeral rites: "Everything concerning the public festivals and obsequies has occurred with such good taste and such great magnificence that Italy must boast no longer that these occasions, which are worthy of being called truly superb, can be found only in her country."[34]

The funeral ceremony for the comte de Vermandois in December 1683 was typical of the obsequies in the reign of Louis XIV. The king selected the Church of Notre-Dame in Arras for the burial place and sent instructions to the bishop. The doors, nave, and choir of the church were draped in black velvet tapestry. The count's body was conveyed from Lens by fifty infantrymen from Arras, three of the king's battalions, and a corps of drummers. The procession was greeted at the church doors by the bishop (dressed in a gold brocade cape), archdeacons, parish clergy, a choir, a group of nobles, and military dignitaries. As the carriage arrived, "the oboes of the army began a lugubrious concert, which was marvelously suited to the funeral ceremony."[35] The concert lasted until the body was taken into the church and placed on a pedestal in the choir beneath twenty-four silver chandeliers. After the prayers, a De Profundis was sung and the body was placed in the Chapel of Mourning. The body was interred two days later during an elaborate service that included a Mass and a concert of Lully's music.

Among the regular ceremonies were those held in connection with the affairs of the Parlement of Paris. When the Parlement convened annually, a ceremony was held that usually culminated in the performance of an oratorio. Marc-Antoine Charpentier, a gifted musician whom the jealous Lully kept in relative obscurity, composed an oratorio entitled *Judicum Salomonis* especially for the convocation of the Parlement in 1702. Because of its revolutionary role during the Fronde, Louis XIV had carefully reduced the power of the Parlement; thus, the musicologist H. Wiley Hitchcock has noted that the subject of Charpentier's oratorio was "singularly—almost mischievously—appropriate for a work to be presented on the assembling of a political group whose sphere of authority had been limited to purely judicial affairs."[36] Other ceremonies were held at the Parlement on occasions such as the registration of the papers that promoted Chancelier Le Tellier to the Grand Conseil.[37] A lit de justice, once a politically meaningful act but now a purely ceremonial chore, was always conducted with great pomp. The *Gazette de France* published an account of the lit de justice of March 23, 1673. Louis left Versailles at eight-thirty in the morning in the company of the Swiss Guards. His arrival at the Parlement was signaled by Sieur de Sainctot, the king's master of ceremonies, who deputed four presidents and six counselors to conduct the royal company to the grand chamber. The procession was accompanied by the drums, fifes, and trumpets of the Écurie, the heralds of arms, and the bailiffs. Louis marched in with the duc d'Enghien, the grand chamberlain, marshals, and other officers of the crown. He mounted a throne under a dais and concluded his business to the accompaniment of a trumpet fanfare.[38] The presence of musicians at the lit de justice unquestionably enhanced the king's splendor.

Dedications of buildings and monuments were among the special state occasions for which the services of the Grande Écurie were also required. In 1665 the king laid the first stone for the façade of the Louvre, "to the sound of drums and trumpets and the acclamations of the people."[39] And in 1685 the musicians of the Écurie marched in procession with the prévôt des marchands, the bishops of Paris, and officers of the crown in a ceremony commemorating the construction of the Pont des Tuileries.[40] The erection of a statue of the monarch was also always an important event. Statues such as the one of Henri IV on the Pont Neuf generate feelings of respect and love in the people and preserve the ruler's image for posterity, according to the *Mercure*.[41] The most refulgent statue of the Sun King was erected in 1686 in the Place des Victoires in Paris. The duc de la Feuillade and the city of Paris (on orders from President de Fourcy, the prévost des marchands) paid for the statue, which was placed on a pedestal twenty-two feet high. Beneath the figure were bronze sculptures of slaves and war trophies. Flanking the pedestal, six bas-reliefs depicted the passage of the Rhine, the conquest of Franche-Comté, the recognition of Spain, the Peace of Nimwegen, the abolition of dueling, and the expulsion of heresy.[42]

The statue was unveiled on March 28, 1686. A platform overlooking the Place was constructed for the dauphin, the duc d'Orléans and Madame, the ducs de Chartres and de Bourbon, and other ladies and gentlemen of the court. Opposite the platform, a stage was erected for the king's musicians. The platform and balconies along the Place were draped with tapestries, and special places were reserved for members of the Académie française and the Académie royale de peinture. The parade assembled at the Place Dauphine at ten in the morning, as hundreds of guardsmen lined the route to the Place des Victoires. The dauphin marched in a special procession via the Quai du Louvre to the accompaniment of distant drums and cannon fire. On arriving, he distributed special medals commemorating the occasion, while the musicians presented a concert. The main procession, which commenced at two-thirty, included twenty-six divisions of fifty soldiers each, numerous officers of the army, special divisions of musketeers and pikemen, and at least one hundred seventy-four musicians, playing drums, trumpets, and oboes. The parade crossed the Pont Neuf, marched down the rue Saint-Honoré and up the rue de Richelieu to the rue des Petits-Champs. Arriving in a carriage attended by twenty liveried servants who drew money from a kettle and threw it to the crowd, the duc de la Feuillade marched

up to the statue and saluted it with a pike. The trumpets sounded
fanfares as military drills were executed in front of the statue. On
a signal from the major, the "warlike noise" of the trumpets gave
way to "a very agreeable symphony of violins, oboes, trumpets,
and kettle drums of the Chambre." The procession continued to
the Hôtel de Ville for another concert of violins and oboes and
then returned for a concluding fanfare at the statue. Throughout
the night, the oboes played periodically at the statue, which was
illuminated by torches and fireworks.[43] The entire affair was
undertaken with a flamboyancy seldom seen, even in Paris.

To instill respect and admiration in the occasional foreign
visitor, the king and his officials exceeded the customary ceremonial routine. This was especially true when the visitors represented a country that the French considered exotic or politically
important. The king believed it was necessary, for example, to
stimulate the esteem and court the favor of the Turks, whose
constant pressure on Imperial Habsburg territory worked to the
benefit of French foreign policy. Thus, the appearance of Turkish
ambassadors in Paris in 1669 prompted an effusion of ceremonial
pomp. Wearing a diamond-encrusted suit made for the ceremony,
Louis received the ambassadors amid the musical din provided
by his trumpeters. Madame de Montespan has described the
occasion: "Being naturally fond of show and display, the King
left nothing undone which might give brilliance to the reception
of so renowned an embassy. The Court wore an air of such splendour and magnificence that these Mussulmans, used though they
were to Asiatic pomp, seemed surprised and amazed at so brilliant
a reception, at which nothing, indeed, had been forgotten."[44]

Louis' reception of delegates from Russia in May 1681 was
equally splendid. The king was moved to put on a special show
for the Russians because they brought their own luxurious company of sixty-two persons, including eight trumpeters, five
drummers, and several oboists and pipe players. The ambassadors
marched into Paris to trumpet fanfares on May 1 and were
received at the Hôtel des Ambassadeurs by officials of the crown.
Louis greeted them in a formal ceremony at Versailles on May 4,
during which they presented gifts and letters from the tsar to the
king. They returned on May 11 for another audience, and on

May 12, after a banquet, a comedy, and some ballet entrées, the ambassadors were taken to a window in the royal apartments to observe a concert with drums, trumpets, and oboes performed in the garden below.[45]

Not long after the Russians departed, Louis XIV entertained emissaries from Morocco, who, after the usual punctilios at Versailles and a symphonically accompanied reception at Saint-Germain, were quoted as saying that "all the miracles of the world are in France."[46] Several years later, the French court regaled another ambassador from Morocco. After a ceremonial round of visits to the Invalides, the Place des Victoires, the Val-de-Grâce, Versailles, and a performance at the opera, the ambassador declared that the rest of the universe was a mere shadow of France. He observed that "the king was the same in games and pleasures as in serious affairs," and he stated that France was unsurpassed in three things: the king, the opera, and the ball of Monsieur.[47]

The most lavish pageantry for foreign visitors was reserved for the most exotic of all the ambassadors to the French court—the Siamese mandarins. The *Mercure* announced their arrival in October 1684, and printed a description of the climate, geography, economy, and customs of Siam.[48] The ambassadors were entertained at the Tuileries on October 13 and were introduced to the king and his court in a dazzling ceremony involving the king's most distinguished musicians. Overcome with this spectacle, the Siamese dropped to the floor before the French king, according to the *Mercure*. Later in the evening at a performance of Lully's opera *Roland*, "they fixed their eyes constantly on His Majesty, because when they prostrated themselves in the *Galerie*, their deep debasement had prevented them from looking at this monarch."[49] In the ensuing days of their visit, the mandarins were exposed to every kind of pageantry that the master of ceremonies could contrive.

In 1685 the Siamese ambassadors returned to France. They were greeted at Brest on June 18 by Louis' confessor, Père de la Chaise, who accompanied them to Paris and took them to the Jesuit Collège Louis-le-Grand, where they witnessed a performance of a ballet entitled *Clovis*. Performed by the students of the

Collège, the ballet extolled the exploits of Hercules, who represented Louis XIV. Successive scenes revealed what Hercules had undertaken for glory, for the well-being of his subjects, for his allies, and for the gods. More specifically, the ballet depicted Louis' conquest of Flanders, the passage of the Rhine, the prohibition of dueling, the promotion of commerce, and the measures taken to destroy Protestantism in France. Although these events were presented allegorically, the Siamese perceived the meaning, according to the *Mercure*, and remarked that *"this Hercules must represent the king, since he triumphs over all his enemies and carries victory everywhere he goes."*[50] During the performance, the ambassadors were greeted by members of the royal family and the nobility. A few days later the Siamese were taken to see the yearly procession of the Day of Assumption at Notre-Dame. They commented on the beauty of the music and asked questions about the organ. On September 1, Louis XIV received them at Versailles. The Siamese marched in a procession with the musicians, the Swiss Guards, officers of the crown, and the master of ceremonies. They were conducted to the foot of the grand staircase, where thirty-six drums and twenty-four trumpets executed flourishes. They were then presented to the monarch, who was sitting on his throne at the top of the staircase. His appearance in this setting was designed to overawe the Siamese.

During the remainder of their sojourn in Paris, the mandarins were occupied with several ceremonial affairs and entertainments. The duc d'Orléans was their host at Saint-Cloud for a comedy, a ballet, and a concert of clavecins, violins, and theorboes. The ambassadors were taken to a performance of Lully's opera *Armide* in Paris; they asked questions about the subject, and having been told that the heroine was not French, they responded: "If she had been French, she would not have needed magic in order to make herself loved, because the French are charming by themselves."[51] When they saw Armide's palace go up in flames in the final act, they reportedly said: "Let us leave; the palace has fallen; we can sleep here no longer." Prior to their departure, the Siamese also participated in some of the ceremonies held to celebrate the king's recovery from a recent illness. The monks of the Order of Saint-Bernard (the Feuillants) decorated their church with tapestries, candles, plaques, and a ruby-encrusted crown, and they employed Lully to conduct his music for the service. In the company of the courtiers and the clergy, the Siamese "looked and listened with an extreme attention; they noticed the different expressions of the music, and during the *Domine salvum fac regem*, which was explained to them, it seemed as if they also prayed for the king."[52] One of the mandarins supposedly said "that his eyes had been enchanted, his ears charmed, and his heart touched." Other Paris churches held equally impressive services and the general celebration of Louis' recovery culminated with an enormous parade to the Place des Victoires, where concerts were performed and wine was served to the public. These additional demonstrations of French eminence were a timely finale to the visit of the Siamese.

From his predecessors, Louis XIV inherited a thriving musical establishment which performed for his regular religious exercises and for religious ceremonies and celebrations. Before Louis, the Musique de la Chapelle Royale included two masters of music, an organist, fourteen singers, a children's choir, a lutists, and a cornetist; after 1660, the organization was augmented by two new masters, three additional organists, and several instrumentalists.[53] Louis presided over the selection of new musicians for the Chapelle. In April 1683, when Henri Dumont and Pierre Robert retired, the king sponsored auditions. He ordered the bishops of France to send their musicians to Versailles to present motets for the court in competition for the jobs. Thirty-five candidates submitted their motets in sealed packets to the king, who drew lots to determine the order of their performance. After six days of competition, Louis selected the winners: Pascal Colasse, a student of Lully; Michel de Lalande, the organist of Saint-Jean; Jean Minoret from Saint-Germain-l'Auxerrois; and Jean Goupillet from Meaux. Each was ordered to serve as master for three months of the year, but since Minoret and Goupillet were priests, they were required to perform for solemn services throughout the year. The salary remained the same as it had been in the 1630's and would remain to the end of Louis' reign: the maîtres were paid 900 livres and most of the singers and instrumentalists received 450 livres.[54]

Louis XIV's personal taste was responsible for important changes in the music performed at royal masses and ceremonies. The king wanted his Mass to be grand and decorous; he wanted diversified motets inserted in the Mass; and he wanted to abandon traditional practice by adding instrumental accompaniment to the motets. One contemporary author has observed: "Occupied constantly with the idea of grandeur, born with the most decided spirit for music, having acquired some extraordinary knowledge in this art through the new genre of composition which the great Lully employed in his Opera, the king imagined that he could introduce the symphony of violins into the motet."[55] Louis informed his masters of music, Dumont and Robert, of his desires, but Dumont protested that the Council of Trent had forbidden the use of instruments in church music. Louis, however, obtained from the archbishop of Paris a judgment that the Council only meant to exclude music disrespectful of the church. Violins were introduced, therefore, at the Chapelle; they accompanied the singing and played ritornelli and little symphonies before and during the motets.

Even before this innovation, the traditional motet style had been changed by Jean-Baptiste Lully to suit the king's taste. He juxtaposed a large choir in tutti sections with a smaller group—two sopranos, an alto, a tenor, and a bass—that performed as a single voice.[56] Lully also composed orchestrally accompanied psalms for eight to ten voices, in which he alternated choral dialogues, recitatives with organ and bass accompaniment, and airs, duets, and trios for soloists. These compositions, which Romain Rolland has called "true religious operas," became prototypes for the motets of Louis' Mass.[57] Compared to earlier church music, the total effect was egregiously massive.

The final transformation of the French motet was the work of Michel de Lalande, who "several times had the honor of composing under the eyes of Louis XIV in the Cabinet itself of His Majesty"; the king "was pleased to communicate to him his ideas on different pieces which he wanted him to set to music."[58] Lalande became Louis' favorite maître de musique. The composer provided the king with seventy motets that were sufficiently grandiose and diversified to make the monarch's religious services harmonize with the opulent tone of the court. The Mass became a *spectacle*. Accompanied by his guards and by the nobles of the court, Louis paraded daily to the royal chapel of Versailles for what was less a demonstration of piety than a musical extravaganza and an exhibition of regal pomp. Sometimes there was no trace of religion left in the service, because the texts of the motets were often unrelated to religious matters. Pierre Perrin's text for a motet on the Elevation of the Host, for example, dealt with the monarch of France rather than the monarch of the heavens:

> Rempli de ton esprit le plus grand des monarques,
> Fay que de son amour il nous donne les marques,
> Et qu'après tant de maux et de troubles divers,
> Enfin le siècle d'or règne sur l'univers.[59]

Performing for religious services at court constituted only part of the duties of the Musique de la Chapelle Royale (Chapelle). The musicians participated in special religious ceremonies and regular celebrations of religious holidays as well. The Day of Saint-Louis was celebrated in August every year with a Mass in the chapel of the Louvre. The holiday was an occasion for pageantry: the oboes, trumpets, and drums of the Grande Écurie marched in the streets; army officers, university scholars, and nobles of the court offered panegyrics to the Saint and to Louis XIV; and motets, whose texts suggested the deeds of the king, were performed during the Mass. The musicians were often placed on a platform at the front of the chapel ornamented with tapestries, multicolored lights, and portraits of the king. The entrance of the monarch was the high point of what was, indeed, an ostentatious exhibition of religiosity and yet another form of musical entertainment for France's most ritualistic ruler.[60]

Pentecost Sunday was also a day of high religious ceremony for the court. The procession at Versailles on June 5, 1681, was typical of this celebration. The officers and musicians of the Chapelle and the Écurie marched through the gardens in a torchlit procession with the king, the Swiss Guards, and the gardes du corps. Proceeding through a specially constructed green arbor filled with water cascades and rock formations, the monarch and his retinue entered the outer court of the château, where the balconies and windows were draped with Persian tapestries, and continued to the grand staircase, which was ornamented with silver vases on marble pedestals. A tabernacle containing religious relics, diamonds, and emeralds, and supporting a crown-shaped dome, had been prepared on the first landing of the staircase. Illuminated cascades of water gushed across the tabernacle and torches lighted the altar. After attending a concert by the musicians of the Chapelle, the entourage marched to the king's stables and to the chapel, where a Mass was held to conclude the religious holiday.[61]

One of the most unusual ceremonies held during Louis' reign was a procession of prisoners at Fontainebleau on September 29, 1700. After he had decided to release sixty-six prisoners of the state and to lodge them in the parish of Père Grégoire de la Forge, Louis gave instructions for a formal observance of the event. Accompanied by a child dressed as an angel, the prisoners gathered in the kitchen of the château at ten in the morning and marched with religious banners to the oval court. Flourishes of trumpets and drums alternated with hymns during the march. The king, the dauphin, and the ducs d'Orléans, de Bourgogne, d'Anjou, and de Berry watched from balconies as the procession moved to the king's chapel, where an anthem was performed. Proceeding to the parish church of Fontainebleau, the prisoners heard a Te Deum, then marched down the broad avenue in front of the Hôtel de la Chancellerie and back to the royal chapel for the celebration of the Mass. The *Mercure* declared that because of the presence of the entire French court and the King of England, "nothing could have been more pompous and more august."[62]

All the ceremonies of Louis XIV's reign were characterized by an ostentation and flamboyance that became the trademark of the French absolutism. The stream of victory celebrations, royal entries, religious festivals, and ceremonies for foreign ambassadors flowed from the court as if the source of the royal spring that fed it would never dry up. Louis' musical establishment kept the waters buoyant and replenished them when the air of celebration was thin and arid. Outwardly banal displays of pomp, these swaggering processions were necessary to perpetuate the mystique of glory, affluence, and power of the royal absolutism.

❧8

The End of the Reign

The 1680's marked the turning point of royal absolutism. The great powers of Europe delivered the first major military defeats to the French monarchy; Louis' depleted treasury showed the drain of years of military adventure; the revocation of the Edict of Nantes deprived France of the productivity of many skilled artisans; and death robbed the nation of its ablest ministers and officers. The death of Jean-Baptiste Lully in 1687, which contributed to the over-all decline of royal grandeur, signaled a deterioration in the traditional associations of music and monarchy. The king seemed to lose interest in his musical establishment. When he did order a musical performance, "it was rather to amuse the Young People, or through policy, than for any pleasure he himself took in it."[1] In these years Louis seldom selected operatic subjects and practically discontinued the lavish operatic productions at Versailles. Instead, he confined his pleasure to concert performances of scenes from Lully's operas, or those of his successors, in the quiet surroundings of Madame de Maintenon's apartments.

Several factors prompted his behavior: the high cost of war necessitated curtailment of opulent musical *spectacles;* the compositions of Lully's successors failed to impress the monarch; and the influence of Madame de Maintenon hung over Louis and the court like a pall. Louis' pious mistress, who disapproved of the accent on pleasures, ceremonial elegance, and theatrical grandeur, managed to turn the king away from his customary entertainments. Relishing her triumph, she wrote: "A taste for Pleasure is extinguished in the King's Heart: Age and Devotion have taught him to make serious reflections on the Vanity and Emptiness of

everything he was formerly fond of; and he daily makes some
Progress in the Ways of God: It is not without Reluctance that he
assists at the Theatres and Festivities, and he bemoans with me
the Necessity which his Dignity lays him under to partake of
Diversions for which he has no longer any Relish."[2] Maintenon
did not extinguish Louis' love of music; she merely drew his
attention away from the flamboyant, outdoor productions of music
dramas, to more sedate recitals in her private rooms at Versailles.
The marquis de Dangeau noted the performances of motets and
chamber pieces for small, select groups of nobles in Maintenon's
apartments. On October 28, 1704, he reported: "This evening,
an ode by the abbé Genest, in praise of the king, was sung at
Madame de Maintenon's. The music is by la Laude [Michel de
Lalande], and the King thought it so good, he encored it."[3]

More elaborate entertainments and *divertissements* were not
abandoned altogether but were transferred from Versailles to
Fontainebleau and Marly, and they were produced on a smaller
scale. Even dancing went out of fashion at the great château.
The duchesse d'Orléans wrote: "The young people do not dance
any more, and as far as I am concerned, I neither dance nor
play."[4] "The court of Versailles," a contemporary observer
declared, "seemed tranquil and grave compared to what it had
been in the most celebrated years of this great monarch's reign."[5]
In the more relaxed atmosphere of Marly, however, the courtiers
held banquets, hunts, balls, and mascarades. In place of operas,
Louis' musicians performed gallimaufries of ballet entrées, songs,
and instrumental pieces, which the *Mercure* regarded as "very
brilliant in spite of the moderate expense."[6] The balls at Marly
were especially colorful, and they were occasionally preceded
by little musical *divertissements*. In February 1700, the *Mercure*
reported a piece entitled *Le roi de la Chine*, in which a dancer
portraying the ruler of China was carried around on a palanquin.[7]
Ingenious and pleasing *divertissements* such as *Le roi* may not match
the grand *spectacles* of the past, the *Mercure* declared, but they are
sufficient to uphold the monarch's magnificence, and they elicit
even stronger admiration for the king, because their moderate
grandeur is a sign of "his prudence and caution."

Louis, however, participated only infrequently in the entertainments that he sponsored for the court at Marly. He "accepted the necessity of denying himself most of the things enjoyed by his court."[8] The king "supervised" the *divertissements*, the *Mercure* wrote in 1705, but he was present only at the beginning of each one, devoting his time, instead, to his ministers or to giving the court an edifying example of religious devotion.[9] Occasionally, the monarch ordered that part of an opera be performed at Marly, and on these occasions he was usually present. In February 1711, for example, the tempest scene from Marin Marais' opera *Alcyoné* (1706) was presented before the king for the first time at Marly.[10] Although the *Mercure* faithfully chronicled the court's *divertissements*, extolled the brilliance of the productions, and carefully pointed to the prosperity and comfort that they presumably reflected, the journal's old enthusiasm was missing. The *divertissements* lacked the luster of former days, and the *Mercure* could not compensate for it with verbiage.

In an effort to restore some of the old splendor, several members of the nobility began sponsoring their own musical entertainments. The control of musical affairs slipped away from the king and became dispersed in two or three "satellite courts."[11] At Versailles, the duchesse de Bourgogne, the princesse de Conti, and the duc d'Orléans promoted new musical productions. In December 1699, they began rehearsals of Lully's opera, *Alceste*, at Conti's home. The ducs de Bourgogne and de Monfort-Biron, the comtes d'Ayen and de Toulouse, Madame de Chartres, and others were invited to participate in the performance. The duc de Bourgogne was persuaded to finance the construction of a theater for this and future productions, at a cost of two or three thousand pistoles. *Alceste* was finally presented on January 9, 1701 before a small, but enthusiastic group of courtiers.

The duc and duchesse du Maine provided another center of entertainment at their château in Sceaux. While the king and some of the nobles were at Marly, the duchesse du Maine often held balls and comedies concurrently during the carnival season. In March 1706 several nobles, including the dauphin and the ducs d'Orléans, de Bourgogne, and de Berry, attended entertainments sponsored by the duchesse, including *La Tarentole*, a comédie-ballet by an ordinaire of the king named Matho.

The duchesse received much praise from her guests for reviving the kinds of *divertissements* that the king had taught them to enjoy.[12] She acquired further prestige by patronizing young musicians such as Colin de Blamont and Jean-Joseph Mouret. Several members of the aristocracy, including the duc de Chartres and the duchesse de la Ferté, followed du Maine's lead, so that at the beginning of the eighteenth century the vacuum in French musical life, which Louis' comparative disinterest had caused, was in some measure filled.

No similar remedy emerged, however, to compensate for the dwindling number of pompous ceremonies and celebrations in the last few years of the reign. The pages of the *Mercure galant* are strikingly barren of accounts of the colorful processions and commemorations which studded the early days of the monarchy. There were fewer victories to celebrate, and even the regular religious holidays inspired only colorless displays. When an especially important occasion arose, however, Louis marshaled the Grande Écurie to provide the appropriate background. For example, when the king and queen of England arrived in Paris in January 1691, they were accorded a parade and a blaring salute by trumpets, cymbals, drums, and organs by Louis' musical establishment.[13] In 1715 the arrival of ambassadors from Persia was celebrated with an elaborate procession conducted by the king's trumpeters on horseback.[14] In short, the king could still turn on the pageantry of the past when it was a question of impressing foreign dignitaries. The last really grandiose show of regal splendor occurred in connection with the duc d'Anjou's accession to the throne of Spain in 1700.

In staking the Bourbon claim to the Spanish kingdom, Louis was embarking on the most perilous foreign adventure of his reign, and he knew it. A coalition of European states just three years earlier had dealt a humbling blow to his territorial aspirations by forcing him to relinquish some previously conquered territory.[15] Laying claim to the crown of Spain in 1700 was, thus, an audacious invitation to the coalition powers to try to halt the new ambitions of the Bourbons. To pull it off, Louis needed a show of power, grandeur, and confidence equivalent to the ceremonial displays that crowned his earlier conquests. He made extensive preparations for Philip V's trip to Spain, so that it would include a steady series of festivals, ceremonies, and *divertissements*. The poet Jean-François Duché de Vancy, who composed librettos for several operas of the period, was ordered to accompany the royal entourage, which included the ducs de Bourgogne and de Berry, and to send back an account of the festivities. On the day of the new king's departure (December 4, 1700), Louis marched through the grand gallery of Versailles, accompanied by the officers of his household, his guard, a group of ambassadors, several ladies of the court, the princes of the blood, and the king of Spain. Upon arriving at the chapel, Louis knelt in the center of the richly decorated tribunal. The princes and courtiers were seated according to rank, "forming the most magnificent and most majestic *spectacle* that could be seen."[16] Michel de Lalande conducted the musicians of the chamber in his motet, *Beati omnes qui timent dominum*. The king, who followed the Latin and French texts during the performance, "felt affected and moved by the words and the excellent music of this motet, especially when the verse, 'Filii tui sicut novellae olivarum in circuitu mensae tuae,' ['your sons sitting around your table are like new olive saplings'] was sung; . . . he was unable to restrain tears of joy and sadness." After the ceremony, the king of Spain and his brothers traveled first to Toury, where they were greeted at the Hôtel de Ville by a cannon salute and fanfares. Subsequent halts at Orléans, Blois, Loches, and Poitiers were marked by public declamations, banquets, and balls. At Lusignan on December 20, the maréchal de Noailles regaled Philip and his company with a musical fete, with verses by Vancy, and music by the comte d'Ayen. The production included ballet entrées for the Muses and songs for Apollo, in which Philip was hailed as the harbinger of peace.[17]

Concerts, banquets, and ceremonial processions were held in Philip's honor in Bordeaux and other cities on the route. At Saint-Jean-de-Luz, where Philip left his companions, the royal entourage was entertained by Basque dancers for three days and four nights. After elegant farewell ceremonies, the ducs de Berry and de Bourgogne began the return trip through Bayonne, Toulouse, Montpellier, Marseilles, Toulon, Avignon, and Lyons.

Everywhere the two princes were treated to sumptuous festivities. At Toulon, they were escorted through the streets by a cavalcade of fifty musicians, and at Toulouse, the Jesuits performed a special ballet (*Les bergers heureux*) at the Collège. Composed by a professor of rhetoric, Père Courties, the ballet eulogized in song and dance the heroic virtues of the two princes and the peace between France and Spain. On March 6, the princes paraded along the coast into the city of Marseilles, where an arch of triumph had been erected. Ceremonies were held at the arsenal, and Lully's operas *Armide* and *Isis* were performed at the local branch of the Académie royale. At the port of Toulon on March 17, the princes watched an unusual marine spectacle: a mechanical whale swam in the bay to the accompaniment of a band of musicians, dressed as sea gods, who emerged from an artificial rock. Neptune sang the following verse:

> Depuis que le dieu du tonnerre,
> se repose sur les Bourbons
> Du soin de gouverner la terre,
> Neptune ne veut plus commander aux Tritons;
> Il nous soumet à vos lois :
> Daignez être nos Rois,
> Et de nos jeux recevez les hommages.[18]

After participating in a procession of boats in the bay, the princes listened to instrumental concerts performed in an aquatic, torch-lit theater. Rockets were fired and machine-driven crocodiles and whales belched fireworks.

The ducs de Berry and de Bourgogne were feted in Avignon on Easter, and on April 6, the Jesuits of Grenoble presented them with verses that praised Louis for extirpating heresy. Elaborate processions and religious services attended the princes' sojourn at Lyons in May, and André Campra's opera *L'Europe galante*, with a special prologue commemorating the union of France and Spain, was performed at the Académie. The long, ceremonious trek concluded at Versailles on April 25, 1701. In his last letter, Vancy reported that on every day of the five-month journey, the princes were regaled with "new and magnificent festivities." He concluded that "only in France can such remarkable things be

seen."[19] The trip once again called attention to the grand flourish
with which the House of Bourbon handled every important event.
It was, however, the final expression of ceremonial grandeur
during Louis' reign. Louis' bold bid to surmount the Pyrenees
resulted in the last, the longest, and the most frustrating war of
his career.

The Académie Royale de Musique

Lully's successors in the Académie lacked the administrative
and musical talent which had made the great master so successful.
Jean-Nicolas de Francine and his partner Hyacinthe Goureault
du Mont were plagued with financial problems, a breakdown of
discipline and musical standards among the performers, and
troublesome audiences. Receipts at the opera fluctuated greatly
from month to month and year to year: in January and February
1706, they averaged about 4,000 livres, but in the spring and
summer fell to between 1,000 and 1,500 livres. In the late autumn
they rose again to about 4,000. Total yearly receipts for 1706 were
just over 30,000 livres.[20] Expenditures were very high, however:
by the Lettres patentes of 1698, the directors of the opera were
obliged to pay 10,000 livres to Lully's children, 3,000 to the
composer Pascal Colasse, 3,000 to the machinist Jean Berain,
and additional prescribed sums to the singers, dancers, and
musicians. Suffering from a mounting debt, Francine and
Du Mont sold a share of the privilège of the Académie in 1704
to a financier, Pierre Guyonet. Divided management and financial
tangles continued to burden the Académie, however, and in 1712,
its total debt was 1,500,000 livres.[21] Absorbed with his own
problems, the king did little to help the Académie, except to
offer moral support. In 1705, the secrétaire d'État, Louis de
Pontchartrain, wrote a letter encouraging Guyonet to re-establish
the Académie on a firm basis: "Continue to apply yourself to it
and be sure that His Majesty will protect you on every matter."[22]

The disintegration of moral standards and discipline at the
Académie after Lully's death created serious problems. Many of
the singers feigned sickness in order to escape rehearsals, and the
high standards of performance set by Lully broke down. Moreover,

in violation of traditional practice, prominent nobles like the
duc de Chartres were admitted to the operas without charge,
and they used the Académie almost as a brothel. The eighteenth-
century writer Bois de Jourdain declared that under Francine
the Académie "served as a depository to recruit the joyful
daughters of debauched, moneyed persons from Paris or the
court."[23] One observer wrote that "the academy of music has
become an academy of love."[24] The predicament of the Académie
was satirized in the verse of a popular song, entitled, "Sur les
filles de l'opéra":

> Voulez-vous scavoir l'histoire
> des beautez de l'opéra?
> Un seul branle suffira
> pour vous remplir la mémoire
> Ah! qu'un branle convient bien
> à tant de filles de bien.
>
> Ce beau lieu fournit de belles
> à tous les gens d'aprésent,
> des matins pour de l'argent
> la morceau pour des dentelles,
> la grand guyard pour son pain
> La Rochois le fait pour rien.[25]

As in Lully's time, the sexual indulgence of the performers
resulted in many pregnancies, which compounded the difficulties
of the Académie. Louis' order that guards be stationed at the
Palais-Royal proved ineffectual. Occasionally, rakes from the
court abducted the ladies of the opera for a few hours' private
entertainment. On the conclusion of the military campaign of
1706, the dauphin, the duc d'Orléans, and the duc de Valentinois
brought several female dancers from the Académie to the duc de
Vendome's country estate near Paris. The marquis de Surville,
Vendome's aide-de-camp, reported what took place: "Their
highnesses were then entertained with a sight which displayed
to their eyes all the beauties of nature; and if the naked charms of
beautiful well made girls could delight their senses, they might
be said to enjoy at once all the pleasures of love to excess. The
dancers, to entertain their lovers, threw off their cloaths, and

danced stark naked all the entrees of the most celebrated operas. Their highnesses, each in their turn, directed the orchestra and musick; nobody but themselves being admitted into this theatre of love and pleasure. It was in this delightful manner that our princes and generals spent the greatest part of the winter at Anet, till towards the opening of the campaign in 1707."[26]

For several years after Lully's death, Louis XIV was indifferent to the Académie's financial plight, the relaxation of discipline, and the open sexual promiscuity and debauchery. He chose to interpret the criticisms aimed at both the Académie and at the Théâtre Italien as applying to the Italian players alone. Token gestures such as stationing guards at the Académie, forbidding anyone to enter the opera without paying, and ordering that no one should disrupt performances (1699) solved few problems.[27] In the last three years of his reign, however, the monarch inaugurated several reforms. In 1712, he ordered the construction of a hôtel for the Académie, which contained administrative offices, a library, a conservatory, a theater for rehearsals, and a ballroom. Built on the rue Saint-Nicaise at a cost of 120,000 livres, the hôtel was also to be used for masked balls. The Académie was given the exclusive privilege to produce these entertainments. It was hoped that tighter control over the disorderly balls could be obtained under the new establishment. Four months after Louis' death, the Regency issued regulations governing the conduct of balls: admission fees were mandatory; one door only was specified for entrance; no one was admitted who was not properly masked; and all persons were instructed not to commit any "violence, insult, or indecency."[28]

On January 11, 1713, Louis XIV issued a comprehensive set of eighteen "rules concerning opera."[29] The document stated: "His Majesty, having been informed that since the death of M. Lully, the regulation and good order of the interior of the Académie royale de musique have been relaxed gradually, . . . and that because of the confusion that is introduced, the said Académie has been found charged with considerable debts and the public exposed to the privation of a *spectacle* which has been quite pleasurable for a long time; and His Majesty, desiring the conduct to prevent similar inconveniences, has settled on the

present regulation, which he wants to be followed and executed."
Articles one and two of the royal mandate gave Francine the
right to select operatic subjects that were appropriate for the
voice, the dance, and the instruments, and accorded to the
composer André Destouches, who was made inspecteur général
of the opera, the right to approve all subjects. In addition, free
schools of music and dance were to be established to raise the level
of artistic standards. Article three decreed that persons employed
in the production of a *spectacle* must be in their proper places at
the time specified by the director, or pay a fine of three livres.
Performers were ordered (Article five) to accept their assigned
roles or suffer dismissal. Furthermore, the regulations specified
that a fine of six livres would be assessed any actor or actress
who disrupted the good order necessary for "the service of the
spectacle," or who was absent without the director's permission.
Several articles dealt with the appointment and payment of
employees of the Académie: Article ten provided for a register of
the salaries of each performer, and Article twelve created a fund
of 15,000 livres to be distributed as rewards to musicians or dancers
whose ability or service merited special consideration. An additional fund of 10,000 livres provided pensions for performers who
had served for fifteen years or who were forced by age or illness
to retire. Article fifteen established a policy for royalty payments
to composers and poets: both would be paid 100 livres for each
of the first ten performances of one of their compositions; 50 livres
were allocated for each of the next twenty performances, after
which all receipts would go to the Académie. The last article
entrusted the administration of the new regulations to the inspecteur général. It also specified that performers should wear only
their opera costumes in the theater and that actors and actresses
were required to stay out of each other's dressing rooms and out of
the orchestra. Finally, the king's regulations stipulated exact
salaries for each performer: the three counter-tenors received a
combined total of 3,700 livres; the chorus, 8,400 livres; twelve
females, 4,800 livres; the ballet master, 2,700; the orchestra,
20,150; and so on, for a grand total of 67,050 livres.

    In August 1714, Louis charged his maître des requêtes Noël de
Lepine d'Alican de Landivisiau with the task of helping the

Académie work out its problems under the new rules. Moreover, on November 19, 1714, the king issued another "règlement au sujet de l'opéra," which supplemented the earlier regulations by setting up the structure for a new opera administration. Many of the earlier articles were also restated. Together, the two sets of regulations represented the reassertion of monarchical control over, and centralization of, the production of dramatic music in France. Thus the king returned at the end of his life to the art form that had so richly contributed to his grandeur in better days.

The Involvement of the Church

While contending with the onerous problems of financial insolvency and royal disinterest, the opera also had to withstand mounting criticism from the Jansenists. Since the Fronde and the invasion of Italian performers, opera had been castigated as an unnecessary and costly exhibition of regal vanity. The musical *spectacle* was clearly linked to the practice of absolutism under Mazarin, so that criticism of the opera was tantamount to resistance to the cardinal. Much of the animadversion was couched in the righteous moralizing of the Jansenists and their sympathizers. Although obloquy was stifled after the Fronde, there was a resumption during Lully's ascendancy of the Jansenist attack on the turpitude of the opera. The criticism culminated in the 1690's in a sharp attack upon all forms of popular entertainment, including opera and drama. During the heyday of Louis' reign the Jansenists had been muffled, and the Jesuits provided support and reinforcement of the king's musical policy. Before considering the Church's sally against opera in the late years of the reign, it is necessary, therefore, to examine the Jesuits' promotion of music drama.

The Collège de Clermont, which was attended by many sons of the nobility, was the principal Jesuit school in Paris during the seventeenth century. From its founding in 1564, the Collège presented dramas in class during the last few days of each carnival season. The major yearly production, however, was given for the public in the courtyard of the Collège every August. In the 1630's, the Jesuits introduced ballets which were performed in conjunction with the dramas. But the ballets soon superseded the dramas in popularity and importance and gradually became full-fledged musical dramas with vocal airs, récits, and subjects resembling those presented at the Académie royale de musique. Indeed, although the Jesuit fathers composed most of the pieces themselves, the Collège also employed musicians and ballet instructors from the academies of dance and opera.[30]

The students of the Collège were trained in the skills and graces expected of persons who were about to enter the society of the court or the Church. They graduated only "after mastering the first qualities of the state."[31] Participation in plays was supposed to develop public-speaking skills and self-assurance in the students. When dancing became popular during Louis XIV's youth, the Jesuits justified their emphasis on ballet on grounds similar to those which the king would later advance in establishing the Académie de danse—it was a useful exercise and a dignified diversion. When opera was established in France, music became more essential in the productions of the Collège. In describing *David et Jonathas*, composed for the Jesuits by Marc-Antoine Charpentier in 1687, the *Mercure* observed that "it is right that the name of opera has been given to this work."[32] Writing in 1682, the Jesuit professor of rhetoric, Claude Menestrier, explained that musical *spectacles* not only enhanced the physical and social graces, but were useful in teaching morality to both performers and spectators. The Jesuit father argued that there was a long tradition of musical-dramatic productions in the Christian Church; and he declared his indifference to those who censured the Jesuits for not confining themselves to purely spiritual works. Dance and music are good for the Church, he asserted: "We are creating public celebrations, . . . in the form of ingenious allegories, in which the events that constitute the welfare of the state are presented, to enable people to enjoy the sweetnesses, through the enticements of pleasure and diversion, which renders them more responsive."[33]

The Jesuits not only concurred with the prevailing monarchical view of the utility of ballet and opera, they helped to reinforce the opulent tone of royal *spectacles* and to propagate the approved image of the king in their own *spectacles*. The future leaders of church, state, and court grew up participating in musical productions which exalted Louis in the manner of Lully and Quinault. The Jesuits' aim was stated quite simply by the professor, Père Jouvancy, in his treatise, *Ratio discendi et docendi* (1685): "If the tragedy has for its subject the peace which two kings have reestablished, the causes and the advantages of the peace will be depicted by the dance. If a war is necessary, the ballet will show the origin and preparation of it. If a Christian hero, triumphing over idolatrous enemies, is put on the stage, the ballet will develop this same idea of the victory of religion over idolatry."[34]

The Jesuit productions followed the events of the reign closely. Many of the performances celebrated royal births, weddings, and special state occasions. *Le mariage du Lys et de l'Impériale* was performed on August 19, 1660 in honor of Louis XIV's marriage and in the presence of the papal nuncio. Composed by Père Dozane de Falaize, the ballet depicted Louis' victory over a serpent representing the Spanish.[35] The Collège commemorated the dauphin's birth in 1662 with the ballet *Destinée de monseigneur le dauphin*. In 1680, the Jesuits presented a work entitled *Les arts, les sciences et les armes, employez par l'Hymenée pour le mariage de monseigneur le dauphin*, in which each of the characters had allegorical significance: the sun represented Louis; Mars was the dauphin; the stars were the Bourbons; and the celestial lion stood for Spain and Flanders.[36] A similar allegorical composition, *La naissance de Mercure*, was performed three years later to honor the birth of the duc de Bourgogne, and in 1697, the duke's birthday was celebrated at the Collège with a performance of *Ballet de la jeunesse*, which specified the proper education for a budding courtier. When the duc de Bourgogne's brother became the king of Spain in 1700, the Jesuits solemnized the event in the ballet *La conquête de la toison d'or*.

The most popular themes of the Jesuit ballets were military conquests and peace treaties. During Louis' second war with the Dutch, the Collège presented *L'empire du soleil* (1673), which depicted allegorically the perpetual success of French arms. The *Ballet de la paix*, in August 1679, was a memorial to the Treaties of Nimwegen: Louis was acclaimed as a virtuous peacemaker, and, in the concluding entrée, France led Spain, Sweden, the Empire, and Holland in a dance of peace.[37] In 1680, the Jesuits presented *France victorieuse sous Louis le Grand* at the Collège de Clermont. In the program accompanying the ballet, four triumphs were attributed to the king: the victory of his laws over disorder and injustice; the victory over ignorance through the advancement of the fine arts; the military victory over his enemies; and the victory over himself which enabled him to promote peace. These triumphs constituted the subjects of the ballet's four parts. Duelers, thieves, and magicians were punished in the first part, and Apollo and the Muses created paintings and sculptures of Louis in the second. Part three represented the French battling snow and wind to defeat the Dutch. The delineation of the dauphin's marriage in the final section celebrated the serenity of the peace.

In the ballet *Les travaux d'Hercule* (1686), Louis XIV was likened to Hercules. This dance depicted the suppression of heresy, the crossing of the Rhine, and the occupation of the Netherlands (see Chapter 7). The *Ballet de la paix* (1698), which solemnized the Treaty of Ryswick, was a blatant piece of propaganda: it stressed the advantages which France would reap by continuing the war against the League of Augsburg and exalted the king's magnanimity in granting peace to Europe. The subjects of all the Jesuit ballets bore striking resemblance to the operas at the Académie. Indeed, while Lully and Quinault presented songs of Louis' greatness at the Palais-Royal for the citizens of Paris, the Jesuits educated the sons of the nobility and the wealthy bourgeoisie to the glorious deeds of their monarch.

The Jesuit productions reached a wide audience, the ballet performances in August being open to everyone. Parents of students at the Collège came, of course, but so did the Parisian public, clerics from other religious orders, officers of the monarchy, courtiers, and, frequently, the king himself. In 1661, Jean Loret described the audience:

> Des Gens de haute extraction
> furent présens à l'action,
> J'y vis des Princes, des Princesses,
> Des Présidentes, des Comtesses,
> Quantité d'Esprits de bon sens,
> Et des Moines plus de deux cens.[38]

In June 1704, the deposed king of England was received at the Collège with great pomp: "He crossed the court to the sound of trumpets, drums, and acclamations from a great number of persons who were there to see this Prince."[39] A special prologue was presented on this occasion, in which "evil forces" were blamed for the revolt of James' subjects. Louis XIV, who often presented awards to the students, regarded himself as the protector of the Collège, and already in 1683 the institutions' name had been changed to the Collège Louis-le-Grand.

Although it was the birthplace and principal home of Jesuit music and drama in France, the Collège in Paris was only one of several Jesuit institutions where ballets were performed. Jesuit schools in Rouen and Poitiers likewise regularly produced works which resembled those of Paris. The *Mercure* reported a rather unusual composition performed in Rouen in the year of the queen's death. In the middle of the first entrée of the ballet, the allegorical character, Genius, interrupted the dancers in order to introduce a scene at a marble tomb. A vision of the queen appeared and verses expressing the king's sorrow were delivered. A chorus of Muses concluded the production with songs about the queen's triumph in heaven.[40] At the Collège de Poitiers, the Jesuit ballets tended to be very elaborate and nearly always alluded to the monarch's glory. The ballet produced there in 1688 dealt entirely with a quarrel among Mars, Peace, and Religion about who had given Louis the title of "le Grand." Each in turn presented his argument in a series of entrées in which the king's justice, piety, and bravery were dramatized. In the final entrée, a parade of deceased monarchs conceded Louis' right to the title.[41]

Charles Robinet characterized the Jesuits as "Pères scavans, bons Casuites, Artisans des beaux esprits.[42]" They were also highly useful servants of the state. They instructed the youth in the great deeds and virtues of the king and prepared them to enter the secure, well-regulated life of the court. We impart to the youth "this ease, this freedom of manners, which, in an aristocratic society, are highly appreciated qualities," declared the Jesuit teacher, Père Porée.[43] The musical dramas and ballets of the Jesuit schools were intended to be more than pleasurable exercises. They constituted a considerable part of the curriculum of the colleges and purportedly fostered desirable habits and talents. The Jesuits did not question the moral rectitude of their productions. Indeed, such advocates of opera and ballet as Père Menestrier contended that by stimulating admiration of the monarchy and promoting the virtues of bravery, benevolence, and magnanimity, the compositions of the Jesuits, like those of Lully, encouraged ethical behavior. During the prosperous years of Louis XIV's reign, the Jesuit view prevailed and Jesuit musical dramas supplemented the *spectacles* of the Académie and contributed to the fatuous image of the monarchy. In the straitened years of the post-Lully period, however, the Jesuit position was sharply challenged. As Louis grew older and became less concerned with grandiose entertainments, the Jansenists came forward to dispute the Jesuits and to contribute to the manifold difficulties of the Académie.

Although it did not become a matter of heated controversy until the 1690's, the question of the moral efficacy, not only of ballets and operas, but of comedies and theatrical productions, had already been raised several times. Not long after ballet first became popular at the French court, a pamphlet entitled *Traitté contre les danses* (1606) denounced dancing for stimulating concupiscence and vanity. The author Jean Boiseul declared that Satan used the dance to "strike up in our hearts his poison and mortal venom, in order to corrupt good morals."[44] Dancing allows too many "lascivious artifices," he asserted; and it fosters vain ostentation and idolatry. His argument found no supporters, however, and most of the literature on music in the first half of the seventeenth century stressed the moral utility of music and drama (see Chapter 1).

The Jansenist position on musical and dramatic productions was first stated by Blaise Pascal. Believing amusements to be dangerous generally for Christians, Pascal held that theatrical entertainments were the most hazardous. While seeming to provide innocent pleasure, they insidiously excite passions and stimulate men to emulate the vanity seen on the stage. Although they may fulfill a need, vainglorious entertainments are not really satisfying, even for kings, Pascal insisted: "I see well that a man is made happy by diverting him from the view of his domestic sorrows so as to occupy all his thoughts with the care of dancing well. But will it be the same with a king, and will he be happier in the pursuit of these idle amusements than in the contemplation of his greatness. ?"[45]

In 1666, Armand de Conti, a prince of the house of Bourbon-Condé and a Frondeur, stirred controversy by publishing a compendium of church canons relating to various types of musical and dramatic *spectacles*. The prince stressed the church's traditionally severe attitude toward *spectacles* and set forth canons attacking them for inciting moral laxity.[46] Almost simultaneously, the Jesuit priest François Hedelin d'Aubignac published a defense of the *spectacles*, in which he reeled off a list of churchmen, including Augustine, who endorsed them.[47] Conti refuted Aubignac's work in 1671, and an anonymous treatise in 1672 attacked the Jesuits for encouraging luxury, deceit, and sensuality in their theatrical pieces.[48] In 1673, the Protestant lawyer Samuel Chappuzeau jumped to the Jesuits' defense in his book *Le théâtre françois*. Insisting that Christians must not deny their emotions, Chappuzeau lauded the dramas and ballets of the Jesuit schools for pointing out the paths to virtue. The productions reveal to our youth, he declared, the triumph of glory, love, and great deeds. The students are given a taste of the valor and zeal of the prince, and they acquire an ardent hope of achieving glory in the king's service. Those who condemn modern *spectacles* are really assailing the gory *spectacles* of the ancients, which disappeared long ago, Chappuzeau contended. Praising operas such as *Cadmus*, the lawyer insisted that even the representations of war are compatible with Christian belief: "War is the noble profession of kings; war is just and commendable when its purpose is the defence of their rights and the preservation of their glory, and the evil purpose to which it can be put has never brought the *Directeurs* of Christianity to condemn it entirely."[49] French theater has reached its apex, he continued. The Italian and French comedians provide honest diversion for the public, and the dramatic poem, which has achieved perfection under Lully, "has charmed the entire court, all of Paris, and every foreign nation which is represented there." The final proof of the utility and uprightness of the modern *spectacle* is its authorization by the monarch.

"Whoever loves his king, loves his pleasures; and whoever loves his pleasures, loves those who give them to him, and who are no less necessary to the state." The great *spectacles* of our era, Chappuzeau concluded, are proof to the foreigner of the felicity which Louis provides for his kingdom.

After Lully's death, the Jesuit and monarchical attitude toward *spectacles*, which, ironically, had been presented so effectively by a Protestant lawyer, was fervidly denounced. A flood of criticism was precipitated by the pamphlet *Lettre d'un théologien illustré par sa qualité et par son mérite*. Written presumably by the Jesuit priest Père Caffaro, the *Lettre*, printed in a collection of dramas published in 1694, restated many of the old arguments for *spectacles*. After contending that the Councils of the Church and the writings of the Saints condoned *spectacles*, Caffaro asserted that it was "not a crime to create them, or a crime to perform them, or a crime to see them."[50] Caffaro denied that Thomas Aquinas and other theologians objected to *divertissements;* they condemned only the excesses of the lewd, libertine productions of the Romans, which have no relevance to modern times. Cypien's criticisms were aimed at Christians who performed wanton dances and lewd songs, "from which it is easy for you to judge that this saintly doctor does not condemn absolutely dances, songs, operas, and comedies, but only the *spectacles* which represented fables in the lascivious manner of the Greeks and Romans, and which were celebrated in honor of idols." If the *spectacles* of our own time are to be condemned, Caffaro asserted, then kings and colleges must also be upbraided for sponsoring them. Are the bishops, cardinals, and nuncios impious because they support *spectacles*, he queried? Does the king entreat his subjects to attend evil performances?

Presented in the post-Lully atmosphere of royal indifference, fiscal uncertainty, and artistic mediocrity, Caffaro's argument evoked virulent rebuttal. In the pamphlet *Réponse à la lettre du théologien défenseur de la comédie*, the Jansenist priest Père Lelevel charged that Caffaro was trying to substitute base human morality for the morality of Christ. Lelevel denied that Saint Thomas opposed only the excessive Roman *spectacles*, and he argued that all the components of modern productions conspire to make men forget God: "All the dances, all the songs from the operas, all the

verses, all the declamations of the comedies, do they give birth
to anything but profane sentiments?"[51] Does a man ever return
from a *spectacle* more religious or more chaste, he asked? Man is
sinful and his pleasures reflect his condition: "I see an Academy
of Music in which pride and self-confidence are the most sublime
virtues, in which one exchanges amorous endearments with
another. Miserable creatures affect power and divine majesty
there; they want to force all of nature to serve their passions;
only profane ideas are aroused there. ... I defy you to find
anything stronger in paganism." As for the *spectacles* of the Jesuit
colleges, Lelevel contended that they were not as evil as Lully's,
and that if priests indulged themselves by such entertainments,
it did not mean that everyone else should do the same. Although
Lelevel called for the excommunication and expulsion of the
Italian comedians, he stopped short of complete condemnation
of French drama, and he added: "If the theater is not closed, it is
through pure politics."

The stalwart proponent of Gallicanism Jacques-Bénigne
Bossuet, bishop of Meaux, jumped into the controversy on the
Jansenist side. In May 1694 he sent a letter to Caffaro urging the
Jesuit to reconsider his position. The bishop asked Caffaro if he,
as a priest, found virtuous "all the perverse endearments, all the
maxims of love, and all those sweet invitations to enjoy the good
times of youth," which are found in the plays of the comedians
and which "resound especially in the operas of Quinault."[52]
After reminding Caffaro that Quinault himself had regretted his
career at the Académie, Bossuet criticized the Jesuit for upholding
compositions even their creator had disavowed. Lully was the real
culprit, however, Bossuet averred, because his pleasing airs and
récits presented the deceiving passions of the text so agreeably.
The great danger of opera is that "while one is enchanted by the
sweetness of the melody or dazed by the marvels of the *spectacle*,
these sentiments creep in while one is not thinking about them,
and conquer the heart without being noticed." Caffaro's reply to
Bossuet was quite simple: he agreed with the bishop's views,
especially his condemnation of the comedians, and he denied
having written the *Lettre* in the first place.[53] Caffaro also asserted
his innocence in a letter to the archbishop of Paris on May 11.[54]

Criticism of drama, opera, and comedy did not abate as a result of Caffaro's denial of authorship. In the treatise *Réfutation d'un écrit favorisant la comédie*, Père de La Grange, theologian and canon of Saint-Victor, congratulated Caffaro for his denial and concluded that the *Lettre d'un théologien* must have been written by one of the actors. La Grange then stated his own objections to the position taken in the *Lettre*. Although the Scriptures may not specifically condemn comedy and opera, he asserted, they do censure the origin and meaning of the *spectacles*. Whether ancient or modern, all *spectacles* "have begun through superstition; they have been refined through pleasure; they have been maintained through politics."[55] Music and dance were originally aspects of pagan sacrifices. Loud symphonies were necessary to drown the piercing cries of the miserable creatures who were murdered and to animate the participants, just as drums and trumpets later spurred soldiers to pitched wrath. In time, these pagan *spectacles* were detached from superstitious rites by the great lords, who dedicated them to pleasure, installed them in their palaces, and displayed them to the public. Although they were transformed into dramatic poems, these new *spectacles* were no less profane than the frantic dances of pagan times, La Grange insisted. Pagan gods are still adored, passions are still enflamed, and, with the addition of récits, men are venerated as if they were gods. The aim of lasciviousness and the mood of idolatrous ritual have not changed. "In what manner does one see most of the operas begin, if not by the invocation of a divinity," La Grange asked. "Accompanied by a perfectly tuned symphony," an actress invokes a false god and makes sacrifices to him. Softened by amorous lovers and bucolic scenes and lured by music that is militant at first but that soon takes on a religious quality, the spectator is at the mercy of the god by the end of the performance. "This God of the Theater appears finally, in the midst of the airs, in a prodigious illumination, seated on the trophies of war; . . . beckoning silence to the entire symphony with his hand, he makes it clear that he approves the hero of the piece and that he has become favorable to his wishes." Is it any wonder, La Grange concluded, that the Church Fathers have called these *spectacles* idolatrous?

Before the end of the year 1694, the controversy over Caffaro's

Lettre and the rectitude of *spectacles* was taken up by the theologians of the Sorbonne. Père Gervais, one of the professors, published his own views prior to the official statement from the faculty. Addressing himself to Caffaro's contention that *spectacles* cannot be evil if the king approves them, Gervais wrote: "If His Majesty has supported the *spectacles* in former times, he may have had political reasons which are not the doctors' affair nor mine."[56] Perhaps the king believed that his presence would inspire sufficient respect to keep actors and spectators within the "bounds of modesty"; perhaps Louis just did not recognize the incompatibility of *spectacle* with Christianity.

The Sorbonne became involved in the controversy when the faculty was informed that one of the French players had been denied absolution by his parish priest for participating in allegedly immoral plays. The Sorbonne report, issued on May 20, 1694, dealt mainly with comedy productions. After upholding the decision to deny absolution to the comedians, the six professors reviewed both the affirmative and negative judgments of church councils. They concluded that comedies feed on the sinful nature of man and are, therefore, a pernicious influence. Moreover, the report declared that opera was much more dangerous than comedy: "There is nothing more suitable for corrupting the heart than those languishing and tender airs of music, adapted to words, [which are] capable of arousing us greatly and which are sustained by gestures and movements suited to this purpose."[57]

The judgment of the Sorbonne professors was upheld in several additional treatises appearing in 1694. Abbé Laurent Pegurier, a priest of Saint-Sulpice, emphasized that the saints of the Church had never criticized particular *spectacles*, but had condemned all *spectacles*. Pegurier urged the king to expel comedy troupes from the kingdom.[58] Père Le Brun of the king's chapel wrote two *Discours sur la comédie* in which he charged that anyone, including a churchman, who participated in or attended the theater was guilty of mortal sin.[59] In an address given to the Séminaire de Saint-Magliore in April, Le Brun did defend the right of Jesuits to produce "pious tragedies" in their schools.[60] Another prominent Jansenist cleric, Antoine Arnauld, also issued an attack on comedy and opera in a letter to Charles Perrault. Arnauld's major concern was that operatic airs were not confined to the Académie, but were spread throughout France and were popular with great numbers of people.[61]

The controversy over *spectacles*, or, more correctly, the criticisms of music and drama launched by the Jansenists, drew slight attention from the court. Madame, the duchesse d'Orléans, suggested that the professors of the Sorbonne might have issued their statement in the belief that it would appeal to the pious king: "We almost stopped having any more plays, because the Sorbonne, thinking to please the King, tried to have them forbidden. The archbishop of Paris and Père La Chaise, however, must have told them that it would be too dangerous to interfere with inoffensive amusements, because that would drive young people to various forms of vice. As far as I am concerned, I shall continue to go to plays until they are abolished altogether."[62] Madame's defiance was echoed by her peers. She also revealed, however, that the court was subjected to sermons criticizing such entertainments. Commenting on one sermon, the duchesse reported that the king said: "He is not preaching at me at any rate, because I do not go to the play nowadays, but at you people who are fond of it and go often."[63] Madame replied that the priest's remarks did not apply to her, "because he is inveighing only against those who allow their passions to be excited by the plays, and I am not one of those." The king, she concluded, "had nothing to say" in return.

One of the principal sermons of criticism was delivered by Père Jean Soanen, a priest of the king's chapel. Entitled *Sur les spectacles*, the homily denounced all forms of *spectacle* as the work of the devil. Arguments that theatrical productions improved morals and that the Church Fathers favored *spectacles* were blasphemous, according to Soanen. The priest charged that the devil undermined Christian piety and simplicity by employing sounds and words to incite lust. He argued that society was mirrored in the theater: "Yes, the theater is the picture of the world, a picture which, through the deeds with which it is filled, is more dangerous than the world itself."[64] All the vanities and errors of the century are paraded at the theater. God will unleash his wrath on those who relish the theater, because the *spectacles* are the symbols of paganism which remain in Christian society: "Yes, my Brothers, these *divertissements* which you excuse, or that you regard as beyond the concern of both religion and morality; these Tragedies which you go to hear with an enthusiasm that can not be expressed; these Operas that you find so magnificent and so marvelous; these Comedies that you call the school of *savoir-vivre*, and of good morals, are the ceremonies of Satan."

Soanen's harsh admonitions and the scorching criticisms leveled against *spectacles* by the Jansenists and their sympathizers had remarkably little effect on the court or the Académie. Louis' austerity had already been felt at Versailles prior to 1694. That the Jansenist position on *spectacles* was expressed so boldly and openly was symptomatic of the decline of elaborate musical productions at court. Nevertheless, the nobles amused themselves elsewhere and the Académie continued to sponsor regal productions. In spite of his personal disinterestedness, the king was never prepared to scuttle his *divertissements* entirely or to abolish the musical and dramatic establishment which had contributed significantly to his public image. Far from being noxious to the king, the morality of the opera sustained the ethics of the royal absolutism. The king did, of course, issue a code of regulations in 1714 designed to tighten discipline. But the operas, themselves, were as valid for reasons of state after Lully's death as they had been during the high point of the absolutism. The strongest evidence of the extent to which music had become an institution of state and an instrument of royal policy is, perhaps, the continuing operation of the Académie royale de musique and the steady presentation of operas glorifying Bourbon policies in a climate of Church hostility, economic retrenchment, and military failure.

The Last Operas

Although many of the essential characteristics of Lully's operas were retained by his successors, the post-Lully period represented a regression. The drama lost its unity and coherence. The plot again became little more than a pretext for ballet entrées and diversion scenes like the tempest in Pascal Colasse's opera *Thétis et Pélée*. Occasionally, as in André Campra's *L'Europe galante* (1697), the entire production resembled a grandiose ballet with multiple plots and numerous exotic effects. In fact, it was often difficult to label the form of a dramatic composition, because operas, ballets, pastorals, and musical comedies so greatly resembled one another. In contrast to Lully, composers such as Campra and Henri Desmarets abandoned the French recitative style and imitated, instead, Italian arias. They employed florid coloraturas, bold modulations, and chromatic harmonies. Italian backgrounds were even used in works such as Campra's *Les fêtes vénitiennes* (1710). Quoting a letter in 1714, which argued that the Italian style had inundated French music and diluted French taste, the *Mercure* stated that Lully "knew perfectly well the necessity of renouncing the taste of his nation in order to accommodate himself to ours; he found that the French judged some things more sanely than the Italians; and he knew that music had no other end than to titillate the ear; it was unnecessary to charge it with affected dissonances."[65]

Several composers competed to fill the musical lacuna created by Lully's death, including Michel de Lalande, Pascal Colasse, André Campra, Marin Marais, André Destouches, and Henri Desmarets. Lalande, who had already attained recognition for his motets, succeeded to the office of superintendent of the music of the king. In 1686 he composed two successful ballets: *Ballet de la jeunesse* and *Épithalame*. Performed for Louis XIV at Versailles in January 1686, *Jeunesse* was a veritable opera with a long prologue, in which a group of shepherds praised the king for providing his people with a "deep tranquillity." A song by one of the shepherds established the theme of the entire ballet (Example 19).[66] Members of the nobility, including the duchesse de Bourbon, Madame de Lafare, and the prince de Rohan, danced many of the principal roles. *Épithalame*, whose thirteen recitatives, fifteen choral passages, and lengthy chaconne indicated the operatic character of the work, was performed on June 28, 1686, to celebrate the marriage of the duc de Bourbon and Mademoiselle de Nantes.

Lully's unfinished opera *Achille et Polixène* (he had composed the overture and the first act), was completed by his industrious secretary Pascal Colasse, whose own undistinguished career

Example 19

Vi-ves vi - ves heur - eux   sous cet em - pire

commenced after the Florentine's death. Colasse retained the style of his mentor, and with the poet Jean Galbert de Campistron he composed a traditional adulatory prologue in which Jupiter recommended resurrecting the memory of the invincible hero, Achilles. Jupiter counseled the Muses to base their characterization of Achilles' valor and wisdom on the model of Louis XIV.[67] It is ironic that Louis' Achilles heel was the passion for glory and conquest which operas such as *Achille et Polixène* celebrated.

Drawn by curiosity about Lully's successor, large crowds fought for seats at the theater in the Palais-Royal. The *Mercure historique et politique* reported that a seat at the first performances of *Achille* in November 1687 had to be obtained at noon and held throughout the day. The dauphin came from Versailles and Maréchal d'Humières rose from a sickbed, despite the remonstrances of his physician, to attend the opera.[68] Colasse disappointed the spectators, however. The *Mercure* noted that the conformity of "our latest composers" to the rules has not guaranteed beautiful music. The journal expressed amazement that Colasse had not absorbed more of the master's style.[69] The actors were less kind. In the parody *Plainte de Priam*, Lully's ghost questioned Colasse and Campistron about the failure of their opera. Colasse blamed the public's low taste. Campistron accused the court of indifference but predicted brighter days:

> Le bon goût des savans du peuple et de la cour,
> Ce retour servira contre la vaine gloire,
> Dont nos Provinciaux sont enflés chaque jour
> Quand ils auront apris ma trop funeste histoire.[70]

In 1688, Lully's two sons, Louis and Jean-Baptiste, made a feeble attempt to carry on their father's work in the three-act opera, *Zéphire et Flore*. The work was performed several times in the spring, but elicited only a weak commendation from the *Mercure*.[71]

In October 1688, Louis XIV's armies invaded the Palatinate. In quick succession, Neustadt, Heidelberg, Mainz, Worms, and other German cities capitulated to France in this first phase of the War of the League of Augsburg. The array of nations which lined up against France was formidable. The *Mercure historique* stated that "the court is overcome with concern and anxiety," but, the journal added that "it acts as if it were profoundly confident."[72] In January, Louis invited the nobles to the Trianon Palace, where the recent siege of Philippsburg, under the nominal command of the dauphin, was celebrated by a performance of Lalande's new ballet, *Le palais de Flore*. In the meantime, Paris was treated to Colasse's and Fontenelle's version of the meaning of the burning and pillaging of the Palatinate. The prologue of the opera, *Thétis et Pélée* (parts of which were sung for Louis and the court on apartment days), began with a lachrymose aria about peace and repose, sung by Night; a shrill trumpet fanfare and a chorus of Victory, however, announced the true mood of the opera: "Let us go, let us not be late; a Young Hero calls us; Let us go and crown him in the horror of combat." Victory persuades the Night to relinquish her somber air, and the Night's steadily paced, quarter-note melody is replaced in the third scene of the prologue by the swift, agitated line of Victory (Example 20).[73] The Sun tells Victory that he will pass from

Example 20

Du Pa-lais du So-leil la bar-rière é-cla-tant - e   S'ou-vre de mo-ment en mo-ment.

battle to battle to illuminate the dauphin's conquests for his father. Thousands of enemies will surrender, the Sun sings, and the new hero will bequeath his exploits to posterity.

Thétis was performed in the festive atmosphere of the carnival season of 1689. The *Mercure galant* reported sanguinely that the people, relying on the king's vigilance, could enjoy their pleasures in the knowledge that the more enemies France had to fight, the greater her glory would be. The *Mercure's* optimism was justified in 1690 when the French routed the Dutch armies as well as the forces of the Duke of Savoy. Disregarding the precarious state of France's finances, the *Mercure* gloated: "All of Europe, leagued against the king for two years, does not prevent everything from continuing as usual in France. Only the states of our enemies feel the effects of the war, and the magnificence which is customary at the opera, seems to have increased this year in the opera, *Énée et Lavinie*, which has just opened. In fact, nothing more sumptuous can be seen than the costumes and the decorations."[74]

The public was enthusiastic about Colasse's *Énée et Lavinie*, according to the *Mercure;* there was unprecedented applause following a prologue that alluded to the prosperity and contentment of the French in the face of adversity. In the final two scenes the trumpets introduced a military motif and a chorus of Titans sang:"We are going to overcome the Empire."[75] Colasse's prologue, composed mainly of extensive choral sections and ballet entrées, lacked the musical diversity and dramatic development characteristic of Lully's works.

The operas produced at the Académie in the 1690's expressed an attitude of complacent optimism about Louis' war against the League of Augsburg. The king was regularly represented as the heroic underdog who overpowers his opponents in the pursuit of the just and honorable goals of French foreign policy. At the same time, in order to mitigate his militancy, the librettos pointed to the domestic tranquillity of France and to the king's promotion of art and entertainment. The prologue to *Orphée* (1690), by Louis and Jean-Baptiste Lully, called for praise of the monarch for preventing the League from despoiling the brilliance of France.[76] An anonymous short opera entitled *La feste universelle à l'honneur de Louis le Grand* reminded the audience that Louis had stamped out heresy, subdued internal strife, and ended dueling. His love for battle is unimportant next to these accomplishments, the chorus declared. His conquests are harmless pursuits, and he obtains them without leaving his court.[77] In the opera *Astrée* (1691) by Colasse and La Fontaine, the performers sang that "terror and fear respect these beautiful lands;" the Rhine witnesses French bravery and the Danube will soon feel that Bourbon sting.[78] And in the verses accompanying Colasse's ballet *Villeneuve Saint-George*, Pan predicts that the French conqueror will soon terminate the war, because he can find no more enemies worthy of him.[79]

The initial successes of the French against the League of Augsburg were extended between 1691 and 1693 by victories over William III in the Netherlands and over the Duke of Savoy. The operas, in turn, attempted to impart an ebullient spirit to the French people and to suggest the rightness of the French cause. In the prologue to *Alcide* by Marin Marais, Louis Lully, and Jean Galbert de Campistron, Victory commits herself to Louis' designs because "his prudence forces me to favor them," while a chorus of French shepherds testify about their happiness and freedom from fear:

> De tous nos ennemis la fureur et les armes
> Ne nous font point sentir d'alarmes;
> Nous ne craignons point leurs projects. . . .
> Cérès pour nous prodigue ses bienfaits.
> Les plus riches moissons brillent sur notre terre.
> Nous joüissons au milieu de la Guerre,
> Des biens d'une profonde paix.[80]

Similarly, in the *Médée* of Marc-Antoine Charpentier and Thomas Corneille, an opera that won rare plaudits from the king, Victory explains that France is her residence because she is attached to the wise ruler who strives to bring peace to the world and is opposed to his enemies who seek to prolong bloodshed.[81]

Operas in 1694 by the female composer E. C. de Laguerre (*Céphile et Procris*) and by Henri Desmarets (*Didon*) also dwelt on the justice of Louis' cause, the odious envy of his enemies, and the well-being of the French people. In 1695 Desmarets and Jean-François Duché de Vancy contrasted the battlefield conquests of French arms in the ballet *Les amours de Momus* with the placidity of the homefront in the operas *Théogène et Cariclée* and *Circé*.[82] *Circé* in particular stressed the idea that only on the banks of the Seine were concord, prosperity, and beauty preserved untouched by "bloody war." Finally in 1696, during the period when Louis was negotiating for a separate peace with Savoy, Pascal Colasse's two ballets *La naissance de Vénus* and *Ballet des saisons* and his opera *Jason* suggested that the war had run its course. The king's pacifistic intentions were underscored, and he was hailed for seeking to extend France's serenity to the rest of Europe.[83]

During a highly successful career in which he enjoyed the recognition of the monarch and the approbation of the Parisian public, Jean-Baptiste Lully was subjected to a constant barrage of scathing satire in popular songs and parodies, emanating chiefly from the Hôtel de Bourgogne where the Italian comedians performed (see Chapter 5). The composers and poets who struggled to succeed to the mantle of Lully and Quinault in the decade of the 1690's were not safe from the comedians' barbs. Indeed, the criticism was perhaps more pointed, because, even though the "proper" image of the king and the "official" view of Louis' wars were presented as before, the Bourbon ruler did not pamper his new sycophantic musical chroniclers as he had the Florentine. Moreover, the practitioners of parody very often presented a clearer picture of the popular reaction to the war than did the creators of the opera; they also offered more accurate appraisals than did the journals of the talents of Colasse, Desmarets, Campistron, and Duché de Vancy. Colasse was the favorite whipping boy. The verses for a satire of his opera *Astrée* suggest the ridicule to which he was subjected:

> Colasse, dont Paris déteste le . . . Ramage,
> Ce ridicule objet d'un grotesque . . . charbon
> Comptoint les opéra parmi son . . . héritage,
> Mais Celadon s'embarque et n'a pas le vent . . . bon.
>
> Malgré ses partisans et leur longue . . . rapière,[84]
> Malgré le fier Pecour et la garde . . . portière,
> On entend rentenir l'équitable . . . sifflet.[85]

In one of the satirical songs, the anonymous composer suggested that with all the jeers which greeted Colasse's operas, a fortune could be made selling whistles at the Académie.[86] The accuracy of such ridicule was attested by the *Mercure*, which, in 1694, noted that opera singers were hooted from the stage by "whistlers" and that the parterre seethed with so much controversy over the operas that it resembled the English Parliament.[87]

The comedians, who lampooned the opera so sharply, were in turn the targets of the Jansenists. The comedians and the Jansenists shared a dislike of opera, but the Jansenists included the parodies of the Italian performers in their general condemnation of *spectacles*. It is ironic that the sole result of the Jansenist-Jesuit controversy over *spectacles* was the expulsion of the Italian comedians. On May 4, 1697, the lieutenant-général of police, acting on the king's instructions, posted a lettre de cachet at the Hôtel de Bourgogne expelling the Italian comedy troupe from France. Although the Italians did not return until 1716, their tradition was perpetuated by the French comedians who, in spite of certain restrictions, continued to compose topical and satirical verses to accompany popular songs and operatic airs.[88]

Soon after the comedians' expulsion, the Treaty of Ryswick terminated the War of the League of Augsburg. Louis' concessions to William III, and later to the emperor, did not substantiate the claims of victory made in the operas. In October 1696, a composition designated simply as *Églogue ou pastorale* by Louis Lully was performed for the king at Fontainebleau. Apollo's air established the theme:

> Louis, près à lancer la foudre
> À ses fiers ennemis, offre une heureuse paix;
> Plus puissant que jamais,
> Il pouroit les réduire en poudre;
> Mais le bonheur du monde ayant lui tant d'attrait,
> Qu'il arreste aujourd'hui le cours de ses hauts faits.[89]

Europe pins its hope on Louis, Glory continued; he extends a hand of friendship to his enemies and he has capped his illustrious achievements on the battlefield with the laurel crown of magnanimous peace.

In December 1696, the *Mercure* printed the text of a short opera
(the composer and poet were not identified) that was being produced in Paris. The scene was Piedmont, where two opposing
armies were dispersed by Mercury, who explained that Louis,
having "touched the heart of your princes," has restored relations
with his former allies, the Piedmontese. The piece concluded
with Mercury's admonition to the nations of Europe to heed the
king's kindly offers of friendship.[90]

Louis invited the Académie to present the opera *Issé* at the
Trianon in December. The music was composed by André
Destouches, who had once prepared to become a Jesuit and had
traveled to Siam with Père Tachard. The text was written by
Antoine Houdar de La Motte, who had abandoned the austere
life of the Trappist monks in favor of more capricious adventures.
The king was probably more impressed with Destouches than
with any composer since Lully. Louis presented Destouches with
a gift of 200 louis d'ors in order to encourage him. Louis also
apparently advised the composer on *Issé*, for Destouches noted
in his dedication that the king had already "listened to a part of
this work" and that a scene had been added "on his orders."[91]
Destouches and La Motte honored their patron with a prologue
in which Hercules killed a dragon who was making war on the
Hesperides (the mythical protectors of the garden of golden
apples). Hercules' victory made the garden accessible to all the
peoples of the earth. According to La Motte, Hercules was "the
exact image of the king, who has conquered so often only in order
to be able to end the war, and to render to his peoples and to his
neighbors the prosperity which they desire."[92]

Aping Lully's musical style, Destouches shifted from the key
of D major, which he used in the choral passages about the
Hesperides, to the relative a minor for references to guarding the
treasure against the profane dragon symbolizing the League of
Augsburg. He employed wide melodic leaps, recurrent fanfare
motifs, dominant seventh chords, and rapid string figures in the
battle scene between Hercules and the dragon; and as Lully
might have done, he passed from minor to major when Hercules
assured the Hesperides that his goal was not plunder but the
opening of fertile fields to commerce. To accompany Jupiter's

descent from the heavens, Destouches introduced a musical filigree of grace notes, grupettos, and mordants, more typical of Italian practice than of Lully's. Destouches' choruses and ballet entrées clearly showed the Florentine's influence, but the vocal airs and orchestral embroideries were cast in a florid style that was unmistakably Italian. The five acts of *Issé* celebrated the ideas of peace, prosperity, and love, and in the last scene, Destouches composed a grand procession of nations in which peoples representing Europe, China, America, and Egypt sang homages to the monarch.

While the court was being indoctrinated in the "mysteries" of Louis' magnanimity, Paris was subjected to similar fare. *Issé* had been running at the Académie since October and a new opera by Henri Desmarets, *Vénus et Adonis*, hailed the extinction of war. André Campra's opera-ballet *L'Europe galante*, with verses by La Motte, was the central attraction of the season. Campra, the master of music at Notre-Dame, composed a score that sufficiently resembled both opera and ballet to defy categorization and to introduce what amounted to a new, combined form.[93] The theme of *L'Europe* was the return of love and the expulsion of discord, but its principal appeal was centered in the exotic costumes and the entrées of the different nations. The duchesse d'Orléans wrote: "The play they are playing now is really only a ballet, but it is very nice. It is called *L'Europe galante*, and it shows how the French, Spanish, Italians, and Turks make love. The characteristics of these nations are splendidly portrayed, which makes it very amusing."[94]

The festive atmosphere pervading the French court continued into 1698. The lavish *tragédies-lyriques* and spectacular *divertissements* which had formerly greeted the end of a war were nowhere in evidence, but Louis XIV sponsored performances at Fontainebleau of the short musical pastorals *Apollon* and *Mirtil* by Louis Lully and Lalande. In Paris, Henri Desmaret's ballet *Les festes galantes*, which celebrated Bacchus' return to the court, was presented at the Académie. Even the usually derisive satirical songs reflected the mood of exultation prevailing in this postwar period. The *Mercure* printed a song "of the times" that the journal contended was sung in every province of France (Example 21).[95]

Example 21

Tout est cal - me sur la ter - re, Nous ne crai-gnons plus les haz-
ards, A - près u - ne si longue et si sang - lan - te
guer - re, La paix a tri - om - phé
- de Mars tou - t Mars. Lou- is le grand en a
tou - te la gloi - re, Heur- eux qui vit
sous sa loy, Et qui peut s'é - cri - er en
ne ces-sant de boi - re. Vi - ve le
Roy Vi - ve Vi - ve Vi - ve le Roy.

In 1699 Louis Lully composed two more pastorals for the court, *Le carnaval mascarade* and *Le triomphe de la raison sur l'amour*, and Destouches offered two new operas, *Marthésie* and *Amadis*. In October the prologue and first act of *Marthésie* were presented at Fontainebleau, and several days later the king heard the prologue again during his supper. *Marthésie* was also performed at Versailles in November in the king's apartment. All the performances were given indoors without elaborate staging, scenery, or costumes. The music alone was sufficient diversion for the monarch. More imposing productions of *Marthésie* and *Amadis*, however, were given at the Palais-Royal. The prologues to both operas were reminiscent of the grandiose style of Lully. Destouches employed harmonic and rhythmic devices to project the text and composed a florid vocal line to embellish key words such as triumph (Example 22)[96] and glory (Example 23).[97] La Motte's librettos

Example 22

d'au-tre   tri - om   -   phe

Example 23

gloi   -   re

dwelt less on the Sun King's olive branch than on the big stick with which he clubbed his enemies into peaceful behavior. For both operas, Destouches wrote dedications in which, like Lully, he likened his heroes to the Bourbon ruler, but he professed his inability to create a drama of bravery and beneficence worthy of the king.

The two works were successful at court and in Paris, but the acclaim did not gag the Italian comedians. One satirical song, composed on the air *Reveillez-vous* from *Amadis*, taunted La Motte for returning to a subject which Quinault had used previously:

> L'auteur avant tout veut écrire
> Et faire au Roi voir son esprit
> Mais il ne scait plus que lui dire
> Car par malheur on a tout dit.[98]

The king was also a target for its barbs:

> Du Roi l'on voit là les devises
> Il est le héros de la paix
> On dit encor d'autres sottises
> Que Termes louë à peu de frais.

In the final verse, Destouches, who had once contemplated a
military career, was mocked:

Pour la musique il faut s'en faire
Je l'ignore mais je scai bien
que jamais mauvais mousquetaire
ne devint bon musicien.

A spate of musical productions appeared at the turn of the
century. Colasse and La Motte composed the ballet *Le triomphe
des arts* and the opera *Canente*. In a tongue-in-cheek dedication of
the ballet to the duc de Bourgogne, La Motte contended that
the duke had inherited his modesty from Louis. Some great men
patronize the arts in order to reap vain eulogies in return; but
you, La Motte assured the duke, possess the monarch's diffidence.[99]
The year 1700 also brought André Campra's first opera, *Hésione*.
Campra, whose ballet *Le dentin de nouveau siècle* was produced
during the carnival season, introduced *Hésione* at the Académie
on December 21. Provided with a dull text by the poet Antoine
Danchet, Campra tried to generate musical interest by sprinkling
his score with the orchestral mimicry of chirping birds and
battle noises. He departed sharply from Lully by composing
several contrapuntally thick choral passages and an unusually
large number of vocal coloraturas. The text, which stated the
standard clichés about Louis' virtues, afforded Campra several
opportunities to indulge in contrapuntal writing to buttress
the message. A choral segment from the end of the prologue is
typical of Campra's technique (Example 24).[100] Instead of illumi-
nating the text, however, Campra often obscured it. The satirists
perceived the weakness:

Quel triomphe : Nouveau Lulli,
Dit Phoebus, quelle gloire!
Moins son sujet est accompli
Plus belle est la victoire
Nous donnans pour t'en päier
Une double Couronne
Europe, prenez du Laurier
Vite qu'on la faconne.[101]

Undaunted by the criticisms, Campra served up the same bag
of musical gimmicks in his new opera, *Aréthuse*.[102] The prologue
of both operas continued to stress the popular support of the
peace.

Example 24

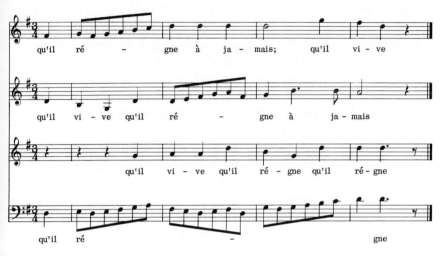

Operas were, thus, in abundant supply in the first few years of the eighteenth century. Writing to the Countess Palatine in 1701, the duchesse d'Orléans asserted: "Every day people say to me, today there is going to be a new opera, or, tomorrow a new play will be produced. This very year there have been—and it has happened thus before—six new comedies and three new operas. I think the Devil has done it on purpose to tease me in my solitude."[103] When deprived of musical fare at Versailles or Fontainebleau, the courtiers went to Paris to see the operas. The king, however, whose own entertainments were restricted, even during this period of celebration, paid scant attention to the new spate of music dramas. When he did hear an opera, it was only in fragments over his meals or in his private quarters. Louis was preoccupied during this period with the problem of the succession to the Spanish crown. In 1698 and 1700 he negotiated treaties of partition with England and the Empire, and in November 1700, on the death of Charles II, Louis proclaimed his grandson, the duc d'Anjou, king of Spain. The event was commemorated in the opera *Danaé* by Anne Philidor, a member of the celebrated Philidor family of musicians. Subtitled "Peace of the Pyrenees," the prologue treated, allegorically, the conjunction of the Tagus and Seine rivers and the efforts of France and Spain to resist the warlike threats of Envy and Discord. Prudence forces the dis-

rupters to "submit to the most beautiful blood in the world."[104]
Envy and Discord (the Empire, England, and Holland) were not
really so obliging, however; they formed a Grand Alliance in
September 1701, and sent armies under Prince Eugene of Savoy
and the Duke of Marlborough into the field against the French.

The War of the Spanish Succession brought an expected shift
in emphasis to the music dramas: glory and valor replaced
beneficence and peacefulness as the paramount attributes of the
monarch; placid bucolic scenes gave way to the turbulence of
battle and the strident fanfares of victory. Campra and Antoine
Danchet pieced together scraps of old ballets by Jean-Baptiste
Lully, entitled the piece *Fragments de Lully*, and presented it at
the Académie on September 10, 1702. An original prologue made
the work timely. The Muse Polymnie emphasized that the
military exploits of "the greatest king of the universe" overshadowed all his other accomplishments, and the other Muses
replied: "Let us sing about the glory of his arms."[105] In November,
Campra and Danchet reiterated this theme in the opera *Tancrède*.
Opening on a tranquil scene before a magnificent palace, the
prologue dealt with the contrast between the jocularity of dancers
on the banks of the Seine and the ominous prophecies of a figure
representing peace. The contrasting moods were harmonized,
however, by the enchantress of the palace, who sang confidently
about Louis' ability to defeat jealous aggressors. The enchantress
called on the dancers to perform concerts depicting the victory of
France over the combined forces of her enemies.[106] *Tancrède* was,
thus, a musical plea to the French people to be sanguine about the
new war.

In spite of the English naval victory over the French in the
Bay of Vigo at the end of the campaign of 1702, Campra and
Danchet composed a ballet, *Les muses*, suggesting that "all the
waves of the universe" lay at Louis' feet.[107] The ballet was the
only major new production at the Académie in 1703; in 1704,
Henri Desmarets and Duché de Vancy composed a new opera,
Iphigénie, which the Académie produced in May. Before he could
complete the opera, however, Desmarets was ordered to go to
Spain to serve as the superintendent of music for Philip V.
Campra and Danchet completed the work. Prior to the defeat at

Blenheim in August 1704, the French had chalked up a string of successes in Italy, Germany, and Holland. The mood of *Iphigénie*, therefore, was buoyant and optimistic. The opera included choral celebrations of the king's conquests and florid depictions of the "flight to victory." Moreover, in another work, the ballet *Alcine* (1704), Campra set forth a musical supplication to the king's soldiers to charge to victory: "Go, go warriors, fly to the midst of alarms."[108] The word "fly" was projected by sudden spurts of ascending eighth notes and subjected to innumerable repetitions which became increasingly imitative as the word passed from the chorus to soloist. The enemies of France were also threatened by Time in Campra's prologue. After assuring the enemies of peace that the sovereign empire under her protection would not succumb easily, Time predicted that she would witness the destruction of the strongest ramparts while sheltering the bastions of her own heroes. *Alcine* was almost a rekindling of the fiery *spectacles* of Lully and Quinault, except that Campra's technique differed substantially from the Florentine's. Instrumental and choral passages were distinctly more contrapuntal; coloraturas peppered the score; and the harmony seldom modulated very far from the tonic.

In spite of Time's prediction, the French did not recover from the defeats of 1704 and 1705. Allied victories at Ramillies and Turin in 1706, at Oudenarde in 1708, and at Malplaquet in 1709 gave the subjects of the Sun King little to celebrate. The Académie suffered from lean years. Only André Campra continued to grind out an occassional music drama. But his pedestrian efforts failed to attract audiences, and he was jeered by the satirists.[109] Campra tried to recoup his failures by switching in 1707 to a new librettist—the poet, Pierre-Charles Roy—but the attempt was feckless. Meanwhile, with the assistance of Charpentier and the marquis de la Fare, the duc d'Orléans attempted an opera. The future regent's *Pentée* was performed at the Palais-Royal on July 16, 1705, but it was never published. Appropriately, the prologue had contemporary relevance only in so far as it dealt with bacchanalian revels, thus anticipating the mien of the duke's court during the Regency.[110]

Very few operas were given at the court or at the Académie

royale de musique between 1707 and 1712. Campra's ballet *Les festes vénitiennes* was the only new composition presented in Paris. Produced on June 17, 1710, and known as *La carnaval de Vénice*, the ballet did not mention Louis XIV or the war.[111] There was, indeed, nothing to celebrate. The economy was in a ruinous condition and the allies inflicted new and heavy losses on the French with each new engagement. As early as 1707, Louis made overtures to the emperor and to England, but the war was not terminated. The Whig's accession to power in England in 1711, which brought Marlborough's removal and more earnest negotiations for peace, was the opportunity Louis needed. The French won a victory over the imperial forces at Denain and recaptured several positions. In 1712 a peace conference opened in Utrecht and soon brought an end to hostilities between France and England, Holland, Portugal, and Savoy. The emperor continued the war, however, until 1714.

Meanwhile, musical productions resumed at the Académie. Campra's opera *Idoménée* was performed on January 12, 1712, and on October 17 *La suite d'Armide ou Jérusalem délivrée* by the duc d'Orléans was presented at Fontainebleau. Recent belated successes by the French on the battlefield not only improved the monarch's position at the conference table, but prompted a tone of complacency and belligerence in the new operas. In the prologue of the duke's opera an old sage called on his ministers to wage an "immortal war" against the injustice of twenty jealous kings. The chorus declared that as long as his enemies consorted against peace, the king would prosecute the inhuman war, while preserving the happiness of his own subjects.[112]

In the same vein, André Destouches' prologue to the opera *Callirhoé* (1712) depicted a battlefield strewn with helmets, shields, weapons, flags, and laurel crowns, symbolizing the French victory. After a vigorous prelude for trumpets and drums, Victory hailed the conquest of her favorite heroes; she entreated the soldiers to be fearless and to rely on her unswerving support. Over imitative figures in the strings and piercing trumpet calls, Victory admonished the troops to "burst out" and "enliven every heart."[113] Louis' strategy of negotiating for peace, while threatening at the same time to continue the war, and indeed, pressing ahead against the emperor, was thus affectively delineated in Destouches' opera.

After the completion of the Treaty of Utrecht in 1713, the new operas once again represented Louis as the victorious peacemaker. In Campra's *Télèphe*, Hercules, Jupiter, Juno, Pluto, and Neptune admit Louis to the rank of the gods and proclaim success for his courageous pursuit of peace.[114] In *Télémaque* (1714) by Destouches and the Marseilles priest, Joseph Pellegrin, Minerva crowns the "beneficent conqueror," and Love is invited to join the Pleasures and the Arts in honoring him.[115] Finally, a new composer, Louis-Thomas Bourgeois, paid homage to the king in his chamber opera *Le divertissement du roi* in 1714, and in the ballet *Les plaisirs de la paix* in 1715. Campra's *L'Europe galante* was also revived for the king's entertainment in the summer of 1715, but the "peacemaker" did not live to enjoy it.

Compared with the 1670's and 1680's, the last years of Louis' reign were somber and colorless. The monarch withdrew into the privacy of his chambers. The war, coupled with his personal inclination, caused him to discontinue the constant regimen of pompous pageants, dazzling *divertissements*, and outdoor musical *spectacles*. He did not disband the musical establishment which he had created for reasons of state, however. Its utility did not cease abruptly just because Maintenon cared little for opera or because Lully's successors could not match the Florentine's genius. The group of musicians and poets who flooded the Académie royale de musique with operas and ballets after Lully's death continued to present the Bourbon view of contemporary history and along with it a beguiling, laudatory portrayal of the king's personality, motivation, and deeds to the good citizens in the parterre. The music was banal and the dramas were limp, but the king was nonetheless well served.

Perhaps realizing that he would soon have to exchange his beloved operas for the music of celestial harps, Louis XIV gathered his musicians around him a few days before his death. On August 25, the festival day of Saint-Louis, the monarch ordered the drums and trumpets to sound their traditional morning fanfare beneath his balcony. He propped himself up in bed to hear them better. During his dinner, the Vingt-quatre violons performed in the antechamber, and the king opened his door to listen. Before retiring, he heard one last concert by the Musique de la Chambre.[116] Seven days later, he died. The glorious epoch of the royal absolutism died with him, but the musical establishment remained as part of his legacy. He had achieved a juncture of French music and government; he had made music a servant of the monarchy. Never again did the Bourbons reach the lofty grandeur of the age of Louis XIV, and many years passed before a worthy successor to Lully appeared. The curious bedfellows of music and absolutism continued for a time to rest comfortably, however, beneath the warm blanket of the ancien regime.

Coda

Since Voltaire first called it the century of Louis XIV, the seventeenth century has belonged to France and, preeminently, to the uncommonly public man who ruled it for half a century. Under her most Apollonian Bourbon, France enjoyed the sort of supremacy she has never regained—as Voltaire explained, it was a supremacy of taste, refinement of manners, and artistic and intellectual brillance. Voltaire was probably right about France's preeminence among the kingdoms of Europe and, as a Frenchman terribly conscious of his empyrean role in leading at least the elite to the heights, he doubtless was in awe of a king who pampered his luminaries and creative people. The celebrated farmer of Ferney also gave proper attention to the diplomatic and political triumphs and defeats of the Dieu-donné, but he failed to analyze the politics of the artistic brilliance and social sophistication he so much admired. Voltaire would not have denied that culture follows politics, that kings can make the arts and sciences flourish, but he would have run from the notion that the artistic servants of "despotism" were, or should be, image-makers, propagandists, and political functionaries.

We know better. We declare that despotism enslaves art, which must enjoy complete freedom if truth and beauty are to be realized. Yet, we also preach that art reflects the society from which it comes; that it can tell us something about our society and our aspirations. We know that the electronic cacophony of our avant-garde composers shows the red noise of a civilization that has forgotten how to be gentle and quiet. Indeed, we deliberately stress the red noise. We duplicate hot dogs on canvas and taxi horns in concert halls.

Somewhere between Voltaire's notion of the polished artistry of the great century and the smart art of today lay the artistic idea of Louis XIV. Art was neither free nor enslaved; it neither proved how advanced the society imagined it was, nor did it portray the nonbeauty of its social dilemmas. It was political in the sense that it served ideal images of the royal establishment and propagated a gospel of classical perfection. It was real in the sense that a vicarious thrill of sexual and heroic conquest is real.

Among the arts, music is thought to have the least relevance to society. Musical sound cannot convey ideas of freedom or tyranny, express precise emotions, or recount events. Its abstract symbols speak only to the initiate; its sounds are an assortment of pitched noise conveying nothing more than what the fancy of player or listener wishes to imagine. Yet in the seventeenth century, music was the most potent weapon in the artistic politicization of royal absolutism. Why? Platonist musical philosophy held that music penetrates the human psyche as nothing else can. Platonism meshed with French taste to suggest that a grand union of sight, sound, and movement was possible. Opera animated the figures of painters and the characters of poets, breathing life into the fabulous heroes of antiquity who were so deliberately construed as the *roi soleil*. Music, French music, provided the sonic glitter for ceremonies designed to inspire public awe of the ruler and for splendid theatrical diversions designed to impress foreigners and occupy courtiers. Above all, music was the medium by which the king's grandeur and his glorious adventures were recounted to all the estates. Louis XIV made music the handmaiden of the politics of absolutism.

Notes

Books and articles are cited in full only the first time they appear. In addition, titles that are excessively long have been abbreviated in the notes and the complete citation given in the bibliography. Articles have been cited the first time they are used but have not been included in the bibliography. The following periodicals, abbreviated as indicated, have been used extensively:

Annales musicologiques (*Ann. mus.*)
L'année musicale (*Année mus.*)
XVIIe siècle
Journal of Renaissance and Baroque Music (*J. Ren. Bar. Mus.*)
Journal of the Warburg and Courtauld Institutes (*Warburg*)
Le mercure musical et bulletin français de la Société Internationale de la Musique (*Mercure mus.*)
Music and Letters (*Mus. Let.*)
Musica Disciplina (*Mus. Disc.*)
The Musical Quarterly (*Mus. Quar.*)
The Music Review (*Mus. Rev.*)
Revue de l'histoire de Versailles et de Seine-et-Oise (*Rev. his. Versailles*)
Revue d'histoire littéraire de la France (*Rev. his. lit.*)
La revue musicale (*Rev. mus.*)

Chapter 1. Musical Philosophy

1. René François, *Essai des merveilles de nature et des plus nobles artifices* (Rouen, 1621), p. 480. François' real name was Étienne Binet.

2. René Descartes, *Excellent Compendium of Musick*, trans. unknown (London, 1653). This work was written in 1619, almost forty years before it was published.

3. Marin Mersenne, *Harmonie universelle* (Paris, 1636), Book VIII, pp. 43-44. Ideas similar to Mersenne's on the utility of music can also be found in technical treatises on musical theory, composition, and performance, such as those of Antoine Parran (*Traité de la musique théorique et pratique contenant les*

préceptes de la composition [Paris, 1639]) and Anibal Gantez (*L'entretien des musiciens* [Auxerre, 1643]).

4. François, p. 481. In his *Dictionnaire universel*, 1690, Antoine Furetière defined *soufre* as a "homogeneous, liquid, oily, sticky and inflammable substance which rises . . . in the form of oil toward the spirit into the distillation which is drawn from all bodies" (quoted in Paul Robert, *Dictionnaire alphabétique et analogique de la langue française* [Paris, 1966], VI, 499). Alchemists believed *soufre* was a condensation of the materials of fire.

5. Plato, *The Collected Dialogues of Plato including the Letters*, ed. Hamilton and Cairns (New York, 1964), *Timaeus* 1175.

6. Plato, *The Works of Plato*, trans. Jowett (4 vols. in 1; New York, n.d.), *Republic* iv. 2, 140-41.

7. Plato (Hamilton), *Laws* ii. 1250.

8. Plato (Jowett), *Republic* iii. 2, 108; see also Plato (Hamilton), *Protagoras* 322.

9. Plato (Jowett), *Republic* iii. 2, 108.

10. Plato (Hamilton), *Epinomis* 1521.

11. *Ibid.*, p. 1520.

12. *Ibid.*, *Philebus* 1092-94.

13. *Ibid.*, *Epinomis* 1521; see also Plato (Jowett), *Republic* vii. 2, 276, 288-90.

14. Plato (Jowett), *Republic* iii. 2, 106.

15. *Ibid.*

16. *Ibid.*, 124.

17. *Ibid.*, iv. 2, 139.

18. *Ibid.*, *Symposium* 3, 348.

19. Plato (Hamilton), *Laws* ii. 1253.

20. *Ibid.*, 1254.

21. *Ibid.*, 1256.

22. *Ibid.*, 1266.

23. *Ibid.*, iii. 1294.

24. *Ibid.*, vii. 1371.

25. *Ibid.*, ii. 1251.

26. *Ibid.*, 1252; see also vii. 1385-65.

27. Frances A. Yates, *The French Academies of the Sixteenth Century* (London, 1947), pp. 87-88.

28. *Ibid.*, pp. 37-39.

29. D. T. Mace, "Musical Humanism, the Doctrine of Rhythmus, and the Saint Cecilia Odes of Dryden," *Warburg*, XXVII (1964), 271.

30. Augustine, *The Confessions*, Book X, chap. xxxiii, as quoted in Yates, *The French Academies*, p. 39.

31. Mace, *Warburg*, XXVII, 284-85.

32. I am relying on Frances Yates' translation (p. 87) of the summary of Boethius' system by Hugo de S. Victore in *Excerptionum allegoricarum*.

33. For this complex and wide-ranging subject, see especially the chapter on the physical tradition in Jean Seznec, *The Survival of the Pagan Gods*, trans.

Sessions (New York, 1953), pp. 37-83. Seznec elaborates a rich iconography to support his theme.

34. Yates, *The French Academies*, p. 40.

35. The best accounts of Ficino's musical philosophy are in the articles of D. P. Walker and Paul-Marie Masson (cited in notes 42, 49, and 66) and the books of Frances Yates, Ernst Cassirer, Paul Kristeller, and Erwin Panofsky. Ficino's aesthetics are especially well handled by Panofsky, on whom I have relied.

36. Erwin Panofsky, *Idea: A Concept in Art Theory*, trans. Peake (Columbia, S.C., 1968), pp. 96-99. Panofsky points out that Ficinian Neo-Platonism did not influence art until the Mannerist period. As a result of the idea that "the visible world is only a likeness of invisible spiritual entities," Mannerist (one must add Baroque) painters gave their works allegorical and symbolical content in order to express the inner and higher ideas they represented. Through God's grace, the artist conveyed the idea of beauty by producing allegories wherein were concealed ideas of supernatural intelligence.

37. Erwin Panofsky, *Renaissance and Renascences in Western Art* (New York, 1969), p. 185.

38. Quoted in Erwin Panofsky, *Studies in Iconology: Humanistic Themes in the Art of the Renaissance* (New York, 1967), p. 140. Ficino, according to Panofsky, has in mind the ecstasy described by Plato as inspired madness, taking four forms—the frenzy of the poet, the raptures of the mystic, the ecstasies of the lover, and the ravishment of the diviner. See also Panofsky, *Renaissance*, p. 183.

39. Quoted in Paul O. Kristeller, *The Philosophy of Marsilio Ficino*, trans. Conant (New York, 1943), pp. 307-308.

40. *Ibid.*, p. 308.

41. Yates, *The French Academies*, p. 40.

42. D. P. Walker, "Ficino's 'Spiritus' and Music," *Ann. mus.*, I (1953), 131-32.

43. *Ibid.*, p. 138; see also D. P. Walker, "Le chant orphique de Marsile Ficin," in *Musique et poésie au XVIe siècle*, Vol. V of *Colloques internationaux du centre national de la recherche scientifique* (Paris, 1954), p. 18.

44. Quoted in Walker, "Ficino," *Ann. mus.*, I, 18.

45. Ernst Cassirer, *The Individual and the Cosmos in Renaissance Philosophy*, trans. Domandi (New York, 1963), pp. 100-101.

46. Walker, "Ficino," *Ann. mus.*, I, 143-44.

47. Walker, in *Musique et poésie*, pp. 18-23.

48. *Ibid.*, p. 20. This is Walker's opinion. There is apparently no evidence to indicate the exact musical nature of Ficino's chant. His lyre, the instrument believed best for the performance of antique music, had a picture of Orpheus casting a spell on the animals.

49. The *Orphica*, along with the *Hermetica*, *Oracula*, and *Chadaica*, the Sybelline prophecies, and writings of early Greek philosophers comprise a body of very ancient texts known as the *prisca theologia* which allegedly formed the basis of Plato's religion and which were believed to be consistent with Christian doctrine. With the revival of Platonic studies, these texts, which were more

available in the late Renaissance period, attracted considerable interest among French and Italian humanists. Including fragments of ancient verse contained in the writings of Proclus and the Church Fathers, the Orphic texts became known in the fifteenth century through George of Trebizond's Latin translation of Eusebius' *Praeparatia Evangelica*, published in 1470. The Orphic hymns, which also formed part of the *Orphica*, were translated by Ficino in 1462, but were not published until 1500. Now believed to date from the second or third century A.D., these hymns were accepted by Renaissance writers as genuine texts coming out of ancient religious beliefs, perhaps older than Pythagoras. It was believed that Orpheus, like Pythagoras and Plato, had studied Moses' writings in Egypt and that his hymns foreshadowed Christian revelation. See D. P. Walker, "The 'Prisca Theologia' in France," *Warburg*, XVII (1954), 204-12.

50. D. P. Walker, "Orpheus the Theologian and Renaissance Platonists," *Warburg*, XVI (1953), 100-104.

51. Quoted in Walker, "Prisca," *Warburg*, XVII, 237.

52. Perhaps the statement should be qualified in light of the power attributed to music by the Romantic movement and in particular by Schopenhauer, Wagner, and the Russian composer Alexander Scriabin. See H. G. Koenigsberger, "Music and Religion in Modern European History," in *The Diversity of History*, ed. Elliott and Koenigsberger (Ithaca, N.Y., 1970), pp. 66-78. Of Schopenhauer's philosophy, Koenigsberger writes: "Never before had music been elevated so high above the other arts nor been identified so unequivocally with the self-expression of the Deity (Schopenhauer's 'will,' at least as popularly understood). Wagner accepted Schopenhauer's philosophy with enthusiasm."

53. For Ficino's influence, the following works have been consulted: Antoinette Huon, "Le thème du Prince dans les entrées parisiennes au XVIe siècle," in *Les fêtes de la Renaissance*, Vol. I of *Colloques internationaux du centre national de la recherche scientifique* (Paris, 1956), pp. 29-30; Kristeller, pp. 19-20; Walker, "Ficino," *Ann. mus.*, I, 148-50; Walker, "Orpheus," *Warburg*, XVI, 101; Walker, "Prisca," *ibid.*, XVII, 204-207; Walker, in *Musique et poésie*, pp. 23-25; Yates, *The French Academies*, pp. 2-13; and Frances A. Yates, "Poésie et musique dans les 'magnificences' au mariage du duc de Joyeuse," in *Musique et poésie*, pp. 241-63. Yates' book also treats other, non-Ficinian Italian influences on French writers, as well as Ficino's influence on later Italian academicians such as Giovanni de' Bardi.

54. La Bodérie, a poet, was the secretary of François d'Anjou, Henri III's brother. His circle included numerous Catholic and Protestant writers and musicians, some of whom later became members of the Académie de musique et de poésie. Champier was a doctor, philosopher, and historian from Lyons.

55. Pointing to the strong influence of Ficino on the Valois, Yates (in *Musique et poésie*, pp. 249-50) suggests the possible influence of Ficinian astrology in the music and poetry of Jean-Antoine de Baïf and Claude Le Jeune (to be discussed in Chap. 2) performed at the Italianate court of the Valois. Miss

Yates cites the well-known addiction to astrology and the occult sciences of Catherine de Medici and her son, Henri III.

56. Sixteenth-century theories of ancient music and their practical application are the subject of D. P. Walker's excellent article "Musical Humanism in the 16th and Early 17th Centuries," *Mus. Rev.*, II, nos. 1-3 (1941), pp. 1-14, 111-21, 220-27, 288-308; and III, no. 1 (1942), pp. 55-71. Walker contends that these two tenets of sixteenth-century musical philosophy resulted in large part from the writings of the musical humanists. These scholars scoured classical sources in order to revive ancient music. The group, largely Italian, included Vincenzo Galilei, Girolamo Mei, G. Zarlino, F. Gafurius, and the French writers Pontus de Tyard and Marin Mersenne.

57. Walker points out (*ibid.*, II, no. 1, p. 2) that of the Greek music now available, only one text (three hymns of Mesomedes from Alypius, printed in the original notation in Vincenzo Galilei's *Dialogo della musica antica e moderna*, 1581) had been discovered.

58. The poets accepted Aristotle's distinction between lyric and dramatic poetry, which had music, and epic and didactic poetry, which did not.

59. Yates, *The French Academies*, p. 41.

60. *Ibid.*, pp. 82-85.

61. For Ronsard, see *ibid.*, p. 50; Raymond Lebègue, "Ronsard et la musique," in *Musique et poésie*, pp. 105-14; and G. Thibault, "Musique et poésie en France au XVIᵉ siècle avant les 'amours' de Ronsard," in *ibid.*, pp. 79-88.

62. Seznec, pp. 84-112.

63. Walker, in *Musique et poésie*, pp. 26-27. Lebègue feels that Walker judges Ronsard too severely. Despite his illogical settings of a single musical air to dozens of different sonnets and his failure to achieve a genuine union of music and poetry, Ronsard, according to Lebègue (in *Musique et poésie*, pp. 111-14), did formulate the first rules of sung poetry.

64. This is D. P. Walker's opinion, as explained in his articles on musical humanism in *The Music Review*.

65. Other avenues to the effects were explored without results in the sixteenth century. Many writers, particularly the Italians Vincenzo Galilei, Girolamo Mei, and J. B. Doni, believed ancient music employed the chromatic and enharmonic genera, and they tried to revive this usage. But lacking any solid classical authority and disagreeing over whose system of intervals most closely approximated the ancient genera, they eventually abandoned this avenue. Mersenne later held that these genera were not essential in producing the effects. Experiments in intonation along Greek lines also proved fruitless, though they generated among the Italian writers a considerable enthusiasm. A more promising approach lay in the use of modes, since all of the musical humanists believed that the modes were essential in attaining ethical effects. But while they were in agreement about the characteristics of each mode, they could not agree on which mode was which. What some thought was the Phrygian, others contended was the Dorian, and so forth. Again, partisanship developed around conflicting modal systems, discouraging most composers

(Walker, *Mus. Rev.*, II, no. 3, pp. 222-26). Besides, in most of the music of the period, it was impossible to tell one mode from another because of the use of accidentals, irrespective of the system embraced by the composer. This increased the importance of the union of music and poetry (see also Yates, *The French Academies*, pp. 47-48).

⁶⁶· The musical philosophy of Baïf and the academicians, who were supported by Charles IX, Catherine de Medici, and a host of literary figures including Tyard, Ronsard, Jean Dorat, Philippe Desportes, and Pierre Ramus, is discussed fully in the following: D. P. Walker, "The Aims of Baïf's *Académie de poésie et de musique*," *J. Ren. Bar. Mus.*, I (1946), 92-100; Walker, *Mus. Rev.*, II, no. 1, pp. 5-9; Yates, *The French Academies*, pp. 22-25, 36-37, 45-46; and Paul-Marie Masson, "L'humanisme musical en France au XVIᵉ siècle," *Mercure mus.*, no. 7 (July 1907), p. 682. In addition to the documents of the Académie, these authors have relied on Mersenne's *Quaestiones Celeberrimae in Genesim* (Paris, 1623).

⁶⁷· Yates, *The French Academies*, p. 23.

⁶⁸· Quoted from the Lettres patentes, in *ibid.*, p. 23.

⁶⁹· Quoted from Artus Thomas, *Philostrate de la vie d'Apollonius Thyanéen . . . enrichie d'amples commentaires* (Paris, 1611), in Mace, *Warburg*, XXVII, 273. See also Yates, in *Musique et poésie*, p. 243.

⁷⁰· Yates, *The French Academies*, pp. 208-209.

⁷¹· *Ibid.*, pp. 214-20; see also Frances A. Yates, "Dramatic Religious Processions in Paris in the Late Sixteenth Century," *Ann. mus.*, II (1954), 215-70.

⁷²· Quoted in Yates, *The French Academies*, p. 288. For the influence of Plato on Mersenne, see also Walker, *Mus. Rev.*, II, no. 1, p. 12.

⁷³· Yates, *The French Academies*, pp. 63-64.

⁷⁴· Quoted in *ibid.*, p. 24.

⁷⁵· Walker, *Mus. Rev.*, II, no. 3, pp. 300-301.

⁷⁶· Quoted in Mace, *Warburg*, XXVII, 285.

⁷⁷· *Ibid.*, p. 287.

⁷⁸· Yates, *The French Academies*, p. 285.

⁷⁹· Seventeenth-century French writers used the word *spectacle*, not only in reference to the parades, contests, and dramas of the ancients, but also as a general term designating all forms of public entertainment, including ballet, opera, and drama, which were popular in their own century. Since the French word *spectacle* carries a rather different connotation (difficult to translate) from that of the English "spectacle," I have retained the French term. For similar reasons, the French *divertissement* has been kept. Moreover, I believe that it is important to use these terms, because French opera and ballet have traditionally stressed the visual appeal of musical productions, which the words suggest, rather than the auditory appeal. Other French words are in roman type to aid readability.

⁸⁰· *A General Collection of Discourses of the Virtuosi of France*, trans. Havers, ed. Renaudot (2 vols.; London, 1663). See especially the following essays: "Why People are Pleased with Music," I, 106-108; "Of Harmony," I, 346-48;

"Of Dancing," I, 399-401; "Whether Musick doth more Hurt or Good," II, 272-74.

81. *Extraordinaire du mercure galant*, July 1680, p. 240.

82. *Ibid.*, Oct. 1680, p. 75.

83. *Ibid.*, April 1680, p. 279.

84. *Ibid.*, p. 304.

85. *Ibid.*, Oct. 1680, pp. 312-50.

86. Letter to Monseigneur Jean-Baptiste Truchi, comte de Saint-Michel and chef du conseil des finances for the duc de Savoy, 1673, as quoted in Samuel Chappuzeau, *Le théâtre françois* (Paris, 1876), p. 1.

87. *Le théâtre de Quinault* (Paris, 1663), I, 8-11.

88. *Mercure*, May 1677, pp. 134-35.

89. *Ibid.*, Feb. 1680, pp. 8-10.

90. *Ibid.*, Feb. 1703, pp. 268-69.

91. Letter to Charles Errard (Paris, July 23, 1671), in Jean-Baptiste Colbert, *Fortifications, sciences, lettres, beaux-arts, bâtiments*, Vol. V. of *Lettres, instructions, et mémoires*, ed. Clément, (Paris, 1868), p. 331. See also *Correspondance administrative sous le règne de Louis XIV*, ed. Depping (Paris, 1850-55), IV, 573.

92. BN ms n.a. fr 402, fol. 694.

93. Henri-Philippe de Limiers, *Histoire du règne de Louis XIV* (2d ed. rev.; Amsterdam, 1718), III, 126.

94. *Le théâtre de Quinault*, I, 11-12.

95. Primi Visconti, comte de San-Maiolo, *Mémoires sur la cour de Louis XIV*, trans. Lemoine (Paris, n.d.), p. 200.

96. Ézéchiel Spanheim, *Relation de la cour de France en 1690*, ed. Schefer (Paris, 1882), p. 10.

97. G. Touchard-Lafosse, *Chroniques de l'œil-de-bœuf des petits appartements de la cour et des salons de Paris (1631-1671)* (Paris, 1830), II, 260-61.

98. *Mémoires de Louis XIV*, ed. Gain-Montagnac (Paris, 1806), p. 37.

99. Louis XIV's brevet of August 1674 to Henri Guichard, intendant of the buildings and gardens of the duc d'Orléans, to set up a Royal Academy of *Spectacles*. From *Correspondance administrative*, IV, 595.

100. *Mercure*, April 1677, p. 86.

101. *Ibid.*, Nov. 1682, pp. 19-20.

102. *Ibid.*, Feb. 1680, p. 6; for additional testimony, see M. de Juvenal, "Dissertation sur l'origine des trois académies," BN ms fr 21732; Jean de La Fontaine, "Épitre à Niert," *Oeuvres complètes* (Paris, 1818), VI, 163; and Roger de Bussy-Rabutin, *Mémoires secrets, 1617-1667* (Amsterdam, 1769), II, 283.

103. *Extraordinaire du mercure galant*, Jan. 1679, pp. 415-16.

104. Pierre Bayle, *Dictionnaire historique et critique* (3d ed.; Rotterdam, 1715), II, 454.

105. Claude-François Menestrier, *Bibliothèque curieuse et instructive de divers ouvrages anciens et modernes de littérature et des arts* (Paris, 1704), p. v.

[106]· Jean Terrasson, *Dissertation critique sur l'Iliade d'Homer* (Paris, 1715), p. 238.

[107]· *Mercure*, April 1689, pp. 52-54.

[108]· Titon du Tillet, *Le parnasse françois* (Paris, 1732), p. xvii.

[109]· Claude-François Menestrier, *Des représentations en musique anciennes et modernes* (Paris, 1681), p. 135.

[110]· BN ms n.a. fr 402; a printed copy of this work may be found in BN ms fr 21625.

[111]· Yates, *The French Academies*, p. 310.

[112]· Additional discussion of historical parallels can be found in the following: Charles Perrault, *Parallèle des anciens et des modernes* (Paris, 1692), IV, 260-97; Perrault, *Mémoires, contes et autres œuvres*, ed. Jacob (Paris, 1842), pp. 320-33; Parran; Gantez; François de La Mothe le Vayer, *De l'instruction de monseigneur le dauphin, à monseigneur l'éminentissime cardinal duc de Richelieu* (Paris, 1640), p. 165; and BN ms fr 19043, fol. 59, 74 v.-84 r.

[113]· Michel de Pure, *Idée des spectacles anciens et nouveaux* (Paris, 1688), p. 96.

[114]· *Ibid.*, p. 211.

[115]· Claude-François Menestrier, *Des ballets anciens et modernes selon les règles du théâtre* (Paris, 1682); Menestrier, *Des représentations*; on Menestrier, see Yates, *The French Academies*, pp. 309-10, and John C. Meagher, "The Dance and the Masques of Ben Jonson," *Warburg*, XXV (1964), 259-66.

[116]· Jacques Bonnet, *Histoire générale de la danse* (Paris, 1723). Additional commentary on the origin, history, and function of the dance may be found in Ch[arles] Compan, *Dictionnaire de danse* (Paris, 1787), and in the *Mémoires de littérature tirées des registres de l'Académie royale des inscriptions et belles-lettres depuis son renouvellement jusqu'en M.DCC.X* (Paris, 1772), I, 121-76.

[117]· Menestrier, *Des ballets*, p. 29.

[118]· Bonnet, p. 2.

[119]· Menestrier, *Des représentations*, p. 1.

[120]· *Ibid.*, p. 18.

[121]· "People would go in processions in front of these princes with the banners of churches: they would sing to their praise some hymns composed from different passages of the scripture, pieced together in order to make allusions to the principal deeds of their reigns" (*Ibid.*, p. 154).

[122]· *Ibid.*, pp. 59-70.

[123]· Jacques Bonnet, *Histoire de la musique et de ses effets* (Paris, 1715), p. 46. According to Warren Dwight Allen (*Philosophies of Music History* [New York, 1939], pp. 23-26), the first three comprehensive histories of music were *Historische Beschreibung der edlen Sing und Klingkunst* by Wolfgang Printz von Waldthurm, *Historia Musica* by Giovanni Bontempi, and Bonnet's book. All three appeared between 1690 and 1715.

[124]· Bonnet, p. 179.

Chapter 2. Music and the Monarchy before the
Reign of Louis XIV

1. Jean Dard, *Principes de la musique* (Paris, 1764), pp. 11-12.

2. Tillet, pp. xxix-xxxvii.

3. Dard, p. 13.

4. Antoine de Leris, *Dictionnaire portatif des théâtres contenant l'origine des différens théâtres de Paris* (Paris, 1754), pp. ix-xiii. See also Pierre-François Godard de Beauchamps, *Recherches sur les théâtres de France, depuis l'année onze cens soixante un, jusques à présent* (Paris, 1735), I, 79-91.

5. Paul Lacroix, "Notice sur les ballet de cour," in *Ballets et mascarades de cour sous Henri IV et Louis XIII de 1581 à 1652*, ed. Lacroix (Geneva, 1868), I, xiii.

6. Donald Jay Grout, "Some Forerunners of the Lully Opera," *Mus. Let.*, XXII (Jan. 1941), 16-18.

7. *Ballets et mascarades*, I, x-xiii. Lacroix' source is the chronicle of Juvenal des Ursins. See also Henry Prunières, *Le ballet de cour en France avant Benserade et Lully suivi du ballet de La délivrance de Renaud* (Paris, 1914), pp. 1-8.

8. The Italian word *ballo* came to mean any kind of dance in which the steps were created anew for each occasion. The French word *ballet* is derived from it. The Italian influence on the development of French ballet has been underscored by Gino Tani in "Le Comte d'Aglié et le ballet de cour en Italie," in *Les fêtes*, pp. 221-33.

9. Frances A. Yates, "Antoine Caron's Paintings for Triumphal Arches," *Warburg*, XIV (1951), 132. See also George R. Kernodle, "Déroulement de la procession dans les temps ou espace théâtral dans les fêtes de la Renaissance," in *Les fêtes*, pp. 443-59.

10. See the following articles in *Les fêtes:* Huon, pp. 21-25; V. L. Saulnier, "L'entrée de Henri II à Paris et la révolution poétique de 1550," pp. 31-59; Kernodle, pp. 443, 458-60.

11. Huon, in *Les fêtes*, p. 28, writes: "The Hercule gaulois, this very special emblem which seems to sum up the entire ideology of the Prince, will take on the traits of Henri IV at Avignon in 1600, and we will come back to it in 1641 symbolizing the arms of France in a ballet given at the Palais-Cardinal." See also Seznec, pp. 27-36.

12. Saulnier, in *Les fêtes*, pp. 43-47.

13. Yates, *The French Academies*, pp. 251-53.

14. *Ibid.*, pp. 254-67.

15. For a full account of the entry, see Frances A. Yates, "Poètes et artistes dans les entrées de Charles IX et de sa Reine à Paris en 1571," in *Les fêtes*, pp. 61-84. Yates relied mainly on an illustrated description of the entry by Simon Bouquet, échevin of Paris.

16. Seznec, pp. 18-20.

17. Yates writes (*Les fêtes*, p. 66): "The Junos, the Arthemise, the Castor and Pollux which Ronsard used spoke a symbolic language which everyone knew how to interpret in terms of the 'new Olympus' of the French court."

[18.] *Ibid.*, p. 78.

[19.] The festivities are described in Yates, *Warburg*, XIV, 133.

[20.] Aubigné, *Histoire universelle*, I, 665, quoted in Prunières, p. 56.

[21.] Yates has a thorough discussion of this whole subject in "Dramatic Religious Processions," *Ann. mus.*, II, 215-62. Her article is accompanied by drawings of religious processions from the cabinet des estampes of the Bibliothèque Nationale which constitute her main source for the processions.

[22.] The first Jesuit confessor of a French king and an important figure in the French Counter Reformation, Father Auger may have been a transmitter of musical philosophy to the seventeenth century. Mersenne mentions him in connection with the effects. Believing in what Frances Yates calls "an 'operatic' style of preaching," Auger contended that musical training could teach priests to deliver affective sermons using three types of speech tones, each of which would produce a different spiritual effect. Auger in fact trained teachers and speakers in the art of sacred oratory, based on Quintilian's principles of oratory and on the doctrine of the effects, at the Congrégation de l'Oratoire de Notre-Dame de Vie Sainte, established by Henri III in the Bois de Vincennes. See Yates, *The French Academies*, pp. 161-67.

[23.] Yates, *Ann. mus.*, II, 222.

[24.] *Ibid.*, p. 247.

[25.] Roy C. Strong, "Festivals for the Garter Embassy at the Court of Henri III," *Warburg*, XXII (1959), 60-70.

[26.] *Ibid.*, p. 64.

[27.] Yates, *The French Academies*, pp. 14-18.

[28.] Masson, *Mercure mus.*, no. 4, pp. 333-35. Masson's article contains the best analysis of Ronsard's poetry from the standpoint of the revival of ancient music. The contrast between the innovations of Ronsard and Baïf is sharply drawn. See also Kenneth Jay Levy, "Vaudeville, vers mesurés et airs de cour," in *Musique et poésie*, p. 196; and Yates, *The French Academies*, pp. 51-59.

[29.] The life of Baïf is fully recounted in Mathieu Augé-Chiquet, *La vie, les idées et l'œuvre de Jean-Antoine de Baïf* (Paris, 1909).

[30.] Masson (*Mercure mus.*, no. 4, pp. 341-45) points out that *vers mesuré* did not begin with Baïf, but had been attempted in the fifteenth century by the Italian poets Leon Battista Alberti and Leonardo Dati and in France by Michel de Boteauville, Étienne Jodelle, and Jacques de la Taille.

[31.] Masson's article provides a detailed explanation of Baïf's problem. He notes that despite its failure, some *vers mesuré* was written by Nicolas Rapin, Gilles Durand, and others at the end of the sixteenth century. Subsequently it became only a "literary curiosity," though strangely, years later, Louis Bonaparte composed some measured verses.

[32.] In his convincing attempt to relate the musical and poetic innovations of the Académie to humanist musical theory, D. P. Walker emphasizes this point in all of his articles on sixteenth-century music. See, for example, "The Influence of *musique mesurée à l'antique* Particularly on the *airs de cour* of the

Early Seventeenth Century," *Mus. Disc.*, II (1948), 142, and "Musical Humanism," *Mus. Rev.*, II, 8-9.

33. The surviving examples of *musique mesurée* can be found in *Maîtres musiciens de la Renaissance Française*, ed. Expert (3 vols.; Paris, 1905-1906).

34. Quoted in Mace, *Warburg*, XXVII, 283.

35. Explanations have been offered by Mace and Walker. Walker (*Mus. Rev.*, II, 295-304) says that since the ancient poets had employed many kinds of feet for a variety of subjects, they had left no concrete guidelines. Whereas the French could speculate freely about the ancients' use of modes because there were no musical survivals from antiquity to confuse them, they could not be sure how to use ancient poetry because they did possess it. Mace (*Warburg*, XXVII, 284-85) says that the French were reluctant to apply their theory of rhythm because they equated soul with number and believed number was the common source of both rhythm and harmony, and because they believed the musician must use his rational powers to discover the mathematical proportions underlying both rhythm and harmony and use those proportions to affect the mind. Thus, classical feet were not to be used as "images of the passions" and for their "affective power," but, following Saint Augustine, as reflections of the proportions and consonances of celestial harmony whose impact was made on the mind rather than on the emotions. Man's love of both harmony and rhythm, as Augustine observed, was based on his love of equally measured intervals. The real aim of Baïf circle, therefore, was not just to arouse emotions, but to use the rhythmic power of literary music to create a perfect proportion in the soul.

36. Copied from Masson, *Mercure mus.*, no. 7, p. 693. See also Walker, *Mus. Disc.*, II, 142; Walker, *Mus. Rev.*; Yates, *The French Academies*, pp. 52-56; and Augé-Chiquet, pp. 333-67.

37. Masson, *Mercure mus.*, no. 7, p. 696.

38. Mace shows the contrast between Italian and French styles of the sixteenth century in *Warburg*, XXVII, 253-57. He makes the point that the monodic experiments of the Camarata grew less out of their efforts to copy the Greeks than out of the practical artistic problems of being unable to express through polyphony the vigorous accents, expressive pathos, and irregular rhythms in the poetry of Torquato Tasso. The attack on polyphony and the upgrading of musical rhythm resulted directly from the rhythmic and poetic incapacity of polyphony. The attack was led chiefly by Vincenzo Galilei, who in his *Dialogo della musica antica e moderna* (1581) argued that a monodic style could imitate in pitch and in rhythm the words of the poem and the gestures of the performers. Walker (*Mus. Rev.*, III, 55-71) also points up the contrast between the Italian and French theories. He suggests that the Italian humanists could not really prove that the ancients had employed a monodic style exclusively and that some humanists (Doni and Salinas) did not believe that ancient music was monodic at all. He concludes that in most respects homophony conformed to the humanists' conception of ancient music and that most sixteenth-century music influenced by humanism, including

musique mesurée, was in fact homophonic, not monodic. See also Masson, *Mercure mus.*, no. 7, pp. 714-18; Levy, in *Musique et poésie*, pp. 193-95.

³⁹· Prunières, *Le ballet*, pp. 60-65; Yates, *The French Academies*, pp. 60-62.

⁴⁰· Yates, *The French Academies*, p. 42. Yates believes that the Medici family served as a link between the Platonic Academy of Florence and the French academy; that Catherine de Medici's sons, Charles IX and Henri III, were carrying on the Medici tradition of supporting an academy and the Platonic thought on which it was based.

⁴¹· Yates makes the following statement: "The chief reason why Charles is anxious to encourage the revival of 'ancient' poetry and music is because he desires to see in his kingdom the good moral effects which should flow from such a revival" (*The French Academies*, p. 23).

⁴²· Quoted from Romain Rolland, *Les origines du théâtre lyrique moderne: Histoire de l'opéra en Europe avant Lully et Scarlatti* (new ed.; Paris, 1931), pp. 236-37. The Lettres and statuts of the Académie are also given in Yates, *The French Academies*, pp. 319-22. The purposes of the Académie are dealt with in Walker, *J. Ren. Bar. Mus.*, I, 92-100. See also Augé-Chiquet, pp. 434-39; Durey de Noinville, Jacques Bernard, and Louis Travenol, *Histoire du théâtre de l'opéra en France depuis l'établissement de l'Académie royale de musique jusqu'à présent* (Paris, 1753), I, 12-18.

⁴³· Quoted in Yates, *The French Academies*, p. 23.

⁴⁴· Walker, *J. Ren. Bar. Mus.*, I, 94.

⁴⁵· Although the evidence is scanty, Yates believes that the Académie had a scientific bent and was probably Copernican in outlook. She points to Dorat's interest in science at the Collège de Coqueret, Tyard's Copernican views, and the fact that since Mersenne was a scientist and was so affirmative toward the Académie long after its demise, the Académie must have been interested in science. Unfortunately the register of members is lost. It is worth noting that Baïf apparently did not believe in astrological determinism. See Yates, *The French Academies*, pp. 95-103.

⁴⁶· Quoted in Walker, *J. Ren. Bar. Mus.*, I, 95.

⁴⁷· Quoted *ibid.*, p. 96.

⁴⁸· Letter to M. du Perrier, Sept. 28, 1581, *Lettres de Catherine de Medicis*, ed. Puchesse, VII, 401, quoted in Prunières, *Le ballet*, p. 89.

⁴⁹· Beaujoyeulx, whose real name was Baldassarino da Belgiojoso, came to France with Catherine de Medici in 1555. Influenced by humanist ideas on music, Beaujoyeulx favored the revival of ancient music and believed in the power of a union of music, poetry, and dance. See Yates, *The French Academies*, p. 268.

⁵⁰· Jean Rousset, "L'eau et les Tritons dans les fêtes et ballets de cour (1580-1640)," in *Les fêtes*, p. 236.

⁵¹· *Mémoires de l'estoile*, I, 134, quoted in Beauchamps, I, 15.

⁵²· Yates demonstrates rather convincingly that some of Le Jeune's music published in a collection in 1608 was composed for the marriage fetes. See Yates, in *Musique et poésie*, pp. 243-48.

⁵³· Baltasar de Beaujoyeulx *et al., Balet comique de la royne,* text by Sieur de la Chesnaye (Paris, 1582). Beaujoyeulx' program for the ballet is in BN ms fr 25515, fols. 48r.–89v. See also Yates, in *Musique et poésie,* pp. 257-63. The dedication has been reprinted in *Ballets et mascarades,* I, 3-7.

⁵⁴· Quoted in *Ballets et mascarades,* I, 5-6.

⁵⁵· Prunières' source for the estimated cost is Theodore Agrippa d'Aubigné (*Histoire universelle* [Amsterdam, 1886], I, 665). Prunières himself believes that the figure of 400,000 écus is probably exaggerated, but that the production did cost a great deal.

⁵⁶· Walker, *Mus. Disc.,* II, 146; Walker, "La musique des intermèdes Florentins de 1589 et l'humanisme," in *Les fêtes,* pp. 134-35, 144. Yates, in *Musique et poésie,* p. 248, is even more adamant on this point than Walker. She suggests that the only reason that the *Ballet* was not completely an Académie project was that the king monopolized its poets and musicians for his contests, leaving the queen to fall back on her own stable for the ballet which she personally supervised.

⁵⁷· Yates, *Ann. mus.,* II, 255.

⁵⁸· Yates, in *Musique et poésie,* pp. 249-52. Yates writes: "It seems hard to believe that the queen mother and the king had taken lightly and as a simple flattering metaphor, the invocation to the stars in the very powerful antique music that Le Jeune composed for the tournament—sinister enough when one thinks that the Ligue was already formed—between the king and the messieurs de Guise" (p. 250).

⁵⁹· Beaujoyeulx *et al.,* p. 13. I have relied on Beaujoyeulx' and on Yates' detailed analyses and interpretations. See especially Yates in *The French Academies,* pp. 253-73, and in *Musique et poésie,* pp. 253-55; *Ann. mus.,* II, 255-56; Rousset, in *Les fêtes,* pp. 236-37; and Meagher, *Warburg,* XXV, 267-69.

⁶⁰· Beaujoyeulx states only that the figures were geometrical. Since the precise nature of the choreography is not known, it is impossible to determine the symbolic or astrological significance the figures might have had. (See Meagher, *Warburg,* XXV, 268).

⁶¹· Yates, *The French Academies,* pp. 248-49.

⁶²· Yates, *Ann. mus.,* II, 255.

⁶³· The role of Pallas was danced by the bride, Henri III's sister.

⁶⁴· In contrast to Augé-Chiquet, who contends (pp. 456-65) that the Académie was replaced by other academies after the death of Charles IX, Yates maintains that the Académie continued to flourish under royal protection until 1585, when it was crushed by the assassination of Henri III and the final phase of the wars of religion. D. P. Walker shares Yates' opinion that the Académie du palais was an extension rather than a replacement of the Académie de poésie et de musique. See Yates, *The French Academies,* pp. 6-7, 27-35, 105-30, 152-76; and Walker, *J. Ren. Bar. Mus.,* I, 97.

⁶⁵· Yates, *The French Academies,* pp. 277-90.

⁶⁶· The position was given to Guillaume Du Manoir, who already held the title of roi du violon in the Confrérie de Saint-Julien des menestriers,

a musicians' guild. The order confirming Du Manoir as roi du violon can be found in BN ms fr 21732, fol. 226. The following sources are relevant to the situation of French music in the first half of the seventeenth century: John E. Borland, "French Opera before 1750," in *Proceedings of the Musical Association, London* (London, 1907), pp. 133-57; Michel Brenet, *Les concerts en France sous l'ancien régime* (Paris, 1900); and Félix Raugel, "La musique à la chapelle du Château de Versailles sous Louis XIV," *XVIIᵉ siècle*, no. 34 (March 1957), p. 19.

[67.] Quoted in *Extraordinaire du mercure galant*, July 1680, p. 42.

[68.] Henry Prunières and Manfred Bukofzer discern an Italian influence in the increasing number of sung récits. The Italian musicians Giulio Caccini and Ottavio Rinuccini, who were instrumental in creating the first Italian operas during this period, were employed at Marie de Medici's court and doubtless influenced musicians like Pierre Guédron, the queen's music master. Since the ballets were given only at court, little of the music and poetry was printed (except the airs de cour), nor does this little remain today. Discussion of musical developments of this period may be found in Manfred F. Bukofzer, *Music in the Baroque Era* (New York, 1947), pp. 143-47; Prunières, *Le ballet*, pp. 98-209; Walker, *Mus. Disc.*, II, 141-63; André Verchaly, "Poésie et air de cour en France jusqu'à 1620," in *Musique et poésie*, pp. 211-24; Rolland, *Les origines*, pp. 243-45; Charles I. Silin, *Benserade and His Ballets de Cour* (Baltimore, 1940), pp. 176-78; *La musique française du moyen âge à la révolution*, compiled by Amédée Gastoué *et al.* (Paris, 1934), pp. 79-81; and BN ms fr 25465.

[69.] Meagher, *Warburg*, XXV, 268-74. In his article Meagher speculates on the possible significance of these dances.

[70.] Walker, *Mus. Disc.*, II, 142-63.

[71.] Verchaly, in *Musique et poésie*, pp. 213-24.

[72.] *Ballets et mascarades*, I, 90-150; Prunières, *Le ballet*, pp. 95-98; Beauchamps, I, 16-28. The precise dates and chronology of the ballets have been difficult to establish until recently. The contemporary editions and manuscript collection of the airs, récits, choruses, and instrumental music from the ballets (see Conservatoire ms rés. F 496) do not always indicate the name or date of the ballet. Nor is the standard edition of the texts by Lacroix, cited above, very reliable. The best source was a collection of airs de cour from the ballets copied in 1620 by Michel Henry, an instrumentalist. Although Henry's collection has been lost, the duc de La Vallière's analysis of it is preserved in his papers at the Bibliothèque Nationale (see BN ms fr 24357). La Vallière's papers have recently been studied by François Lesure, who has reconstructed Henry's titles and dates, beginning with the year 1597, in "Le recueil de ballets de Michel Henry (vers 1620)," in *Les fêtes*, pp. 208-19.

[73.] Excerpts from the mémoires of Bassompierre may be found in BN ms fr 24352, fol. 326; see also "Ballet des barbiers," BN ms fr 20149, fol. 15.

[74.] Called the "Ballet des étrangers," BN ms fr 20149, fol. 16; BN ms fr 24352, fol. 327.

[75.] Music for the grand ballet of the *Ballet de Madame, sœur du roi Henri IV,* 1599, can be found in "Anciens ballets dansez sous le règne de Henri IV et Louis XIII; airs faits sous le règne de Henri III," Conservatoire ms rés. F 496, fol. 7. Compiled by André Philidor in the seventeenth century, this is a collection of musical fragments from the French ballets of the late sixteenth and seventeenth centuries. In this musical example, as in many others presented here, I have transposed the music from the original clef which usually placed C on the second space of the staff rather than in its modern position on the third space. In addition to the ballet fragments given in the Philidor collection, lists of the ballets performed during this period may be found in BN ms fr 20149, fols. 15-31. Verses for these ballets are contained in the Lacroix collection (*Ballets et mascarades,* I, 151-313; II, 1-200) and in BN ms fr 24353, fols. 1, 12-15, 36, 41.

[76.] The *Ballet des argonautes* recalled the *Ballet comique de la reine:* a troop of infernal spirits sent by Circé to stir up discord on the earth were challenged by the god Amphion (a son of Zeus), who warned Circé against flaunting the power of the crown, and were vanquished by the king himself, who forced Circé to pay him homage. See *Ballets et mascarades,* II, 1-9.

[77.] Jacques Vanuxem, "Le carrousel de 1612 sur la Place Royale et ses devises," in *Les fêtes,* pp. 192-201; François-Georges Pariset, "Le mariage d'Henri de Lorraine et de Marguerite Gonzague-Mantoue (1606), les fêtes et le témoignage de Jacques de Bellange," in *Les fêtes,* pp. 153-69.

[78.] François Durand, *Discours au vrai du ballet dansé par le roi* (Paris, 1617), pp. 3-4.

[79.] *Ibid.,* pp. 5-6. That Louis had a lofty view indeed of the power of his performance in this ballet to convey an image of benevolence, might, and unlimited authority is certain. It is less clear whether the spectators could glean this image merely by seeing the ballet, or needed to read Durand's account to clarify the message!

Fire was perhaps the favorite elemental symbol of the Bourbon rulers. Viewed as the most important of the four elements, it stood for light or spiritual and intellectual illumination, for life, for divine grace, and for the sun or Apollo, which both Valois and Bourbon rulers took as a personal image or emblem. Displays of fireworks, both inside and outside the theater, were of course a prominent embellishment in many royal *spectacles.* See Marie-Françoise Christout, "Les feux d'artifices en France de 1606 à 1628," in *Les fêtes,* pp. 247-54.

[80.] Grand ballet from the *Ballet du Roi* (1617), Conservatoire ms rés. F 496, fol. 139.

[81.] *Ibid.,* pp. 1-26; *Ballets et mascarades,* II, 99-119.

[82.] The verses for these and other ballets produced between 1618 and 1640 as well as lists of all the ballets performed in this period may be found in *Ballets et mascarades,* II and III, and in BN ms fr 24355, fols. 70-140, 178-254.

[83.] Concurrently, as the ballet shifted away from drama, a new type of theater piece emerged, which had mythological subjects and exotic characters like nymphs and satyrs and magicians, and which made use of elaborate machinery and scenery to produce magic fountains, apparitions, and phantoms. These plays perpetuated a dramatic tradition formerly associated with the dance, which was initiated by the Italians and which later contributed to the creation of opera in France. See Étienne Gros, "Les origines de la tragédie lyrique et la place des tragédies en machines dans l'évolution de théâtre vers l'opéra," *Rev. his. lit.*, XXV (1928), 160-93.

84. Prunières, *Le ballet*, pp. 119-33; Grout, *Mus. Let.*, XXII, 22-24; Silin, 178-81.

85. For example, see the *Ballet des fées* (1625) in "Recueil de plusieurs anciens ballets dansez sous les règnes de Henri III, Henri IV, et Louis III," Conservatoire ms rés. F. 497, fols. 1-10.

86. Michel de Marolles, *Mémoires* (Amsterdam, 1755), III, 121.

87. "Cérémonies de ville" (fol. 237), and "Extrait des registres de l'Hôtel de Ville" (fol. 114), BN ms n.a. fr 9745. See fol. 246 of the same manuscript for a similar account of a ballet performed at the Hôtel de Ville, February 30, 1621.

88. *Grand bal de la douairière de billebahaut: Ballet dansé par le roy au mois de Février 1626* (Paris, 1626), p. 7; see also *Ballets et mascarades*, III, 153-202.

89. Christout, in *Les fêtes*, p. 252.

90. *Ballets et mascarades*, IV, 191.

91. "Solennités : Fêtes de réjouissances; processions," BN ms n.a. fr 7942, fols. 64r.-65v. A printed copy can also be found on pp. 63r.-74r. of the *Ballet de l'harmonie* (Paris, 1632). See also *Ballets et mascarades*, IV, 207-27.

92. Quoted in BN ms fr 24353, fol. 65.

93. *Ballets et mascarades*, V, 69-70.

94. *Ibid.*, p. 70. The prevalence of aquatic themes in this and earlier ballets is the subject of Rousset's article in *Les fêtes*, pp. 238-42. He suggests that water was a Baroque symbol of change and metamorphoses.

95. *Ballets et mascarades*, V, 85-86.

96. C. V. Wedgwood, *The Thirty Years War* (Garden City, N.Y., 1961), p. 413.

97. BN ms fr 24354, fol. 141r.; *Ballets et mascarades*, V, 229-42.

98. *Ballets et mascarades*, VI, 22; Bonnet (*Histoire générale*, p. 72) believed that Jules Mazarin wrote this preface. See also Marolles, I, 237-39.

99. Conservatoire ms rés. F 497, fol. 106.

100. *Ballets et mascarades*, VI, 37.

101. *Ibid.*, p. 42.

102. *Ibid.*, pp. 34-46.

Chapter 3. Music and the Monarchy during the Youth of Louis XIV

1. André Félibien, *Description du château de Versailles* (Paris, 1696), p. 27.

2. La Mothe le Vayer, pp. 165-68, 218-20; BN ms fr 19043, fols. 59, 74r.-84v.

3. Norbert Dufourcq, "Versailles et la musique française," *XVIIe siècle*, no. 34 (March 1957), pp. 3-6.

4. Bonnet, *Histoire de la musique*, p. 331.

5. Visconti, pp. 191-92, 382-83.

6. Bonnet, *Histoire de la musique*, p. 330. See also Roger de Bussy-Rabutin, *Recueil des histoires galantes* (Cologne, n.d.), pp. 353-54.

7. Maurice Ashley, *Louis XIV and the Greatness of France* (2d ed.; London, 1948), p. 6.

8. Choisy, pp. 80, 111-18.

9. Louis-Pierre Anquetil, *Memoirs of the Court of France during the Reign of Lewis XIV*, trans. unknown (Edinburgh, 1791).

10. Nicolas Goulas, *Mémoires*, ed. Constant (Paris, 1879), II, 204; Limiers, I, 1-8.

11. *Memoirs of Madame la Marquise de Montespan*, trans. unknown (London, 1895), I, 65; see also Bussy-Rabutin, *Recueil*, pp. 360-66.

12. Quoted in Ashley, p. 7.

13. Isaac de Larrey, *Histoire de France sous le règne de Louis XIV* (2d ed.; Rotterdam, 1722), I, 354.

14. *Ibid.*, p. 432.

15. Grouvelle, "Considérations nouvelles sur Louis XIV," in *Oeuvres de Louis XIV*, ed. Grouvelle (Paris, 1806), I, 208-9.

16. Louis de Rouvroi, duc de Saint-Simon, *Louis XIV et sa cour* (Paris, 1853), p. 16.

17. *Ibid.*, pp. 33-34.

18. The impact of the Fouquet episode is discussed in Bonnet, *Histoire de la musique*, pp. 332-35; Marie-Madeleine de La Fayette, *The Secret History of Henrietta, Princess of England . . . together with Memoirs of the Court of France for the Years 1688-1689*, trans. Shelmerdine (New York, 1929), pp. 40-41; Choisy, pp. 170-80; Touchard-Lafosse, II, 183; Olivier Lefèvre d'Ormesson, *Journal et extraits des mémoires* (Paris, 1861), II, lix.

19. *Mémoires de M. de . . . [anonyme] pour servir à l'histoire du XVIIe siècle*, Vol. VII of *Nouvelle collection des mémoires*, ed. Michaud and Poujoulat (3d ser.; Paris, 1839), p. 458.

20. Romain Rolland, *Some Musicians of Former Days*, trans. Blaiklock (4th ed.; London, n.d.), pp. 70-84; Rolland, *Les origines*, pp. 244-45; Alfred Richard Oliver, *The Encyclopedists as Critics of Music* (New York, 1947), p. 3; Bukofzer, pp. 147-48.

21. *Proceedings*, pp. 134-35; Menestrier, *Des représentations*, pp. 231-35.

22. Françoise Bertaut de Motteville, *Mémoires*, Vol. X of *Nouvelle collection des mémoires*, ed. Michaud and Poujoulat (3d ser.; Paris, 1839), p. 98.

23. Margarete Baur-Heinhold, *The Baroque Theatre: A Cultural History of the 17th and 18th Centuries*, trans. Whittall (New York, 1967), pp. 117-33; Rousset, in *Les fêtes*, pp. 235-36; Per Bjurstroem, *Giacomo Torelli and Baroque Stage Design* (Stockholm, 1961); Roger-Armand Weigert, *Jean I Berain* (2 vols.; Paris, 1937).

[24.] Arthur Loewenberg, *Annals of Opera, 1597-1940* (2d ed. rev.; Geneva, 1955), pp. 41, 15-25.

[25.] A discussion of Rossi's career and *Orfeo* can be found in Rolland, *Some Musicians*, pp. 83-127; Menestrier, *Des représentations;* Grout, *Mus. Let.*, XXII, 8; Rolland, *Les origines*, pp. 245-47; and Bjurstroem, pp. 143-47.

[26.] Rolland, *Some Musicians*, pp. 112-13; Luigi Rossi and Francesco Buti, "L'Orfeo," Conservatoire ms rés. 1785, fols. 4r.-7v. (dated 1647).

[27.] *Ibid.*, fol. 4v. The original manuscript score of *Orfeo* is in the Chigi library in Rome. The Bibliothèque du Conservatoire in Paris possesses one of the very rare copies of the manuscript. I have used this copy, in conjunction with the selected group of pieces from *Orfeo* in Hugo Goldschmidt's *Studien zur Geschichte der italienischen Oper im 17. Jahrhundert* (Liepzig, 1901), I, 295-310.

[28.] Rolland, *Some Musicians*, p. 118.

[29.] Goldschmidt, I, 307-308.

[30.] Donald Jay Grout, *A History of Western Music* (New York, 1960), p. 284.

[31.] Goulas, II, 212.

[32.] Quoted in Rolland, *Some Musicians*, p. 100.

[33.] Quoted *ibid.*, p. 102.

[34.] *Mémoires du M. de . . . [anonyme]*, VII, 271.

[35.] Guy Joly, *Mémoires*, Vol. II of *Nouvelle collection des mémoires*, p. 6.

[36.] Goulas, II, 212.

[37.] Most historians agree that French opera grew out of these machine plays and pastorales, the ballets de cour, comédie-ballets, and the Italian opera. Unfortunately many musicologists tend to view French national opera as a potpourri of ingredients that blended together effortlessly, as if the components of musical and dramatic style had a life of their own and simply married each other in order to bear the offspring of the 1670's. The French musicologist Lionel de La Laurencie, for example, asserted blithely (*Lully* [2d. ed.; Paris, 1919], p. 137): "You will understand that historical determinism renders irrevocable the advent of the tragedy in music." Similarly, in estimating the dramatic content of French opera, Philippe Quinault's biographer Étienne Gros designates French opera as a hybrid outgrowth of sundry pastorals, machine plays, and comedies, which were used as models and from which Quinault extracted the ingredients for his unoriginal librettos (Gros, *Rev. his. lit.*, XXXV, 160-93). Unquestionably, French opera had its models, as any historical phenomenon has its precedents. What has escaped the attention of many musicologists is that the machine plays were feeble attempts at music drama, as Manfred Bukofzer has suggested, and, more important, that the originators of French opera consciously created a distinctly French product, which, for all its models, was reared by Colbert and Louis XIV and which reflected in both its music and verse the purposes of the crown.

[38.] Quoted in Bukofzer, p. 149. See also Grout, *Mus. Let.*, XXII, 10-11.

[39.] Charles d'Assoucy, *Andromède, tragédie représentée avec les machines sur le Théâtre royal de Bourbon*, text by Pierre Corneille (Rouen, 1651), p. 2.

40. Charles d'Assoucy, *Les amours d'Apollon et de Daphné, comédie en musique dédiée au roi* (Paris, 1650), p. 6.

41. A few years later when a controversy developed over who could claim to be the originator of French opera, La Guerre cited his pastoral and contended that in 1655 he had "the honor of presenting before Your Majesty a French Comedy in Music entitled the Triumph of Love ... whose style I have created and which is in effect the first work of this kind which has ever appeared in this realm." (From La Guerre's dedication to Louis XIV in *Oeuvres en vers de divers autheurs*, 1662, quoted in Loewenberg, pp. 32-33).

42. Quoted in Silin, p. 234. Translated by the author.

43. Quoted in Silin, p. 236. See also Isaac de Benserade, *Les œuvres* (Paris, 1697), II, 72-73.

44. Silin, p. 236. See also Durand, p. 6. The ballet music may be found in "Les nopces de Pélée et de Thétis," Conservatoire ms rés. 500. Philidor labeled the work a "Comédie italienne en musique entre meslée d'un ballet sur le mesme sujet dansé par sa majesté en 1654."

45. Bukofzer, p. 153.

46. Quoted in Rolland, *Les origines*, p. 251.

47. André Tessier, "Les premiers ballets de Lully," in Jean-Baptiste Lully, *Oeuvres complètes*, ed. Prunières (Paris, 1931), III, xix-xxv. Lully was unusually successful in drilling his musicians to bow uniformly. His methods became known to foreign musicians, some of whom, like Johann Coussu, Pelham Humphrey, and Georg Muffat, came to France to study Lully's techniques. In his *Florilegium Secundum* (Passau, 1698), Muffat analyzed and explained these procedures. A section of the *Florilegium* is printed in Lully, *Oeuvres complètes*, III, xxvii-xliii.

48. The ballet music for *Xerxes* may be found in Conservatoire ms rés. 504, fols. 1-19.

49. Francesco Cavalli, *Xerxes, comédie en musique avec six entrées de ballet qui servent d'intermède de la comédie* (Paris, 1660), p. 15.

50. Jean Loret, *La muze historique*, ed. Ravenel and Pelouze (new ed.; Paris, 1857), III, 284-87, 290. Written in verse, Loret's journal was dedicated and addressed to Mademoiselle de Longueville, the daughter of the governor of Normandy. Although nearly always laudatory of the court and the king, the journal is one of the best sources for the activities of the court in the 1650's and 1660's. On Loret's death in 1665 the journal was continued by La Gravette de Mayolas and Charles Robinet (see *Les continuateurs de Loret*).

51. Designed by Gaspare Vigarani, who had achieved fame for his theater in Modena constructed in 1654, the machine theater was built between 1660 and 1662 in the left wing of the Tuileries. Constructed in a rectangular shape, the theater was exceptionally large for the time, particularly in height, and was so heavily mechanized that the singers could not even hear themselves amid the clanking and rumbling of gears and wheels. See Baur-Heinhold, p. 172; and Bjurstroem, p. 131. There is an illustration of the theater in André Boll's book, *De l'Académie royale à la salle Garnier* (Paris, 1960).

[52] See the bass solo from act 4, scene 1, Goldschmidt, I, 94-97.

[53] Loret, III, 397, 465-67, 471-72, 492. See also the book written in 1715 by Boscheron, "Vie de M. Quinault de l'Académie française, avec l'origine des opéra en France," BN ms fr 24329, fol. 67; Nicholas Boindin, *Lettres historiques sur tous les spectacles de Paris* (Paris, 1719), pp. 35-71; Silin, pp. 301-308.

[54] Francesco Cavalli, *Ercole Amante: Tragedia, representata per le Nozze della Maesta Christianissime*, text by Francesco Buti (Paris, 1662), p. 19; see also Boindin, pp. 10-19.

[55] Letter signed R[obert] Ouvrard, Paris, and dated July 16, 1666; found in BN ms fr 9560.

[56] Bukofzer, p. 141. Lionel de La Laurencie writes (p. 135): "The French taste showed itself strongly hostile to the musical expression of the violent movements of the spirit, loathing the cries, the sobs of the Italians."

[57] Opinions vary on the question of Italian influence upon French opera. Donald Grout argues that Lully did not acknowledge its influence because he feared competition and saw that the future lay in a national music. Grout sees three general influences from the Italians: they prompted the French to experiment with a kind of music suitable for dramatic use, which led to Lully's invention of the French recitative; they stimulated literary men to write dramatic works with scenes in which music might be used; they increased the French fascination with bold staging and machine-propelled scenery. In the final analysis, Grout believes the Italians simply pushed the French composers and poets to create bigger and better ballets in their own style and tradition; French opera sprang quite naturally from the French tragedy, pastoral, machine play, and especially the ballet, Grout concludes (*Mus. Let.*, XXII, 7-25). In his *A Short History of Opera* (New York, 1947), p. 117, Grout writes: "The influence of Italian opera was . . . indirect; it stimulated the French to emulate the Italians by trying to create an opera of their own, and it probably led them to favor a large proportion of machine sets." Romain Rolland also argues that the real influence was slight, a fact which he considers appalling. The French stupidly refused to learn from the Italians because of pride, conceit, and a narrow chauvinism, Rolland declares; as a result, the French had attained by 1670 little more than the Italians had developed in 1600 (*Les origines*, pp. 254-59). Étienne Gros in his biography of Quinault says very little except that the Italian opera "specified the character of the representations in music and contributed in a sizable extent to the future subjection of lyric theater to the royal despotism" (Étienne Gros, *Philippe Quinault, sa vie et son œuvre* [Paris, 1926], p. 523).

[58] The only complete study of Benserade is Silin's. See also Bayle, pp. 565-68, and BN ms fr 25465, fols. 30-56. The manuscript, and the unsigned "Traité du ballet" which provides a commentary on Benserade's career, were probably written in the seventeenth or early eighteenth century. The date, 1893, is penned in on the side of the manuscript but is in ink of a different color from the script of the "Traité." The author refers to Bonnet and Menestrier as if they were contemporaries.

[59.] Louis first danced before the court in a ball following a performance of *Orfeo* on March 4, 1647. The king's maître d'hôtel Jean Vallier reported that Louis also danced at a ball at the Hôtel de Ville which honored his return to Paris in 1649 (Jean Vallier, *Journal de Jean Vallier, maître d'hôtel du roi (1648-1657)* [Paris, 1902], I, 396-97).

[60.] Letter to Godeau, March 2, 1651, quoted in Silin, p. 206. The quotations from the *Gazette de France* are available in *ibid.*, p. 205.

[61.] *Ballets et mascarades*, VI, 267-77; Benserade, II, 3-13.

[62.] Although Loret attributed the *Festes de Bacchus* to Benserade, Charles Silin does not include it among Benserade's works. For a discussion of the problem of the ballet's authorship and a copy of the text, see Victor Fournel, *Les contemporains de Molière* (Paris, 1866), II, 295-324.

[63.] Loret, I, 347, dated March 1, 1653.

[64.] Quoted in Silin, p. 224. See also Benserade, II, 70.

[65.] Conservatoire ms rés. F 501, fol. 27. Attached to the manuscript score of the *Ballet de la nuit* is a printed copy of this récit in which the voice part is transposed into the G clef; this is the version that I have reproduced here.

[66.] Loret, II, 13.

[67.] Lully, *Oeuvres complètes*, I, 10. Other ballets of this period included the *Ballet des proverbes* and the *Ballet du temps*, both performed in the salle des gardes of the Louvre. The music can be found in Conservatoire ms rés. 502, fols. 1-33. For descriptions and accounts of these productions see Loret, I, 468, 573-74; II, 13-17, 47, 57; and Marolles, III, 127-57.

[68.] Loret, II, 291, dated Jan. 20, 1657, and p. 299, dated Feb. 10, 1657. See Lully, *Oeuvres complètes*, I, 5-98; Conservatoire ms rés. F 535, fols. 1-45; and Benserade, II, 173-82.

[69.] Loret, II, 445, dated Feb. 16, 1658.

[70.] *Ibid.*, p. 446, dated Feb. 23, and p. 449, dated March 2, 1658. See also Benserade, II, 183-206.

[71.] The standard biographies of Lully, from which I have drawn material on his life, are La Laurencie, *Lully*; and Henry Prunières, *Lully* (Paris, n.d.). See also Romain Rolland, *Essays on Music* (New York, 1948), pp. 25-30.

[72.] Quoted in Silin, p. 282. See also Benserade, II, 233.

[73.] Quoted in Touchard-Lafosse, II, 257.

[74.] These included the *Ballet des saisons*, which was performed at Fontaine-bleau in June 1660, and the *Ballet des arts* at the Palais-Royal in January 1663.

[75.] Loret, IV, 164, dated Feb. 16, 1664. See also Benserade, II, 300-18.

[76.] Loret, IV, 307-308, dated Feb. 7, 1665. See also pp. 304-306, dated Jan. 31, 1665; and p. 313, dated Feb. 21, 1665.

[77.] *Les continuateurs de Loret*, ed. Rothschild (Paris, 1881), I, 304, dated Oct. 4, 1665; pp. 254-55, 259, dated Sept. 20, 1665.

[78.] Conservatoire ms rés. 505, fols. 1-15.

[79.] *Les continuateurs*, I, 443, dated Nov. 4, 1666.

[80.] *Ibid.*, I, 543, dated Dec. 9, 1666.

[81.] Quoted in Silin, p. 382. See also Benserade, II, 378-79.

⁸². Quoted in Silin, p. 391. See also Benserade, II, 384-85 and BN ms fr 25465, fols. 54-55.

⁸³. *Les continuateurs*, III, 497-99, dated Feb. 21, 1669.

⁸⁴. *Ibid.*, pp. 504-508, dated Feb. 23.

⁸⁵. *Ibid.*, p. 535, dated March 10, 1669.

⁸⁶. Lully, *Oeuvres complètes*, III, 30, 3-33. See also *Les continuateurs*, III, 397-400, dated Oct. 12, 1669.

⁸⁷. Chevalier Laurent d'Arvieux, *Mémoires* (Paris, 1735), IV, 43-107.

⁸⁸. Lully, *Oeuvres complètes*, III, 43-107.

⁸⁹. *Ibid.*, pp. 223 and 154-230.

⁹⁰. In May 1670, the former cook's servant purchased a piece of land on the rue Sainte-Anne and built a hôtel on it. His total expenditure was 22,680 livres.

Chapter 4. The Centralization of Music

¹. The author has treated the subject of this chapter in an article, "The Centralization of Music in the Reign of Louis XIV," *French Historical Studies*, VI (Fall, 1969), 156-71.

². *Mercure*, July 1687, p. 34. Louis' intentions are discussed in the Lettres patentes issued to start a branch of the French academy at Angers in June 1687; as cited in the *Mercure*, July 1687, pp. 22-34. See also Louis Le Gendre's *The History of the Reign of Lewis the Great till the General Peace concluded at Reswick* [*sic*] *in the Year 1697*, trans. unknown (London, 1699), pp. 3-79; and Perrault, *Mémoires, contes*, pp. 41-45.

³. Charles de Bruny, *Examen de ministère de M. Colbert* (Paris, 1774), pp. 62-68; circular to intendants and commissaires, June 19, 1683, *Correspondance*, IV, 606-607.

⁴. Nikolaus Pevsner, *Academies of Art Past and Present* (Cambridge, 1940), p. 99. See also Victor-L. Tapié, *The Age of Grandeur*, trans. Williamson (2d ed.; New York, 1966), p. 133.

⁵. Letter to P. de Bonzy, bishop of Beziers and ambassador from France to Venice, dated June 15, 1663, *Correspondance*, IV, 531.

⁶. Paul Fréart de Chantelou, *Journal du voyage du Cavalier Bernin* (Paris, 1885). See also Perrault, *Characters Historical*, I, 90-95.

⁷. Colbert, *Fortifications*, V, 252.

⁸. Letter to Errard, July 23, 1671, *Correspondance*, IV, 573.

⁹. Tapié, p. 125.

¹⁰. Lettres patentes du roi pour l'establissement d'une Académie royale de danse en la ville de Paris, reprinted in G. A. Crapelet, *Notice sur la vie et les ouvrages de Quinault* (Paris, 1824), p. 39. See also "Documents sur l'Académie de la danse, March 30, 1662," Arsenal ms 10295, dos. 1, fols. 28-43; and "Mémoires pour l'Académie de la danse" (fol. 253), and Lettres patentes (fols. 256-479) of BN ms fr 21732.

¹¹. "Statuts que sa majesté veut et entend être observés en l'Académie royale de danse, qu'elle désire être en la ville et fauxbourgs de Paris," Arsenal ms 10295, dos. 1, fols. 32-35.

12. *Mercure*, June 1680, p. 263; *État actuel de la musique du roi et des trois spectacles de Paris* (Paris, 1772), pp. 27-30; Pure, pp. 317-18; Nicolas de Blegny [Abraham du Pradel], *Le livre commode des adresses de Paris pour 1692*, ed. Fournier (Paris, 1878), I, 127.

13. BN ms n.a. fr 1698, fol. 23.

14. Guillaume Du Manoir, *Le mariage de la musique avec la danse*, ed. Gallay (Paris, 1870), p. 81; see also BN ms fr 22536, fols. 147v.–48v.; Compan, pp. 216-30. The seventeenth-century academies are discussed in Yates, *The French Academies*, pp. 290-308.

15. BN ms fr 21732, fol. 269; see also "Arrêt du Parlement de Paris qui démet les Maîtres violons de l'opposition par eux formée à l'enregistrement des lettres d'établissement de l'Académie de danse," dos. 1, fol. 36 of Arsenal ms 10295.

16. Anon., "Établissement de l'Académie royale de danse en la ville de Paris," BN ms fr 21732, fols. 273r.-273v.

17. "Extraits des registres du Conseil d'État," *ibid.*, fol. 280, dated Apr. 28, 1682; fol. 282, dated Dec. 21, 1682.

18. Paul Tallemant, *Histoire de l'Académie royale des inscriptions et belles-lettres depuis son établissement* (Paris, 1717), I, 2, 2-56. See also Pevsner, pp. 14-18.

19. Rudolf Wittkower, "The Vicissitudes of a Dynastic Monument: Bernini's Equestrian Statue of Louis XIV," *De Artibus opuscula XL: Essays in Honor of Erwin Panofsky* (Zurich, 1960), p. 512.

20. Paris, March 12, 1664, *Correspondance*, IV, 534.

21. *Mercure*, May 1703, pp. 238-39.

22. Quoted in Tallemant, I, 23.

23. Quoted in Charles Perrault, *Mémoires de ma vie* (Paris, 1909), p. 37.

24. The history of the Académie is related in Pevsner, pp. 82-108.

25. Nicolas Bailly, *Inventaire des tableaux du roi* (Paris, 1899), pp. iv-v.

26. Henry Jouin, *Charles Le Brun et les arts sous Louis XIV* (Paris, 1889), pp. 201-204; André Fontaine, "Préface," in *Conférences inédites de l'Académie royale de peinture et de sculpture d'après les manuscrits des archives de l'école des Beaux-arts* (Paris, 1903), pp. lxi-lxiii.

27. Yates, *The French Academies*, pp. 297-99.

28. See, for example, Le Brun's discourse (Jan. 10, 1671) on Poussin's painting "Le ravissement de Saint Paul" in *Conférences inédites*, pp. 77-85.

29. Charles Le Brun, *Conférence de Monsieur Le Breun* [sic] (Amsterdam, 1718), pp. 3-55; Jouin, pp. 371-90.

30. *Mercure*, Feb. 1682, p. 28.

31. *La cour et la ville sous Louis XIV, Louis XV et Louis XVI, ou Révélations historiques tirées de manuscrits inédits*, ed. Barrière (Paris, 1830), p. iv.

32. This vastly complex subject can only be suggested here. There is a great need for an artistic analysis of the *spectacles* of Louis XIV's reign of the sort done on the Valois court by the scholars of the Warburg and Courtauld Institutes. My remarks are based on their writings in addition to those of the following authors: Wittkower; Seznec; Panofsky; Jouin; Eugène Bouvy,

La gravure de portraits et d'allégories (Paris, 1929); Mario Praz, *Studies in Seventeenth-Century Imagery* (2d ed. rev.; Rome, 1964); Agnès Joly, "Le Roi-Soleil, histoire d'une image," *Rev. his. Versailles*, no. 4 (May 1937), pp. 213-35.

[33.] Seznec, p. 321.

[34.] E. H. Gombrich, "*Icones Symbolicae:* The Visual Image in Neo-Platonic Thought," *Warburg*, XI (1948), 173.

[35.] The principal ones were *Iconologia seu de sacris Aegyptiorum aliarumque gentium literis commentarii* (1603) by Ceasare Ripa; *Bibliothecae Alexandrinae Icones Symbolicae* (1626) by Christoforo Giarda; *De Deis Gentium varia et multiplex historia in qua simul de eorum imaginibus et cognominibus agitur* (1548) by Lilio Gregario Giraldi; *L'imagini colla sposizione degli dei degli antiche* (1556) by Vincenzo Cartari; and *Mythologiae sive explicationis fabularum libri decem* (1551) by Natale Conti. For a discussion of these manuals, see Seznec, pp. 229-64.

[36.] Victoria Goldberg, "Graces, Muses, and Arts: The Urns of Henry II and Francis I," *Warburg*, XXIX (1966), 207-208.

[37.] Seznec, pp. 140-42.

[38.] The history of the sun as a royal emblem is recounted by Joly, *Rev. his. Versailles*, pp. 213-35.

[39.] André Félibien, *Description sommaire du chasteau de Versailles* (Paris, 1674).

[40.] Jouin, pp. 258-63.

[41.] *Ibid.*, pp. 273-85, 439-45.

[42.] J. B. Weckerlin, "Notice sur Cambert et son œuvre," in Robert Cambert and Pierre Perrin, *Pomone, Pastorale en 5 Actes et le Prologue* (pp. 12-15), Vol. III of *Les Chefs-d'œuvres* (Paris, n.d.). See also Rolland, *Les origines*, pp. 249-50; and *Proceedings*, pp. 139-40. Because of the rivalry over the founding of the Académie royale de musique, Lully's opponents accused him of having hired assassins to murder Cambert. When Lully died in 1687, this unfounded rumor was satirized in a publication entitled *Lettre de Clément Marot*, in which Cambert, disfigured from his wounds, is depicted challenging Lully's right to enter the Elysian fields.

[43.] Henry Prunières, "Lully and the Académie de musique et de danse," trans. Baker, *Mus. Quar.*, XI (Oct. 1925), 528-30.

[44.] Perrin included some of the verses of the *Pastorale* in his letter, and he noted that the archbishop had gone over the early sketches of the *Pastorale* with him on a prior occasion in Paris. The letter is printed in Pierre Perrin, *Les œuvres de poésie* (Paris, 1661), pp. 273-90, and copied in BN ms fr 12355, fols. 3-4.

[45.] Quoted in Borland, p. 137.

[46.] Perrin, p. 312.

[47.] Loret, III, 51-52, dated May 10, 1659.

[48.] *Ibid.*, p. 61, dated May 31.

[49.] Perrin, p. 277; see also Menestrier, *Des représentations*, pp. 208-11.

[50.] Quoted in Prunières, *Mus. Quar.*, XI (Oct. 1925), 531.

[51.] BN ms fr 2208, fols. 1v.-2r.

[52.] "Ariane et Bacchus," BN ms fr 24352, fol. 183.

⁵³· Lettres patentes du roi, June 28, 1669, quoted in Crapelet, pp. 42-45. See also Noinville *et al.*, 2d ed. rev., pp. 77-81; Jean-Nicolas Du Tralage, *Notes et documents sur l'histoire des théâtres de Paris au XVIIᵉ siècle* (Paris, 1880), pp. 71-72; Gabriel Fictor [Auguste Jal], *Dictionnaire théâtral* (Paris, 1824), p. 959; and BN ms fr 12355, fols. 6-8.

⁵⁴· Sourdéac was known for his eccentric and licentious behavior; his shady past included piracy during the Fronde, possible assassinations, and forgery. His cohort, Champeron, had a prison record for various offenses including tax fraud. See Prunières, *Mus. Quar.*, XI, 533-36.

⁵⁵· Arthur Michel de Boislisle, *Les débuts de l'opéra français à Paris* (Paris, 1875), pp. 6-10.

⁵⁶· The music of the prologue and act 1 is all that remains from *Pomone*.

⁵⁷· Cambert and Perrin, III, 5. The first edition of the musical score may be found in the Bibliothèque Nationale, réserve Vm²-1.

⁵⁸· The order was issued by Achilles du Harlay, conseiller du roi en ses conseils and procureur général du roi, on May 23. See Boislisle, p. 16.

⁵⁹· Chanson on the air of "Quand Florinon les coudes sur la table," BN ms fr 12618, fols. 429-30.

⁶⁰· Accounts of these early months of the Académie royale de musique may be found in Prunières, *Mus. Quar.*, XI, 535-38; Boislisle, pp. 8-13; La Laurencie, pp. 24-27; Boindin, pp. 72-76; and BN ms fr 24329, fols. 73-74.

⁶¹· Robert Cambert, *Les peines et les plaisirs de l'amour*, text by Gabriel Gilbert (Paris, 1672), pp. 3-4. Only the music for the prologue and act 1 is extant. Manfred Bukofzer in his excellent article, "Allegory in Baroque Music," (*Warburg*, III, [1939-40], 1-21), prefers the term "musical allegory." He explains how Baroque composers used an assortment of musical figures to convey the abstract ideas of descent, ascent, speed, slowness, jumping, and other types of movement. These figures were especially meaningful in the seventeenth century, when they were used to project words in a text associated with movement. Lully employed them effectively in all of his operas. Bukofzer's main point is that musical allegory did not convey its meaning through the emotions, but through the intellect. Thus, the same musical figure could be used to allegorize desire in one context and anger in another. Ambiguity could be avoided only when the music was accompanied by a text.

⁶²· Cambert, pp. 10-14.

⁶³· *Ibid.*, p. 6.

⁶⁴· Reprinted in Noinville *et al*, 1753, no pp.

⁶⁵· *Psyché*, in *Recueil des opéra, des ballets, et des plus belles pièces en musique* (Amsterdam, 1690), I, 8-9.

⁶⁶· Perrault, *Mémoires, contes*, p. 92.

⁶⁷· Lully to Colbert, June 3, 1672: "Jean-Baptiste Lully," in *Revue des documents historiques: Suite de pièces curieuses et inédites*, ed. Charavay (Paris, 1875), II, 112.

⁶⁸· Pierre Clément offers this opinion in *Madame de Montespan et Louis XIV* (2d ed.; Paris, 1868), p. 130; see also Boindin, p. 76.

69. *Mercure*, July-Aug. 1673, p. 343.

70. *Mémoires de Louis XIV*, pp. 90-91.

71. Privilège pour l'établissement de l'Académie royale de musique en faveur de Monsieur de Lully, in AN ms O¹613, fol. 1. Additional copies may be found in AN ms O¹16, fols. 94-96; and BN ms fr 12355, fols. 11-13. The Lettres have been printed in Crapelet, pp. 35-38; and in Noinville *et al.*, 1753, pp. 82-87.

72. AN ms O¹613, fols. 1v.–2r.

73. Colbert to Harlay, Versailles, March 24, 1672, BN ms fr 17413, fol. 226. See Colbert, V, 322.

74. Noinville *et al.*, 1753, p. 87.

75. Colbert to Harlay, April 24, 1672, in Colbert, V, 323.

76. Ordonnances of April 14 and 30, 1672, in Noinville *et al.*, 1753, p. 106.

77. *Revue des documents*, II, 110-11.

78. Lully to Colbert, June 3, 1672, *ibid.*, II, 112.

79. Colbert, V, 297.

80. *Ibid.*, p. 298.

81. Privilège du roi, Versailles, Sept. 20, 1672, in *Recueil des opéra*, I, 66. For extracts of this document, see Crapelet, pp. 49-50, and Noinville *et al.*, 1753, p. 88.

82. Loewenberg, p. 51.

83. *Théâtre de Quinault* (new ed.; Paris, 1778), IV, 5.

84. *Ibid.*, p. 14. In addition to its availability in *ibid.*, pp. 9-50, the text of *Les fêtes de l'amour et de Bacchus* may be found in BN ms fr 24352, fols. 121-28. The musical score was printed in 1717 and is available in the BN.

85. Noinville *et al.*, 1753, p. 2.

86. Letter to Madame de Grignan, Paris, Dec. 1, 1673, in Marie de Sévigné, *Lettres de sa famille et de ses amis* (Paris, 1820), III, 157.

87. Letter to Madame de Grignan, Paris, Jan. 8, 1674, *ibid.*, IV, 203.

88. Perrault, *Characters Historical*, I, 186.

89. A general analysis of Quinault's drama may be found in the excellent biography by Étienne Gros, pp. 542-43.

90. Lully, *Cadmus et Hermione*, *Oeuvres complètes*, I, 7-50.

91. *Ibid.*, p. 195.

92. A very good discussion of Lully's style in *Cadmus* that has contributed to and reinforced my own findings has been written by Henry Prunières in the preface to his edition of Lully's works (*ibid.*).

93. Quoted from the preface, *ibid.*

94. Loewenberg, pp. 51-52.

95. Perrault, *Mémoires, contes*, p. 93.

96. Prunières, *Mus. Quar.*, XI, 538-40. See also Baur-Heinhold, pp. 161-72.

97. Colbert's note is difficult to decipher. See "Requête de J.-B. Lulli au nom de l'Académie royale de musique, relative à des réparations à faire à son local avec note de Colbert," BN ms fr 165, fol. 1.

[98.] Blegny, I, 270. See also Prunières, *Mus. Quar.*, XI, 541-46; and Leris, pp. xxvi–xxvii.

[99.] Quoted in Prunières, *Mus. Quar.*, XI, 541.

[100.] "Épître," in La Fontaine, VI, 23. See also Prunières, *Mus. Quar.*, XI, 540-41.

[101.] See, for example, J. L. de Freneuse Lecerf de la Viéville, *Comparaison de la musique italienne et de la musique française* (Brussels, 1705), pp. 295-310.

[102.] Du Tralage, p. 86.

[103.] Lully, *Oeuvres complètes*, III, 79; Viéville, *Comparaison*, pp. 327-28.

[104.] Leris, p. xxvii. The archives of the opera (AN ms AJ^{13}, cartons 1-44) and the archives of secrétariat d'État of the maison du roi (AN ms O^{1}613-29) contain a wealth of information on every aspect of the Académie's administration during the eighteenth century, but yield few details about the seventeenth century.

[105.] BN ms fr 16750, fols. 175-76.

[106.] This figure is a guess based on the fact that Lully offered to pay the machinist Sieur Angelo 1,000 écus, but was turned down by Angelo, who demanded 5,000 livres annually. See Du Tralage, p. 5.

[107.] Noinville *et al.*, 2d ed. rev., p. 38; Blegny, I, 285.

[108.] Leris, p. xxvii.

[109.] Noinville *et al.*, 2d ed. rev., pp. 118-20.

[110.] Ordonnance, Apr. 22, 1673, AN ms O^{1}17, fol. 72. See also AN ms O^{1}618, pièce 1; and Colbert, V, 545-46, item LIV. Accounts of the activities of the comedians can be found in Leris, pp. xix–xxiv; Beauchamps, pp. 94-100; Donald J. Grout, "The Music of the Italian Theater at Paris, 1682-97," in *Papers of the American Musicological Society, Dec. 30, 1941,* ed. Reese (1946), pp. 160-62.

[111.] Ordonnance portant défenses d'établir des opéra dans le royaume, sans la permission de Sieur de Lully, Versailles, Aug. 17, 1684, fol. 47; and Ordonnance, Saint-Germain, March 21, 1675, fol. 51 of Arsenal ms 10295, dos. 2. See also Ordonnance portant défenses d'établir des opéra dans le royaume sans la permission du Sr. Lully, AN ms O^{1}28, fol. 272.

[112.] *Papers*, pp. 160-62. Grout points out that the comedians tried to compensate for their loss by creating musical scenes for their regular actors, resulting in the semimusical productions with simple airs or popular tunes known as vaudevilles.

[113.] In 1672 Quinault's pension was raised from 800 to 1200 livres a year, and in 1674 it was 1500. Few artistic or literary figures were paid more. See Colbert, V, 466-98.

[114.] *Nouvelles parodies bachiques mêlées de vaudevilles ou rondes de table*, coll. and ed. Ballard (Paris, 1700), I.

[115.] *Factum pour Jean de Ganoüilhet . . . contre Jean-Baptiste Lully* (Paris, n.d.), p. 8.

[116.] "Brevet en faveur de Henry Guichard," in *Correspondance*, IV, 595-96. See also Colbert, V, 551-52. A popular madrigal of the time chided Lully and compared him to Chausson, a sodomist who had been burned for his crime. The madrigal suggested that burning Lully would make a fine fireworks. (BN ms fr 12619, fol. 101).

[117.] *Requeste d'inscription de faux en forme de factum, pour Sieur Guichard ... contre Jean-Baptiste Lully* (Paris, 1676). An account of the incident can be found in Prunières, *Lully*, pp. 40-46; and La Laurencie, pp. 40-49.

[118.] Gabriel Fictor, *Dictionnaire critique de biographie et d'histoire* (Paris, 1867), p. 814.

[119.] AN ms O^{1}613, pièce 1, fol. 3; "Anecdotes historiques de l'opéra de Paris en 1672 jusqu'en 1749," Arsenal ms 3308, fols. 140v.-141v.; and Noinville *et al.*, 1753, pp. 88-92.

Chapter 5. The Operas of Lully

[1.] Viéville, *Comparaison*, p. 218.

[2.] *Ibid.*, pp. 217-18. Viéville states that Lully made only one exception: the comte de Fièsque, an esteemed friend of Lully's, who was occasionally permitted to hear parts of the score. He adds that the count was so trustworthy that he "would not have allowed to slip through his hands for four smiles and six kind glances of a goddess the least song of Lully before the first public performance of the opera had been presented." In addition to Viéville, see *Mercure*, Feb. 1695, p. 216; BN ms fr 24329, p. 76; Noinville *et al.*, 1753, pp. 39-43; and Tallemant, I, 6-7.

[3.] Oliver, pp. 4-5. Donald J. Grout (*A Short History of Opera*, p. 118) has made a similar observation: "Interest in the poem of an opera, and insistence that it should be of respectable dramatic quality, was one of the basic differences between the French and Italian viewpoints in the seventeenth and eighteenth centuries."

[4.] Madeleine de Scudéry, *Conversations nouvelles sur divers sujets* (new ed.; The Hague, 1710), I, 61-62.

[5.] Gros, p. 662. Gros' book provides a good comprehensive discussion of Quinault's librettos; see pp. 541-712. See also La Laurencie, pp. 137-46; Grout, *Mus. Let.*, XXII, 3-6; and Rolland, *Les origines*, pp. 260-69.

[6.] Jean-François Marmontel, *Éléments de littérature* (Paris, 1846), III, 241.

[7.] Saint-Simon, p. 4.

[8.] The following works contain useful analyses of Lully's operatic music: Bukofzer, pp. 156-61; La Laurencie, pp. 157-223; Lionel de La Laurencie, "L'opéra français au XVIIe siècle," *Rev. mus.* (Jan. 1, 1925), pp. 29-42; Grout, *Mus. Let.*, XXII, 1-7; Grout, *A Short History*, pp. 121-25; Prunières, *Lully*, pp. 95-120; *Proceedings*, pp. 140-43; and Rolland, *Some Musicians*, pp. 185-250.

[9.] Antoine Furetière, *Dictionaire universel, contenant généralement tous les mots françois, tant vieux que modernes, et les termes de toutes les sciences et des arts* (The Hague, 1690), II, no pp.

[10.] Lully, *Amadis, Oeuvres complètes*, III, 63-64.

11. *Ibid.*, p. 150.

12. *Ibid.*, pp. 120-22.

13. Grout, *Mus. Let.*, XXII, 2.

14. Maurice Barthélemy, "La musique dramatique à Versailles de 1660-1715," *XVIIᵉ siècle*, no. 34 (March 1957), p. 10.

15. The reference is to the appearance of Charon's dog, Cerbère, act 4, scene 4, of *Alceste*.

16. "Sur le nouvel opéra d'Alceste," Arsenal ms 6542, no. 172, fol. 259.

17. Charles Perrault, *Critique de l'opéra ou examen de la tragédie intitulée Alceste, ou le Triomphe d'Alcide* (Paris, 1674), pp. 2-6.

18. Quoted in Prunières, "Preface: Les représentations d'Alceste," in *Lully, Oeuvres complètes*, II, vii.

19. Lully, *Alceste*, *ibid.*, I, pp. 72-74.

20. *Ibid.*, p. 87.

21. *Ibid.*, p. 16.

22. *Ibid.*, p. 6. The dedication was actually written for Lully by Quinault.

23. Jean-Baptiste Lully, *Thésée*, Vol. XXVI of *Les chefs d'œuvre*, pp. 1-48.

24. *Théâtre de Quinault*, IV, 276.

25. Letter to Madame de Grignan, May 6, 1676, Sévigné, IV, 285.

26. Letters to Madame de Grignan, June 15, 1677, and June 23, 1677, *ibid.*, V, 93, 104. See also Touchard-Lafosse, II, 312.

27. The "cloud music" at the beginning of act 2 is a cogent example of Lully's attempt at graphic, musical delineation. The music for the frost people and the contrasting fire music in act 4 are also good examples of early atmospheric music. See Jean-Baptiste Lully, *Isis* (Paris, 1719), pp. 113, 220-21.

28. *Théâtre de Quinault*, IV, 355-412.

29. BN ms fr 12687, fol. 463.

30. *Théâtre de Quinault*, IV, 347-52.

31. Jean-Baptiste Lully, *Bellerophon* (Paris, 1679), "Au Roy."

32. Yates, *The French Academies*, p. 130.

33. Lully, *Bellerophon*, p. 146.

34. *Mercure*, Jan. 1679, p. 332; Oct. 1679, Pt. 1, pp. 329, 350-51. See also March 1679, pp. 1 and 184-87; May 1679, pp. 182-85; June 1679, p. 59; and Jan. 1680, pp. 300-302.

35. *Ibid.*, Nov. 1680, pp. 191-94; Jan. 1680, Pt. 1, pp. 302-303; Feb. 1680, pp. 7-8.

36. *Théâtre de Quinault*, V, 8.

37. Jean-Baptiste Lully, *Proserpine* (Paris, 1680), p. 43.

38. *Théâtre de Quinault*, V, 16.

39. Letter to Madame de Grignan, Feb. 5, 1680, Sévigné, VI, 157.

40. The pro-Jansenist poet, Nicolas Boileau-Despréaux, who did not like Lully, Quinault, or opera, was less impressed. In his "Épître IX à monsieur le Marquis de Seignelay," *Oeuvres complètes*, ed. Chéron (new ed.; Paris, 1860), p. 80, he lampooned the performance and castigated Lully's morals:

En vain par sa grimace un bouffon adieux
Une table nous fait rire et divertit nos yeux :
Ses bon mots ont besoin de farine et de plâtre
Prenez la tête à tête, ôtez-lui son théâtre;
Ce n'est plus qu'un cœur bas, un coquin ténébreux
Son visage essuyé n'a plus rien que affreux.
J'aime un esprit aisé qui se montre, qui s'ouvre
Et qui plaît d'autant plus, que plus il se découvre.
Mais le seule vertu peut souffrir la clarté :
Le vice, toujours sombre, aime l'obscurité;
Pour paroître au grand jour il faut qu'il se déguise;
C'est lui qui de nos mœurs a banni la franchise.

41. Viéville, *Comparaison*, II, 207.

42. "Soumission à Lully pour la charge de conseiller-secrétaire du roi," AN ms V⁷47, pièce 153, Dec 29, 1681.

43. Viéville, *Comparaison*, II, 209-10. In addition to J. L. de Fresneuse Lecerf de la Viéville's account, the following sources treat Lully's ennoblement: Noinville *et al.*, 1753, pp. 51-53; BN ms fr 24329, fols. 83-85; Émile Campardon, *L'Académie royale de musique au XVIIIᵉ siècle* (Paris, 1884), III, 144-47; La Laurencie, pp. 58-60; Prunières, *Lully*, pp. 53-55.

44. *Mercure*, Dec. 1681, pp. 328-29.

45. *Ibid.*, April 1682, p. 329.

46. *Théâtre de Quinault*, V, 127-28.

47. Jean-Baptiste Lully, *Persée* (Paris, 1682), "Au Roy."

48. *Mercure*, July 1682, p. 354.

49. *Ibid.*, p. 358.

50. "Fragment d'un prologue d'opéra" (avertissement au lecteur), Boileau-Despréaux, p. 152.

51. *Théâtre de Quinault*, V, 193.

52. Du Tralage, p. 82.

53. *Mercure*, Jan. 1684, p. 327; March 1685, pp. 221-22.

54. Lully, *Amadis, Oeuvres complètes*, III, "Au Roy."

55. *Ibid.*, pp. 20-21.

56. *Ibid.*, p. 26.

57. *Ibid.*, p. 35.

58. Philippe de Courcillon de Dangeau, *Memoirs of the Court of France from the Year 1684 to the Year 1720*, trans. unknown (London, 1825), I, 17, dated Jan. 16, 1685.

59. Louis-François de Bouchet de Sourches, *Mémoires sur le règne de Louis XIV*, ed. Bertrand (Paris, 1882), I, 168.

60. *Mercure*, Jan. 1685, pp. 317-18; June 1685, p. 313.

61. Jean-Baptiste Lully, *Roland* (Paris, 1685), "Au Roy."

62. *Théâtre de Quinault*, V, 309.

63. *Ibid.*, p. 402.

64. Quoted in Prunières, *Mus. Quar.*, XI, 540.

65. Jean-Baptiste Lully, *Armide* (Paris, 1686), "Au Roy."

66. *Mercure*, Feb. 1686, Pt. 2, p. 295.

67. Dangeau, I, 69-70, dated April 5, 1686.

68. Jean-Baptiste Lully, *Acis et Galatée*, text by Jean Galbert de Campistron (Paris, 1686), "Au Roy."

69. Sourches, II, 10; Noinville *et al.*, 1753, pp. 55-62; *Mercure*, March 1687, Pt. 1, pp. 361-68.

70. Copied from the tomb and translated by the author. An unsigned verse entitled "Sur le superbe mausolée élevée à Lulli dans l'Église des Petits Pères" appeared shortly after the composer's death. The author criticized the erection of such an elaborate monument to "a notorious libertine, unworthy of memory" ("Apostrophe à la mort, sur le mausolée de Lully," in BN ms fr 15226, fols. 250-94).

71. Dangeau, I, 96, dated March 12, 1687. See also Prunières, *Lully*, pp. 76-77; and La Laurencie, pp. 87-89. Lully's will, dated March 10, 1687, has been published in Campardon, II, 148-51.

72. Viéville, *Comparaison*, Préface.

73. BN ms fr 12669, fol. 359.

74. François de Callières, *Histoire poëtique de la guerre nouvellement déclarée entre les anciens et les modernes* (Paris, 1688), p. 274.

75. Arsenal ms 6542, no. 173, fol. 260. Henry Prunières has edited this manuscript for *La revue musicale* ("Le triomphe de Lully aux Champs-Élysées" [Jan. 1925], pp. 92-105). Prunières states that the work was by an obscure writer named Nodot.

76. Antoine Bauderon de Senecé, "Lettre de Clément Marot à Monsieur de S . . . ," *Oeuvres choisies*, ed. Chasles and Cap (new ed.; Paris, 1855), pp. 295-334.

77. *Mercure*, June 1683, p. 263.

78. The best account of the parodies of this period is Donald J. Grout's two-part article, "Seventeenth-Century Parodies of French Opera," *Mus. Quar.*, XXVII (April and Oct. 1941), pp. 211-19 and 514-26. See also Grout's "The Music of the Italian Theatre at Paris, 1682-97," in *Papers*, pp. 158-70; and Louis Riccoboni, *Observations sur la comédie et sur le génie de Molière* (Paris, 1736), pp. 275-348.

79. BN ms fr 12619, fol. 121, and 12621, fols. 19, 21, 23, 25, 26, and 98.

80. BN ms fr 12619, fol. 322; and ms 12620, fols. 425-29. See also BN ms fr 12668, fols. 80, 201, 202, 208, 210, 215, 225; ms 12669, fols. 109, 318, 359; and ms 12689, fols. 49-51.

81. BN ms fr 12687, fol. 321.

82. La Fontaine, VI, 103.

83. *Ibid.*, p. 163.

84. Boileau-Despréaux, "Réflexions critiques," pp. 204-40, and "Épître IX à monsieur le Marquis de Seignelay," pp. 78-80. See also Oliver, pp. 5-10.

85. Jean de La Bruyère, *Les caractères de Théophraste, et la suite* (11th ed.; Lyons, 1730), pp. 20-40.

[86.] Saint-Évremond recorded his opinions in a celebrated letter concerning opera to the duke of Buckingham. It was published by the *Mercure* (Feb. 1683, pp. 72-105), and that is the version quoted here. See also Saint-Évremond's *Oeuvres mêlées* (Paris, 1689), XI, 77-119. The letter was also published in London: Charles de Marguetel de Saint-Denis de Saint-Évremond, *Miscellanea: or Various Discourses upon Tragedy, Comedy, the Italian, the English comedy, and operas to his Grace, the Duke of Buckingham*, trans. Spence (London, 1686), pp. 41-61.

[87.] Charles de Marguetel de Saint-Denis de Saint-Évremond, *Oeuvres mêlées*, ed. Gourmont (3d ed.; Paris, 1909), pp. 238 and 274-76.

[88.] The following essays are relevant: Perrault, *Parallèle*, III, 237-42, and IV, 260-67; and Terrasson, pp. 206-29.

[89.] François Raguenet, *Parallèle des Italiens et des François en ce qui regarde la musique et les opéra* (Paris, 1702).

[90.] Viéville, *Comparaison*, pp. 348-49.

[91.] La Laurencie, p. 235.

Chapter 6. *Divertissements*

[1.] Furetière, I, no pp. The word *divertissement* has also been used to designate the ballets, dances, or short musical interludes in the French Baroque opera (see Willi Apel, *Harvard Dictionary of Music* [Cambridge, 1951], p. 214). The more general, sociological significance of *divertissement* as a diversion or recreation, however, will be used in this chapter, unless otherwise indicated.

[2.] *Mémoires de Louis XIV*, pp. 19-20.

[3.] Norbert Dufourcq, "Versailles et la musique française," *XVIIe siècle*, no. 34 (March 1957), pp. 5-6.

[4.] André Félibien, *Les divertissements de Versailles donnez par le roy à toute sa cour au retour de la conqueste de la Franche-Comté en l'année M.DC.LXXIV* (Paris, 1676), pp. 4-5.

[5.] Le Gendre, p. 25.

[6.] *Mercure*, Dec. 1686, Pt. 2, no pp. See also *Relation des assemblées faites à Versailles dans le grand apartement du roi pendant ce carnaval de l'an 1683* (Paris, 1683), no pp.

[7.] Limiers, III, 126-27.

[8.] *Mercure*, Jan. 1690, p. 290.

[9.] *Ibid.*, Mar. 1690, pp. 9-10.

[10.] *Ibid.*, Feb. 1708, pp. 294-95, 297-306.

[11.] Michel Brenet states that a concert at Saint-Germain in 1679 cost the king 2,766 livres, after the performers' salaries, food, and transportation were figured. See Brenet, p. 67.

[12.] A list of the king's musicians, their residence, rank, and works may be found in Blegny, I, 204-16.

[13.] "Recueil de quittances signées par des musiciens et maîtres de chapelle des rois de France (1471-1680)," BN ms n.a. fr 7835, fols. 49-58.

¹⁴· "Cour des aides," AN ms Z¹ᵃ and "Violons de la chambre du roi, 1638-1761," AN ms Z¹ᵃ 487. There was no change in the salary figure between 1677 and 1706.

¹⁵· "Comptes des Menus-plaisirs du roi," AN ms KK 213-16, fols. 10-27, list salaries paid to the chamber musicians for the years 1661 and 1707.

¹⁶· "Roles de placets au roi," AN ms O¹356, fol. 81. Marcelle Benoit has published several of these petitions in her article "Placets au Rois," *XVIIᵉ siècle*, no. 34 (March 1957), pp. 52-54. My information is derived from Benoit's sampling and from my own examination of these documents in the AN.

¹⁷· *Mercure*, Jan.-March 1677, pp. 55-65. The *Mercure* referred specifically to a ball given by the prince de Furstemberg in the Palais-Royal in January or February 1677.

¹⁸· Compan, pp. 12-25; Bonnet, *Histoire générale*, pp. 129-60.

¹⁹· *Mercure*, March 1683, pp. 318-38.

²⁰· *Ibid.*, Feb. 1700, pp. 155-215.

²¹· *La gazette d'Amsterdam*, Jan. 13, 1673 (Amsterdam, 1673), II, no pp.

²²· Dangeau, I, 36. Inevitably, there were some, like the dauphine Marie, who did not enjoy the royal *divertissement*. In her *Mémoires* she wrote: "Those like me who did not dance, remained there for two hours seated without leaving their place for a second and seeing or hearing nothing but an interminable minuet. ... Some danced the *contre-danse* one after the other like children reciting their catechism" (quoted in Gros, p. 152).

²³· *Gazette de France*, Jan. 31, 1671, no. 4, in *Recueil des gazettes nouvelles ordinaires et extraordinaires* (Paris, 1672), p. 107.

²⁴· *Les continuateurs*, III, 535, dated March 10, 1669.

²⁵· *Mercure*, March 1683, p. 316.

²⁶· Letter to Wilhelmine Ernestine, Electress Palatine, Dec. 6, 1682, Versailles (*The Letters of Madame*, trans. and ed. Stevenson [New York, 1924], pp. 60-62).

²⁷· Short musical dramas or pastorales were also frequently performed in the "appartements." The *Mercure* relates one such performance of the *Idille dramatique* by Marin Marais in which victory sang about the peace and pleasure of the court in spite of the war (April 1686, pp. 170-87).

²⁸· Scudéry, I, 12 and 15.

²⁹· *Relation des assemblées*, pp. 29-30.

³⁰· *Mercure*, Dec. 1682, pp. 62-63. See also the duc de Saint-Aignan's description of the jour d'appartements in *ibid.*, Nov. 1682, pp. 355-68.

³¹· *Ibid.*, Oct. 1705, p. 370.

³²· *Ibid.*, July 1685, pp. 269-83.

³³· *Ibid.*, May 1680, pp. 81-89.

³⁴· Sourches, I, 273.

³⁵· *Mercure*, Oct. 1714, pp. 310-25.

³⁶· "Le canal de Versailles," Conservatoire ms rés. F 522, fol. 3.

³⁷· Antoine Furetière (*Dictionaire*, I, no pp.) defined a course de bague as "an exercise of horsemanship which enables gentlemen to display their skill,

when, racing with a lance at full speed, they catch a ring suspended from a gibbet in the middle of a course."

[38]. BN ms fr 6203, fols. 1v.-2v.; see also "Carrozel du mariage du Roi Louis XIV," fols. 309-18 of BN ms fr 17460.

[39]. Sourches, I, 228-48; Dangeau, I, 23-25; *Mercure*, March 1685, pp. 216-21; *Gazette de France*, June 9, 1685, no. 29, in *Recueil des gazettes*, pp. 343-44. Jean-Baptiste Lully composed music for the Grande Écurie, and some of it was used for Louis' carrousels. His music for the dauphin's carrousel in May 1686 has been published: *Fanfares royales de J. B. Lully, Josquin des Prés, et J. J. Mouret*, transcribed for orchestra by Robert Chérisse (Paris, 1954), pp. 2-5; see also Sourches, I, 387-92.

[40]. *Mercure*, July 1677, p. 285.

[41]. Letter to the duc de Montausier, Toul, Feb. 19, 1678, in *Lettres de Louis XIV aux princes de l'Europe, à ses généraux, ses ministres*, col. Rose, ed. Morelly (Paris, 1756), p. 68.

[42]. *Mercure*, Feb. 1678, p. 189.

[43]. *Ibid.*, Sept. 1688, Pt. 2, pp. 26-27.

[44]. BN ms fr 24353, fol. 194r.

[45]. *Mercure*, Feb. 1706, p. 15.

[46]. Tapié, p. 106. In addition to Tapié, brief accounts of the 1664 festival have been given in the following works: James Eugene Farmer, *Versailles and the Court under Louis XIV* (London, 1906), pp. 120-23; Paul Heuzé, *La cour intime de Louis XIV d'après les manuscrits du temps et les documents de la Bibliothèque de Versailles* (Paris, 1902), pp. 52-63; Barthélemy, *XVIIᵉ siècle*, no. 34, pp. 8-9; Yolande de Brossard, "Les premiers musiciens de Versailles d'après Loret et ses continuateurs," *ibid.*, pp. 47-48; André Maurois, *Louis XIV à Versailles* (Paris, 1955), pp. 11-22; Antoine Parmentier, *La cour du roi soleil* (Paris, 1909), pp. 106-14. The description given in this study, however, is based on several seventeenth-century sources, which include Jacques Charpentier de Marigny, *Relation des divertissemens que le roy a donnés aux reines dans le parc de Versailles* (Paris, 1664); "Les plaisirs de l'isle enchantée," Conservatoire ms rés. F 531; Bizincourt, "Les plaisirs de l'isle enchantée, ordonnez par Louis XIV roi de France et de Navarre, à Versailles le 6 Mai, 1664," BN ms fr 7834, fols. 2-72; Loret, IV, 197, dated May 10, 1664; Menestrier, *Des ballets*, pp. 75-78; Ormesson, II, 142-43; and *Mercure*, Aug. 1679, pp. 100-105.

[47]. As part of the Peace of the Pyrenees ending the Franco-Spanish War in 1659, Louis' wife relinquished her claim to the Spanish inheritance, but on condition that a dowry of 500,00 écus be paid. Since Spain did not satisfy this part of the agreement, Louis felt justified in lodging a claim to the Spanish crown, which he subsequently backed up with an invasion of the Spanish Netherlands and ultimately with the acquisition of the Spanish crown itself for his grandson in 1700. Benserade's verse at the carrousel of 1664 represented Louis' first public declaration of his ambition.

[48]. The unidentified author, Bizincourt, wrote the dedication and commen-

tary for a special edition of the music drama and verses given during the 1664 festival (see BN ms fr 7834, fols. 2-3).

49. Marigny, p. 31. Lully's music for these entertainments has been printed in *Les plaisirs de l'île enchantée, Oeuvres complètes*, II, 3-12.

50. *Ibid.*, 38-45.

51. Marigny, pp. 39-40.

52. Lully, *Les plaisirs, Oeuvres complètes*, II, 70-75.

53. Loret, IV, 197, dated May 10, 1664.

54. *Mercure*, Aug. 1679, pp. 103-105.

55. Bussy-Rabutin, *Mémoires secrets*, II, 88.

56. The *Ballet des muses* had been performed several times during the preceding carnival season: on February 12, 14, and 16, foreign ministers and ambassadors had been entertained by it (see Charles Robinet's accounts in *Les continuateurs*, II, 620, dated Jan. 23, 1667; II, 655, dated Feb. 13, 1667; and II, 672-73, dated Feb. 20, 1667. Molière wrote three short comedies (*Pastorale comique, Mélicerte*, and *Le sicilien*) to accompany various performances of the ballet (see Lully, *Oeuvres complètes*, II, 81-150), and Benserade wrote several verses praising the king (Benserade, II, 357-81).

57. *Les continuateurs*, II, 1055, dated Oct. 22, 1667.

58. *Ibid.*, III, 16, dated Jan. 7, 1668.

59. Menestrier, *Des représentations*, pp. 223-25.

60. *Les continuateurs*, III, 198, dated July 21, 1668.

61. "Projet pour un feu dans l'île de l'Étang de Versailles," Colbert, V, 273-74, dated July 1668.

62. *Mercure*, Aug. 1679, pp. 107-109.

63. "Relation de la feste de Versailles," Arsenal ms 675, Vol. V, fols. 582r.-584v. The principal account of the festivities was written by André Félibien, *Relation de la feste de Versailles du 18 Juillet mil six cens soixante-huit* (Paris, 1674).

64. Lully's ballet *Georges Dandin, ou Le grand divertissement royal de Versailles* may be found in Lully, *Oeuvres complètes*, II, 160-225.

65. Félibien, *Relation*, p. 22.

66. A complete account of the undertaking and of the celebration which followed it appeared in the *Gazette de France*, May 24, 1671 (*Recueil des gazettes*, pp. 533-44).

67. Félibien, *Les divertissemens*, p. 3. The original version of Félibien's account of the festivities of 1674 is in BN ms fr 24353, fols. 259-84.

68. Félibien, *Les divertissemens*, p. 5.

69. "La grotte de Versailles," Conservatoire ms rés. 532.

70. Félibien, *Les divertissemens*, p. 11.

71. The Versailles grotto, which was constructed by André le Nôtre, was decorated in 1672 with several pieces of sculpture, including a figure of the sun surrounded by nymphs, by Jean Girardon. See *Mercure*, April 1672, pp. 248-51.

72. Félibien, *Les divertissemens*, p. 11.

73. *Ibid.*, July 1685, pp. 263-96.

[74] Jean-Baptiste Lully, *Idylle sur la paix avec l'églogue de Versailles et plusieurs pièces de symphonie* (Paris, 1685), pp. 28-29.

[75] *Mercure*, Feb. 1686, Pt. 2, p. 293.

[76] Jean-Baptiste Lully, *Ballet du temple de la paix* (Paris, 1685), "Au Roy."

[77] Roland Mousnier, *Les XVIᵉ et XVIIᵉ siècles*, Vol. IV of *Histoire générale des civilizations* (Paris, 1954), p. 235; quoted in *The Greatness of Louis XIV— Myth or Reality?* ed. Church (Boston, 1959), p. 95.

Chapter 7. Ceremony and Celebration

[1] Abbé François Duffo, *Le cérémonial de France à la cour de Louis XIV* (Paris, 1936), p. 10. A valuable source for the history and description of ceremony is Denys and Théodore Godefroy's book *Le cérémonial françois* (Paris, 1649). A list of all the important ceremonies of Louis XIV's reign, organized by type, may be found in BN ms n.a. fr 818. A similar list, as well as the rules and regulations for royal ceremonies, is in "Solennités en général: Sacres et couronnements des rois et reines de France; Sacres et couronnements des souverains étrangers," BN ms n.a. fr 7938.

[2] Louis-Charles d'Hautefort, marquis de Surville, *Memoirs*, trans. unknown (London, 1763), p. 140.

[3] "Marche pour les hautbois" in Conservatoire rés. ms 671, fol. 1. The original manuscript of this rare collection is in the Bibliothèque de Versailles.

[4] *Ibid.*

[5] Loret, II, 247, dated Oct. 7, 1654.

[6] Information about the composition and function of the musical forces of the Grande Écurie has been drawn principally from a collection of documents in the Archives Nationales: "Trompettes" and "Oboes," dos. 1, pièces 5-28 and 121-232; "Tambours and fifres," dos. 3, pièces 265-395; and "Cromornes," dos. 4, pièces 396-428, from AN ms O¹878. Two other works have also been very useful: Eugène Borrel, "Notes sur la musique de la Grande Écurie de 1650 à 1789," *XVIIᵉ siècle*, no. 34 (March 1957), pp. 33-40; and Émile Rhodes, *Les trompettes du roi* (Paris, 1909). See also *État actuel*.

[7] See especially AN ms O¹878, dos. 1, pièces 17 and 23.

[8] *Ibid.*, pièces 11 and 25.

[9] *Ibid.*, dos. 3, pièce 248.

[10] "La marche du roi pour le Te Deum, August 14, 1672," *ibid.*, dos. 2, pièce 111.

[11] BN ms n.a. fr 7942, pp. 102-108.

[12] "Description d'un second feu qui se fera jeudi, Vᵉ juillet dans la place du Palais-Royal pour l'heureux retour de sa majesté," Paris, 1674, *ibid.*, pp. 105r.–v.

[13] The orders for many of these ceremonies, including proclamations of the treaties, may be found in AN ms K 1001, dos. 3, pièces 200-219.

[14] *Mercure*, Sept. 1678, p. 376.

[15] *Ibid.*, Oct. 1678, pp. 92-113.

16. *Ibid.*, Jan. 1679, pp. 9-16, 179-81.

17. *Ibid.*, April 1679, pp. 38-49.

18. *Ibid.*, May 1679, pp. 1-15; June 1679, pp. 184-86.

19. BN ms fr 141, fols. 38v.–43v.

20. AN ms K 1002, dos. 3, pièces 178-202.

21. Orders and accounts of the ceremonies during the final years of the reign may be found in AN ms K 1719, nos. 9-13; *Mercure*, Feb. 1704, pp. 27-64, and June 1707, pp. 192-201; and *Les musiciens de la Sainte-Chapelle du Palais*, unedited documents collected and annotated by Brenet (Paris, 1910), pp. 263-73.

22. A more detailed description of this and the other arches along the procession route may be found in Tapié, pp. 96-102; Theodore Reff, "Puget's 'Gallic Hercules,' " *Warburg*, XXIX (1966), 259-60; and Jouin, pp. 137-38.

23. Tapié, p. 100.

24. *Ibid.*, p. 102. In addition to Tapié, the author has relied on two contemporary accounts of the 1660 processions: *L'entrée triomphante de leurs majestés* (Paris, 1662), pp. 1-32; and BN ms a.f. fr 5884.

25. AN ms K 1000, pièce 342.

26. *Les continuateurs*, pp. 91-95, dated April 7, 1668.

27. *Mercure*, Aug. 1682, pp. 151-52; see also AN ms K 1001, dos. 3, pièces 266-67.

28. *Mercure*, Oct. 1682, Pt. 2, pp. 25-43.

29. *Mercure*, July 1704, Pt. 2, p. 84; AN ms K 1002, dos. 4, pièces 232-324.

30. *Mercure*, July 1704, Pt. 2, p. 102.

31. *Ibid.*, p. 159.

32. *Ibid.*, p. 288.

33. Claude-François Menestrier, *Des décorations funèbres* (Paris, 1682).

34. *Mercure*, April 1695, pp. 57-58. Victor Tapié has described the artistry and pomp of Baroque funerals (pp. 144-60).

35. *Mercure*, Dec. 1683, p. 197. Accounts of similar ceremonies for Chancelier Séguier of the Parlement of Paris and for Maréchal Boufflers can be found in a letter dated May 6, 1672, to Madame de Grignan from Marie de Sévigné, II, 422-24, and in Dangeau's book, II, 265. Madame de Sévigné's remarks on the funeral of Séguier point up the importance of music at these ceremonies: "The music was fine beyond expression. Baptiste exerted his utmost effort, and was assisted by the King's musicians. There was an addition made to that fine Miserere and there was a Libera which filled the eyes of the entire gathering with tears; I can hardly conceive that in Heaven there can be heard a nobler harmony."

36. H. Wiley Hitchcock, "The Latin Oratorios of Marc-Antoine Charpentier," *Mus. Quar.*, LXI (Jan. 1955), 41-65.

37. *Mercure*, Feb. 1678, pp. 214-17.

38. *Gazette de France*, Mar. 25, 1673, no. 35, in *Recueil des gazettes*, pp. 278-80. See also BN ms fr 16633, fols. 45-49.

39. BN ms n.a. fr 9745, fol. 235r.

[40.] *Gazette de France*, Sept. 25, 1685, no. 54, in *Recueil des gazettes*, p. 640.

[41.] *Mercure*, April 1686, pp. 223-24. Celebrations accompanying the erections of statues at Poitiers in 1687 and at Caen in 1685, for example, are discussed in *ibid.*, Oct. 1685, pp. 13-30.

[42.] *Mercure*, April, 1686, pp. 237-45. The statue was smashed during the French Revolution, but the bas-reliefs may still be seen in the Louvre.

[43.] *Ibid.*, pp. 257-92. Illness prevented the French monarch from attending the ceremony, which was given in his honor.

[44.] *Memoirs of Madame*, I, 136; see also Ormesson, II, 575-76. One of the best sources for the ceremonial treatment of foreign dignitaries is the journal of M. de Sainctot, the maître des cérémonies du roi, BN ms fr 6679, fols. 1-688.

[45.] *Mercure*, May 1681, pp. 228-312; *Memoirs of Madame*, I, 144-47.

[46.] *Mercure*, Feb. 1682, p. 302.

[47.] *Ibid.*, April 1699, pp. 57-102, and May 1699, pp. 63-92.

[48.] *Ibid.*, Oct. 1684, pp. 219-81. In addition an account of the Siamese visit can be found in Choisy, pp. 33-59.

[49.] *Mercure*, Jan. 1685, pp. 317-18.

[50.] The italics are the *Mercure's*, Sept. 1686, Pt. 2, pp. 112, 171-88; see also BN ms fr 16633, fols. 459-65.

[51.] *Mercure*, Jan. 1687, Pt. 2, pp. 186-87.

[52.] *Ibid.*, pp. 257-58.

[53.] Félix Raugel, "La musique à la chapelle du château de Versailles sous Louis XIV," *XVIIᵉ siècle*, no. 34 (March 1957), pp. 19-20; *Mercure*, June 1678, pp. 193-94, April 1683, pp. 310-18, May 1683, pp. 230-34.

[54.] "Cour des aides," AN ms Z¹ᵃ; "Musique de la chapelle," AN ms Z¹ᵃ 486.

[55.] *État actuel*, p. 5.

[56.] Jean-Baptiste Lully, *Motets à deux chœurs pour la chapelle du roi* (17 vols.; Paris, 1684), La Laurencie, pp. 123-24. In La Laurencie's opinion, the grandiose and dramatic harmonic style of Lully's motets "corresponded to the desires of a sovereign loving the vast displays of sonority in which he saw the musical symbols of his reign and of his politics" (p. 125).

[57.] Rolland, *Some Musicians*, p. 124; Raugel, *XVIIᵉ siècle*, no. 34, p. 20.

[58.] *État actuel*, p. 9.

[59.] Perrin, p. 235.

[60.] The celebrations of Saint Louis Day are chronicled in the *Mercure*. See especially Sept. 1679, pp. 55-64; Sept. 1681, pp. 153-57; Aug. 1682, pp. 319-22; Sept. 1689, pp. 210-21; Sept. 1693, pp. 211-24; Sept. 1697, pp. 8-13. See also Loret, II, 91, dated Aug. 28, 1655.

[61.] *Mercure*, June 1681, pp. 4-11. See also June 1682, pp. 10-17, and Aug. 1680, pp. 70-84.

[62.] *Ibid.*, Oct. 1700, pp. 171-85.

Chapter 8. The End of the Reign

[1] [Gatien de Courtilz], *Memoirs of the Court of France and City of Paris*, trans. unknown (London, 1702), p. 121.

[2] Letter to Madame de St. G . . . , Dec. 10, 1697, in Françoise d'Aubigné de Maintenon, *Letters*, trans. unknown (London, 1759), I, 209.

[3] Dangeau, II, 117 and 297. See also the letter to the Duchess of Hanover, Oct. 26, 1704, in *The Letters of Madame*, pp. 243-44. The French musicologist Pierre Citron contends that the decline of dramatic music was accompanied by the concurrent emergence of French chamber music. Thanks to Maintenon and to a drained treasury, the sonata was able to blossom in France and was developed by composers such as François Couperin, Joseph Marchan, Jean-François Dandrieu, and others. Maintenon's "evenings" also gave Couperin the chance to present his instrumental suites known as concerts royaux (Pierre Citron, "Notes sur la musique de chambre à Versailles," *XVIIe siècle*, no. 34 [March 1957], pp. 31-32).

[4] Letter to Louise, Comtesse Palatine, May 14, 1695, in *The Letters of Madame*, p. 120.

[5] Bois de Jourdain, *Mélanges historiques, satiriques et anecdotiques* (Paris, 1807), I, 2. Jourdain, director of Louis XV's Grande Écurie, quoted a writer named Masillon.

[6] *Mercure*, Feb. 1699, pp. 284-85.

[7] *Ibid.*, Feb. 1700, pp. 151-54.

[8] *Ibid.*, p. 153.

[9] *Ibid.*, Jan. 1705, pp. 396-98, and April 1707, pp. 374-75.

[10] Sourches, XIII, 38.

[11] Barthélemy, *XVIIe siècle*, no. 34, p. 17; Dangeau, I, 401-402.

[12] *Mercure*, March 1706, pp. 257-65.

[13] Dangeau, I, 208.

[14] *Mercure*, Feb. 1715, Pt. 2, pp. 264-70.

[15] The Treaty of Ryswick (Sept. 1697) stipulated that France restore to Spain most of the territory obtained since the Treaty of Nimwegen and that the Dutch garrison the main fortresses in the Spanish Netherlands as a barrier between Holland and France. In addition, by a separate treaty (October 1697) Louis was obliged to relinquish Philippsburg, Breisach, and Freiburg to the emperor and to restore all the territory claimed by his Chambers of Reunion. The best account in English of Louis' foreign policy and, indeed, the best biography of the king in any language is John B. Wolf's *Louis XIV* (New York, 1968).

[16] Tillet, p. 641.

[17] *Lettres inédites de Duché de Vanci* (Paris, 1830), p. 70.

[18] *Ibid.*, p. 280; see also *Mercure*, March 1701, pp. 308-16.

[19] *Lettres inédites de Duché de Vanci*, p. 395; see also *Mercure*, May 1701, Pt. 2, pp. 144-52.

20. "État du produit de l'opéra et de la comédie, en faveur des pauvres," BN ms fr 16750, fol. 176.

21. "Anecdotes historiques de l'opéra de Paris en 1672 jusqu'en 1749," Arsenal ms 3308, portefeuille K2, fol. 141v.

22. Letter to Guyonet, Jan. 12, 1705, from *Correspondance*, IV, 636. See also Noinville *et al.*, 1753, pp. 90-97; and Du Tralage, pp. 91-92.

23. Jourdain, I, 35. See also Du Noyer, I, 13; II, 237; and V, 132-36.

24. Du Tralage, p. 87.

25. BN ms fr 12747, fol. 314. (Marthe de la Rochois was a singer at the Académie).

26. Hautefort, pp. 216-17.

27. "Mœurs," BN ms fr 21625, fols. 241-42.

28. Noinville *et al.*, 1753, pp. 148-49; Nérée Desarbres, *Deux siècles à l'opéra (1669-1868)* (Paris, 1868), pp. 221-22.

29. Noinville *et al.*, 1753, pp. 108-21.

30. The development of the Jesuit theater has been treated in Ernest Boysse's book, *Le théâtre des Jésuites* (Paris, 1880). The music for many of the Jesuit ballets can be found in "Les ballets des Jésuites composés par messieurs Beauchant, Desmatins et Colasse," Conservatoire rés. ms F 516. See also Baur-Heinhold, p. 45. In the reign of Louis XIV there were about a hundred Jesuit colleges in France giving public performances of ballets and dramas like those given at Clermont.

31. *Mercure*, March 1687, p. 317.

32. *Ibid.*, p. 319.

33. Menestrier, *Des ballets*, Préface.

34. Quoted in Boysse, p. 37.

35. *Ibid.*, pp. 135-43; Loret, III, 243-44, dated Aug. 21, 1660.

36. *Mercure*, June 1680, pp. 67-87.

37. Boysse, pp. 171-77; *Mercure*, Aug. 1679, pp. 333-35.

38. Loret, III, 397, dated Sept. 3, 1661. See also Mayolas' account, in *Les continuateurs*, I, 171, dated Aug. 16, 1665.

39. *Mercure*, July 1704, Pt. 1, p. 36.

40. *Ibid.*, Oct. 1683, Pt. 1, pp. 54-62.

41. Foucault, pp. 227-40; *Mercure*, Sept. 1688, Pt. 1, pp. 36-46.

42. *Les continuateurs*, II, 153, dated Aug. 1666.

43. Quoted in Boysse, p. 101.

44. Jean Boiseul, *Traitté contre les danses* (La Rochelle, 1606), p. 6.

45. Blaise Pascal, *Thoughts*, trans. Trotter, Vol. XLVIII of *The Harvard Classics*, ed. Eliot (New York, 1938), p. 57; see also *ibid.*, pp. 13 and 53.

46. Armand de Bourbon, prince de Conti, *Traité de la comédie et des spectacles selon la tradition de l'église tirée des conciles et des saints pères* (Paris, 1666).

47. François Hedelin d'Aubignac, *Dissertation sur la condamnation des théâtres* (Paris, 1666). See also *Le journal des sçavans* (Paris, 1713), XXXIII, 392-96, dated Aug. 23, 1694.

48. Both works are cited in Ambroise Lallouètte's *Histoire et abrégé des ouvrages*

Latins, Italiens et François, pour et contre la comédie et l'opéra (Paris, 1697), pp. 60-66.

49. Chappuzeau, p. 32.

50. "Lettre d'un théologien," Edme Boursault, *Oeuvres* (new ed. rev.; Amsterdam, 1721), I, 68.

51. Père de Lelevel, "Réponse à la lettre du théologien, défenseur de la comédie," in *Recueil de divers écrits pour et contre la comédie* (Paris, 1694), I, 8.

52. Jacques-Bénigne Bossuet, *Maximes et réflexions sur la comédie précédées de la lettre au Père Caffaro et de deux lettres de ce religieux suivies d'une épître en vers adressée à Bossuet*, intro. and notes by Gazier (new ed.; Paris, 1881), p. 2.

53. Letter to Bossuet, May 11, 1694, *ibid.*, pp. 18-21. Caffaro's reply was published in *Le journal des sçavans*, XXII, 262-63, dated June 7, 1694.

54. Printed in Lallouètte, p. 81. Whether or not Caffaro wrote the Lettre is a moot question. There is little evidence to substantiate the matter, or to disprove it. Bossuet and other critics accepted his denial. The anonymous editor of a collection of pamphlets dealing with the dispute about *spectacles* in 1694 maintained that Caffaro did admit privately that he was the author, but insisted that he did it for his own amusement and not for publication. One of his Jesuit colleagues then obtained the Lettre and had it published (see the editor's preface to *Recueil de divers*, III, x). The important thing is not whether Caffaro was guilty, but that the Lettre did trigger strong criticism of *spectacles* (operas, ballets, comedies, parodies, and tragedies), and that it would have gone unnoticed if it had been published ten years earlier.

55. Père de la Grange, "Réfutation d'un écrit favorisant la comédie," in *Recueil de divers*, I, 10-11.

56. M. Gervais, "Lettre d'un docteur de Sorbonne à une personne de qualité sur le sujet de la comédie," *ibid.*, p. 95.

57. "Décision faite en Sorbonne, touchant la comédie" (Paris, 1694), printed in Lallouètte, p. 87.

58. Pegurier's treatise was printed as an addendum to one of the copies of the Sorbonne report.

59. Pierre le Brun, "Discours sur la comédie," in *Recueil de divers*, I, 20-94.

60. Printed in *ibid.*, pp. 139-50.

61. Cited in Rolland, *Some Musicians*, p. 245.

62. Letter to the Duchess of Hanover, Dec. 23, 1688, *The Letters of Madame*, p. 115.

63. *Ibid.*

64. Jean Soanen, *Sermons sur différents sujets prêchés devant le roi* (Lyons, 1767), I, 47.

65. *Mercure*, Nov. 1714, p. 202. See also Antoine-Louis Le Brun, *Théâtre lyrique: Avec une préface où l'on traite du poëme de l'opéra* (Paris, 1712), pp. 4-18.

66. Michel de Lalande, "Ballet de la jeunesse," Arsenal ms mus. 896, p. 23.

67. Pascal Colasse and Jean-Baptiste Lully, *Achille et Polixène* (Paris, 1687), pp. i-xxxiii.

68. *Mercure historique et politique contenant l'état présent de l'Europe* (Parma, 1688), III, 504-505, dated Dec. 1687.

69. *Mercure*, Nov. 1687, pp. 267-74.

70. BN ms fr 12621, fol. 182.

71. "Zéphire et Flore," in *Recueil des opéra* (Amsterdam, 1700), IV, 1-16; *Mercure*, March 1688, pp. 323-24. The opera was ridiculed in a *brunette* (*Brunettes ou petits airs tendres, avec les doubles et la basse-continue: mêlées de chansons à danser*, col. and ed. Ballard [Paris, 1703], I, 110-15).

72. *Mercure historique*, VI, 164, dated Feb. 1689.

73. Pascal Colasse, *Thétis et Pélée* (2d ed.; Paris, 1716), p. 9.

74. *Mercure*, Nov. 1690, pp. 252-53.

75. Pascal Colasse, *Énée et Lavinie, tragédie mise en musique* (Paris, 1710), p. xxxvi.

76. "Orphée," in *Recueil des opéra*, IV, 4-5.

77. *Mercure*, April 1691, pp. 40-58.

78. "Astrée," in *Recueil des opéra*, IV, 608. See also "Coronis," *ibid.*, p. 509.

79. Pascal Colasse, *Ballet de Ville-Neuve Saint-George* (Paris, 1699), pp. 35-37.

80. "Alcide," in *Recueil des opéra*, V, 3.

81. "Médée," in *Recueil des opéra*, V, 6-7; *Mercure*, Dec. 1693, p. 334.

82. Henri Desmarets, *Les amours de Momus* (Paris, 1695), p. xxvii.

83. Pascal Colasse, *Les saisons, opéra-ballet en 4 entrées et prologue*, Vol. VIII of *Les chefs d'œuvre* (Paris, n.d.), pp. 28-29.

84. Colasse's supporters included several nobles of the sword such as the comte de Fièsque.

85. BN ms fr 12690, fol. 361.

86. BN ms fr 12669, fol. 404.

87. *Mercure*, Dec. 1694, pp. 283-85.

88. The following sources contain good accounts of the Italian comedies in France and the origin of French vaudevilles: *Papers*, pp. 160-62; Georges Cucuel, *Les créateurs de l'opéra-comique français* (Paris, 1914); Bukofzer, pp. 257-60; and Antoine Jean-Baptiste-Abraham d'Origny, *Annales du Théâtre Italien, dupuis son origine jusqu'à ce jour* (Paris, 1788).

89. BN ms fr 24354, fol. 44r.

90. *Mercure*, Dec. 1696, pp. 132-46.

91. André Destouches, *Issé, pastorale héroïque*, Vol. XI of *Les chefs d'œuvre*, p. 4.

92. *Ibid.*, p. 8.

93. André Campra, *L'Europe galante* (3d ed. rev.; Paris, 1699). The archbishop of Paris, who objected to opera on the grounds that it fostered immorality, discharged Campra from Notre-Dame in 1700 for composing operatic music. A satirical song expressed the glee of the comedians (BN ms fr 12751, fol. 59): "Quand notre archevêque scaura, / Que Campra fait des opéra, / Alors Campra decampera; / Alleluia."

94. Letter to Louise, Comtesse Palatine, Nov. 10, 1697, in *The Letters of Madame*, p. 160.

95. *Mercure*, June 1698, pp. 241-42.

96. André Destouches, *Marthésie, première reine des Amazons* (Paris, 1669), p. 33.

97. André Destouches, *Amadis de Grèce, tragédie mise en musique* (3d ed. rev.; Paris, 1712), p. 23.

98. BN ms fr 12671, fol. 89.

99. "Le triomphe des arts," in *Recueil des opéra*, VIII, 5-6.

100. André Campra, *Hésione* (Paris, 1700), p. li.

101. BN ms fr 12671, fols. 106-107.

102. André Campra, *Aréthuse, ou la vengeance de l'amour* (Paris, 1701).

103. Dec. 8, 1701, in *The Letters of Madame*, p. 218.

104. BN ms fr n.a. 4676, fol. 3r.

105. André Campra, *Fragments de Monsieur de Lully* (Paris, 1702), pp. v-xxvii.

106. André Campra, *Tancrède* (Paris, 1702), pp. iv-xlv.

107. "Les muses," in *Recueil des opéra*, IX, 3-5.

108. André Campra, *Alcine* (Paris, 1704), p. ii.

109. See the derogatory songs in BN ms fr 12672, fols. 18, 73, and 74.

110. Duc d'Orléans, "Penthée, opéra," Arsenal ms 6639, fols. 6-74.

111. André Campra, *Les festes vénitiennes* (Paris, 1714), pp. 1-30.

112. Duc d'Orléans, "Suite d'Armide, ou Jérusalem délivrée, opéra," Arsenal ms mus 901, fols. 4-50.

113. André Destouches, *Callirhoé* (Paris, 1712), pp. xviii-xix.

114. "Télèphe," in *Recueil des opéra*, IX, 3-5. See also M. Salomon and M. de la Roque, "Médée et Jason," *ibid.*

115. André Destouches, *Télémaque et Calypso* (Paris, 1714), pp. viii-xxxvi.

116. *Mercure*, Oct. 1715, pp. 9-12.

❧

Bibliography

MANUSCRIPTS

Archives Nationales

Curzon, Henri de. État sommaire des pièces et documents concernant le théâtre et la musique, conservés aux Archives Nationales. Paris: n.p., 1899.

Rambaud, Mireille. Les sources de l'histoire de l'art aux Archives Nationales. Paris: Imprimerie Nationale, 1955.

AJ¹³1-44. Opéra, opéra-comique, théâtre Italien.

E 1684-92. Conseil d'État du roi : Conseil des dépêches.

H². Bureau de la ville de Paris, Intendance et généralité en Paris.

K and KK. Monuments historiques.

    1000-1002. Ville de Paris : fêtes et cérémonial.

    1030-31. Ville de Paris : arts et métiers.

    1719-20. Cérémonies publiques, pompes, entrées.

    KK 1-227. Comptes royaux.

O¹. Maison du roi.

    1-749. Secrétariat d'État de la maison du roi.

    820-54. Papiers du grand chambellan.

    878. Grande Écurie du roi.

    2806-3276. Direction intitulée argenterie, Menus plaisirs et affaires de la chambre, communément appelée les menus.

V⁷. Commissions extraordinaires du Conseil.

Z. Jurisdictions spéciales et ordinaires.

Z¹ᵃ472-523. Cour des aides : États de la maison du roi et des maisons des princes.

Z¹ᴴ657. Bureau de Ville : Rôles des maîtres à danser et des joueurs d'instruments.

Bibliothèque de l'Arsenal

675. Suite des précédents : recueil le Cadmus.

896, musique. Michel de Lalande, "Ballet de la jeunesse."

901, musique. Duc d'Orléans. "Suite d'Armide ou Jérusalem délivrée, opéra."

2905. Mélanges concernants les sciences et les arts.

3308. Recueil de Fevret de Fontette.

3438. Fonds d'Espagnac : fragments d'histoire de France.

6334. Archives des ducs de Longueville et autres papiers.

6541-45. Recueil de Jean-Nicolas du Tralage.

6609. Bernard le Bouyer de Fontenelle, "Diane et Endimion, pastorale héroïque."

6639. Duc d'Orléans, "Panthée, opéra."

6829. Recueil de pièces du règne de Louis XIV.

10295. Divers arrêts sur l'Académie royale de musique.

Bibliothèque du Conservatoire

F 494-537, rés. Collection Philidor.

F 671, rés. Partition de plusieurs marches et batteries de tambour tant françoises qu'étrangères avec les airs de fifre et de hautbois à 3 ou 4 parties et des marches de timballes et de trompettes à cheval avec les airs du carousel en 1686, et les appels et fanfares de trompe pour la chasse.

1785, rés. Luigi Rossi and Francesco Buti, "L'Orfeo."

1838, rés. Fragments d'opéras et cantates (XVIIe et XVIIIe siècles); chansons à louange de Louis XIV.

Bibliothèque Nationale

Collection des cinq cents de Colbert.

141. Relation originale de diverses cérémonies du règne de Louis XIV par Desgranges maître des cérémonies (1672-1698) suivie d'extraits des registres de Sainctot autre maître des cérémonies (1646-1663).

165. Correspondance de Juillet et Août 1673.

167. Correspondance de Janvier à Mars 1674.

394, a.f. Les noms et armes de tous les princes et seigneurs nommés par sa majesté au grand carouzel et course de bague, le cinquième jour de Juin 1662.

402, n.a. Abbé Du Guet et Louis, duc d'Orléans, "Réflexions sur les spectacles."

818, n.a. Collection générale des cérémonies qui ont été observées et des fêtes qui ont été données sous le règne de Louis XIV.

1359. Nicolas Borgier, "La musique spéculative."

1563, n.a. Mélanges historiques.

1698, n.a. Recueil de chansons diverses.

2208. Pierre Perrin, "Recueil des paroles de musique . . . dédié à Monseigneur Colbert."

2842-3060, n.a. Collection de pièces de théâtre.

4137, n.a. Deux lettres de Jacques Villery.

4673, n.a. Sébastien de Brossard, "Recueil d'extraits d'ouvrages imprimés sur la musique."

4676, n.a. M. Le Noble and M. Anne Philidor, "Danaé, opéra, mis au théâtre."

5269, n.a. Mélanges et extraits relatifs à l'histoire de la musique.

5884, a.f. Relation de ce qui s'est passé au mariage du roy.

6203. Charles Perrault, "Courses de testes et de bagues, faites par le roy, et par les princes et seigneurs de sa cour en l'année 1662.

6326, n.a. Charles-Havoi Blainville, "Abrégé de tous les différents systèmes de musique, depuis l'origine de cet art, jusqu'au temps présent."

6355, n.a. Sébastien de Brossard, "Mélanges et extraits de divers auteurs sur la musique."

6356, n.a. Notes et extraits divers sur la musique.

6679. Journal du Sieur de Sainctot, introducteur des ambassadeurs.

6815-17. Extraits et dépouillements de toutes les gazettes de France, contenant ce qui s'est passé de plus remarquable depuis l'année 1631 jusqu'en 1723.

7009. Mémoire adressé à Louis XIV sur l'état politique et sur l'état des finances de la France à la fin du XVIIe siècle.

7561-978, n.a. Collection de copies de pièces sur l'histoire de France, connue sous le nom de "Portefeuilles de Fontanieu."

9359-63. Correspondance de l'Abbé Nicaise.

9632-826, n.a. Portefeuilles d'Antoine Lancelot.

10265. Gazettes historiques et anecdotiques, du 20 Février 1682 au 13 Mars 1687.

10279. Journal de tout ce qui s'est passé au sacre de Louis XIV.

11768. Extraits des sciences et des arts libéraux.

12355. Claude et François Parfaict, "Histoire de l'Académie royale de musique depuis son établissement jusqu'à présent.

12499. Receuil de vers, épîtres, stances, épigrammes, sonnets, etc. relatifs au règne de Louis XIV.

12515-31. L.-François Beffara, "Recueil de matériaux pour une histoire de la vie et une bibliographie des œuvres de Molière."

12616-59. Chansonnier dit de Maurepas, "Recueil de chansons, vaudevilles, sonnets, épigrammes, épitaphes et autres vers satiriques et historiques, avec des remarques curieuses."

12666-72. Recueil de chansons anecdotes satiriques et historiques (1514-1708).

12686-743. Recueil de chansons historiques, critiques, et chronologiques avec des notes sur les différens événemens arrivés depuis 1549 jusqu'en 1781.

12747. Recueil de chansons historiques sous le règne de Louis Quatorze.

12751-52. Recueil de chansons historiques du tems, sous le règne de Louis XIV.

12801. Recueil de pièces diverses sur le règne de Louis XIV, en prose et en vers.

13648. Mélanges historiques, de la fin du XVIIe siècle.

13679-90. Journaux historiques des années 1711-1722.

15012. Recueil de poésies diverses et de quelques pièces relatives à l'histoire du règne de Louis XIV.

15226. Mélanges.

15333. Mélanges.

16216. Recueil de pièces, manuscrits et imprimés, relatifs au conseil d'État, à l'office de chancelier, à la maison du roi à différentes charges; extraits de registres de la chambre des comptes.

16633. Cérémonies du règne de Louis XIV, recueil formé, au moins en partie, d'après le journal de M. de Sainctot.

16750-51. Papiers du Président Achille III de Harlay.

17413. Correspondance de Achille III de Harlay.

17460. Nicolas de Brichanteau, marquis de Beauvais-Nangis, "Mémoires ou histoire des favoris, depuis Henri II jusqu'à Louis XIII."

18540. Mélanges historiques; cérémonial, sacres, et obsèques; papiers de divers Bénédictins, principalement de religieux de l'abbaye de Saint-Denis.

19043. Maximes d'éducation et direction puérile, des dévotions, mœurs, actions, occupations, divertissemens, jeux et petite estude de monseigneur le daufin jusques à l'age de sept ans.

19100. Louis Chaveneau, "Traités de musique."

19229-30. Mélanges historiques et littéraires; procès politiques et autres, du XVe au XVIIe siècle; mémoires secrets de la cour de Louis XIV.

19347. Mélanges théologiques.

20149. Mélanges généalogiques et bibliographiques sur l'histoire de France.

20862-64. Recueil de pièces en prose et en vers du règne de Louis XIV.

21545-808. Collection formée par Nicolas Delamare sur l'administration et la police de Paris et de la France.

22536-38. Philippe-Josephe Caffiaux, "Histoire de la musique depuis l'antiquité jusqu'en 1754."

22566-69. Recueil de chansons, épigrammes, satires, épitaphes, sur les personnages et sur les événements des règnes de Louis XIV et Louis XV.

24329. Boscheron, "Vie de M. Quinault de l'Académie française, avec l'origine des opéras en France."

24352-57. Recueil de ballets, d'opéras, pastorales et de tragédies.

24446. Recueil de pièces satiriques (épîtres, sonnets, madrigaux, épigrammes), en vers et en prose en français et en latin relatives au régne de Louis XIV.

24807. Lettres à une religieuse sur les fêtes de l'année.

24851. Sermons et instructions religieuses pour une mission.

25465. Traité du ballet; du progrès que ce spectacle a fait en France et comment il a donné lieu à l'opéra.

25515. Recueil des plus excellens ballets dansez en 1612.

25554-55. Recueil de pièces fugitives sur divers événements et personnages du règne de Louis XIV.

PRINTED SOURCES

The operas and ballets used for this book are listed below alphabetically by composer with publication dates. The authors of the texts are given when known. With the two exceptions noted, Philippe Quinault wrote all the texts of Lully's operas. Unless otherwise noted, the operas were published by Robert or Christophe Ballard, the king's printers.

Assoucy, Charles d'. *Les amours d'Apollon et de Daphné, comédie en musique dédiée au roi* (Paris: Raffle, 1650); *Andromède, tragédie représentée avec les machines sur le Théâtre royal de Bourbon*, text by Pierre Corneille (Rouen: Maurry, 1651).

Beaujoyeulx, Baltasar de, Lambert de Beaulieu, and Jacques Salmon. *Balet comique de la royne, faict aux nopces de Monsieur le Duc de Joyeuse et Mademoiselle de Vaudemont sa sœur*, text by Sieur de la Chesnaye (Paris: Roy, Ballard, and Patisson, 1582).

Bourgeois, Louis-Thomas. *Les plaisirs de la paix* (Paris: Ribou, 1715).

Cambert, Robert. *Les peines et les plaisirs de l'amour*, text by Gabriel Gilbert: Vol. III of *Les chefs d'œuvres classiques de l'opéra français* (Paris: Michaelis, n.d.); *Pomone, pastorale mise en musique*, text by Pierre Perrin (1671).

Campra, André. *Alcine* (printed by the author, 1704); *Aréthuse, ou la vengeance de l'amour* (1701); *Le carnaval de Vénise* (1699); *L'Europe galante*, text by Antoine Houdar de La Motte (3d ed. rev., 1699); *Fragments de Monsieur de Lully*, text by Antoine Danchet (1702); *Les festes vénitiennes*, text by Antoine Danchet (1714); *Hésione*, text by Antoine Danchet (1700); *Idoménée*, text by Antoine Danchet (1712); *Tancrède*, text by Antoine Danchet (1702).

Campra, André, and Henri Desmarets. *Iphigénie en Tauride*, text by Jean-François Duché de Vancy and Antoine Danchet (1711).

Cavalli, Francesco. *Ercole Amante: Tragedia, representata per le Nozze della Maestà Christianissime*, text by Francesco Buti (1662); *Xerxes, comédie en musique avec six entrées de ballet qui servent d'intermède de la comédie* (1660).

Cesti, Marc-Antonio. *Il Pomo d'Oro*, prologue and act I: Vol. III of *Denkmäler der Tonkunst in Österreich* (Vienna: Artaria, 1896).

Colasse, Pascal. *Ballet de Ville-Neuve Saint-George* (1699); *Canente, tragédie mise en musique*, text by Antoine Houdar de La Motte (1700); *Énée et Lavinie, tragédie mise en musique* (1710); *Les saisons, opéra-ballet en 4 entrées et prologue*: Vol. VIII of *Les chefs d'œuvre*; *Thétis et Pelée*, text by Bernard Le Bovier de Fontenelle (2d ed., 1716).

Colasse, Pascal, and Jean-Baptiste Lully. *Achille et Polixène*, text by Jean Galbert de Campistron (1687).

Desmarets, Henri. *Les amours de Momus*, text by Jean-François Duché de Vancy (1695); *Didon, tragédie mise en musique* (1693); *Les festes galantes*, text by Jean-François Duché de Vancy (1698); *Théagène et Cariclée, tragédie mise en musique*, text by Jean-François Duché de Vancy (1695); *Vénus et Adonis*, text by Jean-Baptiste Rousseau (1697).

Destouches, André. *Amadis de Grèce, tragédie mise en musique*, text by Antoine Houdar de La Motte (3d ed. rev., 1712); *Callirrhoé*, text by Pierre Charles Roy (1712); *Le carnaval et la folie, comédie-ballet* (Paris: Marchand, 1704); *Issé, pastorale héroïque*, text by Antoine Houdar de La Motte, Vol. XI of *Les chefs d'œuvre*; *Marthésie, première reine des Amazons* (1699); *Omphale, tragédie en musique*, text by Antoine Houdar de La Motte, Vol. XII of *Les chefs d'œuvre; Télémaque et Calypso*, text by Joseph Pellegrin (1714).

Fanfares royales de J. B. Lully, Josquin des Prés, et J. J. Mouret, transcribed for orchestra by Robert Chérisse (Paris: Éditions musicales, 1954).

Lully, Jean-Baptiste. *Acis et Galatée*, text by Jean Galbert de Campistron (1686); *Armide* (1686); *Atys* (1689); *Ballet du temple de la paix* (1685); *Bellerophon*, text by Thomas Corneille (1679); *Les festes de l'amour et de Bacchus* (1717); *Idylle sur la paix avec l'églogue de Versailles et plusieurs pièces de symphonie* (1685); *Isis* (1719); *Motets à deux chœurs pour la chapelle du roi* (17 vols., 1684); *Persée* (1682); *Phaéton* (1683); *Proserpine* (1680); *Roland* (1685); *Te Deum* (London: Schott, 1955); *Thésée*, Vol. XXVI of *Les chefs d'œuvre; Le triomphe de l'amour* (1681). For a modern edition of Lully's works, see *Oeuvres complètes*. Edited by Henry Prunières. 10 vols. (Paris: Revue musicale, 1930-39).

Anquetil, Louis-Pierre. *Memoirs of the Court of France during the Reign of Lewis XIV*. Translator unknown. 2 vols. Edinburgh: Bell and Bradfute, 1791.

Arvieux, Chevalier Laurent d'. *Mémoires*. Vol. IV. Paris, Delespine, 1735.

Aubignac, François Hedelin d'. *Dissertation sur la condamnation des théâtres*. Paris: Pepingue, 1666.

Bailly, Nicolas. *Inventaire des tableaux du roi*. Paris: Leroix, 1899.

Ballets et mascarades de cour sous Henri IV et Louis XIII de 1581 à 1652. Edited by Paul Lacroix. 6 vols. Geneva: Gay, 1868.

Bayle, Pierre. *Dictionnaire historique et critique*. 3 vols. 3d ed.; Rotterdam: n.p., 1715.

Beauchamps, Pierre-François Godard de. *Recherches sur les théâtres de France, depuis l'année onze cens soixante un, jusques à présent*. 3 vols. in 1. Paris: Prault, 1735.

Benserade, Isaac de. *Les œuvres*. 2 vols. Paris: Sercy, 1697.

Blegny, Nicolas de [Abraham du Pradel]. *Le livre commode des adresses de Paris pour 1692*. Edited by Édouard Fournier. 2 vols. Paris: Daffis, 1878.

Boileau-Despréaux, Nicolas. *Oeuvres complètes*. Edited by Paul Chéron. New ed.; Paris: Garnier, 1860.

Boindin, Nicolas. *Lettres historiques sur tous les spectacles de Paris*. Paris: Prault, 1719.

Boiseul, Jean. *Traitté contre les danses*. La Rochelle: Holtin, 1606.

Bonnet, Jacques. *Histoire de la musique et de ses effets*. Paris: Cochart, 1715.

———. *Histoire générale de la danse, sacrée et prophane; ses progrès et ses révolutions depuis son origine jusqu'à présent*. Paris: Houry, 1723.

Bontempi, Andrea Angelini. *Historia musica*. Perugia: Costantini, 1695.

Bossuet, Jacques-Bénigne. *Maximes et réflexions sur la comédie précédées de la lettre au Père Caffaro et de deux lettres de ce religieux suivies d'une épître en vers adressée à Bossuet*. Introduction and notes by A. Gazier. New ed.; Paris: Bolin, 1881.

Boursault, Edme. *Oeuvres*. 2 vols. Rev. ed.; Amsterdam: Duvillard et Changuion, 1721.

Brossard, Sébastien de. *Dictionnaire de musique*. 6th ed.; Amsterdam: Mortier, n.d.

Brunettes ou petits airs tendres, avec les doubles et la basse-continue; mélées de chansons à danser. Collected and edited by Christophe Ballard. 3 vols. Paris: Ballard, 1703.

Bussy-Rabutin, Roger de. *Correspondance.* Edited by Ludovic Lalanne. 6 vols. Paris: Charpentier, 1859.

——. *Histoire amoreuse des Gaules suivie de la France galante.* Vol. II. New ed.; Paris: Garnier, n.d.

——. *Mémoires.* 2 vols. Paris: Anisson, 1696.

——. *Mémoires secrets, 1617-1667.* 2 vols. Amsterdam: Gosse, 1769.

——. *Recueil des histoires galantes.* Cologne: Le Blanc, n.d.

Callières, François de. *Histoire poëtique de la guerre nouvellement déclarée entre les anciens et les modernes.* Paris: Auboüin, 1688.

Cérémonies observées pour l'érection de la statue équestre du roi. Paris: Chardon, 1699.

Chantelou, Paul Fréart de. *Journal du voyage du Cavalier Bernin.* Paris: Beaux-Arts, 1885.

Chappuzeau, Samuel. *Le théâtre françois.* Paris: Bonnassies, 1876.

Les chefs d'œuvre classiques de l'opéra français. 40 vols. Paris: Michaelis, n.d.

Chevrement, Jean-Baptiste de. *La connoissance du monde ou l'art de bien élever la jeunesse pour les divers états de la vie.* Paris: Guignard, 1694.

Choisy, François-Timoléon de. *Mémoires pour servir à l'histoire de Louis XIV.* Utrecht: Wan-de-Vater, 1727.

Choix de Mazarinades. Edited by Célestine Moreau. 2 vols. Paris:Renouard, 1853.

Colbert, Jean-Baptiste. *Fortifications, sciences, lettres, beaux-arts, bâtiments.* Vol. V of *Lettres, instructions, et mémoires.* Edited by Pierre Clément. Paris: Impériale, 1868.

——. *The Political Last Testament.* Translated by John Augustine Bernard. London: Brome, 1695.

Colbert, Jean-Baptiste, marquis de Torcy. *Journal* (1709-1711). Edited by Frédéric Masson. Paris: Plon et Nourrit, 1884.

Les comédiens du roi de la troupe française pendant les deux derniers siècles. Unedited documents collected in the Archives Nationales by Émile Campardon. Paris: Champion, 1879.

Compan, Ch[arles]. *Dictionnaire de danse, contenant l'histoire, les règles et les principes de cet art, avec des réflexions critiques et des anecdotes curieuses concernant la danse ancienne et moderne.* Paris: Cailleau, 1787.

Conférences inédites de l'Académie royale de peinture et de sculpture d'après les manuscrits des archives de l'école des Beaux-arts. Paris: Fontemoing, 1903.

Conti, Armand de Bourbon, prince de. *Les devoirs des grands.* Paris: Barbin, 1666.

——. *Traité de la comédie et des spectacles selon la tradition de l'église tirée des conciles et des saints pères.* Paris: Billaine, 1666.

Les continuateurs de Loret, lettres en vers de La Gravette de Mayolas, Robinet, Boursault, Perdou de Subligny, Laurent et autres (1665-1689). Edited by James de Rothschild. 3 vols. Paris: Morgand et Fatout, 1881.

Correspondance administrative sous le règne de Louis XIV. Edited by G. P. Depping. 4 vols. Paris: Nationale, 1850-55.

The Correspondence of Madame, Princess Palatine, mother of the Regent; of Marie-Adelaide de Savoie, Duchesse de Bourgogne; and of Madame de Maintenon, in relation to Saint-Cyr. Translated by Katherine Prescott Wormeley. Boston: Hardy and Pratt, 1902.

La cour et la ville sous Louis XIV, Louis XV et Louis XVI, ou Révélations historiques tirées de manuscrits inédits. Edited by Jean-François Barrière. Paris: Dentu, 1830.

Courtilz, Gatien de. *Annales de la cour et de Paris.* 2 vols. Cologne: Marteau, 1711.

[Courtilz, Gatien de]. *Memoirs of the Court of France and City of Paris.* Translator unknown. London: Lincott, 1702.

——. *La vie de Jean-Baptiste Colbert, ministre d'État.* Cologne: n.p., 1695.

Crapelet, G. A. *Notice sur la vie et les ouvrages de Quinault, suivie de pièces relatives à l'établissement de l'opéra.* Paris: Crapelet, 1824.

Crousaz, J. P. de. *Traité du beau, où l'on montre en quoi consiste ce que l'on nomme ainsi, par des exemples tirez de la plûpart des arts et des sciences.* Amsterdam: Honoré, 1715.

Dangeau, Philippe de Courcillon de. *Memoirs of the Court of France from the Year 1684 to the Year 1720.* Translator unknown. 2 vols. London: Colburn, 1825.

Dard, Jean. *Principes de la musique qui seuls doivent suffire pour l'apprendre parfaitement auxquels l'auteur à joint l'histoire de la musique et de ses progressions, depuis son origine jusqu'à présent.* Paris: Auteur, 1764.

Desarbres, Nérée. *Deux siècles à l'opéra (1669-1868).* Paris: Dentu, 1868.

Descartes, René. *Excellent Compendium of Musick.* Translator unknown. London: Harper, 1653.

Documents historiques sur Versailles. Edited by Victor Bart. Versailles: Cerf, 1885.

Dufresny, Charles. *Oeuvres.* 4 vols. Rev. ed.; Paris: Barrois, 1779.

Du Manoir, Guillaume. *Le mariage de la musique avec la danse.* Edited by J. Gallay. Paris: Bibliophiles, 1870.

Du Noyer, Anne-Marguerite. *Lettres-historiques et galantes.* 6 vols. Rev. ed.; London: Nourse, 1739.

Durand, François. *Discours au vrai du ballet dansé par le roi le dimanche XXIX jour de janvier 1617, avec les desseins, tant des machines et apparences différentes, que de tous les habits des masques.* Paris: Ballard, 1617.

Du Tralage, Jean-Nicolas. *Notes et documents sur l'histoire des théâtres de Paris au XVIIe siècle.* Paris: Bibliophiles, 1880.

L'entrée triomphante de leurs majestés Louis XIV roi de France et Navarre, et Marie-Thérèse d'Autriche, son épouse, dans la ville des rois, capitale de leur royaume, en retour de la signature de la paix générale et de leur heureux mariage. Paris: Le Comte, 1662.

L'esprit de la France et les maximes de Louis XIV. Cologne: Marteau, 1688.

État actuel de la musique du roi et des trois spectacles de Paris. Paris: Vente, 1772.

Factum pour Jean de Ganoüilhet escuyer Sieur de Sablières, intendant de la musique de monsieur, Duc d'Orléans, et Henry Guichard Gentilhomme de S. A. R. Opposants et Demandeurs. Contre Jean-Baptiste Lully, l'un des intendants de la musique du roi et le Sieur Perrin Demandeurs. Et encore contre Messire Alexandre de Rieux, Marquis de Sourdéac, et Laurent de Bersac Sieur de Champeron Défendeurs. Paris: n.p., n.d.

Félibien, André. *Description du château de Versailles, de ses peintures, et d'autres ouvrages faits pour le roi.* Paris: Mariette, 1696.

——. *Description de la grotte de Versailles.* Paris: Royale, 1679.

——. *Description sommaire du chasteau de Versailles.* Paris: Desprez, 1674.

——. *Les divertissemens de Versailles donnez par le roy à toute sa cour au retour de la conqueste de la Franche-Comté en l'année M.DC.LXXIV.* Paris: Royale, 1676.

——. *Mémoires pour servir à l'histoire des maisons royalles et bastimens de France.* Paris: Saur, 1874.

——. *Relation de la feste de Versailles du 18 Juillet mil six cens soixante-huit.* Paris: Royale, 1674.

Feuillet, Raoul-Anger. *Chorégraphie ou l'art de décrire la dance par caractères, figures et signes démonstratifs, avec lequels on apprend facilement de soi-même toutes sortes de dances.* 2d ed. rev.; Paris: Brunet, 1701.

Fontenelle, Bernard le Bovier de. *L'histoire du théâtre françois.* Vol. II of *Oeuvres.* New ed.; Amsterdam: Compagnie, 1754.

François, René [Étienne Binet]. *Essai des merveilles de nature et des plus nobles artifices.* Rouen: Beauvais, 1621.

Furetière, Antoine. *Dictionnaire universel, contenant généralement tous les mots françois, tant vieux que modernes, et les termes de toutes les sciences et des arts.* 3 vols. The Hague: Leers, 1690.

Gantez, Anibal. *L'entretien des musiciens.* Auxerre: Bouquet, 1643.

La gazette d'Amsterdam. 6 vols. Amsterdam: Zwoll, 1667-85.

A General Collection of Discourses of the Virtuosi of France upon Questions of all Sorts of Philosophy and other Natural Knowledge made in the Assembly of the Beaux Esprits at Paris by the Most Ingenious Persons of That Nation. Translated by G. Havers, edited by Eusebius Renaudot. 2 vols. London: Morice, 1663.

Godefroy, Théodore, and Godefroy, Denys. *Le cérémonial françois.* 2 vols. Paris: Cramoisy, 1649.

Goulas, Nicolas. *Mémoires.* Edited by Charles Constant. Vol. II. Paris: Renouard, 1894.

Grand bal de la douairière de billebahaut: Ballet dansé par le roy au mois de Février 1626. Paris: Henault, 1626.

Le grand carousel du roi, ou la course de bague ordonnée par sa majesté. Paris: Besongne, 1662.

Hautefort, Louis-Charles de, marquis de Surville. *Memoirs.* Translator unknown. London: n.p., 1763.

Heuzé, Paul. *La cour intime de Louis XIV d'après les manuscrits du temps et les documents de la Bibliothèque de Versailles.* Paris: Charles, 1902.

Joly, Guy. *Mémoires.* Vol. II of *Nouvelle collection des mémoires pour servir à l'histoire de France depuis le XIIe siècle jusqu'à la fin du XVIIIe.* Edited by M. M. Michaud and Poujoulat. 3d ser.; Paris: Commentaire analytique du code civil, 1838.

——. *Recueil de maximes véritables et importantes pour l'institution du roi.* Paris: n.p., 1653.

Jourdain, Bois de. *Mélanges historiques, satiriques et anecdotiques.* Vol. I. Paris: Chèvre et Chanson, 1807.

Le journal des sçavans. 35 vols. Paris: Cusson, 1666-1715.

La Bruyère, Jean de. *Les caractères de Théophraste, et la suite; avec les caractères ou les mœurs de ce siècle.* 11th ed.; Lyons: Baritel, 1730.

La Fayette, Marie-Madeleine de. *The Secret History of Henrietta, Princess of England, First Wife of Philippe, Duc d'Orleans, together with Memoirs of the Court of France for the Years 1688-1689.* Translated by J. M. Shelmerdine. New York: Dutton, 1929.

La Fontaine, Jean de. *Oeuvres complètes.* Vol. VI. Paris: Lefèvre, 1818.

Lallouètte, Ambroise. *Histoire et abrégé des ouvrages Latins, Italiens et François, pour et contre la comédie et l'opéra.* Paris: Robustee, 1697.

La Mothe le Vayer, François de. *De l'instruction de monseigneur le dauphin, à monseigneur l'éminentissime cardinal duc de Richelieu.* Paris: Cramoisy, 1640.

Larrey, Isaac de. *Histoire de France sous le règne de Louis XIV.* 2 vols. 2d ed.; Rotterdam: Bohn, 1722.

Le Brun, Antoine-Louis. *Théâtre lyrique; avec une préface où l'on traite du poème de l'opéra.* Paris: Ribou, 1712.

Le Brun, Charles. *Conférence de Monsieur Le Breun, [sic] premier peintre du Roy de France, Chancelier et Directeur de l'Académie de peinture et sculpture, sur l'expression générale et particulière.* Amsterdam: De Lorane, 1718.

Le Gendre, Louis. *The History of the Reign of Lewis the Great till the General Peace concluded at Reswick [sic] in the Year 1697.* Translator unknown. London: Brown, 1699.

Leris, Antoine de. *Dictionnaire portatif des théâtres contenant l'origine des différens théâtres de Paris.* Paris: Jombert, 1754.

Leti, Gregorio. *La monarchie universelle de Louis XIV.* Translated from the Italian. 2 vols. in 1. Amsterdam: Wolfgang, 1689.

The Letters of Madame: The Correspondence of Elizabeth-Charlotte of Bavaria, Princess Palatine, Duchess of Orleans, called "Madame" at the Court of King Louis XIV, 1661-1708. Translated and edited by Gertrude Scott Stevenson. New York: Appleton, 1924.

Lettres du Cardinal Mazarin pendant son ministère. Edited by M. Le Vᵗᵉ G. d'Avenal. 9 vols. Paris: Nationale, 1906.

Lettres du Duc de Bourgogne au Roi d'Espagne Philippe V et à la reine. Edited by Alfred Baudrillart and Léon Lecestre. 2 vols. Paris: Renouard, 1912.

Lettres inédites de Duché de Vanci, contenant la relation historique du voyage de Philippe d'Anjou, appelé au trône d'Espagne, ainsi que des ducs de Bourgogne et de Berry, ses frères, en 1700; précédées de l'exposé de ce qui s'est passé à la cour de Versailles depuis la mort de Charles II jusqu'au départ du nouveau roi. Paris: Lacroix, 1830.

Lettres inédites de Mme de Maintenon et de Mme la Princesse des Ursins. 2 vols. Paris: Bossange, 1826.

Lettres de Louis XIV. Edited by Pierre Gaxotte. Paris: Tallandier, 1930.

Lettres de Louis XIV aux princes de l'Europe, à ses généraux, ses ministres. Collected by M. Rose, edited by M. Morelly. 2 vols. in 1. Paris: Bassompierre, 1756.

Limiers, Henri-Philippe de. *Histoire du règne de Louis XIV.* 12 vols. 2d ed. rev.; Amsterdam: La Compagnie, 1718.

Loret, Jean. *La muze historique ou recueil des lettres en vers contenant des nouvelles du temps écrites à son altesse Mademoizelle de Longueville, depuis Duchesse de Nemours (1650-1665).* Edited by M. M. J. Ravenel and Ed. V. de la Pelouze. 4 vols. New ed.; Paris: Jannet, 1857.

Maintenon, Françoise d'Aubigné de. *Letters.* Translator unknown. 2 vols. London: Davis, 1759.

Maîtres musiciens de la Renaissance Française. Edited by H. Expert. 3 vols. Paris: Senart, 1905-1906.

Marigny, Jacques Charpentier de. *Relation des divertissemens que le roy a donnés aux reines dans le parc de Versailles.* Paris: Barbin, 1664.

Marolles, Michel de. *Mémoires.* 3 vols. Amsterdam: n.p., 1755.

Masson, Ch. *Nouveau traité des règles pour la composition de la musique.* 2d ed. rev.; Paris: Ballard, 1699.

Maugars, Jean-André. *Response faite à un curieux sur le sentiment de la musique d'Italie.* Rome: Maroscotti, 1639.

Mémoires de littérature tirées des registres de l'Académie royale des inscriptions et belles-lettres depuis son renouvellement jusqu'en M.DCC.X. Vol. I, Paris: Panckoucke, 1772.

Mémoires de Louis XIV, écrits par lui-même, composés pour le grand dauphin, son fils, et adressés à ce prince. Edited by J. L. M. de Gain-Montagnac. Paris: Garnery, 1806.

Mémoires de M. de ... [anonyme] pour servir à l'histoire du XVIIe siècle. Vol. VII of *Nouvelle collection des mémoires pour servir à l'histoire de France, depuis le XIIIe siècle jusqu'à la fin du XVIIIe.* Edited by M. M. Michaud and Poujoulat. 3d ser.; Paris: Commentaire analytique du code civil, 1839.

Mémoires du Maréchal d'Estrées sur la régence de Marie de Médicis (1610-1616) et sur celle d'Anne d'Autriche (1643-1650). Edited by Paul Bonnefon. Paris: Renouard, 1910.

Memoirs of the Duc de Saint-Simon on the Times of Louis XIV and the Regency. Translated by Katherine Prescott Wormeley. Vol. IV. Boston: Hardy and Pratt, 1902.

Memoirs of Madame la Marquise de Montespan. Translator unknown. 2 vols. London: Nicols, 1895.

Memoirs of Ninon de l'Enclos with her Letters to the Marquis de Sévigné and Mons. de St. Évremond. Translated by M. Griffith. Philadelphia: Manning, 1806.

Menestrier, Claude-François. *Des ballets anciens et modernes selon les règles du théâtre.* Paris: Guignard, 1682.

———. *Bibliothèque curieuse et instructive de divers ouvrages anciens et modernes de littérature et des arts.* Paris: Ganeau, 1704.

———. *Des décorations funèbres.* Paris: n.p., 1682.

———. *Des représentations en musique anciennes et modernes.* Paris: Guignard, 1681.

Le mercure galant, contenant plusieurs histoires véritables et tout ce qui s'est passé depuis le premier janvier 1672 jusques au départ du Roy. Paris: Girard, 1672-74, 1677-1715.

Mercure historique et politique, contenant l'état présent de l'Europe, ce qui se passe dans toutes les cours, l'intérêt des princes, leurs brigues, et généralement tout ce qu'il y a de curieux. Vols. I-VI. Parma: Batanar, 1686-89.

Mersenne, Marin. *Harmonie universelle, contenant la théorie et la pratique de la musique, où il est traité de la nature des sons et des mouvements, des consonances, des dissonances, des genres, des modes, de la composition, de la voix, des chants, et de toutes sortes d'instruments harmoniques.* 8 bks. Paris: Cramoisy, 1636.

Montglat, François de Paule de Clermont, marquis de. *Mémoires.* Vol. V of *Nouvelle collection des mémoires pour servir à l'histoire de France, depuis le XIIIe siècle jusqu'à la fin du XVIIIe.* Edited by M. M. Michaud and Poujoulat. 3d ser.; Paris: Commentaire analytique du code civil, 1839.

Motteville, Françoise Bertant de. *Mémoires.* Vol. X of *Nouvelle collection des mémoires pour servir à l'histoire de France, depuis le XIIIe siècle jusqu'à la fin du XVIIIe.* Edited by M. M. Michaud and Poujoulat. 3d ser.; Paris: Commentaire analytique du code civil, 1839.

Les musiciens de la Sainte-Chapelle du Palais. Unedited documents collected and annotated by Michel Brenet. Paris: Picard, 1910.

Naudé, Gabriel. *Jugement de tout ce qui a été imprimé contre le Cardinal Mazarin depuis le sixième Janvier, jusques à la déclaration du premier Avril mil six cens quarante neuf.* Paris: Sainct-Ange, 1649.

——. *Science des princes ou considérations sur les coups d'État.* Strasbourg: n.p., 1673.

Nemours, Marie d'Orléans-Longueville, duchesse de. *Mémoires.* Cologne: n.p., 1709.

Noinville, Durey de, Jacques Bernard, and Louis Travenol. *Histoire du théâtre de l'opéra en France depuis l'établissement de l'Académie royale de musique jusqu'à présent.* 2 vols. in 1. Paris: Barbou, 1753. See also 2d ed. rev.; Paris: Duchesne, 1757.

Nouveaux caractères de la famille Roïale, des ministres d'État et des principales personnes de la cour de France. Ville Franche: Pinceau, 1703.

Nouvelles parodies bachiques mêlées de vaudevilles ou rondes de table. Collected and edited by Christophe Ballard. 3 vols. Paris: Ballard, 1700.

Oeuvres de Louis XIV. Edited by M. Grouvelle. 6 vols. Paris: Treuttel et Wurtz, 1806.

Origny, Antoine Jean-Baptiste-Abraham d'. *Annales du Théâtre Italien, depuis son origine jusqu'à ce jour.* 3 vols. Paris: Duchesne, 1788.

Ormesson, Olivier Lefèvre d'. *Journal et extraits des mémoires.* 2 vols. Paris: Cheruel, 1860-61.

Parran, Antoine. *Traité de la musique théorique et pratique contenant les préceptes de la composition.* Paris: Ballard, 1639.

Pascal, Blaise. *Thoughts.* Translated by W. F. Trotter. Vol. XLVIII of *The Harvard Classics.* Edited by Charles W. Eliot. New York: Collier, 1938.

Pegurier, Laurent. *Décision faite en Sorbonne touchant la comédie, avec une réfutation des sentimens relâchez d'un nouveau théologien sur le même sujet.* Paris: Coignard, 1694.

Pellisson-Fontanier, Paul. *Histoire de Louis XIV depuis la mort du Cardinal Mazarin en 1661 jusqu'à la Paix de Nimègue en 1678.* 3 vols. Paris: Rollin, 1749.

——. *Lettres historiques.* 3 vols. Paris: Didot, 1729.

Perrault, Charles. *Le cabinet des beaux arts ou recueil d'estampes gravées d'après les tableaux d'un plafond où les beaux arts sont représentés avec l'explication de ces mêmes tableaux.* Paris: Edelinck, 1690.

——. *Characters and Criticisms upon the Ancient and Modern Orators, Poets, Painters, Musicians, Statuaries and Other Arts and Sciences, with an Heroick Poem entitled the Age of Lewis the Great.* Translated by Captain Bladen. London: Smith, 1705.

——. *Characters Historical and Panegyrical of the Greatest Men that have appeared in France during the last Century.* Translated by F. Ozell. 2 vols. London: Lintott, 1704-1705.

——. *Critique de l'opéra ou examen de la tragédie intitulée Alceste, ou le Triomphe d'Alcide.* Paris: Barbin, 1674.

——. *Mémoires, contes et autres œuvres.* Edited by Paul L. Jacob. Paris: Gosselin, 1842.

——. *Mémoires de ma vie.* Paris: Bonnefon, 1909.

——. *Parallèle des anciens et des modernes.* 4 vols. Paris: Coignard, 1692.

Perrin, Pierre. *Les œuvres de poésie.* Paris: Loyson, 1661.

Plato. *The Collected Dialogues of Plato including the Letters.* Edited by Edith Hamilton and Huntington Cairns. New York: Bollingen Foundation, 1964.

——. *The Works of Plato.* Translated by B. Jowett. 4 vols. in 1. New York: Tudor, n.d.

La poëtique d'Aristote. Edited and translated by André Dacier. Paris: Barbin, 1692.

La pompe et magnificence faite au mariage du roi et de l'enfante d'Espagne. Tolosa: Ordinaires du roi, 1660.

Pure, Michel de. *Idée des spectacles anciens et nouveaux.* Paris: Brunet, 1668.

Quelques lettres de Louis XIV et des princes de sa famille, 1688-1713. Paris: Aubry, 1862.

Raguenet, François. *Parallèle des Italiens et des François en ce qui regarde la musique et les opéra.* Paris: Moreau, 1702.

Recueil de divers écrits pour et contre la comédie: pièces concernant la querelle de la morale et du théâtre. 2 vols. Paris: Guignard, 1694.

Recueil des gazettes nouvelles ordinaires et extraordinaires, relations et récits des choses avenues tant en ce royaume qu'ailleurs 1671. Paris: Louvre, 1672.

Recueil des opéra, des ballets, et des plus belles pièces en musique qui ont été représentées depuis dix ou douze ans jusques à présent devant sa majesté très-chrestienne. Vols. I, V and VI. Amsterdam: Schelte, 1690-1700.

Relation des assemblées faites à Versailles dans le grand apartement du roi pendant ce carnaval de l'an 1683 et des divertissements que sa majesté y avoit ordonnées. Paris: Cottard, 1683.

Relazioni degli stati Europei lette al senato dagli ambasciatori Veneti nel secolo deci-mosettimo. Collected and annotated by Barozzi and Berchet. 3 vols. Venice: Naratovich, 1859-63.

Requeste d'inscription de faux en forme de factum, pour Sieur Guichard, intendant général des bastimens de son altesse royale, monsieur. Contre Jean-Baptiste Lully, faux accusateur, Sébastien Aubry, Marie Aubry, Jacques du Creux, Pierre Huguenet, faux témoins, et autres complices. Paris: n.p., 1676.

Revue des documents historiques: Suite de pièces curieuses et inédites. Edited by Étienne Charavay. 2 vols. Paris: Lemerre, 1874-75.

Riccoboni, Louis, *Observations sur la comédie et sur le génie de Molière.* Paris: Pissot, 1736.

——. *Réflexions historiques et critiques sur les différens théâtres de l'Europe.* Paris: Guerin, 1738.

Riencourt, Simon de. *Histoire de la monarchie françoise sous le règne de Louis le Grand (1643-1654).* 2 vols. 2d ed. rev.; Paris: Cavelier, 1691.

Saint-Évremond, Charles de Marguetel de Saint-Denis de. *Miscellanea: or Various Discourses upon Tragedy, Comedy, the Italian, the English comedy, and operas to his Grace, the Duke of Buckingham.* Translated by Ferrand Spence. London: Pall-Mall. 1686.

——. *Oeuvres mêlées.* Vol. XI. Paris: Barbin, 1689.

——. *Oeuvres mêlées.* Edited by Rémy de Gourmont. 3d ed.; Paris: Mercure de France, 1909.

Saint-Maurice, Thomas-François Chabod, marquis de. *Lettres sur la cour de Louis XIV (1667-1673).* Edited by Jean Lemoine. 2 vols. Paris: Calman-Lévy, 1910.

Saint-Simon, Louis de Rouvroi, duc de. *Louis XIV et sa cour; portraits, jugements et anecdotes extraits des mémoires authentiques du Duc de Saint-Simon (1694-1715).* Paris: Hachette, 1853.

Scudéry, Madeleine de. *Conversations nouvelles sur divers sujets.* 2 vols. New ed.; La Hague: Voys, 1710.

Senecé, Antoine Bauderon de. *Oeuvres choisies.* Edited by Émile Chasles and P. A. Cap. New ed.; Paris: Jannet, 1855.

Sévigné, Marie de. *Lettres de sa famille et de ses amis.* 10 vols. Paris: Blaise, 1820.

Soanen, Jean. *Sermons sur différents sujets prêchés devant le roi.* Vol. I. Lyons: Duplain, 1767.

Sourches, Louis-François de Bouchet de. *Mémoires sur le règne de Louis XIV.* Edited by Arthur Bertrand. 13 vols. Paris: Hachette, 1882.

Spanheim, Ézéchiel. *Relation de la cour de France en 1690.* Edited by C. Schefer. Paris: Renouard, 1882.

Tallemant, Paul. *Histoire de l'Académie royale des inscriptions et belles-lettres depuis son établissement, avec les éloges des académiciens morts depuis son renouvellement.* 13 vols. Paris: Guerin, 1717-40.

Terrasson, Jean. *Dissertation critique sur l'Iliade d'Homer, où à l'occasion de ce poëme on cherche les règles d'une poëtique fondée sur la raison, et sur les exemples des anciens et des modernes.* Paris: Fournier, 1715.

Le théâtre de Quinault. 2 vols. Paris: n.p., 1663.

Théâtre de Quinault. Vols. IV and V. New ed.; Paris: Associés, 1778.

Le théâtre Italien, ou le recueil de toutes les comédies et scènes françoises qui ont été jouées sur le Théâtre Italien. Edited by Evariste Gherardi. 3 vols. Paris: Mabre-Cramoisy, 1695-98.

Tillet, Titon du. *Le parnasse françois*. Paris: Coignard, 1732.

Touchard-Lafosse, G. *Chroniques de l'œil-de-bœuf des petits appartements de la cour et des salons de Paris (1631-1671)*. Vol. II. Paris: Garnier, 1830.

Vallier, Jean. *Journal de Jean Vallier, maître d'hôtel du roi (1648-1657)*. 4 vols. Paris: Renouard, 1902.

Viéville, J. L. de Freneuse Lecerf de la. *L'art de décrier ce qu'on n'intend point ou le médecin musicien*. Brussels: Foppens, 1706.

——. *Comparaison de la musique italienne et de la musique française*. 3 vols. in 1. Brussels: Foppens, 1705.

Visconti, Primi, comte de San-Maiolo. *Mémoires sur la cour de Louis XIV*. Translated by Jean Lemoine. Paris: Calmann-Lévy, n.d.

SECONDARY WORKS

Allen, Warren Dwight. *Philosophies of Music History*. New York: American, 1939.

André, Louis. *Louis XIV et l'Europe*. Paris: Michel, 1950.

Apel, Willi. *Harvard Dictionary of Music*. Cambridge: Harvard University Press, 1951.

Ashley, Maurice. *Louis XIV and the Greatness of France*. 2d ed.; London: Hodder and Stoughton, 1948.

Augé-Chiquet, Mathieu. *La vie, les idées et l'œuvre de Jean-Antoine de Baïf*. Paris: Hatchette, 1909.

Baur-Heinhold, Margarete. *The Baroque Theatre: A Cultural History of the 17th and 18th Centuries*. Translated by Mary Whittall. New York: McGraw-Hill, 1967.

Bjurstroem, Per. *Giacomo Torelli and Baroque Stage Design*. Stockholm: Wiksell, 1961.

Boislisle, Arthur-Michel de. *Les débuts de l'opéra français à Paris*. Paris: Société de l'histoire de Paris, 1875.

Boll, André. *De l'Académie royale à la salle Garnier*. Paris: Perrin, 1960.

Boudot, Pierre-Jean. *Bibliothèque du théâtre françoise depuis son origine*. 3 vols. Dresden: Groell, 1768.

Bouvy, Eugène. *La gravure de portraits et d'allégories*. Paris: Van Oest, 1929.

Boysse, Ernest. *Le théâtre des Jésuites*. Paris: Vaton, 1880.

Brenet, Michel. *Les concerts en France sous l'ancien régime*. Paris: Fischbacher, 1900.

Bruny, Charles. *Examen du ministère de M. Colbert*. Paris: D'Houry, 1774.

Bukofzer, Manfred F. *Music in the Baroque Era*. New York: Norton, 1947.

Campardon, Émile. *L'Académie royale de musique au XVIIIe siècle*. 2 vols. Paris; Berger-Levrault, 1884.

Cassirer, Ernst. *The Individual and the Cosmos in Renaissance Philosophy.* Translated by Domandi. New York: Harper and Row, 1963.

Catalogue des livres de musique (manuscrits et imprimés) de la Bibliothèque de l'Arsenal à Paris. Compiled and edited by Lionel de La Laurencie and Amédée Gastoué. Paris: Société française de musicologie, 1936.

Clément, Pierre. *Madame de Montespan et Louis XIV.* 2d ed.; Paris: Didier, 1868.

Cucuel, Georges. *Les créateurs de l'opéra-comique français.* Paris: Alcan, 1914.

Darle, Françoise. *Marly ou la vie de cour sous Louis XIV.* Paris: Lenore, 1959.

De Artibus opuscula XL: Essays in Honor of Erwin Panofsky. Edited by Paul Weiss. Zurich: Buehler Buchdruck, 1960.

Despois, Eugène. *Le théâtre français sous Louis XIV.* 2d ed.; Paris: Hachette, 1882.

The Diversity of History. Edited by J. H. Elliot and H. G. Koenigsberger. Ithaca, N. Y.: Cornell University Press, 1970.

Duffo, François. *Le cérémonial de France à la cour de Louis XIV.* Paris: Lethielleux, 1936.

Écorcheville, Jules. *De Lulli à Rameau, 1690-1730, l'esthétique musicale.* (Doctoral dissertation, University of Paris). Paris: Imp. artistiques, 1906.

Farmer, James Eugene. *Versailles and the Court under Louis XIV.* London: Nash, 1906.

Les fêtes de la Renaissance. Vol. I of *Colloques internationaux du centre national de la recherche scientifique.* Paris: Centre national de la recherche scientifique, 1956.

Fictor, Gabriel [Auguste Jal]. *Dictionnaire critique de biographie et d'histoire.* Paris: Plon, 1867.

——. *Dictionnaire théâtral.* Paris: Barba, 1824.

Fournel, Victor. *Les contemporains de Molière.* Vol. II. Paris: Didot, 1866.

Fromageot, Paul. *Les compositeurs de musique à Versailles.* Versailles: Aubert, 1906.

Goldschmidt, Hugo. *Studien zur Geschichte der italienischen Oper im 17. Jahrhundert.* Vol. I. Leipzig: Breitkopf und Härtel, 1901.

The Greatness of Louis XIV: Myth or Reality. Edited by William F. Church. Boston: Heath, 1959.

Gros, Étienne. *Philippe Quinault, sa vie et son œuvre.* Paris: Champion, 1926.

Grout, Donald Jay. *A History of Western Music.* New York: Norton, 1960.

——. *A Short History of Opera.* New York, 1947.

Hassall, Arthur. *Mazarin.* London: Macmillan, 1903.

Heyer, Anna Harriet. *Historical Sets, Collected Editions and Monuments of Music.* Chicago: American Library Association, 1957.

Jouin, Henry. *Charles Le Brun et les arts sous Louis XIV.* Paris: Imprimerie Nationale, 1889.

Kristeller, Paul O. *The Philosophy of Marsilio Ficino.* Translated by Virginia Conant. New York: Columbia, 1943.

La Laurencie, Lionel de. *Lully.* 2d ed.; Paris: Alcan, 1919.

Langlois, Marcel. *Louis XIV et la cour, d'après trois témoins nouveaux: Bélise, Beauvillier, Chamillart.* Paris: Michel, 1926.

Lassus, L. Augé de. *Les spectacles antiques*. Paris: Hachette, 1888.

La Vallière, Louis-César de la Baume, duc de la Blanc de. *Ballets, opéras, et autres ouvrages lyriques, par ordre chronologique depuis leur origine, avec une table alphabétique des ouvrages et des auteurs*. Paris: Bauche, 1760.

Lavisse, Ernest. *Louis XIV (1643-1715)*. Vol. VII of *Histoire générale du IVe siècle à nos jours*. Edited by Ernest Lavisse and Alfred Rambaud. Paris: Colin, 1895.

Lejeune, André, and Wolff, Stéphane. *Les quinze salles de l'opéra de Paris, 1669-1955*. Paris: Coulouma, 1955.

Loewenberg, Arthur. *Annals of Opera, 1597-1940*. 2d ed. rev.; Geneva: Societas Bibliographica, 1955.

MacPherson, Harriet Dorothea. *Censorship under Louis XIV*. New York: Pubs. Inst. French Studies, 1929.

Marmontel, Jean-François. *Éléments de littérature*, 3 vols. Paris: Didot, 1846.

——. *Essai sur les révolutions de la musique en France*. Paris: n.p., 1777.

Maurois, André. *Louis XIV à Versailles*. Paris: Hachette, 1955.

Musique et poésie au XVIe siècle. Vol. V of *Colloques internationaux du centre national de la recherche scientifique*. Paris: Centre national de la recherche scientifique, 1954.

La musique française du moyen âge à la révolution. Catalogue compiled by Amédée Gastoué, V. Leroquais, André Pirro, Henry Expert, and Henry Prunières. Paris: Bibliothèque Nationale, 1934.

Oliver, Alfred Richard. *The Encyclopedists as Critics of Music*. New York: Columbia, 1947.

Panofsky, Erwin. *Idea: A Concept in Art Theory*. Translated by Joseph J. S. Peake. Columbia: University of South Carolina Press, 1968.

——. *Renaissance and Renascences in Western Art*. New York: Harper and Row, 1969.

——. *Studies in Iconology: Humanistic Themes in the Art of the Renaissance*. New York: Harper and Row, 1967.

Papers of the American Musicological Society, December 30, 1941. Edited by Gustave Reese, Printed by the Society, 1946.

Parmentier, Antoine. *La cour du roi soleil*. Paris: Colin, 1909.

Pevsner, Nikolaus. *Academies of Art Past and Present*. Cambridge Press: 1940.

Praz, Mario. *Studies in Seventeenth-Century Imagery*. 2d ed. rev.; Rome: n.p., 1964.

Proceedings of the Musical Association, London, 33d session, 1906-1907. London: Novello, 1907.

Prunières, Henry. *Le ballet de cour en France avant Benserade et Lully suivi du ballet de la Délivrance de Renaud*. Paris: Laurens, 1914.

——. *Lully*. Paris: Renouard, n.d.

——. *La vie illustrée et libertine de Jean-Baptiste Lully*. Paris: Plon, 1929.

Rhodes, Émile. *Les trompettes du roi*. Paris: Picard, 1909.

Riemann, Hugo. *Das Generalbasszeitalter*. Vol. II of *Handbuch der Musikgeschichte*. Leipzig: Breitkopf und Härtel, 1912.

Robert, Paul. *Dictionnaire alphabétique et analogique de la langue française.* Vol. 6. Paris: Société du Nouveau Littré de Robert, 1966.

Rolland, Romain. *Essays on Music.* New York: Allen, Towne, and Heath, 1948.

———. *Les origines du théâtre lyrique moderne: histoire de l'opéra en Europe avant Lully et Scarlatti.* New ed.; Paris: Boccard, 1931.

———. *Some Musicians of Former Days.* Translated by Blaiklock. 4th ed.; London: Kegan Paul, Trench, and Trubner, n.d.

Seznec, Jean. *The Survival of the Pagan Gods.* Translated by Barbara F. Sessions. New York: Pantheon, 1953.

Silin, Charles I. *Benserade and His Ballets de Cour.* Baltimore: Johns Hopkins, 1940.

Storz, Walter. "Der Aufbau der Tànze in den Opern und Ballets Lully's vom musikalischen Standpunkte aus betrachtet." (Doctoral dissertation, University of Göttingen.) Göttingen: Buchdruckerei, 1928.

Tapié, Victor-L. *The Age of Grandeur: Baroque Art and Architecture.* Translated by A. Ross Williamson. 2d ed.; New York: Praeger, 1966.

Valensi, Theodore. *Louis XIV et Lully.* Nice: Dervyl, 1951.

Wedgwood, C. V. *The Thirty Years War.* Garden City, N. Y.: Doubleday, 1961.

Weigert, Roger-Armand. *Jean I Berain.* 2 vols. Paris: Éditions d'art et d'histoire, 1937.

Wolf, John B. *Louis XIV.* New York: Norton, 1968.

Yates, Frances A. *The French Academies of the Sixteenth Century.* London: Warburg, 1947.

———. *The Valois Tapestries.* London: Warburg, 1959.

Index

MUSIC IN THE SERVICE
OF THE KING

Designed by R. E. Rosenbaum.
Composed by The St. Catherine Press, Ltd.
in 11 point monotype Baskerville, 2 points leaded,
with display line in monotype Garamond.
Printed offset by Vail-Ballou Press, Inc.
on Warren's 1854 text, 60 pound basis,
with the Cornell University Press watermark.
Bound by Vail-Ballou Press.

Library of Congress Cataloging in Publication Data
(For library cataloging purposes only)

Isherwood, Robert M   date.
  Music in the service of the King.

  Bibliography: p.
  1. Music—France—History and criticism.
2. Music—History and criticism—17th century.
3. France—History—Louis XIV, 1643-1715.   I. Title.
ML270.2.I8   780'.944   72-8467
ISBN 0-8014-0734-6